STUDIES IN IMPERIALISM

General editor: Andrew S. Thompson
Founding editor: John M. MacKenzie

When the 'Studies in Imperialism' series was founded by Professor John M. MacKenzie more than thirty years ago, emphasis was laid upon the conviction that 'imperialism as a cultural phenomenon had as significant an effect on the dominant as on the subordinate societies'. With well over a hundred titles now published, this remains the prime concern of the series. Cross-disciplinary work has indeed appeared covering the full spectrum of cultural phenomena, as well as examining aspects of gender and sex, frontiers and law, science and the environment, language and literature, migration and patriotic societies, and much else. Moreover, the series has always wished to present comparative work on European and American imperialism, and particularly welcomes the submission of books in these areas. The fascination with imperialism, in all its aspects, shows no sign of abating, and this series will continue to lead the way in encouraging the widest possible range of studies in the field. 'Studies in Imperialism' is fully organic in its development, always seeking to be at the cutting edge, responding to the latest interests of scholars and the needs of this ever-expanding area of scholarship.

The Germans in India

Manchester University Press

SELECTED TITLES AVAILABLE IN THE SERIES

WRITING IMPERIAL HISTORIES
ed. Andrew S. Thompson

EMPIRE OF SCHOLARS
Tamson Pietsch

HISTORY, HERITAGE AND COLONIALISM
Kynan Gentry

COUNTRY HOUSES AND THE BRITISH EMPIRE
Stephanie Barczewski

THE RELIC STATE
Pamila Gupta

WE ARE NO LONGER IN FRANCE
Allison Drew

THE SUPPRESSION OF THE ATLANTIC SLAVE TRADE
ed. Robert Burroughs and Richard Huzzey

HEROIC IMPERIALISTS IN AFRICA
Berny Sèbe

The Germans in India

ELITE EUROPEAN MIGRANTS IN THE BRITISH EMPIRE

Panikos Panayi

MANCHESTER UNIVERSITY PRESS

Copyright © Panikos Panayi 2017

The right of Panikos Panayi to be identified as the author of this work has been asserted by him in accordance with the Copyright, Designs and Patents Act 1988.

Published by MANCHESTER UNIVERSITY PRESS
Oxford Road, Manchester M13 9PL

www.manchesteruniversitypress.co.uk

British Library Cataloguing-in-Publication Data
A catalogue record for this book is available from the British Library

ISBN 978 1 5261 1933 9   hardback
ISBN 978 1 5261 9124 3   paperback

First published 2017
Paperback published 2025

The publisher has no responsibility for the persistence or accuracy of URLs for any external or third-party internet websites referred to in this book, and does not guarantee that any content on such websites is, or will remain, accurate or appropriate.

EU authorised representative for GPSR:
Easy Access System Europe, Mustamäe tee 50, 10621 Tallinn, Estonia
gpsr.requests@easproject.com

Typeset
by Toppan Best-set Premedia Limited

CONTENTS

List of figures—page vi
List of tables—viii
Preface—ix
Acknowledgements—xv
Abbreviations—xvii
Nineteenth-century Indian place names with contemporary variants and twenty-first-century equivalents—xviii

1	The Germans in India as elite European migrants	1
2	Passages to India	40
3	Everyday life	73
4	Community	111
5	Interethnic perceptions and interactions	145
6	The impact of the Great War	187
7	Endings, new beginnings and meanings	229

Bibliography—245
Index—273

FIGURES

1.1 Map of Basel Mission activity in India, based on Wilhelm Schlatter and Hermann Witschi, *Geschichte der Basler Mission*, Vol. 4 (Basel, 1965), p. 316. — page 15

1.2 Locations of Leipzig mission stations, based on *Zweiundneunzigster Jahresbericht der Evangelisch-lutherischen Mission zu Leipzig* (Leipzig, 1911), p. 24. — 17

1.3 Map of Gossner Mission activity in India, based on Hans Kausch, *Festschrift zum 75. jährigen Bestehen der Gossnerschen Mission* (Friedenau-Berlin, 1911), p. 51. — 19

2.1 Madras Harbour at the end of the nineteenth century, from Alwin Gehring, *Erinnerungen aus dem Leben eines Tamulenmissionars* (Leipzig, 1906), p. 3. — 45

2.2 Map of the German Empire, 1871–1918, based on www.edmaps.com/html/germany.html. — 59

3.1 A missionary preaching in the temple city of Chidambaram, from E. R. Baierlein, *Unter den Palmen: Im Lande der Sonne* (Leipzig, 1890), p. 197. — 81

3.2 Plague and cholera in Bombay, 1910, from Oscar Kauffmann, *Aus Indiens Dschungeln: Erlebnisse und Forschungen*, Vol. 1 (Leipzig, 1911), p. 6 — 85

3.3 The first Gossner mission house in Ranchi, from Hans Kausch and F. Hahn, *50 Bilder aus der Goßnerschen Kols-Mission mit erläuterndem Text und Karte* (Berlin, 1894), p. 34. — 89

4.1 The German Crown Prince in Bombay, December 1910, from Oscar Bongard, *Die Reise des Deutschen Kronprinzen durch Ceylon und Indien* (Berlin, 1911), p. 55. — 115

4.2 The Basel mission house in Kety, from Evangelische Missions-Gesellschaft, *Album der Basler Mission: Bilder aus Indien* (Basel, 1860). — 126

LIST OF FIGURES

4.3	The Gossner church in Purulia, from Hans Kausch and F. Hahn, *50 Bilder aus der Goßnerschen Kols-Mission mit erläuterndem Text und Karte* (Berlin, 1894), p. 52.	128
4.4	Gossner Mission parish elders, catechists and clergymen, from Hans Kausch and F. Hahn, *50 Bilder aus der Goßnerschen Kols-Mission mit erläuterndem Text und Karte* (Berlin, 1894), p. 86.	135
4.5	Indian Gossner Mission pastors, from Hans Kausch and F. Hahn, *50 Bilder aus der Goßnerschen Kols-Mission mit erläuterndem Text und Karte* (Berlin, 1894), p. 84.	136
5.1	A classic Orientalist image, from Emil Schlagintweit, *Indien in Wort und Bild*, Vol. 1 (Leipzig, 1880), p. 7.	149
5.2	A sympathetic image of two Indian girls, from Oscar Kauffmann, *Aus Indiens Dschungeln: Erlebnisse und Forschungen*, Vol. 2 (Leipzig, 1911), p. 198.	152
6.1	Waltair sanatorium and internment camp, from Otty Jessen, *Vertrieben* (Breklum, 1917), p. 18.	203
6.2	Location of major internment camps in India, 1914–20.	205
6.3	The *Golconda*, from Therese Zehme, *Heimkehr mit der Golconda: Wie es den Kindern unserer vertriebenen indischen Missionare erging* (Leipzig, 1916), p. 1.	215
6.4	George Kenner, 'Returned German Missionaries in Alexandra Palace', courtesy of Christa Kenner Bedford.	217

TABLES

1.1	Foreign-born population of India	page 27
1.2	Major German populations on the outbreak of the First World War	28
2.1	Origins of Indian-based Basel missionaries and their wives born in Germany, 1818–1914	60
2.2	Major origins of Indian-based Leipzig missionaries sent to India before 1914	61
3.1	Time spent by German-born Leipzig missionaries in India	82
4.1	Origins of Basel Mission employees working in Mangalore in 1885	123
5.1	Nationality of the wives of German-born missionaries employed by the Church Missionary Society	170
5.2	Ethnicity of the wives of German-born missionaries employed by the Basel Mission, 1820–1918	172
5.3	Ethnicity of marriage partners exempted from internment in India in 1916	174

PREFACE

The origins of this book essentially lie in my recent Manchester University Press volume *Prisoners of Britain*. During my research for that book, it became obvious that internment operated upon an imperial level. One of the camps that constantly surfaced in discussions involving the British and German governments, via US and then Swiss intermediaries, consisted of Ahmednagar in present day Maharashtra. I unsuccessfully tried to persuade an undergraduate student of South Asian origin to undertake a dissertation on this camp in the early summer of 2010, and increasingly came to realise that I would have to reconstruct its story myself. In July of that year, I found myself in the Staatsbibliothek zu Berlin carrying out further research on internment in Britain when I came across a book entitled *Unter indischer Sonne: 19 Monate englischer Kriegsgefangenschaft in Ahmednagar* written by the German missionary Hans Georg Probst and published in 1917. Discovering this volume on a blisteringly hot Berlin summer day hundreds of miles away from the pressures of subject leadership at De Montfort University acted as a turning point for this project. I finally reached my decision to proceed further when, during a trip to New Delhi with my wife Mundeep in January 2011, the duty archivist allowed me to spend a few hours searching through the catalogue at the National Archives of India and I discovered several hundred files on the position of Germans in India during the Great War. By this time I had also come across further material which would allow me to trace the history of the Germans in the preceding century, culminating in their internment and deportation between 1914 and 1920.

What follows is essentially the story of a few thousand people who found themselves living in India between c1815 and 1920. On the one hand their experience resembles that of German minorities that sprang up throughout the world during these years. However, the Germans in India differ because of their much smaller numbers compared, for example, with the millions who progressed to the USA. The Germans in India constitute an elite migration made up particularly of highly educated missionaries, academics, businessmen and travellers. While some Germans from lower down on the social scale, especially sailors, certainly visited India between 1815 and 1914, they have left little trace. This contrasts especially with the missionaries, travellers and academics (sometimes the same) who left a rich record of their experiences and perceptions of their Indian lives. Indeed, the project has made use of the Basel and Leipzig mission archives. More particularly, it has relied upon the numerous biographies, memoirs and travelogues of those Germans in India between 1815 and 1920. The narrative has the key aim of demonstrating the experiences of an elite European group within the British Empire which remained distinct from the British ruling minority and whose difference led to its persecution by the Government of India during the First World War.

Although we might dismiss the Germans as part of the 'European elites' which controlled India in the century before the First World War, this would prove misleading. 'European' society during this period consisted essentially of Britons with a small minority of people from other European states, of which Germans counted the largest national group. While interaction took place between Germans and Britons, the different groups of Germans developed their own distinct communities in which interaction with Indians became at least as important as their relationships with Britons, especially in the case of missionaries.

Divided into six chapters with a concluding seventh, the book has the key aim of addressing the experiences of German elite migrants in India from 1815–1920, especially against the perspective of both their fellow nationals – elite and non-elite – in other parts of the world, as well as the white British minority in India. German identities in India before 1914 became just as complex as those of the larger German communities in other parts of the world. The volume will provide much detail about the uniqueness of the German experience in India. It distinguishes between different groups of Europeans who lived in the British colony along national lines rather than simply accepting the term 'Europeans'. This case study tackles elite groups within the British Empire distinct from the ruling classes (despite the relationships which developed), which became clear during the Great War when the Germans faced persecution and expulsion.

Chapter 1 is essentially introductory in nature and has a series of aims. First, it points to the wealth of information which the German migrants left and which allowed this book to emerge, as well as interrogating the nature of the sources. Second, it stresses the need to differentiate between the history of the Germans *and* India and the Germans *in* India. This is not another book about German indology but a study of Germans in India, which only examines those academics who spent time in the country. The chapter then goes back to the sixteenth century to identify the first German merchants in the country and focuses more especially upon the first German (and Protestant) missionaries who arrived in 1706. The chapter then identifies the nineteenth-century Germans divided into missionaries, scholars and

PREFACE

scientists, travellers and businessmen and other professionals. Although poorer Germans lived there, Chapter 1 concludes by arguing that the Germans in nineteenth-century India best fit into the description of an elite migrant group, which distinguishes them from the mass of the German diaspora during the nineteenth century. However, the type of migrants who made their way to India also progressed to other parts of the world as the *Kaiserreich* went global. The chapter also stresses the need to distinguish between different groups of Europeans in India.

The second chapter, 'Passages to India', investigates the reasons for the migration of Germans to India under three headings. First, structural factors linked with the globalisation which took place during the nineteenth century. These include the European population explosion and, more especially, the transport revolution which facilitated international migration more generally. While the opening of the Suez Canal made the journey to India easier, missionaries in particular recorded details of their travel in great detail, often constructing epic accounts of a trip around the Cape of Good Hope. The issue of German Pietism also receives consideration as a structural factor because the growth of this strand of Protestantism helped to persuade thousands of Germans to emigrate – not just to India but to destinations throughout the world. The chapter then deals with the networks which proved fundamental in sending German elites to India. For the missionaries, family, geographical origin and the group which employed them all played central roles while academics and scientists developed their own networks. The chapter then examines the role of individual agency. It concludes by placing the experience of the German elites migrating to India within the experience of those German elites and non-elites moving to other parts of the world.

'Everyday life' essentially offers an examination of the realities of German existence in India, before moving on to the two key chapters dealing with community and interethnic perceptions and relationships. It begins by pointing out that, even after arrival in India, the missionaries in particular – together with academics and, more obviously, travellers – lived mobile lives, whether this meant travelling in the search for converts or sources or moving from one mission station to another or returning home to recover for the purpose of recuperating from a spell in India. The chapter then examines the health of the Germans in India pointing out that, in common with other Europeans, it improved during the course of the nineteenth century due to advances in scientific knowledge. It then considers the housing of the Germans, which, once again, reflected their elite status, as did the work which they undertook. Although this chapter remains the most narrative in approach, it again places German elite experiences within the context of similar migrating lives in the nineteenth century.

Chapter 4 on 'Community' examines the complex identities of the Germans in India in the century before the First World War. It begins by trying to establish whether or not they constituted part of the German diaspora, as claimed by nationalist groups in the decades after unification in 1871. Although a few German clubs had emerged in Bombay, Calcutta and Madras by the outbreak of the First World War, they counted just a handful of members, on a completely different scale to similar organisations in other parts of the world. Those Germans who lived as individuals often became assimilated into British society, especially through their marriage and citizenship choices. The chapter also examines the importance of community through family, especially in the case of missionaries, and then moves on to address the role of religion for this group. It points to the fact that German identities played a secondary role to Lutheranism in the century before 1914, although the communities that emerged developed a racial hierarchy despite the multilingual and multiracial elements which they needed to function in their interaction with the Indians they converted. The chapter contrasts the experience of these elites with others, both Germans and British, as well as with the mass ethnic bodies which emerged in the USA and, on a smaller scale, in Britain and Australia, for example.

Chapter 5 'Interethnic perceptions and interactions' opens with a discussion of the role of racism, orientalism and Christianity, but also points to the fact that missionaries and scholars came into contact with Indians which inevitably broke down some of these prejudices. The narrative then discusses the stereotypes which emerged in memoirs, biographies and travelogues which include: an admiration of Indian landscapes; contempt for Hinduism; criticism of the plight of women; and repulsion at cityscapes. The chapter also examines basically positive attitudes towards the British, with some criticisms of their rule. It then addresses the complexities of interaction between Germans and Indians and Germans and Britons in which racial and religious affiliation played an important role. This becomes most obvious through interethnic relationships which, in the case of Germans and Indians, remained rare, especially when they involved missionaries. At the same time, those involving Germans and Britons also remained relatively unusual. The chapter further examines the hostility faced by missionaries which could result in violence, peaking in the 1857 Mutiny, although only Gossner Mission employees became caught up in this. It concludes by pointing to the complexities of interethnic interaction. The chapter, like the previous one, demonstrates the clear difference

PREFACE

between the Germans and the British, again questioning the idea of a European identity.

'The impact of the Great War' focuses upon the transformation which took place as a result of this conflict, mirroring the plight of Germans in other parts of the world. Two underlying changes took place in India. First, all Germans, including missionaries, became conscious of their national identity because the British authorities imposed it upon them as part of the marginalisation process. Consequently, this impacted upon the racial hierarchy, which shocked some Indians and Germans. Backed up by a hostile British-Indian public opinion and copying actions towards enemy aliens elsewhere in the Empire, the Government of India marginalised and eliminated the Germans in a four-stage process. First, it introduced a series of measures labelling them enemies and also controlling their movements and other aspects of their lives. Second, it confiscated their property, including some belonging to missionary groups, primarily through trading with the enemy legislation. Third, it introduced internment for males in particular, in which the Ahmednagar camp became central. Finally, virtually all Germans, almost without exception, faced deportation by the end of 1920. The marginalisation which took place closely mirrored the plight of the German communities throughout the British Empire. The unique aspect of the experience in India consisted of the birth of a national identity.

The concluding seventh chapter has a series of aims, as suggested in its title, 'Endings, new beginnings and meanings'. First, it points to the totality of exclusion which continued into the early 1920s. However, by the second half of the 1920s and into the 1930s, German community – both religious and secular – had re-emerged, although internment followed again in 1940. The conclusion also places the experience of the Germans in India into four broader contexts: the global history of the nineteenth and early twentieth centuries; German history; the history of the British Empire in India; and Indian history. In this way the story of a small grouping forms part of broader developments which its experiences help us to emphasise.

The chronological and geographical parameters of the book need explanation. It begins in in the early nineteenth century because the Basel Mission, which sent the largest group of Germans to India, came into existence in 1815. Its first workers went out shortly afterwards, initially employed by the London-based Church Missionary Society. The use of the British Empire in the subtitle also refers to East India Company rule. Whether under the control of the East India Company or not, the takeover by the British state from 1857 did not significantly impact upon the Germans – in contrast to the Great War. The book

PREFACE

ends in 1920 because of the totality of the ethnic cleansing which took place at the end of the First World War.

The geographical parameters also need explanation. India excludes both Burma and Ceylon, which went on to become separate states, although the narrative pays some attention to territories which would become Pakistan. The volume uses the place names of the time. The concept of German might appear problematic because such a state did not come into existence until 1871, but those individuals examined before 1871 came from the areas which the German nation state would cover. It therefore does not deal with Austrians and Swiss Germans.

ACKNOWLEDGEMENTS

I would first like to thank the funding bodies which made this book possible. It initially formed part of a broader project supported by the Higher Education Innovation Fund via De Montfort University under the title of 'Internment during the First World War: Remembering, Forgetting and Experiencing on a Local, National and Global Scale' which looked at Ahmednagar in wider context and which financed two conferences on internment open to the public held at the Manx Museum (covering the local) and the Imperial War Museum North (examining the global). This grant also allowed me to make trips to the library of the School of Oriental and African Studies and the British Library and to devote teaching and administration free time to completing the research and much of the writing. The final stages of writing became possible because of a reduction of teaching under De Montfort's Individual Research Plan scheme. A grant from the Gerda Henkel Foundation held with Stefan Manz for a project entitled 'Interning German "Enemy Aliens" in the British Empire during World War I: Global, National and Local Perspectives' allowed me to make two research trips to Berlin, where I used the Bundesarchiv and the Staatsbibliothek zu Berlin, as well as another journey to use the Militärarchiv in Freiburg. This funding further covered my journey to the National Archives of India in New Delhi as well as allowing numerous trips to London to use the National Archives and the British Library. Most importantly, a three-month resumption of my Alexander von Humboldt Fellowship at the end of 2014 meant that I could visit the following institutions: the Münster and Osnabrück University libraries; the Institut für vergleichende Städtegeschichte in Münster; the Bundesarchiv, the Evangelisches Zentralarchiv, the Geheimes Staatsarchiv Preußischer Kulturbesitz and the Staatsbibliothek in Berlin; the Deutsche Bibliothek in Leipzig; the archive and library of the Studienzentrum August Hermann Francke in Halle; the Institut für Auslandsbeziehungen and the Württembergische Landesbibliothek in Stuttgart; and the Basel Mission Archive and Library and the University Library in Basel. I am particularly grateful to Salome Marschall, Anke Schürer Ries and Claudia Wirthlin who helped me to navigate the collections of the Basel Mission Archive and Library.

I would also like to thank many other individuals for their support with this project. At Manchester University Press Emma Brennan persevered with the project. I am also grateful to Andrew Thompson, the series editor of 'Studies in Imperialism', and to the anonymous

ACKNOWLEDGEMENTS

referee who helped me to think about the broader meaning of my project. I am especially thankful to the staff of the Institut für Migrationsforschung und Interkulturelle Studien at the University of Osnabrück who supported the resumption of my Alexander von Humboldt Fellowship there (after an absence of 13 years and even though I only spent two weeks in Osnabrück on this occasion), especially Jochen Oltmer, Jutta Tiemeyer and Sigrid Putsch. During my two-week stay I also had useful and constructive chats over lunch and coffee with 'Junior Professor' Jannis Panagiotidis. Other academics who helped me in various ways include: Elizabeth Buettner, Kathy Burrell, Dave Dee, Richard Evans, Andreas Fahrmeier, Elizabeth Lambourne, Tony Kushner, Christoph Lorke, Heidi MacPherson, Stefan Manz, David Maxwell, Maren Möhring, Gavin Schaffer, Matthew Stibbe and Karl-Heinz Wüstner. My PhD students Christopher Zembe and Vimal Patel also listened to my thoughts on Germans in nineteenth-century India. I would especially like to thank my fellow De Montfort historian Pippa Virdee who, as a South Asian specialist, encouraged me to pursue this project from the moment I mentioned it to her and answered numerous questions about Indian history and Indian sources throughout its duration.

Above all I would like to thank my wife Mundeep. Fifteen years ago I could not have imagined undertaking research on any aspect of the history of India, just as I could not have conceived travelling to the country. While dragging my feet about initially visiting, I was overwhelmed with a combination of positive and negative feelings (rather like some of the Germans described in this book) during my first trip in November 2006. During our second holiday, in January 2011, I paid the decisive brief visit to the National Archives of India in Delhi, where I realised that sufficient material existed to allow me to write a book on the Germans in India. Mundeep came with me when I made my extended trip to the archives in February 2015, as I couldn't really visit her spiritual and ancestral homeland without her. In any case, I felt much more comfortable travelling with her: while I laboured in the archives, Mundeep explored Delhi. She also remained relaxed about my absences from home, including the resumption of my Alexander von Humboldt Fellowship – although the latter meant she could visit me for a surreal birthday weekend in Berlin in October 2014 and also meant she could come to Basel and Freiburg. Mundeep has taken an interest throughout and I hope she remains true to her promise to read the published book. Clearly, I would like to dedicate it to her.

ABBREVIATIONS

AA   Auswärtiges Amt
AFST   Archiv der Frankeschen Stiftung
BA   Bundesarchiv
BL   British Library
BMA   Basel Mission Archives
CMS   Church Missionary Society
CO   Colonial Office
CRL   Cadbury Research Library
EZA   Evangelisches Zentralarchiv
FO   Foreign Office
Gsta   Geheimes Staatsarchiv
IOR   India Office Records
LMW   Leipziger Missionswerk
MA   Militärarchiv
NA   National Archives
NAI   National Archives of India
PK   Preußischer Kulturbesitz
UB   University of Birmingham

NINETEENTH-CENTURY INDIAN PLACE NAMES WITH CONTEMPORARY VARIANTS AND TWENTY-FIRST-CENTURY EQUIVALENTS

Nineteenth-century name	*Nineteenth-century variants*	*Twenty-first-century name*
Anamagalam		Annamagalam
Andimadam		
Arkonam		Arakkonam
Bancoorah		Bankura
Bangalore	Bangalur	Bengaluru
Baroda		Vadodara
Benares		Varanasi
Betegeri	Betgeri/Bettighery/Bettigeri	Gadag-Betageri
Bodinayakanur		
Bombay		Mumbai
Burdwan		Bardhaman
Bussahir		Bushahr
Calcutta		Kolkata
Calicut		Kozhikode
Cannanore	Cannanur/Kannanur	Kannur
Cape Comorin		Kanyakumari
Ceylon		Sri Lanka
Chinsurah		Hooghly
Chota Nagpur	Chotanagpur	Chota Nagpur
Coorg	Kurg/Kurgland	Kodagu
Dhawar	Dharward	Dharward
Dindigal		Dindigul
Gorockpur		Gorakhpur
Hoobly		Hubali

TWENTY-FIRST-CENTURY EQUIVALENTS

Nineteenth-century name	Nineteenth-century variants	Twenty-first-century name
Jeypur	Jaipur	Jeypore
Kaimbatur		Coimbatore
Kairkal		Karaikal
Kalashti		Srikalahasti
Kanara	Canara/Karnataka	Kanara/Canara/Karnataka
Keti	Kety/Kaity	Ketti
Kotageri		Kotagiri
Kudelur		Cuddalore
Kumbakonam		
Lahore		Lahore
Madras		Chennai
Madura		Madurai
Mayavang		Mayiladuthurai
Mannargudi		
Mangalore	Mangalur	Mangalore
Mayavaram		Mayiladuthurai
Mercara		Madikeri
Motupatti		
Nayudupetta		Naidupeta
Negapatam		Nagapattinam
Nilgiri	Nilgiris/Nilagiri	Nilgiri
Palghat		
Panrutti		Panruti
Pegu		Bago
Peshawar		Peshawar
Pollachi		Palakkad
Pondicehri		Puducherry
Pudukotei		Pudukkottai
Puna	Poona	Pune
Ramandroog	Ramandrog	Ramandroog

TWENTY-FIRST-CENTURY EQUIVALENTS

Nineteenth-century name	Nineteenth-century variants	Twenty-first-century name
Sadras		
Sengelpa		Chengalpattu
Sholapur	Shalapoor	Solapur
Sidambaram		Chidambaram
Sind		Sindh
Sivaganga		
Tandshur		
Taliparambu		Taliparamba/ Thaliparamba
Tanjore		Thanjavur
Talatscheri		Thalassery
Tinnevelly		Tirunelveli
Tirhoot		Tirhut
Tirumangalam		
Tirupatur		Tirupattur
Tiruppur		
Triwallur	Tiruwalur	Tiruvallur
Tranquebar		Tharangambadi
Trichinopoli	Trichinopoly	Tiruchirappalli
Tripumtura		Thrippunithura
Tuticors		Tuticorin/ Thoothukudi
Udapi	Udipi	Udupi
Udumalpet		
Umballa		Ambala
Utakamand		Udhagamandalam/ Ootacamund/ Udhagai/Ooty
Vilupuram	Villupuram	Viluppuram
Virudalpati		
Virrutasalem		Virudhachalam
Yercard	Yercaud	Yercaud

CHAPTER ONE

The Germans in India as elite European migrants

A small minority with a large footprint

This book constitutes a history of a few thousand Germans who lived in India from the early nineteenth century until their expulsion during the First World War. It may seem that, on the surface, such a small minority does not deserve an entire volume devoted to it. Except for the fact that it has left an enormous footprint. I first came across this group while carrying out research on the internment of Germans in Britain during the First World War. While most of those who suffered this fate lived within British shores, the Royal Navy brought Germans from throughout the world to face incarceration in the network of camps established in Britain. These included individuals seized from ships sailing throughout the world and also people captured in both the British and German empires.[1] The most important groups transported to Britain included Germans who had lived in west Africa after the near instant defeat of the German armies in the summer and autumn of 1914.[2] In addition, German missionaries who had lived in India for years or decades also experienced transfer to Britain, some of them in the camp established in Alexandra Palace in north London.[3] They included J. Maue, initially interned in Ahmednagar in today's Gujarat.[4] The experiences of Maue point to the two areas of the history of the Germans in India which have left the largest footprints: the experiences of German missionaries; and interment during the First World War.

Beginning with the missionaries themselves, an enormous source base has survived. In the first place, the two major mission groups who sent Germans to India during the nineteenth century have their own archives. The most important of these consists of the Basel Mission. While located on the Swiss side of the German/Swiss border, a significant majority of those it sent overseas originated in Germany and, in particular, the southern German state of Württemberg, which had become a major population exporter by the beginning of the nineteenth century.[5] The Basel Mission Archive contains an extraordinary wealth of material outlining the activities of its missionaries throughout the world, ranging from letters to reports outlining activity on a daily basis including teaching, preaching and healing.[6] The Leipzig Mission has a similar set of material held in the Archiv der Franckeschen Stiftungen in Halle. Furthermore, some German missionaries worked for English groups, meaning that information survives about them in, for example, the archive of the Church Missionary Society (CMS) at the Cadbury Library at Birmingham University.

While these archival sources do not quite represent the tip of the iceberg, they form just one element of the mass of material which the German missionaries, in common with their English counterparts, kept. As several scholars of the German proselytisers have recognised, they formed a highly literate and educated group, who carried out advanced academic-style research in a variety of areas[7] and seem to have recorded their every movement while abroad, partly for the purpose of sending details of their activities back to Europe for fundraising purposes.[8] Together with the Basel Mission, the Leipzig Mission and the CMS, several other groups sent Germans out as missionaries in the form of: the Schleswig Holstein Evangelical Lutheran [Breklum] Mission;[9] the Gossner Mission[10] and the Hermmansburg Mission.[11] In addition, German Jesuits also laboured in India during the nineteenth and early twentieth centuries.[12]

Collectively, these groups published a record of their activities in the following ways. First, annual reports, especially by the large Basel and Leipzig missions, which ran for much of the nineteenth and early twentieth centuries. The former produced material in both German and English, at least for some of the nineteenth century. Together with these annual accounts, the German missionary organisations also published periodicals, which appeared more regularly.[13] These journals contain extraordinary detail about the lives of German missionaries, often repeating archival material.

In addition, these organisations issued more irregular publications, probably as part of their money-raising efforts. For example, in 1860 the Basel Mission published the *Album der Basler Mission*, subtitled *Bilder aus Indien*, a narrative of the activities of the organisation in south India, accompanied by a set of exquisite line drawings presenting an exotic portrait of the landscape and indigenous and newly arrived architecture of the areas in which the missionaries worked.[14] Three decades later, the Gossner Mission, working further north, issued a publication entitled *50 Bilder aus der Gossnerschen Kols-Mission*. Once again, this consisted of a narrative of the activies carried out by this society, together with photographs which, by this time, had become normal in such missionary publications. The subjects covered included the missionaries themselves, the people among whom they worked, the schools and churches and other buldings in which they worked, and the landscape and the people who lived within it.[15]

The German missionaries also wrote their own history, a process which began during the course of the nineteenth century. On the one hand there emerged narratives describing the evolution of the activities of German and other missionaries on a global scale, published either by English or German writers. A good example consists of *Dr. G. E. Burkhardt's Kleine Missions-Bibliothek*, anything but small as suggested in the title, regularly reissued and consisting of several volumes outlining the history of missionary activity on a global scale.[16] This publication emerged from, and linked to, the work of Reinhold Grundemann, who particularly concentrated upon producing atlases of missionary activity.[17]

But the individual missions also produced their own histories, usually through their own publishing house. This applies to the Basel Mission which issued a series of such narratives, emerging from the nineteenth century and crowned with the epic, five-volume *Geschichte der Basler Mission* begun by Wilhelm Schlatter and emerging during the First World War.[18] The publishing house in Basel also issued a series of more localised studies.[19] The other missionary societies also produced histories of their activities from the nineteenth century, especially the Leipzig Mission which, like its sister in Basel, issued both national and international studies[20] as well as more local accounts.[21] In addition, the smaller German missionary societes also produced their own stories.[22]

The missionaries also liked writing about themselves, their experiences and their perceptions of what they saw around them.[23] Perhaps the most monumental of these accounts consists of the five volumes produced by Karl Graul, first director of the Leipzig Mission, about his journey to India.[24] In addition, what can only merit the description of hagiographies also appeared. Some of these focused upon the founding fathers of the German missions; especially, within the Basel Mission, Samuel Hebich,[25] but also, in the case of the Leipzig Mission, Karl Graul,[26] as well as Johannes Evangelista Gossner who founded the eponymous Gossner Mission.[27] Also, in the early twentieth century, Johann Wörrlein wrote a series of short biographies of ordinary men working for the Hermannsburg Mission.[28]

The size of the footprint which the German missionaries have left has meant that historians have devoted much attention to them. In recent decades, academics have taken a critical primary source-based approach to their activities. They include Heike Liebau, who has looked at a variety of aspects of the Tranquebar Mission (especially interaction with the local population) which landed the first German missionaries in eighteenth-century India.[29] Judith Becker has taken a similarly rigorous and critical approach to the activities of the Basel missionaries.[30] Both of these authors have essentially focused upon the relationship between missionaries and Indians. Similarly, Andreas Nehring examined the orientalist perceptions of the Leipzig workers.[31] The activities of women have also received attention.[32]

At the same time as these critical academic studies have appeared, the more narrative approaches taken by the missionaries themselves have continued into the twentieth century with, for example, straightforward accounts of the Basel and Gossner churches in India.[33] On the other hand, Arno Lehmann and Hugald Grafe took more sophisticated approaches while outlining the evolution of German/Danish Protestantism in India.[34] Albrecht Frenz has concentrated on the activities of missionaries in India, especially those of the Basel Mission and one of its founding fathers, Hermann Gundert, through a series of biographies, collections of primary sources and edited books.[35]

Clearly, an enormous source base has survived, which would allow a study to focus simply upon the German missionaries in India. Scholars such as Heike Liebau, Judith Becker and Dagmar Konrad have used just a selection of the wealth of information available to simply focus upon one aspect of the activities of specific groups. The second area where a significant footprint has remained – the First World War experience, especially internment and deportation – has received virtually no attention from historians. Admittedly, the source base remains much smaller, without specific archives devoted to the theme, but it attracted an enormous amount of contemporary attention. In one sense it represents a sub theme within the study of German missionaries in India, although those affected included the entire German presence in the country. The information focuses upon the internment and deportation of the German population in India during the First World War.

Information on this episode survives in the national archives of the UK, Germany and India. Furthermore, the Basel Mission also holds papers, while those belonging to the Leipzig Mission have survived in the Archiv der Franckeschen Stiftungen. This issue became something of a *cause célèbre* among missionary circles during the First World War symbolising, above all, the way in which nationalism had undermined Christianity. Both English and German missionary magazines carried stories about the plight of the Germans, especially at the time of their mass internment and deportation in 1915 and 1916,[36] an episode which also resulted in the publication of numerous volumes, especially by missionaries[37] – although others who experienced life behind wire, especially in the major Indian camp at Ahmednagar, also published accounts of their experiences.[38]

The two themes of missionary studies and the experiences of both missionaries and other Germans during the Great War have therefore left a large footprint. This finds explanation not only in the fact that missionaries and their supporters recorded what appears to be their every movement on a daily basis, but also in the fact that they formed the largest element of the German presence in India. The only other significant groups in the country fit into the following categories: scholars and scientists; travellers; businessmen and other professionals; and those at the lower end of the social scale, especially sailors. Travellers have left a significant historical record because they wrote about their experiences and impressions. The activities of businessmen and the few working-class individuals remain much more difficult to reconstruct because of a lack of obvious sources.

The nature of the sources has determined the development of this project. The availability of material produced by missionaries means that they play a leading role in the story which follows and that we see much through their eyes. Their 'ego sources', whether memoirs or articles in missionary magazines, allow the construction of personal stories, in contrast to some of the histories of Germans in larger communities such as the USA or even Great Britain which, while they may have counted significantly more people, provide no more opportunities for constructing these types of rich personal narratives. The story which follows takes the type of prosopographical approach utilised by Stefan Manz in his microstudy of the Germans in Glasgow, allowing the tracing of individual lives.[39] This applies not simply to missionaries but also to academics, many of them short-term visitors, who produced memoirs of their journeys.

The use of 'ego documents' raises a series of methodological problems connected with subjectivity and the presentation of the self in an almost inevitably positive manner,[40] even though missionaries have a level of self-reflection. At the same time, the number of sources used, as well as the utilisation of other material, allows a more balanced approach. One of the main advantages of personal sources for this book lies in the richness of the descriptions they provide. Above all, some of the material used here – including that produced by the musician A. Anton[41] and the tea plantation administrator Oscar Flex[42] – proves unique, meaning that the experiences of such individuals would remain lost. On the other hand, ego documents exclude the illiterate. Winfried Schulze views this as one of their main weaknesses.[43] The less educated could also not construct elaborate narratives.

One type of personal source which this book particularly uses consists of travelogues, ultimately the impressions of Germans in India about the world around them. This applies both to those who made short trips to the country and longer term residents. Casey Blanton has pointed to the 'narrative power' of travelogues 'both literal and symbolic'.[44] While some remain 'impersonal' others resemble literary works.[45] Many of these travelogues focus upon otherness, especially in the case of Europeans in Africa, India and elsewhere during the nineteenth century, as Tim Youngs has demonstrated in his study of travellers in Africa – although his analysis recognises that such narratives have far more complexity to them.[46] In fact, Germans in India, especially missionaries, who lived in the country for long periods of time, became embedded in the civilisation which they experienced and, while they may ultimately have remained wedded to the idea of the superiority of Christian European culture, they revealed profound insights into the societies in which they lived, especially as they learnt local languages. Such travelogues, whether written by short- or long-term residents, prove important both for revealing the ideologies of those who wrote them, and for providing information on the societies which they observed.

The Germans and *India*

While historians have devoted relatively little attention to the German missionaries in India, scholars and scientists have attracted significant consideration. Much writing in both German and English has focused upon the connections between India and Germany, especially in the research and intellectual sphere, but, in reality, relatively few of the great and less well-known German scholars and writers who constructed this 'symbiosis' spent any time in India during the course of the nineteenth and early twentieth century.

The connection between the Germans *and* India has a long intellectual tradition, recognised by many scholars writing today, which we need to examine. In the first place, we can recognise 'indology'[47] as an academic discipline, as outlined by Douglas McGetchin, who points out that by the beginning of the twentieth century 'Germany had more university professors studying Sanskrit than all other European countries combined. By 1903 in Germany there were forty-seven professors, including twenty-six full professors, of "Aryan" studies, a category that included, as its major component, Indology.'[48] Indra Sengupta has traced the development of the academic fascination of Germans with India back to the eighteenth century. She points out that the German Halle (subsequently Leipzig) missionaries had 'discovered' India in this century, but that 'it was the Romantic interest in India that was directly relevant for the transformation of nebulous ideas about the particular kind of scholarship that was to become academic Indology'.[49] Sengupta stresses the role of German states and the establishment of relevant chairs in the evolution of indology as an academic discipline.

If we take another perspective on this, German scholars played a central role in the growth of orientalism, which Edward Said recognised but essentially ignored, for which he reproached himself. However, he made two fundamental points. First, many German Orientalists spent no time in the East. As he points out: 'the two most recognised German works on the Orient, Goethe's *Westöstlicher Diwan* and Friedrich Schlegel's *Über die Sprache und Weisheit der Inder* were based respectively on a Rhine journey and on hours spent in Paris libraries'. At the same time, Said also stressed that 'at no time in German scholarship during the first two-thirds of the nineteenth century could a close partnership have developed between Orientalists and a protracted, sustained *national* interest in the Orient. There was nothing in Germany to correspond to the Anglo-French presence in India, the Levant or North Africa.' However, the German Orientalists, like those from Britain, France and the USA, constructed 'a kind of intellectual *authority* over the Orient within western culture'.[50] The most monumental study of German orientalism comes from Suzanne Marchand. She not only takes a longer chronology than, for example, Sengupta, but also broadens her geographical perspective to include perceptions of the orient in Germany from the Ottoman Empire to the German Pacific Empire, encompassing everything in between. Additionally, she does not simply focus upon the views of intellectuals and scholars, but also upon the importance of such perceptions for the development and practice of German colonialism and expansionism.[51] This points to the fact that German scholars working on India did not operate in isolation but formed part of a wider fascination with 'the East' which incorporated not simply German researchers but also broader groups of elites with an interest in the Orient. Perry Myers takes a more focused approach, concentrating upon *German Visions of India* during the Kaiserreich and pointing to the contradictory reasons why German thinkers focused upon India in this period, whether because they wanted to use it to undermine the protestant-based Bismarckian and Wilhelminian great power politics by focusing upon alternative religions, or whether, in contrast, this knowledge became part of the justification for imperial expansion.[52]

In fact, this recent sophisticated academic research on German views of India, which utilises the orientalist paradigm, builds upon earlier, perhaps more innocent, philosophically based studies which tended to focus upon the views of India held by the canon of German philosophers including Kant, Herder, Hegel, Schelling and Schopenauer[53] – an approach which has not disappeared.[54] Such approaches in one sense trace the origins of German academic indology but, on the other hand, also appear to simply extract any thoughts which the figures examined held about India.

These studies of German ideas have run parallel to others which have focused upon what we might describe as research on German literary perceptions of India. An important scholar here is Vidhagiri Ganeshan, who published a book focusing upon well-known and less-famous writers who travelled to India,[55] as well as producing a volume which focused upon the engagement of Hermann Hesse (the grandson of the pioneer Basel missionary Hermann Gundert) with India.[56] Veena Kade-Luthra has also edited an anthology of German writers who have engaged with India, from Herder to Günther Grass and beyond.[57]

Such research points to a German intellectual and literary fascination with India, which fed the growth of the academic discipline that scholars have described as indology, driven forward by three factors in particular in the form of the German missionary discovery of India, the support of German states for the growth of this discipline – reflecting broader backing for education in this period – and the evolution of German nationhood with a perspective which looked beyond German borders. However, this fascination proves relatively limited in helping to explain the presence of Germans in India. Despite the growth of indology, many German scholars solely relied upon manuscripts in German libraries, especially during the early nineteenth century. Much travelling simply took place between different European University libraries which held relevant texts.[58] Sengupta recognises the second half of the nineteenth century as a turning point in the travelling of German indologists to India, partly because of the opening of the Suez Canal but also because of the desire of the British Imperial Government to employ experts in educational institutions.[59]

Apart from Sengupta, two other recent studies have recognised the connection between the German fascination for India and the presence of Germans in the country. A collection of essays edited by Joanne Miyang Cho, Eric Kurlander and Douglas T. McGetchin focuses upon a variety of *Transcultural Encounters* over the past 200 years.[60] More importantly, Kris Manjapra has examined the variety of ways in which German and Indian intellectuals became 'entangled' from 1815 to the present. While his volume, like most of those outlined above, focuses upon the realm of ideas, it includes an important chapter on 'German Servants of the British Raj' which pays particular attention to scholars who made their way to the country and, as the subtitle suggests, those who worked for the British Government, especially, as Ulrike Kirchberger and others have demonstrated, in the field of forestry.[61] Slightly earlier than Manjapra, Kamakshi Murti took an approach encompassing the fascination of German Orientalists and missionaries – whether working from Europe or present in India – which argued that, in many ways, this interest worked on a gendered basis.[62]

Clearly, much discourse has surfaced on the fascination of German intellectuals and scholars with India. This study will only consider this theme to the extent that it motivated individuals to make their way to work and live in the country. In fact, as the above discussion has suggested, the eighteenth-century missionaries acted as a spark which led to the fire of fascination which engulfed German thought over the next 200 years and which caused some writers to make their way to the country.

The first Germans in India

Most histories of the German presence in India do not begin with Bartholomäus Ziegenbalg and Heinrich Plütschau, the first missionaries who arrived in the Tamil port of Tranquebar in 1706, but, instead, tend to go back to the early sixteenth century, when Nuremberg and Augsburg merchants in Lisbon made their way to India with the Portuguese explorers and colonisers of the time. However, Walter Leifer suggests that some pilgrims may have travelled to the site where St Thomas died in Kerala during the Middle Ages.[63]

But most attention has focused upon the German merchants who moved to Lisbon and then on to the west coast of India in the early sixteenth century, reflecting an engagement of German elites with the Spanish and Portuguese empires in the Early Modern period which has been stressed by David Blackbourn.[64] Wolfgang Knabe has suggested the presence of 21 merchants in Lisbon between 1502 and 1619,[65] although earlier works trace the first journey of Germans to Portuguese India to 1505.[66] They included the prosperous Fuggers, Welsers and Hoechstetters. Hermann Kellenbenz has focused upon the activities of Jorg Imhoff, a Rothenberger who worked for the Herwarts of Augsburg and set sail for India in 1526, where he visited Goa, Cannanore, Cochin and Vijayanagara.[67]

Michael Mann, in an essay forming part of a collection on German elite migrations, has also recognised these early merchants as a group who made their way to India from the sixteenth to the eighteenth centuries. He views them, together with the mercenaries which he examines, as individuals who moved to India in order to escape the threat of poverty and to reinvigorate their careers or to begin a new course in life, prepared to take the risk of moving despite the high mortality rates of the journey and resettlement. His analysis also focuses upon those who moved further east than the Indian subcontinent to present-day Malaysia, demonstrating the fact that India provided just one destination for elites. Mann has also examined botanists and doctors who travelled to India during the eighteenth century. However, he devotes more attention to mercenaries and soldiers, as does Chen Tzoref-Ashkenazi. Both point to the fact that people from German-speaking Europe, as well as from elsewhere on the continent, served the British Empire throughout the world during the eighteenth century. Germans also worked for both the Dutch and British East India companies during this period. The dynastic connection proved especially important as several thousand Hanoverians fought in India.[68]

The eighteenth century also witnessed the beginning of German Protestant missionary activity in south India, which has a 'birthday'[69] of 9 July 1706 when Bartholomäus Ziegenbalg and Heinrich Plütschau landed in Tranquebar, where a memorial to commemorate this event now exists. Their arrival there took place against the background of the rise of Pietism in Germany, with an evangelical zeal which wanted to see not only the improvement of social conditions in Germany but also the sending of missionaries to carry out conversions in the wider world. In fact, Ziegenbalg and Plütschau arrived in the service of the Danish King and the Danish East India Company. They spent much of their time learning Portuguese and Tamil, with Ziegenbalg concentrating on the latter, meaning that he not only created Tamil dictionaries, but also wrote studies of the people he observed around him. In addition, and perhaps most importantly, Ziegenbalg scripted the first Indian translation of the *New Testament*, published in 1714. Conversion work started fairly instantly so that by the end of 1706 German services took place in Tranquebar. By 1720, the community counted about 250 members from a variety of backgrounds including converts from the already existing Roman Catholic communities. This set in train a development which would continue into the nineteenth century, as did the establishment of charity schools by Ziegenbalg, based upon the model of those opened by the Franckeschen Stiftung in Halle and established by August Francke who had influenced Ziegenbalg. As the century progressed, the congregation set up by Ziegenbalg – who died in 1719 – became truly multilingual such that Danish, German, Portuguese and Tamil all played a role in the communication between Europeans and Indians. This multilingualism became essential in the growth of Lutheranism in Tranquebar as the incoming church employed native catechists in order to spread the word. By 1718, the imposing New Jerusalem Church, the first Protestant place of worship in India, had come into existence. Europeans from several countries played a role in its establishment with help from a variety of European states. Christianity consolidated in Tranquebar during the eighteenth century and spread to other parts of southern India, partly due to the efforts of native catechists but also because of the activities of a series of Germans with a similar dynamism to Ziegenbalg. These included Johann Ernst Gründler, Benjamin Schultze and Johann Philip Fabricius. Christian Friedrich Schwartz, who arrived in 1750 and remained until his death in 1798, played a particularly important role. By this time, Pietist congregations had reached the southern tip of India in Cape Comorin, 503 kilometres from Tranquebar. By 1806, Lutheran missionaries had baptised 36,970 Indians. Those who carried out this work included dozens of Germans. The Tranquebar Mission declined and fizzled out by the early 1840s, partly because of a lessening support from the Danish Crown, although by this time new Anglican missions had moved into the areas it covered and had taken over the old stations. Other Germans began working for British-based groups, including the early Society for Promoting Christian Knowledge, the London Missionary Society and the CMS.[70]

The nineteenth-century missionaries

These early arrivals set in motion some of the patterns which would continue into the nineteenth century. In the hundred years before the outbreak of the First World War, thousands of missionaries would make their way to the territories controlled by the East India Company and the British Government. Some histories of Christianity and Christian missionaries do not distinguish between the national origins of those who made their way to India, preferring to focus upon key themes in the relationship between European and North American missionaries with Indians and other peoples with whom they came into contact.[71] Furthermore, while distinctive German missionary organisations evolved during the course of the nineteenth century, the example of the Danish-backed society which emerged in Tranquebar and employed Germans in some of the leading positions indicates the international nature of this grouping, transcending state and linguistic boundaries even after the formation of the German nation state in 1871, as the Basel Mission also attests.

Although Germans may have constituted some of the first Protestant missionaries to travel to India in the early eighteenth century, 100 years later British, American and Swiss organisations had also moved into the country. By the 1830s, the Church Mission Society (CMS), the London Mission Society, the Basel Mission, together with Baptist and Wesleyan groups, had all become active in India.[72] In the earlier nineteenth century, most Germans worked either for the British groups or for the Basel Mission, with the latter continuing to employ a predominance of Germans, especially from nearby Württemberg. The *Register of Missionaries* produced by the CMS included, by 1875, 86 Germans from the 834 sent out not just to India but also to the other areas in which this organisation became active – including Africa, New Zealand and the Middle East – meaning over 10 per cent in these years; although after this time, when German organisations had become established and carved out their own niches throughout the world, no Germans went out with the CMS. In fact, the further back we go in the nineteenth century, the higher the percentage of Germans – standing, for instance, at 22 from 56 (39 per cent) between 1804 and 1819.[73] The classic work on the CMS by Eugen Stock pointed to the fact that, of the 98 men who went from Europe by 1824, 'thirty-two were English clergymen; thirty-two were English laymen (including a few who were ordained afterwards); thirty were in Lutheran orders (sixteen from the Berlin Seminary, nine from the Basel Seminary, two from the University of Jena, and three others) and four were German laymen'. The Basel Mission continued to supply 'some of the noblest and most devoted missionaries in to the 1840s'.[74] Returning to the overall figure of the 86 German missionaries sent out by the CMS by 1875, over 50 per cent, at 47, carried out activities in the different areas of India in which the CMS became involved. We can give the example of John Fuchs, from Plieningen in Württemberg, trained in Basel, who went to India in 1847, aged 28, and served in Lucknow and Benares – dying in the latter in 1878 after catching smallpox in nearby Chunar.[75] Meanwhile, Henry Stern – born in Karlsruhe and also trained in Basel – went out in 1849 at the age of 23 and worked in Benares and Goruckpur, where he led a mission for 41 years.[76] Some of the German-born missionaries who went to India with the CMS have left accounts of their experiences. The most monumental is the life story of John Jakob Weitbrecht (compiled by his widow), who travelled to London in 1828 and then went to Burdwan in North India in 1830, perishing of cholera in Calcutta in 1852.[77] Similarly, we have the equally epic hagiography of Charles Rhenius, produced by his son. Educated at the Berlin Seminary, Rhenius spent much of his 21-year missionary life working in the Tinnevelly Mission station in south India.[78] As well as the CMS, Germans also worked for a series of other British-based groupings in the first half of the nineteenth century, including 32 for the London Missionary Society as well as others employed by the Baptist Missionary Society. Ulrike Kirchberger has described them as 'fellow-labourers in the same vineyard' as their British brethren.[79]

Although the phenomenon of Germans working for British groupings characterised the early nineteenth century, their work for the Swiss-based grouping in Basel lasted until their expulsion during the First World War. In fact, while based in Basel, the majority of the Mission employees actually consisted of Germans, particularly originating from nearby Baden and, more especially, Württemberg, which had its own migratory tradition that sent people all over the world, including towards England.[80]

Perhaps above all other missionary organisations, the German Evangelical Mission Society encapsulates the global activities of the Christian Church during the nineteenth century, focusing not simply upon its southern Indian base, but also on a series of locations in West Africa, China and North Borneo.[81] This body emerged gradually towards the end of the eighteenth century from south German and Swiss Pietism, initially as the Christian Society in Basel, and would become formalised at a meeting in the city in September 1815. Much of its initial efforts focused upon activities in Germany and Switzerland. The mission school developed courses for potential missionaries. After their initial training, 'brothers' started moving into service abroad in Africa and the Caucasus where Basel mission stations became established during the course of the 1820s.[82]

Self-standing Basel mission stations did not open in India until the following decade. The standard histories of the development of Basel activity in India present the same narrative. In 1833, Parliament renewed the Charter of the East India Company with an additional clause allowing foreigners to establish their own organisations. Foreigners also obtained equal rights with Britons, including protection if they pursued Protestant religious activity in the country, meaning that those trained in Basel could now move to India to open up their own stations, which happened fairly instantly because of the desire and enthusiasm of the hierarchy in Switzerland, helped by the connections between Basel and the CMS. The Inspector of the Basel Mission at the time, Christian Gottlieb Blumhardt, actually found himself in London when Parliament reached its decision and returned to India instantly in order to begin work on establishing self-standing stations. Although plans emerged for activity in north India, these did not materialise. Instead, the Basel Mission decided to focus upon the south-west coast, where a series of concentrations evolved. The first missionaries actually arrived in Calcutta in October 1834, having originally travelled to London to make their onward journey, consisting of the Württemberg-born Samuel Hebich and Christian Leonhard Greiner, together with Johann Christian Lehner from Rhein Hessen.[83]

Over the next 80 years, until expulsion during the First World War, the Basel Mission would develop a detailed network of missionary activity involving churches, schools and charitable organisations (Figure 1.1). As already mentioned, their work concentrated upon the south-west coast of India revolving around four major diocese in the form of Kanara (including Kurg), South Maharatta, Malabar and Niligiri. Hebich, Greiner and Lehner founded the first of these diocese after arriving here in 1834, while Hermann Gundert established the second in 1839 when he moved here with his wife. Activity in south Maharatta began in 1837 and in Niligiri in 1846.[84] These individual locations would expand over the course of the nineteenth century, establishing stations within them, reaching 17 by 1871 and 19 by 1890. A snapshot from 1871 reveals 61 schools, including 15 seminaries and 16 middle schools.[85] A directory of the property of the Mission in south India from 1890 helps us to understand the scale of the activity. For example, the station of Udapi, which came under South Kanara included: 'a great compound', which had a church, two mission houses, a middle school, two homes for the middle-school teachers, a boys school, a sick room, a widow's home, a palm garden and fields, together with a girls school in the city of Udapi. In fact, this list simply refers to Udapi city and excludes the property owned by five further branches (Filiale) connected with it.[86] Such figures only provide an indication of the activities of the Basel Mission in south-west India. Apart from its religious and charitable activities, it also developed an industrial branch, which meant the opening of workshops and factories, especially in weaving.[87]

The range of activities carried out by the Basel Mission could only operate on the basis of conversion and co-operation from local populations, as becomes clear when examining the small numbers of European-born missionaries who actually made their way there in the century before the outbreak of the First World War. To return to another snapshot, a report from 1871 suggested that 5,586 people came 'under the care of the mission', which included 2,193 'communicants', 147 'non-communicants' and 1,964 children all described as 'members of the Church', together with 231 catechumen and 1,146 schoolmasters and scholars. The missionaries totalled 55 brethren and 33 sisters.[88] In fact, a table of the missionaries sent to India by the Basel Mission in the Basel Mission Archives (BMA) gives a total of just 438 who travelled here before the First World War. A majority of these, 287, actually came from locations in Germany, especially Württemberg and, to a lesser extent, Baden, while the rest came mostly from Switzerland, together with some – with German names – born in India, presumably to already established missionary families, and a few from Alsace.[89] The number of women which the Basel Mission sent out during this period totalled 297 including 180 from Germany, again mostly from Württemberg, with the rest coming from similar origins to the males.[90]

GERMANS IN INDIA AS ELITE EUROPEAN MIGRANTS

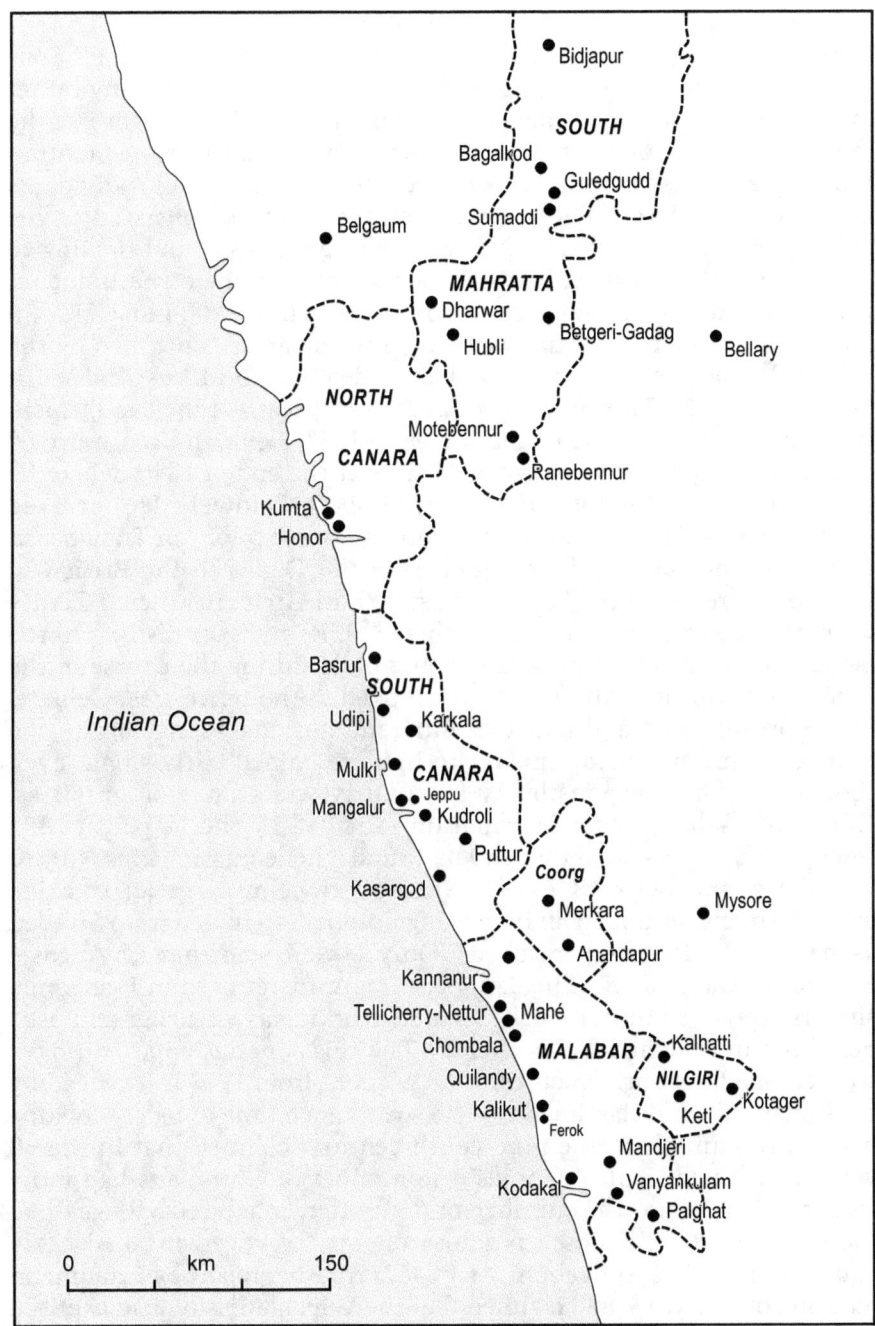

Figure 1.1 Map of Basel Mission activity in India

Such figures provide an indication of the small number of Germans who made their way to India. The other German missionary organisations sent out even fewer people, but did have their base in Germany rather than Switzerland, which made them more purely German both in the sense of the location of their headquarters and because of the fact that the people they sent to India consisted almost entirely of individuals from German states. The most important of these consisted of the Leipzig Mission, founded initially in Dresden in 1836 and moving to a headquarters in Leipzig in 1848. As well as carrying out missionary work in Germany, it focused its efforts on Australia and India. Within the last of these, it essentially moved into the areas controlled by the Danish Mission in Tranquebar and expanded into south-east and south India (Figure 1.2). This process began after the death of the last Danish-Halle missionary, Friedrich Caemmerer, in 1837. Heinrich Cordes arrived as the first Leipzig missionary in Madras at the end of 1840, where he stayed with the London missionary, Robert Caldwell. He received instructions to concentrate on the declining Danish colony in Tranquebar. Following the selling of Tranquebar by the Danes to the British in 1843, the Director of the Leipzig Mission, Karl Graul, instructed Cordes to move forward with his efforts there.[91] Like the Basel Mission, the Leipzig Mission would expand exponentially during the course of the nineteenth century. An 1888 report looked at the territories (Gebiete) of the organisation and listed 23 different stations.[92] Once again, the number of missionaries sent out to India remained fairly small, even though they had responsibility for a fairly wide range of activities. Christoph Gäbler, using information provided by the Leipziger Missionswerk, has suggested that 130 male and female missionaries worked in India in the years 1846–1915. The overwhelming majority came from Germany, although an increasing number originated from Sweden as the First World War approached.[93] Only 23 were women, with Auguste Hensolt as the pioneer. The daughter of a minister born in Franconia, she first travelled to India in 1895 after working as a teacher and used her skills in several schools there.[94] The missionaries appear to have worked in a target-driven culture. An account from 1903 by the leading missionary Richard Handmann – who spent much time in India – looking back to the middle of the nineteenth century, claimed that in the 20 years after the arrival of Cordes 'the number of Christians had more than trebled' while the number of 'Christian inhabited villages had increased fourfold'. These grandiose claims, however, masked fairly small numbers in a 'soul count' of 4,846.[95] Another report by Handmann focusing on the year 1888 claimed that the Leipzig Mission had baptised 15,749 'heathens' in the previous 46 years and established 149 schools.[96] By the end of 1910, these figures had increased significantly to: 30

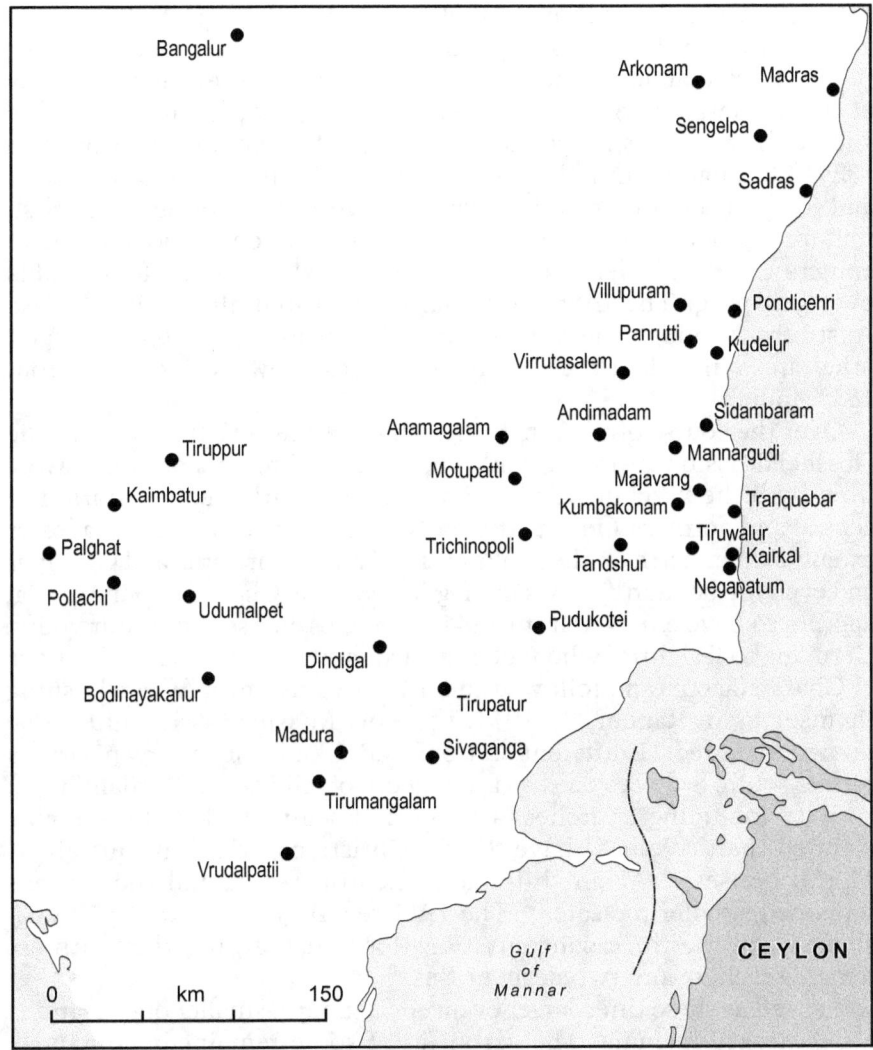

Figure 1.2 Locations of Leipzig mission stations

main stations and 230 subsidiary stations; 33 missionaries, including 30 ordained, one doctor and two others; 13 European sisters; 187 native helpers; and 11,740 pupils.[97]

The other significant German evangelical missionary grouping in India consisted of the Gossner Mission, named after its founder, Johannes Evangelista Gossner. Born in Bavaria in 1773, he initially became ordained as a Roman Catholic priest in 1796 but gradually moved over to

Protestantism after working in south and west Germany, St Petersburg and a variety of locations in north Germany. He eventually reached Berlin in 1826 and, despite some initial hostility from the main body of the Lutheran clergy here, he took the exams necessary to convert and became responsible for the Bethlehem Lutheran congregation in 1829. Although he initially worked for the Berlin Missionary Society and focused upon domestic missionary work, his reading of English missionary tracts persuaded him of the need to look beyond German borders. In 1836, he left the Berlin Missionary Society and founded his own grouping. The first missionaries ventured abroad in 1837 to Australia, although the organisation also focused its attention upon other areas including the Dutch East Indies, New Zealand and, from 1838, India.[98]

Over the course of the nineteenth and early twentieth centuries, the Gossner Mission in India would focus upon three major areas, away from both the Basel or Leipzig groupings and with a concentration in central and northern India, particularly in Chota Nagpur and, to a lesser extent, further north on the banks of the Ganges near Patna and Ghazipur and even further north in Assam (Figure 1.3). The Chota Nagpur Mission appears to have emerged from 1844 when Gossner sent out four young Germans to Calcutta, who made the acquaintance of Kols, the natives of Chata Nagpur, and followed them westwards, initially establishing themselves in Ranchi. By 1911, the Kols Mission, as it came to be known, counted 21 different stations and, like its sister organisations further south, had developed a vast network of religious and philanthropic activity including churches, schools and seminaries. A 1911 report claimed that: 'We now have 91,500 Christians, which means about 12,500 houses.'[99] Meanwhile, activities in Assam and the Ganges remained smaller in scale.[100] The 1911 report gives a total of 50 missionaries in the three concentrations for that year, together with six female teachers and two deaconesses.[101]

As well as these three larger evangelical groups, smaller organisations also emerged in India. The activities of some remained short-lived, including the Berlin Missionary Society, which worked in Ghazipur on the Ganges from 1842–7, but withdrew to focus upon South Africa. The North German Missionary Society operated further south in Rajahmundry from 1843, but then passed its work on to American German Lutherans in 1848. Meanwhile, the Women's Association for the Education of Females in the Orient (Morgenländische Frauenverein) worked with the CMS at a girl's orphanage in Sigra, near Benares and then at Sicandra, near Agra from 1863.[102] The Schleswig-Holsteinischer evangelisch-lutherischer Missionsgesellschaft, with its German headquarters in Breklum in Schleswig, concentrated its efforts in Jeypur and

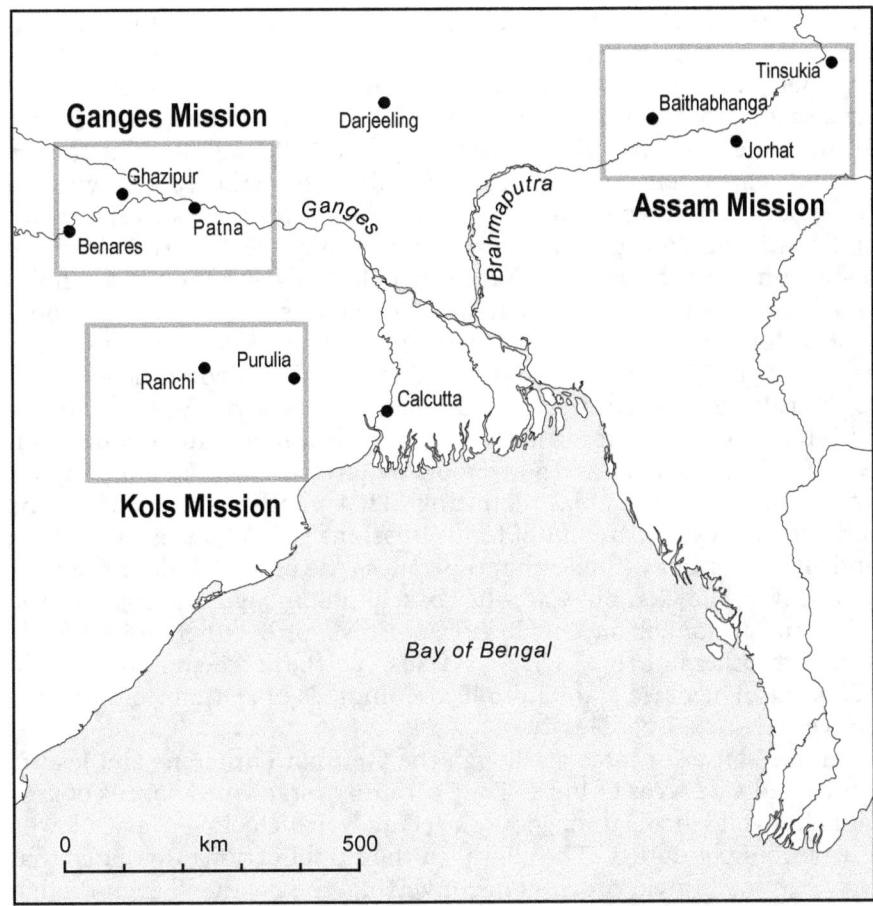

Figure 1.3 Map of Gossner Mission activity in India

the Teluguland from 1876, and developed the whole range of religious and welfare activities. By 1901, it claimed to have baptised 4,944 people and also taught 718 children in the seven stations it had established. It only counted 15 missionaries, consisting of 11 men and four women.[103] The only other German Protestant group worth mentioning consists of the Hermannsburg Society, which first sent out missionaries to south Telugu during the 1860s, opening stations in Salurpetta, Nayudupetta, Gudur, Rupur, Vakadu, Venkatagiri, Kalashti, Tirupati and Kodur.[104]

Together with the Lutheran groups established during the course of the nineteenth century, German Jesuits also became similarly active in India during the same period, building upon the work of their

Portuguese brethren from the seventeenth century. While Roman Catholic decline had occurred here during the eighteenth century, especially following the suppression of the Society of Jesus in 1773, a renaissance took place after its re-establishment by Pope Gregory XVI, allowing Jesuits to land in India from 1837.[105] The German Jesuits became particularly important in Bombay from the 1850s, where a series of Germans served as bishop, beginning with Athanasius Hartmann and continuing with John Meurin. In the same decade, the Sisters of Jesus and Mary became active there. The most important Catholic achievements in Bombay included the establishment of educational institutions such as St Xavier's College, a higher education institute, as well as boys' and girls' schools. In addition, following the example of their Protestant brethren, the German Jesuits carried out missionary activity in other parts of India, again with a focus upon education, establishing as many as 154 schools as far away as Karachi, Gujerat and Tamil speaking areas, counting 3,204 pupils at one stage. This reflected the establishment of Jesuit missions in Sind, Dhawar, Gujerat and efforts amongst the Kathkari peoples. At the outbreak of the First World War, the German Catholics based in Bombay-Puna counted the following personnel: one archbishop, one bishop, 92 fathers, 16 scholars, and 23 brothers of the Society of Jesus. To these we should also add 123 nuns. They also claimed to have hundreds of stations and to have converted 42,207 people.[106]

In one sense it seems as though the German Lutherans and Jesuits controlled vast areas of India. They certainly established dozens of new churches and schools throughout the country, which often overshadowed surrounding buildings. The claims in their publications suggested that they had made great progress in converting 'the heathen', even though a closer inspection of figures suggests that the total number of people baptised by German missionaries probably totalled no more than a few hundred thousand, which needs contextualisation against the background of an Indian population of hundreds of millions. Clearly, the German Protestant missionaries remained one piece in a vast jigsaw of Christian activity, which also emanated from Britain, America and Scandinavia in particular. The Germans usually co-operated with other national groupings so that, at the same time as European states carved up the world in the age of empire, European and North American Missionary societies divided up spheres of influence and produced maps, mirroring the political cartography of the world, to demonstrate their prowess and success.[107] India formed just one piece of the jigsaw while the German missionaries formed just one image in this particular piece. While some scholars asserted that the flag often followed missions,[108] the situation remained more complex in India, gradually taken over

Scholars and scientists

While missionaries constituted a significant percentage of the Germans in India by the First World War, other occupational groupings also lived here. The first includes scholars and scientists. While many indologists never made their way to India, their numbers increased as the nineteenth century progressed. An early example was Hans Roer. Born in Brunswick in 1805, he studied Sanskrit in Berlin and then moved to Calcutta in the service of the East India Company, becoming the librarian of the Asiatic Society of Bengal in 1841 and establishing a tradition of Germans in the development of research libraries in India during the nineteenth century – especially in Bombay. He remained in the country until his death in 1861. This sketch of Roer's life comes from the set of biographies of *Scholars in Indian Studies Writing in German*, compiled by Valentina Stache-Rosen in 1981. While her list includes people who had interests in the East beyond India, of the 101 people who became academics before the First World War (i.e. born between 1767 and 1881), only 27 actually appear to have travelled to India. Interestingly, she includes missionaries such as Gundert and Graul. Travel to India certainly became more common as the century progressed. If we ignore some of the missionaries who spent the bulk of their lives in India, we can distinguish those who simply made research trips to the country from those who took up academic posts in India. In the first category we can include Richard Pischel, who actually died in Madras in 1908 after taking up an invitation to lecture in Calcutta in that year. Meanwhile, Richard von Garbe travelled to India on an 18-month research trip in 1885 and published his experiences in a book.[109] Those who took up posts in India included Georg Thibaut, born in Heidelberg in 1848. He went to England to work with Max Mueller in 1871, moved to a Chair in Anglo-Sanskrit in Benares Hindu College in 1875 and eventually became Principal of Muir Central College in Allahabad in 1895.[110]

Together with these humanities scholars, we can also mention a category of Germans who come under the broad definition of scientists. One of the most famous consisted of the ground-breaking bacteriologist and epidemiologist Robert Koch who, like some of his fellow researchers working in the humanities, made research trips to India. Thus, in 1897, he travelled to Bombay on behalf of the German Government to investigate an outbreak of the bubonic plague in both India and East Africa. This followed an earlier journey to Calcutta at Christmas of

1883, when he investigated cholera and then attended an international exhibition in the city in January 1884. Koch further travelled to Java and New Guinea to pursue his research. Those who accompanied Koch on this trip included Georg Gaffky, who helped to draw up a report on the expedition.[111]

Ulrike Kirchberger has also identified German natural scientists in India, above all the Schlagintweit brothers (Adolphe, Hermann and Robert), who left Southampton in September 1854 and would travel through the country until 1857. Following in the tradition of the earlier nineteenth-century German natural explorer, Alexander von Humboldt,[112] the Schlagintweits carried out research for the magnetic survey of India in a trip from Bombay to Madras, which they published, and also produced a lavishly illustrated three-volume work about their travels, completed by Hermann Schlagintweit. One of the brothers, Adolphe, was actually murdered in Central Asia following an outbreak of rioting. Like many travel accounts published at this time, and resembling the anthropological work of some of the missionaries, they contain extraordinary details of the vast areas which the brothers visited.[113]

While the Schlagintweit brothers remained in India for a relatively short time, other natural scientists spent much longer in the country. Particular attention has rightly focused upon the role of Germans in the development of forestry there, where a whole series of individuals participated. The most important and pioneering figure consisted of Dietrich Brandis, the son of a philosophy professor in Bonn. He became known to the Governor-General of the time, Lord Dalhousie, through a family connection – as his wife's sister was married to Major General Sir Henry Havelock, who would help to suppress the Indian Mutiny. Dalhousie appointed him Superintendent of the Pegu Teak forests in Burma in 1856, following the annexation of Pegu by the British 1852, after which he became responsible for all Burmese forests from 1857–62. From 1864 he became the first Inspector General of Forests to the Government of India and would hold this position until he retired in 1883.[114] Two immediate successors of Brandis were German, namely Sir William Schlich, who held the position from 1883–5, and Berthold Ribbentrop, who would remain in post from 1889 until 1900. Schlich had completed a PhD in forestry at Gießen University in 1866 and would initially work in Burma before transfer to Sind and then the Punjab. Similarly, Ribbentrop, having studied forestry in Germany, initially worked in the Punjab and then Burma.[115] Ulrike Kirchberger has also identified a series of botanists who worked for the Indian Forest Service, as well as scientists such as Hugo Warth who moved to India to become the leading expert in the saline industry during the 1870s.[116] We should also mention John Augustus Voelcker, a German trained chemist, who held a series of positions in Britain, including consulting chemist to the Royal Agricultural Society. This took him to India on three different occasions between 1889 and 1891, where he spent 13 months touring the whole country and produced his lengthy *Report on the Improvement of Indian Agriculture*.[117]

Travellers

Voelcker might fall into a third category of Germans in nineteenth-century India in the form of travellers, as might some of the other scholars and students who visited the country, such as the Schlagintweit brothers. In fact, this group of professional and upper-class individuals remains rather miscellaneous. Not only did the Schlagintweits keep accounts of their travels through the country, but so did many of the missionaries, including, for example, Karl Graul,[118] Karl Heinrich Plath, who worked for the Gossner Mission,[119] the German Jesuit Joseph Dahlmann[120] and Waldemar Bonsels, working for a short period for the Basel Mission before he publicly declared his resignation.[121] Other academics also produced accounts of their journeys to India, including the Kiel Philosophy Professor, Paul Deussen, the biologist Ernst Haeckel and the engineer Franz Reuleaux. While some of these accounts may contain scientific observation, others focus primarily upon the experience of travelling through, residing in and observing India. Haeckel's account falls into the first category, with observations which we can describe as scientific, although he spends much of his narrative observing the urban and human, as well as the natural, environment he encounters. Deussen, on the other hand, certainly devotes some attention towards Indian religion but also, for example, focuses upon his hotel when he arrives in Bombay.[122]

In addition to these individuals who recorded their experiences partly or largely in connection with their professional lives, others travelled to India as high-class tourists. This would apply, for instance, to Eugenie Schaeuffelen, who recorded her experiences in India in 1903,[123] or to Max Zimmer,[124] who also made a journey to India in the same decade. Count Hans Von Koenigsmarck, meanwhile, focused specifically upon his observations on the British and their administration in India.[125] In 1911, there emerged an account of the visit of the German crown princes in India, written by Oscar Bongard.[126] Several decades earlier a slightly different aristocratic narrative had emerged, written by Countess Nostiz, who had accompanied her husband, Dr Helfer, to India in 1835–6.[127]

Clearly, these travellers spent a relatively short period of time in India and, in some cases, the accounts which they produced devoted much attention to the journey, as well as their experiences and impressions once they arrived and travelled around the country. In terms of the length of their stay, they resemble some of the academics. They number fewer people than the missionaries, but they constitute an important section of our Germans in India for two reasons. First, because they form one of the groups in the essentially elite populations which travelled from Germany to India in our period. Second, the impressions which they produced, taken together with those of the missionaries and scientists, provide an important insight into the opinions of the elite German mind towards India, Indians, Britain and British rule.

Businessmen and other professionals

As the nineteenth century progressed, and German industrialisation evolved, representatives of German firms ventured into India. Consulates of the individual pre-unification German states opened up to assist this process from the earlier part of the nineteenth century. German-based ships had begun sailing to India in the final decades of the eighteenth century. The first trade representative appeared in 1844 when A. H. Huschke of Hesse established a business in Bombay, where he also acted as consul for both Hesse and Hamburg. In the same year, a consulate opened in Calcutta. During the course of the 1850s, Prussia, Hanover, Bremen and Saxony established consulates in India. German unification resulted in the opening of Imperial consulates, above all in Bombay, Calcutta and Madras. The introduction of free trade in India in 1882 aided the growth of business with Germany. By the end of the nineteenth century, firms such as Krupps, Siemens and Thyssen had representatives in India. For example, German engineers from Siemens played a role in the construction of the Tata Steelworks in Jamshedpur. Meanwhile, the Berlin firm of Borsig and Orenstein together with Koppel helped in the construction of railways in India at the beginning of the twentieth century. Smaller firms also sent representatives to India, including Heinrich König from Bumb and König. He travelled from Berlin to Bombay in 1905 for the purpose of gathering recordings of Indian artists and managed to produce over 300 records of music and singing in Hindustani, Urdu, Maharati, Gujurati and Bengali. Meanwhile, the German dye firm of Meister, Lucius and Brüning, based in Höchst am Main, opened a branch in Bombay. In 1896 the first German bank branch became established in Calcutta in the form of the Deustch-Asiatische Bank, which had outlets throughout the Orient with a particular concentration upon China.[128]

While the presence of businessmen largely receives explanation from the growth of trade between India and Germany, many other miscellaneous German professionals who would not fit into any of the categories outlined above also lived in India during the course of the nineteenth and early twentieth centuries. For example, Robert Vincent, born in Teterow in the Grand Duchy of Mecklenburg-Schwerin, served on a British ship in the late 1860s after fighting for Garibaldi in Italy and then facing capture as a prisoner of war. After landing in India he served in the British Indian army and learnt local languages and dialects. He then became a policeman in Bombay and eventually rose to the position of Police President.[129] Similarly, after advertising the post of City Architect and Surveyor, the Corporation of Calcutta appointed Otto Pöthig, who made an application directly from Germany where he held the position of 'Government Architect on one of the Local Boards of Berlin'.[130] A selection of files connected with internment and deportation during the First World War also reveals the miscellany of German professionals in India in this period. A list of deportees from January 1916, while dominated by Jesuit priests from Bombay, also includes: Ernst Schroder, a 53-year-old schoolmaster; 57-year-old August Schunemann, an engineer from Madras; and Hermann Johann Christian Bentzien, a 57-year-old piano maker from Puna.[131] Another list of internees at Ahmednagar, again dominated by missionaries, includes, for example: Otto Schrader, a 56-year-old photographer; and 62-year-old Gustav Jelke, owner of a soda water and ice factory in Belgaum.[132]

'Low and licentious Europeans'

The majority of Germans in India formed part of elite networks. Nevertheless, focusing particularly upon the British in India, Harald Fischer-Tiné has identified what he describes as 'low and licentious' Europeans in an attempt to move away from the image of Europeans in India as a purely elite group. He has even constructed a 'white varna pyramid' with six layers, beginning with the Viceroy and the Indian civil service at the top and Eurasians at the bottom. The second and third groups consist of army officers and 'planters, merchants, surgeons, clergymen, teachers and lawyers' respectively. In group four he includes soldiers, sailors, skilled workers, servants, musicians and missionaries, while group five, 'white subalterns', lists 'orphans/widows, lunatics, convicts, vagrants/loafers, prostitutes' and 'distressed seamen'.[133] Fischer-Tiné does not concentrate on identifying the nationalities of Europeans but his book, together with other primary sources, reveals the presence of low-class Germans, following the fourth and, more especially, the fifth category of his pyramid. This would exclude missionaries. While some may have originated in the lower strata of German society, the level of education they obtained resulted in social mobility[134] and places them among the European elites in India. Sarmistha De's almost simultaneously published *Marginal Europeans in Colonial India* focused upon 'the vagrants, the prostitutes and the convicts',[135] paying a similar amount of attention to the continental origins of Europeans as Fischer-Tiné. De's vagrants include an Italian and two Greeks,[136] while he also identifies prostitutes 'from lower Danubian countries' and a 'Yiddish speaking girl' from Geneva.[137] He further provides an appendix containing a list of 33 foreign prostitutes, the overwhelming majority of whom were Russian (with no Germans).[138] Ultimately, like Fischer-Tiné, De does not deconstruct Europeaness.

There seems little doubt that German sailors found themselves in Indian ports by the end of the nineteenth century, as they did in ports throughout the world,[139] because of the increasing number of German ships which docked in India. An official list of 51 which landed in Calcutta in 1895 reveals a total crew membership of exactly 2,000 personnel who would have landed here, and therefore had some experience of Indian soil, in this year alone.[140] Some of these sailors may have come into contact with Europeans, including German prostitutes who worked in India in the late Victorian and Edwardian years. Some sexual encounters would have involved Indian and even Japanese women, as recounted by the ship's doctor Erwin Rosenberger who kept a diary of his visits to Indian brothels before and after the First World War, but there also existed European-run establishments which employed Germans.[141] Fischer-Tiné has identified a 'German barracks' in Calcutta and has also pointed to a decline in the number of European prostitutes in Bombay from 126 to 67 due to the large number of deportations of Germans and Austrians during the First World War.[142] Some Germans fell on hard times and became destitute. Fischer-Tiné identified a Schlansbrusch of Holstein, who moved to India and initially worked in a variety of manual occupations.[143] Similarly, Isabella Schraut found herself reliant upon the Calcutta District Charitable Society in 1841 following the death of her husband after he contracted cholera.[144]

German elite migrants as a distinct European group

In view of the relatively small numbers of German lower-class individuals we can identify in India and the lack of documentation they have left, it seems accurate to describe the bulk of those in the country in the century before the First World War as elites. The last few censuses before the outbreak of war provide figures on the number of foreign-born residents in India. In 1891, the total population stood at 287,223,431. All but 661,637 had been born in India, of whom 538,815 originated in other Asian countries, including 236,398 from Nepal. A total of

107,772 consisted of Europeans, with 100,551 born in the UK. Only two other European states counted more than 1,000 in the form of France with 1,258 and Germany with 1,458, making Germans the largest European group after the British. Similar figures emerge from the 1911 census.[145] Publications concerned with the German diaspora in the early twentieth century mention around 200 Germans in Calcutta and 150 in Bombay, together with 750 missionaries.[146]

What do these figures reveal about India and its foreign-born population in the late nineteenth and early twentieth centuries? First, India counted a foreign-born percentage of just 0.23 per cent in 1891 and 0.2 in 1911, which remains low in terms of any global comparison, but in keeping with the immigration history of India (Table 1.1).[147] When we turn to European populations, it becomes clear that the overwhelming majority (over 93 per cent) were British.[148] While some Germans became integrated into and interacted with Britons until the ethnic cleansing of the First World War, distinct German communities also evolved.[149]

The Germans in India need contextualisation against both more general nineteenth-century emigration of Germans and the consequent development of German settlements throughout the world, and the evolution of elite migration on a global scale in the age of empire. Between 1815 and 1930, 4.8 million people left Germany.[150] By 1914, one of the most visible German minorities lived in Russia, although this amorphous group had actually emerged over several centuries and some of its members constituted part of the third or even fourth generation.[151] But most of the German groups which existed by 1914 emerged as a result of emigration from Germany during the course of the eighteenth[152] and, more especially, the nineteenth century.[153] Table 1.2

Table 1.1 Foreign-born population of India

Year	1891	1911
Total population	287,223,431	315,156,396
Foreign population	661,637	650,768
Population born in other Asian countries	538,815	504,113
European population	107,772	131,968
UK-born population	100,551	122,919
German-born population	1,458	1,860

Sources: *Census of India 1891: General Tables for British Provinces and Feudatory States.* Vol. 1, *Statistics of Area; Population; Towns and Villages; Religion; Age; Civil Condition; Literacy; Parent-tongue; Birth- place; Infirmities, and Occupation* (London, 1892), pp. 390–2; *Census of India, 1911,* Vol. 1, Part II – *Tables* (Calcutta, 1913), p. 125.

Table 1.2 Major German populations on the outbreak of the First World War

Country	Census Year	German population	Germans per 1,000 inhabitants
Luxembourg	1910	22,000	81
Switzerland	1910	222,000	47
United States	1910	2,501,000	27
Denmark	1911	35,000	13
Australia	1911	33,000	7
Belgium	1910	57,000	7
Netherlands	1909	38,000	6
Austria	1910	126,000	4
Chile	1907	11,000	3
France	1901	90,000	2
British Isles	1911	56,000	1
Argentina	1914	27,000	0.3
Italy	1911	11,000	0.03

Source: F. Burgdorfer, 'Migration Across the Frontiers of Germany', in Walter F. Wilcox (ed.), *International Migrations* (London, 1961 reprint).

indicates the major foci of Germans by 1914. The table excludes one of the most significant German exile populations, in the form of those living in Brazil, which totalled approximately 400,000,[154] as well 'the 1.8 million people who gave German as their mother tongue in the Russian census of 1897'.[155]

In addition, it does not include some of the small German communities which had emerged as a result of colonial expansion, either German or British. This table actually points to the ethnic concentrations which had emerged of Germans from primarily agrarian backgrounds, with the classic example consisting of the USA and leading to the development of concentrations settled in rural areas in the mid-west[156] as well as the emergence of the type of working-class urban concentrations identified and analysed by Stanley Nadel in his study of Germans in New York.[157] In Australia, meanwhile, the settlement of Germans also took place to a significant degree in rural areas, especially in south Australia.[158] In the case of Great Britain, the migrants from primarily rural backgrounds settled almost exclusively in urban areas. The German community which emerged in Britain in the century before 1914 included a significant number of what we might describe as elites, including businessmen, foreign correspondence clerks, teachers and academics.[159] Stefan Manz devoted particular attention to businessmen, industrialists and educators in his microstudy of the Germans in Glasgow.[160]

In his exploration of the Germans in Australia, Jürgen Tampke actually identified scientists and explorers together with missionaries as distinct groups which progressed to that country.[161] This points to the global nature of the German elite migration during the course of the nineteenth century. The missionary enterprise became international, as revealed in the maps of their activity. The German missions did not simply operate in India but in several other locations. For Basel these incorporated China, North Borneo and west Africa, especially the Gold Coast, Cameroon and Togo.[162] In his history of the German evangelical mission, Wilhelm Oehler identified seven areas in which German missionary organisations operated: Africa, India, the Dutch East Indies, China and Japan, Australia and the Pacific, America and the Polar lands and the Near East.[163] British and US religious activity operated in a similarly global way, leading to the World Missionary Conference of 1910.[164]

The migration of German elites did not, therefore, simply take place towards India but to other parts of the world, a process which had a long history as scholars such as Michael Mann[165] and Margrit Schulte Beerbühl[166] have recognised. While Mann examined a variety of groups who made their way to India, Beerbühl focused upon German merchants in seventeenth-century London, whom she describes as a 'forgotten majority' because of their central role in the development of foreign trade during this period. Similarly, a collection of essays edited by Dittmar Dahlmann and Carmen Scheide has demonstrated the range of commercial and industrial activity in which Germans in Russia became involved during the nineteenth and early twentieth centuries, which covered much of this vast country.[167] While educated German migrants may have settled throughout the world, they became especially important in the German Empire that emerged in the decades immediately preceding the First World War, where they settled not simply as missionaries but also as administrators and businessmen – as the 897 Germans who lived in New Guinea just before the outbreak of the First World War would indicate. Only 294 of the 37,903 people on Samoa consisted of Germans. The 499 whites, who also counted 129 Britons, worked in the following areas: 31 government officials; 56 missionaries; 78 planters and settlers; and 115 'businessmen, merchants, landlords, etc'.[168] Even Cameroon counted just 1,871 whites out of a total population of 2,649,000, while the same figures for Togo stood at 368 and 1,032,000 respectively. German South West Africa revealed a significantly higher proportion of Germans, at 12,292, while Africans totalled 83,204[169] which meant the emergence of the type of German communities characterising areas where more significant numbers had settled.[170] In this sense they mirror the British ruling elites who lived in India during the nineteenth century, who, however, remained overwhelmingly British.

The Germans in India therefore form one element of a globally mobile elite group with origins dating back to the Early Modern period. While the reasons for their emigration may resemble those which sent millions of other people away from their homeland during the course of the nineteenth century, they mirror those missionaries, businessmen and scholars who travelled to destinations throughout the world. At the same time as the mass migration initially identified by German commentators during the nineteenth century emerged, so did a simultaneous stream of elite migration based on networks.

It is important to stress the uniqueness of the Germans in India. They certainly resemble other German communities which emerged in the British Empire, including those in Australia, New Zealand and parts of Africa.[171] This means that in all of these locations they both formed part of the wider European population, whether as elites or as part of a larger urban or rural population, but, at the same time, retained a distinct German – particularly religious – identity which the British Empire emphasised during the First World War.[172]

Notes

1 Panikos Panayi, *Prisoners of Britain: German Civilian and Combatant Internees during the First World War* (Manchester, 2012), especially Chapter 2.
2 Hew Strachan, *The First World War*, Vol. 1, *To Arms in Africa* (Oxford, 2004), pp. 495–643. Several contemporary accounts appeared from those captured by British forces here, including: Wilhelm Kröpke, *Mein Flucht aus englishcher Kriegsgefangenschaft 1916: Von Afrika über England nach Deutschland zur Flandern-Front* (Flensburg, 1937), pp. 7–20; Otto Schimming, *13 Monate hinter dem Stacheldraht: Alexandra Palace, Knocakaloe, Isle of Man, Stratford* (Stuttgart, 1919), pp. 1–7; Heinrich Norden, *In englischer Gefangenschaft* (Kassel, 1915); and Gotthilf Vöhringer, *Meine Erlebnisse während des Krieges in Kamerun und in englischer Kriegsgefangenschaft* (Hamburg, 1915).
3 See, for example: Maggie Butt, *Ally Paly Prison Camp* (South Pool, 2011); and Janet Harris, *Alexandra Palace: A Hidden History* (Stroud, 2005).
4 J. Maue, *In Feindes Land: Achtzehn Monate in englischer Kriegsgefangenschaft in Indien und England* (Stuttgart, 1918).
5 See, for example, F. G. Huber, 'Auswanderung and Auswanderungspolitik im Königreich Württemberg', in Eugen von Philippovich, ed., *Auswanderung und Auswanderungspolitik in Deutschland* (Leipzig, 1892), pp. 233–84.
6 For the full catalogue, see: www.bmarchives.org, accessed on 29 April 2015.
7 See, for example: Albrecht Frenz, *Eine Reise in die Religionen: Herrmann Mögling (1811–1881), Missionar und Sprachforscher in Indien, zum 200. Geburtstag* (Heidelberg, 2011); Christian Triebel, ed., *Der Missionar als Forscher: Beiträge christlicher Missionare zur Erforschung fremder Kulturen und Religionen* (Gütersloh, 1988); and Heike Liebau, 'Deutsche Missionare als Indienforscher: Benjamin Schultze – Ausnahme oder Regel', *Archiv für Kulturgeschichte*, vol. 76 (1994), pp. 111–33.

8 See, for example, Julia Ulrike Mack, *Menschenbilder: Anthropologische Konzepte und stereotype Vorstellungen vom Menschen in der Publizistik der Basler Mission 1816–1914* (Zurich, 2014).
9 Otto Waack, *Indische Kirche und Indien-Mission*, two volumes (Erlangen, 1994).
10 As an introduction, see: Hans Kausch: *Festschrift zum 75. jährigen Bestehen der Gossnerschen Mission* (Friedenau-Berlin, 1911); and Hans Kausch and F. Hahn, *50 Bilder aus der Goßnerschen Kols-Mission mit erläuterndem Text und Karte* (Berlin, 1894).
11 See a series of publications authored by Johann Wörrlein including: *Christian Kohlmeier: Von 1888–1892 Missionar in Indien* (Hermannsburg, 1901); *Hermann Ernst Jügenmeier: Von 1888–1892 Missionar in Indien* (Hermannsburg, 1901); *Ist in Indien eine besondere Frauenmission nötig?* (Hermannsburg, 1902); *Paul Otto Petersen: Von 1875 bis 1888 Missionar in Indien* (Hermannsburg, 1901); *Peter Wilhelm Heinrich Lüchow: Von 1880–1893 Missionar in Indien* (Hermannsburg, 1901); and *Vierzig Jahre in Indien: Erinnerungen eines alten Missionars* (Hermannsburg, 1913).
12 Ernest R. Hull, *The German Jesuit Fathers of Bombay: By an Englishman who Knows Them* (Bombay, 1915); Alfons Väth, *Die deutschen Jesuiten in Indien: Geschichte der Mission von Bombay-Puna* (Regensburg, 1920).
13 These include: *Der evangelische Heidenbote* (1828–1955); *Allgemeine Missions Zeitung* (1845–9); *Allgemeine Missions Zeitschrift* (1874–1923); *Evangelisch-lutherisches Missionsblatt* (1846–1941); *Evangelisches Missions-Magazin* (1857–1939) which began as *Magazin für die neueste Geschichte der evangelischen Missions- und Bibelgesellschaften* (1816–56); and *Die Biene auf dem Missionsfelde* (1834–1941). In addition, German Catholics issued *Echo aus Indien: Mitteilungen d. Deutschen Jesuiten-Mission in Britisch-Indien*, although this only lasted from 1912–14, but the more general *Die katholischen Missionen* contained much information about German Jesuit activities throughout the world.
14 Evangelische Missions-Gesellschaft, *Album der Basler Mission: Bilder aus Indien* (Basel, 1860).
15 Kausch and Hahn, *50 Bilder*.
16 Gustav Emil Burkhardt, *Dr. G. E. Burkhardt's kleine Missions-Bibliothek*, three volumes (Leipzig, 1879–1880).
17 See, for example: *Kleine Missions-Geographie und-Statistik zur Darstellung des Standes der evangelischen Mission am Schluss des 19. Jahrhunderts* (Stuttgart, 1901); *Allgemeiner Missions-Atlas nach Originalquellen* (Gotha, 1869).
18 Wilhelm Schlatter and Hermann Witschi, *Geschichte der Basler Mission*, five volumes (Basel, 1916–70). Earlier histories include Paul Eppler, *Geschichte der Basler Mission 1815–1899: Mit vier Kartenskizzen* (Basel, 1900).
19 See, for example: H. Mögling and C. Weitbrecht, *Das Kurgland und die evangelische Mission in Kurg* (Basel, 1866); C. Stolz, *Die Basler Mission in Indien: Zugleich als Festschrift zum 50 jährigen Jubiläum der Kanara-Mission* (Basel 1884).
20 E. R. Baierlein, *Die evangelische lutherische Mission in Ostindien* (Leipzig, 1874); D. Paul, *Die Leipziger Mission Daheim und Draussen* (Leipzig, 1914); Richard Handmann, *Umschau auf dem Gebiete der evangelisch-lutherischen Mission in Ostindien* (Leipzig, 1888); Richard Handmann, *Die Evangelisch-lutherische Tamulen-Mission in der Zeit ihrer Neubegründung* (Leipzig, 1903).
21 E. R. Baierlein, *The Land of the Tamulians and its Missions* (Madras, 1875). As the title suggests, this volume covered all missionary activity here but Baierlein worked for the Leipzig Mission.
22 Ernst Gloyer, *Jeypur, das Haupt-Arbeitsfeld der Schleswig-Holsteinischen evangelisch-lutherischen Missionsgesellschaft zu Breklum auf der Ostküste Vorderindiens* (Breklum, 1901).
23 See, for example: Alwin Gehring, *Erinnerungen aus dem Leben eines Tamulenmissionars* (Leipzig, 1906); Otto E. Ehlers, *An Indischen Fürstenhöfen* (Berlin, 1894); Severin Noti, *Reisebriefe eines Missionars* (New York, 1908); Wörrlein, *Vierzig Jahre in Indien*.

24 Karl Graul, *Reise nach Ostindien über Palästina und Egypten von Juli 1849 bis April 1853* (Leipzig, 1854–6).
25 See, for example: Hermann Gundert and H. Mögling, *The Life of Samuel Hebich: By Two of His Fellow-Labourers* (originally London, 1876; Memphis, TN, 2012); Traugott Schölly, *Samuel Hebich: Der erste Sendbote der Basler Mission in Indien* (Basel, 1911); Johann Jakob Jaus, *Samuel Hebich: Ein Zeuge Jesu Christi aus der Heidenwelt* (Stuttgart, 1922); G. N. Thomssen, *Samuel Hebich of India: A Master Fisher of Men*, 2nd Edition (Mangalore, 1915); and Alfred Mathieson, *Hebich of India: A Passionate Soul-Winner* (Kilmarnock, 1936).
26 G. Hermann, *Karl Graul und seine Bedeutung für die lutherische Mission* (Halle, 1867).
27 Johann Dettloff Prochnow, *Johannes Gossner: Biographie aus Tagebüchern und Briefen* (Berlin, 1874); Hermann Dalton, *Johannes Goßner: Ein Lebensbild aus der Kirche des neunzehnten Jahrhunderts* (Berlin, 1878).
28 Wörrlein: *Christian Kohlmeier; Hermann Ernst Jügenmeier; Paul Otto Petersen; Peter Wilhelm Heinrich Lüchow*.
29 Heike Liebau, *Cultural Encounters in India: The Local Co-workers of the Tranquebar Mission, 18th to 19th Centuries* (New Delhi, 2013).
30 Judith Becker, *Conversio Im Wandel: Basler Missionare Zwischen Europa und Südindien und die Ausbildung Einer Kontaktreligiosität, 1834–1860* (Göttingen, 2015).
31 Andreas Nehring, *Orientalismus und Mission: Die Repräsentation der tamulischen Gesellschaft und Religion durch Leipziger Missionare 1840–1940* (Wiesbaden, 2003).
32 See, especially, Dagmar Konrad, *Missionsbräute: Pietistinnen des 19. Jahrhunderts in der Basler Mission* (Münster, 2001).
33 K. Hartenstein, *Das Werden einer jungen Kirche im Osten: 100 Jahre Basler Missionsarbeit in Indien* (Stuttgart, 1935); Hans Lokies, *Die Gossner-Kirche in Indien: Durch Wachstumskrisen zur Mündigkeit* (Berlin, 1969).
34 Arno Lehmann, *Es begann in Tranquebar: Die Geschichte der ersten evangelischen Kirche in Indien* (Berlin, 1955); Hugald Grafe, *Evangelische Kirche in Indien: Auskunft und Einblicke* (Erlangen, 1981).
35 The publications of Albrecht Frenz include: *Eine Reise in die Religionen; Hermann Gundert: Tagebuch aus Malabar, 1837–1859* (Stuttgart, 1983); *Hermann Gundert: Reise nach Malabar* (Ulm, 1998); *Hermann Gundert: Schriften und Berichte aus Malabar* (Stuttgart, 1983).
36 See especially: *Allgemeine Missions Zeitung; Evangelisch-lutherisches Missionsblatt; Harvest Field*.
37 Karl Foertsch, *Unter Kriegs-Wettern: Kriegserlebnisse der Gossnerschen Missionare in Indien* (Berlin-Friedenau, 1916); Johann Jakob Jaus, *Als Kriegsgefangener: Von Indien nach Deutschland* (Stuttgart, 1916); Johann Jakob Jaus, *Kriegsgefangene Missionskinder* (Stuttgart, 1916); E. Langholf, *Die Gefangenschaft und Heimkehr unserer Indischen Missionare* (Hermannsburg, 1916); Carl Paul, *Vom Missionsfeld vertrieben: Ein Kriegserlebnis der Leipziger Mission* (Leipzig, 1916); Christian Roemer, *Heimkehr aus Feindesland: Begrüßungsfeier f. die aus engl. Gefangenschaft freigewordenen Basler Missionsgeschwister in d. Stiftskirche zu Stuttgart 12. Juni 1916* (Stuttgart, 1916); Therese Zehme, *Heimkehr mit der Golconda: Wie es den Kindern unserer vertriebenen indischen Missionare erging* (Leipzig, 1916); Otty Jessen, *Vertrieben* (Breklum, 1917); Marie Elisabeth Schäfer, *Was vier kleine Kriegsgefangene erlebten: Erzählung aus dem Weltkrieg* (Leipzig, 1917); Hans Georg Probst, *Unter indischer Sonne: 19 Monate englischer Kriegsgefangenschaft in Ahmednagar* (Herborn, 1917); Maue, *In feindes Land*; Albrecht Oepke, *Ahmednagar und Golconda: Ein Beitrag zur Erörterung der Missionsprobleme des Weltkrieges* (Leipzig, 1918).
38 Albert Achilles, *Erinnerungen aus meiner Kriegsgefangenschaft im Mixed-Transit-Camp Ahmednagar und Erholungslager Ramandrog in Indien während des ersten Weltkrieges 1914–1920* (Berlin, 1977).

39 Stefan Manz, *Migranten und Internierte: Deutsche in Glasgow, 1864–1918* (Stuttgart, 2003).
40 These issues are tackled by: Mary Fulbrook and Ulinka Rublak, 'The "social self" and ego-documents', *German History*, vol. 28 (2010), pp. 263–72; and Marijke van der Wal and Gijsbert Rutten, 'Ego-Documents in a Historical-Sociological Perspective', in Marijke van der Wal and Gijsbert Rutten, eds, *Touching the Past: Studies in Historical Sociolinguisstics and Ego-Documents* (Amsterdam, 2013), pp. 1–17.
41 A. Anton, *Von Darmstadt nach Ostindien: Erlebnisse und Abenteuer eines Musikers auf der Reise durch Arabien nach Lahore: Die denkwürdigen Ereignisse der letzten Jahre* (Darmstadt, 1860).
42 Oscar Flex, *Pflanzerleben in Indien: Kulturgeschichtliche Bilder aus Assam* (Berlin, 1873).
43 Winfried Schulze, 'Ego-Dokumente: Annäherung an den Menschen in der Geschichte', in Winfried Schulze, ed., *Ego-Dokumente: Annäherung an den Menschen in der Geschichte* (Berlin, 1996), pp. 25–7.
44 Casey Blanton, *Travel Writing: The Self and the World* (Abingdon, 2002), p. 2.
45 Ibid., p. 4.
46 Tim Youngs, *Travellers in Africa: British Travelogues, 1830–1900* (Manchester, 1994).
47 For a purely intellectual history of German Indology, see Vishwa Adluri and Joydeep Bagchee, *The Nay Science: A History of German Indology* (Oxford, 2014).
48 Douglas T. McGetchin, *Indology, Indomania and Orientalism: Ancient India's Rebirth in Modern Germany* (Madison, NJ, 2009), p. 17.
49 Indra Sengupta, *From Salon to Discipline: State, University and Indology in Germany, 1821–1914* (Würzburg, 2005), p. 1. For the importance of the Romantic movement, see Arnos Leslie Willson, *A Mythical Image: The Ideal of India in German Romanticism* (Durham, NC, 1964). The indology of the Halle missionaries receives attention in Hanco Jürgens, 'German Indology avant la Letter: The Experiences of the Halle Missionaries in Southern India', in. Douglas T. McGetchin, Peter J. Park and Damodar Sardesai, eds, *Sanskrit and Orientalism: Indology and Comparative Linguistics in Germany, 1750–1958* (New Delhi, 2004), pp. 41–82.
50 Edward Said, *Orientalism* (London, 2003 reprint), pp. 17–19.
51 Suzanne L. Marchand, *German Orientalism in the Age of Empire: Religion, Race, and Scholarship* (Cambridge, 2009).
52 Perry Myers, *German Visions of India, 1871–1918: Commandeering the Holy Ganges during the Kaiserreich* (Basingstoke, 2013).
53 See, for example: Jean W. Sedlar, *India in the Mind of Germany: Schelling, Schopenauer and their Times* (Washington, DC, 1982); Dietmar Rothermund, *The German Intellectual Quest for India* (New Delhi, 1986); Pranabendra Nath Ghosh-Shantinikaten, 'Johann Gottfried Herder's Image of India', in Heinz Mode and Hans-Joachim Peuke, eds, *Indien in der deutschen Literarischen Tradition* (Halle, 1979), pp. 4–17; Helmuth von Glasenapp, *Indien in der Dichtung und Forschung des deutschen Ostens* (Königsberg, 1930); Helmuth von Glasenapp, *Image of India* (New Delhi, 1973).
54 Robert Cowan, *The Indo-German Identification: Reconciling South Asian Origins and European Destinies, 1765–1885* (Rochester, NY, 2010).
55 Vidhagiri Ganeshan, *Das Indienbild deutscher Dichter um 1900: Dauthendey, Bonsels, Mauthner, Gjellerup, Hermann Keyserling und Stefan Zweig: Ein Kapitel deutsch-indischer Geistesbeziehungen im frühen 20. Jahrhundert* (Bonn, 1975).
56 Vidhagiri Ganeshan, *Das Indienerlebins Hermann Hesses*, 2nd Edition (Bonn, 1980).
57 Veena Kade-Luthra, ed., *Sehnsucht Nach Indien: Ein Lesebuch von Goethe bis Grass* (Munich, 1991).
58 For details, see Valentina Stache-Rosen, *German Indologists: Biographies of Scholars in Indian Studies Writing in German* (New Delhi, 1981).
59 Sengupta, *Salon to Discipline*, p. 135.

60 Joanne Miyang Cho, Eric Kurlander and Douglas T. McGetchin, eds, *Transcultural Encounters between Germany and India: Kindred Spirits in the Nineteenth and Twentieth Centuries* (London, 2014).
61 Kris Manjapra, *Age of Entanglement: German and Indian Intellectuals across Empire* (London, 2014); Ulrike Kirchberger, 'Deutsche Naturwissenschaftler im britischen Empire: Die Erforschung der außereuropäischen Welt im Spannungsfeld zwischen deutschem und britischen Imperialismus', *Historische Zeitschrift*, vol. 271 (2000), pp. 621–60; Ulrike Kirchberger, 'German scientists in the Indian Forest Service: A German contribution to the Raj?', *Journal of Imperial and Commonwealth History*, vol. 29 (2001), pp. 1–26.
62 Kamakshi Pappu Murti, *India: The Seductive and Seduced 'Other' of German Orientalism* (Westport, CN, 2001). Susanne Zantop, *Colonial Fantasies: Conquest, Family, and Nation in Precolonial Germany, 1770–1870* (London, 1997) has utilised some of these ideas in the context of more general German colonial desire.
63 Walter Leifer, *India and the Germans: 500 years of Indo-German Contacts* (Bombay, 1977), p. 20.
64 David Blackbourn, 'Germans abroad and Auslandsdeutsche: places, networks and experiences from the sixteenth to the twentieth century', *Geschichte und Gesellschaft*, vol. 41 (2015), pp. 321–46.
65 Wolfgang Knabe, *Auf den Spuren der ersten deutschen Kaufleute in Indien: Forschungs Expedition mit der Mercator entlang der Westküste und zu den Aminen* (Anhausen, 1993), pp. 100–1.
66 Franz Hümmerich, *Die erste deutsche Handelsfahrt nach Indien 1500/6* (Munich, 1922); Friedrich Kuntsmann, *Die Fahrt der ersten Deutschen nach dem portugiesischen Indien* (Munich, 1861).
67 Hermann Kellenbenz, 'The Herwarts of Augsburg and their Indian Trade during the First Half of the Sixteenth Century', in K. S. Mathew, ed., *Studies in Maritime History* (Pondicherry, 1990), pp. 69–83.
68 Michael Mann, 'Indien ist eine Karriere: Biographische Skizzen deutscher Söldner, Ratsherren und Mediziner in Südasien, 1500–1800', in Markus A. Denzel, ed., *Deutsche Eliten in Übersee (16. bis frühes 20. Jahrhundert)* (St Katharinen, 2006), pp. 249–89; Chen Tzoref-Ashkenazi, 'German Auxilliary Troops in the British and Dutch East India Companies', in Nir Arielli and Bruce Collins, eds, *Transnational Soldiers: Foreign Military Enlistment in the Modern Era* (Basingstoke, 2013), pp. 32–49.
69 Julius Richter, *A History of Missions in India* (Edinburgh, 1908), p. 103.
70 The above account of the Tranquebar Mission is based upon: Lehmann, *Es begann in Tranquebar*; Liebau, *Cultural Encounters*, pp. 40–103; Baierlein, *Die Ev.-luth. Mission in Ostindien*, pp. 75–109; Robert Eric Frykenberg, *Christianity in India: From Beginnings to the Present* (Oxford, 2008), pp. 14–68; Richter, ibid., pp. 102–27, 161–73; Leonard Fernando and G. Gispert-Sauch, *Christianity in India: Two Thousand Years of Faith* (London, 2004), pp. 157–60; A. Devanesan, 'The Lutheran Mission', in B. Sobhanan, ed., *A History of the Christian Missions in South India* (Thiruvananthapuram, 1996), pp. 159–60; Stephen Neill, *A History of Christianity in India: 1707–1858* (Cambridge, 1985), pp. 28–58.
71 See, for example, Frykenberg, ibid; Henriette Bugge, *Mission and Tamil Society: Social and Religious Change in South India (1840–1900)* (Richmond, 1994); Hartmann Tyrrell, '"Organisierte Mission": Protestantische Missionsgesellschaften des "langen 19. Jahrhunderts"', in Klaus Korschorke, ed., *Etappen der Globalisierung in christentumsgeschichtlicher Perspektive* (Wiesbaden, 2012), pp. 255–71.
72 Richter, *History of Missions*, pp. 128–61.
73 Church Missionary Society, *Register of Missionaries, Clerical, Lay, & Female, and Native Clergy, from 1804 to 1904* (London, 1904), pp. 1–152.
74 Eugene Stock, *The History of the Church Missionary Society: Its Environment, Its Men and Its Work*, Vol. 1 (London, 1899), pp. 243, 263.
75 CMS, *Register of Missionaries*, p. 69.
76 Ibid., p. 83.

GERMANS IN INDIA AS ELITE EUROPEAN MIGRANTS

77 Mary Weitbrecht, *Memoir of the Rev. J. J. Weitbrecht: Compiled from his Journals and Letters by his Widow* (London, 1854).
78 J. Rhenius, *Memoir of C. T. E. Rhenius, Comprising Extracts from His Journals and Correspondence, with Details of Missionary Proceedings in South India* (London, 1841).
79 Ulrike Kirchberger, '"Fellow-Labourers in the Same Vineyard": Germans in British Missionary Societies in the First Half of the Nineteenth Century', in Stefan Manz, Margrit Schulte Beerbühl and John R. Davis, eds, *Migration and Transfer from Germany to Britain* (Munich, 2007), pp. 81–92.
80 Huber, 'Auswanderung and Auswanderungspolitik'; Wolfgang von Hippel, *Auswanderung aus Südwestdeutschland: Studien zur württembergischen Auswanderung und Auswanderungspolitik im 18. und 19. Jarhundert* (Klett-Gotha, 1984); Panikos Panayi, *German Immigrants in Britain during the Nineteenth Century, 1815–1914* (Oxford, 1995), pp. 56–8.
81 See volumes 2–4 of Schlatter and Witschi, *Geschichte der Basler Mission*.
82 Schlatter and Witschi, *Geschichte der Basler Mission*, Vol. 1, pp. 1–58; Eppler, *Geschichte der Basler Mission*, pp. 1–61.
83 Hartenstein, *Das werden einer jungen Kirche im Osten*, pp. 17–18; Schlatter and Witschi, *Geschichte der Basler Mission*, Vol. 2, pp. 1–15.
84 Schlatter and Witschi, ibid, pp. 16–53; Hartenstein, ibid; Richter, *History of Missions*, p. 196; Stolz, *Die Basler Mission in Indien*.
85 Basel German Evangelical Missionary Society, *Report of the Basel German Evangelical Mission in South-Western India for 1870* (Mangalore, 1871), p. 8; Evangelische Missionsgesellschaft (Basel), *Verzeichnis der Basler Missions-Stationen in Indien: Mit Bezeichnung der Eigentumsverhältnisse* (Basel, 1888–91).
86 Evangelische Missionsgesellschaft, ibid., pp. 10–11.
87 Jaiprakash Raghaviah, *Basel Mission Industries in Malabar and South Canara, 1834–1914: A Study of its Social and Economic Impact* (New Delhi, 1990); Rudolf Fischer, *Die Basler Missionsindustrie in Indien 1850–1913: Rekrutierung und Disziplinierung der Arbeiterschaft* (Zürich, 1978).
88 Basel German Evangelical Missionary Society, *Report of 1870*, p. 8.
89 BMA/Q-30.3,5, Gebietslisten, Indien, Männer 1. See Chapter 2 for further details.
90 BMA/Q-30.3,5, Gebietslisten, Indien, Frauen. See Chapter 2 for further details.
91 Nehring, *Orientalismus und Mission*, pp. 55–6; Handmann, *Die Evangelisch-lutherische Tamulen-Mission*, pp. 1–148; Baierlein, *Die Ev.-luth. Mission in Ostindien*, pp. 159–69.
92 Handmann, *Umschau*.
93 Gaebler, Info und Genealogie, 'Liste der IndienmissionarInnen der Leipziger Mission', www.gaebler.info/india/leipziger_indienmissionare-1.htm, accessed 23 April 2015.
94 Leipziger Missionswerk, www.lmw-mission.de/de/missionar-136.html, 'Auguste Hensolt, geb.1864, gest.1923', accessed, 23 April 2015.
95 Handmann, *Die Evangelisch-lutherische Tamulen-Mission*, p. 367.
96 Handmann, *Umschau*, p. 47.
97 AFST/LMW/II.31.11.29.I, 'Statistik der Ev.-Luth. Mission zu Leipzig, Ende Nov. 1910'.
98 Dalton, *Johannes Goßner*; Lokies, *Die Gossner-Kirche in Indien*, pp. 9–16; Eyre Chatterton, *The Story of Fifty Years' Mission Work in Chhota Nagpur* (London, 1901), pp. 1–4; Klaus Rober, 'Johannes Evangelista Goßner (14.12.1773–30.3.1858): Skizze eines Lebens', in Ulrich Schöntube, ed., *Zwischen Wort und Tat: Beiträge zum 150. Todestag von Johannes Evangelista Goßner* (Neuendettelsau, 2009), pp. 21–9; Walter Holsten, *Johannes Evangelista Goßner: Glaube und Gemeinde* (Göttingen, 1949).
99 Kausch, *Festschrift*, p. 74. For further detail, see also Kausch and Kahn, *50 Bilder*.
100 Kausch, *Festschrift*.
101 Ibid., p. 180.
102 Julius Richter, *Nordindische Missionsfahrten: Erzählungen und Schilderungen von einer Missions-Studienreise durch Ostindien* (Gütersloh, 1903), pp. 103–15; Richter, *History of Missions*, p. 198.

103 Waack, *Indische Kirche und Indien-Mission*, I; *Bericht über die Arbeit der Schleswig-Holsteinischen Evangelisch Lutherischen Missionsgesellschaft für die Zeit vom 1. April 1900 bis dahin 1901* (Breklum, 1901).
104 Richter, *History of Missions*, p. 213 Wörrlein, *Vierzig Jahre in Indien*.
105 See: Frykenberg, *Christianity in India*, pp. 116–41, 344–79; Neill, *History of Christianity in India*, pp. 121–4, 276–306.
106 Väth, *Die deutschen Jesuiten in Indien*, pp. 68–228; Hull, *German Jesuit Fathers*, pp. 8–31; James H. Gense, *The Church at the Gateway of India, 1720–1960* (Bombay, 1960), pp. 276–300; P. Beda Kleinschmidt, *Auslanddeutschtum und Kirche*, Vol. 2, *Die Auslanddeustchen im Übersee* (Münster, 1930), pp. 231–6.
107 For German missionary maps, see: Karl Heilmann, *Missionskarte der Erde nebst Begleitwort: Mit besonderer Berücksichtigung der deutschen Kolonien* (Gütersloh, 1897); Grundemann, *Allgemeiner Missions-Atlas*.
108 These issues are considered in: Andrew Porter, *Religion Versus Empire? British Protestant Missionaries and Overseas Expansion, 1700–1914* (Manchester, 2004); and Jeffrey Cox, *Imperial Fault Lines: Christianity and Colonial Power in India, 1818–1940* (Stanford, 2002).
109 Stache-Rosen, *German Indologists*, pp. 5–201; Richard Garbe, *Indische Reiseskizzen* (Berlin, 1889); Kaushik Bagchi, 'An Orientalist in the Orient: Richard Garbe's Indian Journey, 1885–1886', *Journal of World History*, vol. 14 (2003), pp. 281–325; Ernst Waldschmidt, 'Richard Pischel zum Gedächtnis', *Zeitschrift der Deutschen Morgenländischen Gesellschaft*, vol. 109 (1959), pp. 26–30; Donald Clay Johnson, 'German influences on the development of research libraries in nineteenth century Bombay', *Journal of Library History*, vol. 21 (1986), pp. 215–27.
110 Stache-Rosen, ibid., p. 112. See also the list of Germans holding posts in India provided by Joachim Oesterheld, 'Zum Spektrum deustcher Eliten im kolonialen Indien: Ein erster Überblick', in Denzel, *Deutsche Eliten in Übersee*, p. 379.
111 Robert Koch, *Reiseberichte über Rinderpest, Bubonenpest in Indien und Afrika, Tsetse- oder Surrakrankheit, Texasfieber, tropische Malaria, Schwarzwasserfieber* (Berlin, 1898), pp. 1–3; Benhard Möllers, *Robert Koch: Persönlichkeit und Lebenswerk* (Hannover, 1950), pp. 140–7; Wolfgang Genschorek, *Robert Koch* (Leipzig, 1975), pp. 154–72; Georg Gaffky, Richard Pfeiffer, Georg Sticker and Adolf Dieudonné, *Bericht über die Thätigkeit der zur Erforschung der Pest i. J. 1897 nach Indien entsandten Kommission* (Berlin, 1899).
112 See, most recently, Andrea Wulf, *The Invention of Nature: The Adventures of Alexander von Humboldt, the Lost Hero of Science* (London, 2015).
113 Adolphe Hermann and Robert Schlagintweit, *Report on the Proceedings of the Officers Engaged in the Magnetic Survey of India* (Madras, 1855); Adolphe Hermann and Robert Schlagintweit, *Report upon the Progress of the Magnetic Survey of India, and of the Researches Connected with it in the Himalaya Mountains, from April to October 1855* (Agra, 1856); Hermann von Schlagintweit, *Reisen in Indien und Hochasien Basirt auf die Resultate der wissenschaftlichen Mission von H., A. und R von Schlagintweit ausgefuhrt in den Jahren 1854–1858*, three volumes (Leipzig, 1869–80); Ulrike Kirchberger, *Aspekte deutsch-britischer Expansion: Die Überseeinteressen der deutschen Migranten in Großbritannien in der Mitte des 19. Jahrhunderts* (Stuttgart, 1999), pp. 388–90; Leifer, *India and the Germans*, p. 200.
114 S. S. Negi, *Sir Dietrich Brandis: Father of Tropical Forestry* (Dehra Dun, 1991); Herbert Hesmer, *Leben und Werk von Dietrich Brandis, 1824–1907: Begründer der tropischen Forstwirtschaft, Förderer der forstlichen Entwicklung in den USA, Botaniker und Ökologe* (Opladen, 1975); Kirchberger, 'German Scientists', p. 3; Ramachandra Guha, 'Dietrich Brandis: A Vision Revisited and Reaffirmed', in Mark Poffenberger and Betsy McGean, eds, *Village Voices, Forest Choices: Joint Forest Management in India* (Oxford, 1996), pp. 86–100; Indra Munshi Saldanha,'Colonialism and professionalism: a German forester in India', *Environment and History*, vol. 2 (1996), pp. 195–219; Ajay S. Rawat, 'Brandis: The Father of Organized Forestry in India', in Ajay S. Rawat, ed., *Indian Forestry: A Perspective* (New Delhi, 1993), pp.

85–101; David Prain and M. Rangarajan, 'Brandis, Sir Dietrich (1824–1907)', *Oxford Dictionary of National Biography*, www.oxforddnb.com/view/article/32045?docPos=1, accessed 27 April 2015.
115 Kirchberger, ibid., pp. 3–4; *The Times*, 1 October 1925; R. S. Troup and Andrew Grout, 'Schlich, Sir William Philipp Daniel (1840–1925), *Oxford Dictionary of National Biography*, www.oxforddnb.com/view/article/35970, accessed 27 April 2015; Berthold Ribbentrop, *Forestry in British India* (Calcutta, 1900).
116 Kirchberger, ibid., p. 5.
117 Nicholas Goddard, 'Voelcker (John Christopher) Augustus (1822–1884)', *Oxford Dictionary of National Biography*, www.oxforddnb.com/view/article/28345?docPos=1, accessed 27 April 2015; John Augustus Voelcker, *Report on the Improvement of Indian Agriculture* (London, 1893).
118 Graul, *Reise nach Ostindien*
119 Karl Heinrich Christian Plath, *Eine Reise nach Indien: Für kleine und große Leute beschrieben* (Berlin, 1880).
120 Joseph Dahlmann, *Indische Fahrten*, two volumes (Freiburg im Breisgau, 1908).
121 Waldemar Bonsels: *Indienfahrt* (originally 1912; Gloucester, 2008); *Mein Austritt aus der Baseler Missions-Industrie und seine Gründe: Ein offener Brief an die Baseler Missions-Gemeinde in Württemberg und der Schweiz* (Munich-Schwabing, 1904).
122 Aurélie Choné, 'Die Stadt des Lichts, eine für den Fremden unsichtbare Stadt? Probleme der Wahrnehmungsperspektive von Benares in deutschsprachigen Indienreiseschriften (1880–1930)', in Manfred Durzak, ed., *Bilder Indiens in der deutschen Literatur* (Frankfurt, 2011), pp. 41–54; Paul Deussen, *Erinnerungen an Indien* (Leipzig, 1904); Ernst Haeckel, *Indische Reisebriefe* (Berlin, 1883); Franz Reuleaux, *Eine Reise quer durch Indien im Jahre 1881: Erinnerungsblätter* (Berlin, 1884).
123 Eugenie Schaeuffelen, *Meine indische Reise* (Munich, 1904).
124 Max Zimmer, *Unsere Reise durch Indien, Java u. Ceylon im Jahre 1910* (Baden-Baden, 1911).
125 Hans Von Koenigsmarck, *Die Engländer in Indien: Reiseeindrücke* (Berlin, 1909).
126 Oscar Bongard, *Die Reise des Deutschen Kronprinzen durch Ceylon und Indien* (Berlin, 1911).
127 Grafin Pauline Nostitz, *Travels of Doctor and Madame Helfer in Syria, Mesopotamia, Burmah and other Lands*, two volumes (London, 1878).
128 Oesterheld, 'Zum Spektrum deutscher Eliten im kolonialen Indien', pp. 383–4; Leifer, *India and the Germans*, pp. 273–6; Joachim Oesterheld and Günther Lothar, *Inder in Berlin* (Berlin, 1997), p. 9; August Eggers, *Die Deutsch-Asiatische Bank und ihre Aufgaben* (Berlin, 1890); Maximilian Müller-Jabusch, *Fünfzig Jahre Deutsch-Asiatische Bank: 1890–1939* (Berlin, 1940); BA/R901/9294.
129 Hans-Joachim Rehmer, 'Ein Mecklenburger – Polizeipräsident von Bombay', *Carolinium*, vol. 64 (2000), pp. 25–7.
130 BA/901/5552 traces the whole process of his appointment, from advertisement through application to taking up the post.
131 BL/IOR/L/PJ/6/1445, File 2600: Nov 1915–June 1916, Permits, with photographs, of Germans and Austrians over military age intending to proceed from India on the SS Golconda.
132 NA/F0383/237, List of hostile aliens in civil charge after repatriation. In the Civil Camp at Ahmednagar, n.d.
133 Harald Fischer-Tiné, *Low and Licentious Europeans: Race, Class and 'White Subalternity' in Colonial India* (Hyderabad, 2009), p. 59.
134 Jon Miller, *The Social Control of Religious Zeal: A Study of Organizational Contradictions* (New Brunswick, NJ, 1994), pp. 41–58.
135 Sarmistha De, *Marginal Europeans in Colonial India, 1860–1920* (Kolkata, 2008), p. 11.
136 Ibid., p. 106.
137 Ibid., p. 200.
138 Ibid., pp. 297–9.

139 See, for example, Christiaan Engberts, 'The rise of associational activity: early twentieth century German sailors' homes and schools in Antwerp and Rotterdam', *Immigrants and Minorities*, vol. 32 (2014), pp. 293–314.
140 BA/R901/53018, 'Verzeichniss der im Jahre 1895 im Hafen von Calcutta angelaufenen Schiffe der Deutschen Handels-Marine'.
141 Erwin Rosenberger, *In indischen Liebesgassen: Aus dem Tagebuch eines Schiffsarztes* (Vienna, 1924).
142 Fischer-Tiné, *Low and Licentious Europeans*, pp. 209–11.
143 Ibid., p. 149.
144 GSta PK, III. HA MdA, III. 13903, letter to D. McFurlan, 8 September 1841.
145 *Census of India 1891: General Tables for British Provinces and Feudatory States. Vol. 1, Statistics of Area; Population; Towns and Villages; Religion; Age; Civil Condition; Literacy; Parent-tongue; Birth- place; Infirmities, and Occupation* (London, 1892), pp. 390–2; *Census of India, 1911*, Vol. 1, Part II – *Tables* (Calcutta, 1913), p. 125.
146 *Deutsche Erde*, vol. 1 (1902), p. 138; Friedrich Wilhelm Mohr and Walter von Hauff, *Deutsche im Ausland* (Breslau, 1923), p. 262; Alfred Geiser, *Deutsches Reich und Volk*, 2nd Edition (Munich, 1910), p. 360.
147 Most research on Indian migration history focuses upon those who left. See, for example, Judith M. Brown, *Global South Asians: Introducing the Modern Diaspora* (Cambridge, 2006), which concentrates on the years since 1947. Tirthankar Roy, *India in the World Economy: From Antiquity to the Present* (Cambridge, 2012), contains two chapters on 'Trade, Migration and Investment' covering the years 1800–1920, which, despite their title, devote little attention to migration.
148 See, for example, Elizabeth Buettner, *Empire Families: Britons and Late Imperial India* (Oxford, 2004); Christopher Bayly, *Indian Society and the Making of the British Empire* (Cambridge, 1988); Michael Edwardes, *Bound to Exile: The Victorians in India* (London, 1969); David Gilmour, *The Ruling Caste: Imperial Lives in the Victorian Raj* (London, 2005).
149 See Chapters 4–6.
150 Dudley Baines, *Emigration from Europe 1815–1930* (London, 1991), p. 9.
151 Dittmar Dahlmann, 'The Russian Germans: A Heterogeneous Minority during the First World War', in Panikos Panayi, ed., *Germans as Minorities During the First World War: A Global Comparative Perspective* (Farnham, 2014), pp. 171–3.
152 As an introduction to eighteenth-century German emigration, see Hans Fenske, 'International migration in the eighteenth century', *Central European History*, vol. 13 (1980), 332–47.
153 See Chapter 2 for an outline of the causes of emigration from Germany.
154 Frederick C. Luebke, *Germans in the New World: Essays in the History of Immigration* (Chicago, 1990), p. 123.
155 Stefan Manz, *Constructing a German Diaspora: The 'Greater German Empire', 1871–1914* (London, 2014), p. 145.
156 Ibid., pp. 93–109.
157 Stanley Nadel, *Little Germany: Ethnicity, Religion, and Class in New York City, 1845–80* (Chicago, 1990).
158 Jürgen Tampke, *The Germans in Australia* (Cambridge, 2006), pp. 72–89.
159 Panayi, *German Immigrants*, pp. 129–42.
160 Manz, *Migranten und Internierte*, pp. 48–110.
161 Tampke, *Germans in Australia*, pp. 33–71.
162 See Schlatter and Hermann Witschi, *Geschichte der Basler Mission*.
163 Wilhelm Oehler, *Geschichte der deutschen evangelischen Mission*, two volumes (Baden-Baden, 1949–51).
164 Brian Stanley, *The World Missionary Conference, Edinburgh, 1910* (Grand Rapids, 2009).
165 Mann, 'Indien ist eine Karriere'.
166 Margrit Schulte Beerbühl, *The Forgotten Majority: German Merchants in London, Naturalization and Global Trade, 1660–1815* (Oxford, 2015).

167 Dittmar Dahlmann and Carmen Scheide, eds, '... *das einzige Land in Europa, das eine große Zukunft vor sich hat'. Deutsche Unternehmen und Unternehmer im Russischen Reich im 19. und frühen 20. Jahrhundert* (Essen, 1998).
168 *Deutsches Kolonial-Handbuch*, 13th Edition (Berlin, 1913), pp. 1, 35.
169 *Hansard* (Commons), fifth series, LXXX, 1390–3, 7 March 1916.
170 Klaus H. Rüdiger, *Die Namibia-Deutschen: Geschichte einer Nationalität im Werden* (Stuttgart, 1993); Martin Eberhardt, *Zwischen Nationalsozialismus und Apartheid: Die deutsche Bevölkerungsgruppe Südwestafrikas 1915–1965* (Münster, 2007); Daniel Joseph Walther, *Creating Germans Abroad. Cultural Policies and National Identity in Namibia* (Athens, OH, 2002), pp. 1–108.
171 Tampke, *Germans in Australia*; Andrew Francis, *'To Be Truly British We Must Be Anti-German': New Zealand, Enemy Aliens and the Great War Experience, 1914–1919* (Oxford, 2012), pp. 15–46; Daniel Steinbach, 'Power Majorities and Local Minorities: German and British Colonials in East Africa during the First World War', in Panayi, *Germans as Minorities*, pp. 263–88.
172 These issues receive more attention in Chapters 4 and 7.

CHAPTER TWO

Passages to India

The Germans who moved to India in the century before the First World War therefore did so in an age when global migration had reached an unprecedented level. Population growth in Europe, combined with the development of rapid means of transport, acted as the underlying factors which pushed people out of the continent to the rest of the world.[1] Much of the movement from Europe tended to follow two paths, as scholars have recognised. First, North America, evidenced especially in the German case, as the USA became the nation state which housed the largest German diaspora community by the outbreak of the First World War. A spurt of growth in the US economy during the nineteenth century would result in a significant rise in the number of people who left Germany.[2] The second path involved what we might describe as 'following the flag', a process established during the Spanish, Portuguese and British imperial expansions from the late fifteenth century, whereby people emigrated towards the areas which the country of their birth seized.[3] During the course of the nineteenth century, this became obvious in the migration of Britons towards the English speaking world – an issue addressed by Charlotte Erickson decades ago,[4] but also tackled in volumes by Marjory Harper and Stephen Constantine,[5] Gary B. Magee and Andrew S. Thompson[6] and Tanja Bueltmann, David T. Gleeson and Don MacRaild.[7]

Such approaches offer limited help in explaining German movement to India both because these migrants represented elite groups and because they did not follow their flag. While some German elites progressed towards the territories acquired by the newly created German Empire after 1870,[8] they did not do so on the scale of either those who moved to the New World or the British who emigrated during the nineteenth century.[9] While structural factors need consideration, networks offer a more precise tool. As we have already seen, religious and academic settlers and visitors developed their own communities. The missionary networks originated at a local level, mirroring the picture of overall movement out of Germany, especially from Württemberg. Nevertheless, the information available, especially on missionaries, also allows a consideration of personal motivations. An investigation of the causes and processes that conveyed Germans to India therefore needs to consider structures, networks and individual choice.

Structural factors

Before pinpointing these structural issues, we might also wish to tackle the issue of the global history of the nineteenth century, especially as put forward by the German scholars Sebastian Conrad and Jürgen Osterhammel, whose work built upon the efforts of British researchers such as Eric Hobsbawm and Chris Bayly. Hobsbawm pioneered the idea of globalisation in his *Age of Empire* in which he recognised imperialism as the driver of the internationalisation of ideas, goods and institutions. If Hobsbawm concentrated on the period 1875–1914,[10] Bayly moved backwards towards 1780 and while – as a specialist on British India – he stressed the role of imperialism in the growth of global interconnectedness, his approach also incorporated new directions in historiography in the two decades since Hobsbawm's book, such as the history of the body.[11] Perhaps most useful for us is Osterhammel's global history of the nineteenth century which is even more all-encompassing in terms of the themes he covers than that of his predecessors.[12] Osterhammel includes migration which involves, like the rest of the book, moving away from a purely Eurocentric approach to examine the movement of people in all directions throughout the world as a result of the rise of capitalism, political reconfiguration and slavery.[13] Like his predecessors, Osterhammel stresses the importance of empire and also the interconnectedness of ideas, politics, political institutions, transport developments and demographic change. Sebastian Conrad has applied globalisation theory to his study of Germany from unification to the outbreak of the First World War. Conrad views imperialism as a process which took place not just beyond Europe but also in Germany's own internal colony in Poland. Significantly, he brings migration into his equation, not simply of Poles towards Germany at the end of the nineteenth century, but also the use of cheap Chinese labour on a global scale. Conrad further tackles emigration and the growth of German trade in the decades leading up to the First World War as indicators of a globalised Germany.[14]

We should therefore consider the migration of Germans to India during the nineteenth century against this background of globalisation, where we can focus on a series of structural factors, the most deep-rooted motivations for movement, which help us to contextualise our migratory stream against broader nineteenth-century developments. They act as the preconditions for emigration and divide further into economic and social factors and ideological and political determinants. While the vast majority of movement took place on a voluntary basis, the First World War meant forced migration of Germans from Siam and East Africa towards India as the British Empire established a global system of internment camps.

At the end of the twentieth century, scholars such as Klaus Bade, Peter Marschalck and Dirk Hoerder[15] investigated the underlying causes of German migration in the previous century, building upon some of the work which had emerged at the time.[16] The deepest factor consists of the population explosion which took place in nineteenth-century Germany, meaning an increase from 24,831,000 in 1816 to 64,568,000 by 1910.[17] Population growth resulted in smaller plots in the predominantly rural economy that existed until the end of the nineteenth century, which could no longer sustain the same number of people as previously. Therefore, a plot which had previously sufficed for one family would have to support more as the population continued to grow. Demographic change worked in the same way in areas where inheritance took place equally among sons (especially in south-west Germany), and areas such as East Prussia where the eldest inherited everything, as the remaining sons would often have to find alternative employment which frequently meant emigration.[18] A clear link exists between the population growth of the nineteenth century, internal migration and emigration. German industrialisation could not have taken place without a supply of mobile domestic labour. For much of the nineteenth century, the latter exceeded the number of jobs available, leading to emigration – mostly to the USA. Only from the end of the 1880s did jobs match labour supply and, in fact, exceed them, leading to immigration.[19]

How do these structural factors in Germany link with migration to India? For much of the nineteenth century, the German state with the highest emigration rates was Württemberg,[20] precisely the source of a significant percentage of our Basel missionaries, many of whom came from humble rural backgrounds. Württemberg may have lost a quarter of its population during the course of the nineteenth century, when emigration became a social movement in a locality with a strong tradition of population loss dating back to the eighteenth century.[21] These demographic and economic structural factors also help to explain emigration from other parts of Germany.

Another structural factor consisted of improvements in transportation during the course of the nineteenth and twentieth centuries, above all the impact of the steam engine, which not only made travel on the high seas safer, cheaper and quicker, but also, because of the growth of the railway, transported Germans to emigration ports, such as Bremen and Hamburg. The main function of these ports was facilitating transatlantic mass migration.[22]

Nevertheless, for much of the nineteenth century Germans on their way to the USA passed through Great Britain, which played a major role as a point of transhipment. This helped the development of the German community in Britain, because some Germans decided to stay rather than travel on to North America.[23] At the same time, it also assisted the evolution of the German elite migration to India because many of those who travelled there did so through Great Britain. Ships of the East India Company played a large role in transporting people and goods to India, although later in the century new companies emerged including the British India Steam Navigation Company.[24]

Many accounts survive of the multistage journey of Germans to India during the nineteenth century. We can begin with Basel missionary Hermann Gundert, who travelled to the Malabar Coast using several ships. His voyage began with an overland journey from Stuttgart to Mannheim on 3 October 1835, from where he boarded a steamship which sailed up the Rhine to Rotterdam. On 11 October, he transferred to the *Ramona* and sailed to London. Gundert then spent several months in London and Bristol, where he networked with British missionaries and clerics before boarding a ship to Madras in Milford Haven at the end of March. At this time the journey to India involved travelling around Africa via the Cape of Good Hope, eventually arriving in Madras on 7 July.[25] Meanwhile, the journey of CMS employee J. J. Weitbrecht, from Württemberg to Calcutta, involved a different route and took longer, partly because he spent more time in England before travelling to India. On 11 December 1828 'I gladly stepped into the coach at Stuttgart' after saying farewell to relatives 'and proceeded to Strasburg, where I remained a day for rest, held a meeting and then went forward to Paris'. On 20 December he left for Calais 'from whence he embarked in an English steamer bound to Ramsgate'. He then travelled to London where he spent several months in the company of clergymen. He had originally intended to go to Abyssinia as he had learnt the Tigree language. As he did not like the London air he stayed with a friend in Brixton in Devon. After seven months here, he returned to London, where the Bishop of London ordained him. On 27 August he left the capital and reached Portsmouth on 4 September via Gravesend. He then sailed south via the Bay of Biscay and the Cape of Good Hope, eventually reaching India at the beginning of 1830.[26] Charles Rhenius made a similar journey. Born in Graudens in West Prussia in 1790, he moved to Berlin in May 1812[27] where he prepared himself 'for usefulness among the negroes of Sierra Leone'. After ordination in Berlin, he actually made his way to London via Denmark in the same year 'for the wars of that time had rendered the more direct road impracticable'.[28] He remained there for some time, during which Parliament and the East India Company passed legislation allowing missionaries to proceed to India.[29] On 4 February 1814, Rhenius left London for Portsmouth and then boarded 'the Marquis of Huntly, bound for Madras' on 21 February.[30] He reached his destination on 4 July.[31] Similarly, the Basel missionary Hermann Mögling sailed down the Rhine to London in March 1836 and then proceeded to India via Portsmouth. By this time, the Basel Mission sent its own agents abroad, rather than using English groupings, which meant that he did not spend the same amount of time networking in London as his predecessors, arriving in Bombay by the end of 1836, after a four-month journey, and then proceeding to Mangalur.[32]

Not all journeys to India involved a stopover in southern England, especially after the completion of the Suez Canal in 1869, although even before this development some Germans had made the trip without the necessity of sailing around Africa.[33] Karl Graul's epic description of his visit to India also outlined his journey there which involved sailing from Port Said to Bombay in 1849, although he does not recount the trip to Port Said. His party boarded a ship in the town of Suez, after presumably travelling from Port Said to this location overland. He then described proceeding along the Red Sea and then on to Aden before reaching Bombay.[34] Karl Plath's 1877 journey, which began on 18 September, involved first travelling by railway from Berlin to Genoa and then sailing from there to Naples, after which he reached the Suez Canal on 3 October, pausing in Aden and then moving on to Bombay, where he landed on 20 October – taking months off the journey which Plath's earlier nineteenth-century missionary predecessors had made.[35] Georg Stosch took a slightly different route 11 years later, again using the Suez Canal, but on this occasion utilising the traditional transhipment location of England and sailing from Port Said to Colombo in a journey time lasting about six weeks in total, rather than the four to six months before the opening up of the Suez Canal and the arrival of rail and steamships.[36] Alwin Gehring made a similar journey in 1877, initially travelling from Rotterdam to Harwich and then proceeding to London, where he remained for a short spell, before boarding a ship in the 'London-docks' on 1 September and arriving in Madras on 9 October, recalling that: 'Our sea journey was very comfortable from beginning to end' (Figure 2.1).[37]

Many of the travel accounts outlined above remain fairly matter of fact, with relatively little personal, and even less emotional, reflection

Figure 2.1 Madras Harbour at the end of the nineteenth century

on the enormity of the journey and the fate to which individuals committed themselves. Jennifer M. Jenkins has suggested, when examining the 1857 journey of Fanny Würth-Leitner, that travelling to India 'was a commitment to life',[38] or so it appeared for much of the nineteenth century. Her journey involved an initial coach trip from Basel to Lucerne after which she proceeded to Trieste through a combination of ship and overland routes. 'Delays were particularly worrying, because the timetable worked out for them in the Basel Mission headquarters allowed very little latitude.'[39] Würth-Leitner's party arrived in Trieste a week after leaving Basel and caught a steamship for Alexandria the following day.[40] They then proceeded overland to Suez, via Cairo and a visit to the Pyramids, and boarded a steamer bound for Bombay, which they reached on 8 December having set out on 2 November.[41] The main anxieties of Fanny Würth-Leitner's journey, as described by Jennifer M. Jenkins, consisted of the novelties of visiting unknown places and the fear of missing connections. Marie Hesse focused upon different issues to Würth-Leitner. The daughter of Hermann Gundert, she was actually born in Talatscheri in the southern Indian mission station where her father worked, but made the journey between India and Europe on several occasions. She spent much of her childhood in Europe because her parents had to return to Stuttgart for health reasons, leaving Marie and her siblings. Her parents then left again in 1846, and she found herself in the care of the Ostertag family – a period upon which she looked back fondly, despite the trauma of separation from parents. She then spent time in a Christian girls institute in Korntal in Württemberg.[42] She left an emotional account of her first departure for India on 21 November 1857, the same month as Würth-Leitner, in a diary entry of that day:

> It has arrived, the long desired yet feared day of departure and parting. The way in which mother (Ostertag) embraced and gazed at me with tears on the station – I will never be able to forget. Oh parting, parting, you hurt me. Gundeldingen, the home of my childhood, farewell – forever.[43]

Despite the rawness of the separation described here, Hesse's mood changed during the journey via Marseilles and again through Egypt. The arrival in Bombay on 23 December resulted in more crying when reunited with her mother.[44] Dagmar Konrad has examined the female experience of migration more generally by focusing upon those women who went out as wives of Basel missionaries, outlining a series of stages from the betrothal to the departure and the journey itself, which she divides into three phases: the first consisted of a desire to hold on to the past as the day of departure approached; the second developed on the ship, when the brides began to normalise the 'exceptional'; the third involved acceptance of both the new environment and husband as the ship neared India and excitement developed.[45]

Despite this fairly sanitised argument constructed by Konrad, some male missionaries left accounts of traumatic journeys, especially from the earlier nineteenth century, involving sailing around the Cape of Good Hope which, as the pioneering Dresden missionary Carl Ochs recalled, took several months. He left London on the *Queen Mary* on 10 August 1842, and 'finally' arrived in Madras on 11 December. The journey had involved one of the crew falling overboard and drowning, drunken sailors who would not work after celebrating the birthday of one of their colleagues, intense heat and the loss of two sails.[46] Meanwhile, the Basel missionaries Johannes Müller, Johannes Ammann, Gottfried Weigle, Johannes Fritz and Johannes Meugert left London on 18 February 1840 and spent 111 days at sea, arriving in Bombay on 18 June. Just four days into their journey they experienced a storm in the Bay of Biscay which meant that the 'ship really was almost buried between the waves'.[47] Similarly, the Gossner missionaries Heinrich Höppner and Friedrich Dodt left London on 16 August 1853 and did not arrive in Calcutta until 'the first day of Christmas'. The journey once again involved storms, a sailor falling overboard and drowning, tropical heat and a collision with another ship.[48] Although the journey of Hermann Gäbler, who travelled from Hirschfelde in Saxony to Madras in August and September of 1891, did not contain quite this level of excitement in view of the transportation improvements which had taken place in the second half of the nineteenth century, he recorded a sad departure in which 'with heavy heart and many tears' he left his parental home. He recorded seeing his father for the last time in Hirschfelde station, while his mother and brother accompanied him to Dresden station. 'Here, after lunch another tearful departure took place. They stood on the station and looked at the train in front of them with tear stained eyes.' Gäbler's journey involved a boat from London through the Suez Canal and his diary paints a positive picture after the farewells to family members.[49]

By the beginning of the twentieth century, a direct route also existed between Germany and India as trade between the two countries grew. By 1912, Germany had become the second most important trading partner for India, even if it remained considerably behind Great Britain. Ultimately, as Conrad has demonstrated, while German trade became globalised, by this time 'three quarters of German exports went to Europe, mostly to Britain'.[50] The most important products which made their way to Germany from India included raw cotton, animal hides and skins, jute and rice.[51] This direct trade had evolved in the previous decades, as consular reports from individual ports reveal. For example, in 1881 the main product exported from Cochin to Hamburg consisted of coconuts and coconut oil.[52] Meanwhile, the most important goods which made their way from Germany to the Madras Presidency in 1903–4 included: chemicals, drugs and medicines; tobacco; iron, engineering goods, cameras and typewriters; matches; metals; and condensed milk.[53] Such statistics find reflection in the number of ships which sailed between Germany and India in the late nineteenth and early twentieth centuries. Thus, in 1900, a total of 56 German merchant vessels landed in Calcutta, including 37 directly from Hamburg and seven from Bremen.[54] Nine years earlier the figures stood at 33 German ships of which 31 had sailed from Hamburg.[55] In 1911–12, meanwhile, a total of 757 foreign ships had sailed into Bombay. The country of origin which counted the largest was Great Britain, followed by Germany with 82. At the same time, 588 merchant ships left Bombay including 400 bound for Great Britain and 35 for Germany (behind Austria-Hungary with 38).[56] Meanwhile, in 1913, 55 German ships visited Cochin together with 48 which docked at the other ports on the Malabar Coast. The major companies facilitating these journeys were the German Australian Steam Ships, the Hamburg America Line and the Bremen Hansa.[57] These developments help to explain the presence of German companies and their representatives in India before the First World War.[58]

With the opening of the Suez Canal, the development of a German merchant fleet following German unification in 1870 and the replacement of sail by steam, it became easier to reach India. Rather than sailing via Great Britain and over the Cape of Good Hope, those who made the journey could travel either directly from Hamburg or Bremen or from another European port and proceed though the Suez Canal. While the trip had taken months at the beginning of the nineteenth century, it had fallen to weeks at the start of the twentieth. But the impact of these developments does not prove easy to measure. One of the problems consists of the lack of accurate figures of people born abroad who lived in India before 1891, as the Indian census did not ask for place of birth earlier. Nevertheless, we have previously seen that the number of academics progressing to India increased during the course of the nineteenth century, as did the number of those connected with business. Direct sailing to India certainly had an impact upon the presence of German businessmen in the country by the end of the nineteenth century, as they often found themselves there in connection with the types of goods imported and exported. Lists of merchant ships sailing from Cochin during the 1880s also include details of the products and firms involved in the exportation.[59]

Apart from the mechanics of transportation, another important factor facilitating migration to India, which can also merit the description of structural, consists of the power of Christianity, which scholars have explained through the prism of Pietism or even zeal, although a more mundane explanation might focus upon the importance of religious belief in the nineteenth century.[60] Pietism or zeal, combined with missionary organisations, would have directed people into activity outside their home states. Jon Miller, in his study of the Basel Mission, has suggested that Pietism remained 'close to the heart of dominant Protestant beliefs' but was 'emotionally intense'. It 'placed especially strong emphasis on spiritual rebirth, close reading of scripture, personal asceticism, discipline and ... social conservatism ... These beliefs included a strong commitment to missionary evangelism.'[61] Würtemburg, from where many of the Basel missionaries originated, became a centre of Pietism.[62] When analysing the motivations of those who went abroad in the service of the Basel and Rhineland missions, Judith Becker has focused upon the religious belief which the sending groups provided to those who travelled thousands of miles beyond Europe despite the dangers involved, whether sickness or persecution, and the fact that they might not see their families and friends for years or decades. This belief included an element of millenarianism and the desire to convert as many people as possible before the arrival of the kingdom of God.[63]

The language of the missionaries indicates the concrete nature of their belief in the Christian message and its superiority over the religions with which they came into contact. The centrality of Christianity as a belief system comes across especially in everyday discourse as revealed in the accounts of several missionaries who travelled to India. A full understanding of the role of belief in the life of John Weitbrecht requires appreciation that Christianity essentially controlled his every thought and action, including the most mundane. A letter to his mother from Basel on 4 February 1827 began: 'Our Faithful God and Saviour has hitherto kept me in good health, and He causes his Sun of Grace to shine upon me, and on all of you too I hope, for his Mercy endureth for ever.'[64] This type of language permeates the entire memoir, compiled by his wife, whether referring to everyday events or to the activities he undertakes in connection with his missionary work. On New Year's Day 1834, he wrote:

> I have now spent three years in India, and depending on the Almighty hand which has hitherto so graciously and faithfully guided me, I enter on the fourth. O Lord, let thy Favour preserve my breath, for in this land we sensibly feel that in the midst of life we are in death. Give me, blessed Jesus, new faithfulness, new zeal, new strength, and new blessings in my work in this vineyard wherein Thou hast called me to labour.[65]

The same language appears in the memoirs of Charles Rhenius. For example, on 10 January 1815 he set 'out in the evening, praying the Lord to protect and guide us on our way'.[66]

The mention of the Lord in, what seems, virtually every other word, characterised the earlier rather than later nineteenth century missionaries against the background of 'a new sociocultural paradigm' influenced by Darwinism and social and economic change.[67] However, such transformations had not undermined the fundamental beliefs of the missionaries. While the accounts of visits to India by Gehring, Plath and Stosch[68] contain somewhat different language to that of Weitbrecht and Rhenius, the belief in the superiority of Christianity remains strong, otherwise the whole purpose of missionary activity disappears. Thus Stosch concludes his 1896 account of his visit to India by outlining the tasks of the missionary:

> The struggle of the mission in India is a spiritual struggle in the sense that two world views fight against each other, monotheism against a multi-coloured polytheism, the belief in the living personal God, the creator and saviour of the world, with the melancholic, frivolously tinged stoic, epicurean polytheism.[69]

Stosch essentially speaks the same language as his earlier nineteenth-century predecessors. While he may not continuously mention God, the strength of his belief remains unflinching as he regards missionary work as a clash of civilisations.

Such beliefs partly evolved from the training acquired from the organisations for which the missionaries worked, providing the networks which sent them to India. A final structural factor which needs consideration is the role of the state in influencing the nature of migration. Clearly an important turning point in the history of missionary activity came with the decision of the British Parliament in 1833, when renewing the Charter of the East India Company, to allow foreigners to establish their own organisations in India.[70] This had followed the earlier easing of East India Company attitudes towards British missions in 1813 – in connection with the renewal of the charter – which had allowed a growth of British missionary activity, in which Germans served.[71]

If we proceed forward to the First World War, we see the Government of India, working in tandem with the foreign office and war office in London, as part of a grand imperial strategy to control the activities of German subjects in the Empire, transporting them from East Africa and Siam to face internment in the country. While the overwhelming majority of Germans who went to India between 1800 and 1920 did so voluntarily, forced migration took place during the Great War, characterising policy towards Germans throughout the Empire. Most would simply face internment in the country in which they resided in 1914, including the Germans in India, but forced migration symbolised the global nature of British internment policy.[72]

As well as the two major transportations which took place towards India from East Africa and Siam, other Germans captured in the Middle East proceeded to internment camps in India in the early stages of the War. At the beginning of 1915, seven men arrested in Basra and Bahrain experienced transportation to the most important camp in Ahmednagar.[73] They included G. Harling, seized in the office of his employer Robert Douckbans & Co. in Bahrain on 28 October 1914, who complained that this event had taken place in 'an independent country'.[74]

Those Germans residing in East Africa before the outbreak of the Great War included plantation owners, traders and missionaries. The majority initially endured incarceration in Nairobi, but would face transportation to the major Indian camps of Ahmednagar and Belgaum from November 1914 once shipping became available.[75] For example, 'John Booth, born in the year 1863, owner of a plantation upon the isle of Mafia, German East Africa, was taken prisoner there by the British about the beginning of January 1915. He was taken to Nairobi, British East Africa, and from that place to Ahmednagar in British India.'[76] In addition, German troops stationed and captured in East Africa also experienced transportation to Ahmednagar, including Albert Achilles.[77] Meanwhile, a Herr von Busse, living in Lamu in the Sultanate of Zanzibar at the outbreak of war, became a prisoner of war in Lamu on 6 August and faced imprisonment after the Battle of Tanga when German forces captured British soldiers. Busse then experienced transportation upon a ship to Mombassa on 4 December, and then went to Bombay on another vessel together with 89 Germans and Austrians. On 27 December, a train took them to Ahmednagar. Although Busse seems to have returned to Germany during the course of the War,[78] over 200 internees brought from East Africa still resided there at the beginning of 1918, by which time they constantly complained about their incarceration and their desire to return to East Africa, where many had lived for decades.[79]

In 1918, Germans (together with a smaller number of Austrians) also experienced transportation from Siam to Ahmednagar or, in the case of women and children, to a specially constructed camp in Sholapur. The journey to India took place in February 1918 upon the SS *Pinsamud* and the SS *Dinsamud*. In addition, a further 12 internees arrived from the Straits Settlement in June 1918. The total of 286 consisted of 251 Germans and 35 Austrians.[80] This forced migration proves particularly interesting because Siam remained an independent state which did not constitute part of the British Empire, rather like Bahrain. While in both cases there exists an element of the two territories falling within the British sphere of influence – and while, in the former case, the British seem to have muscled in to arrest the local Germans – this did not happen in Siam. The Siamese Government had already asked the British Government to send its entire enemy alien population to Australia even before it declared war on Germany on 22 July 1917, leading to a decision to send the internees to India and the eventual establishment of the Sholapur camp. Those arrested included not simply Germans already resident in the country on 22 July, but also those seized upon German ships docked in Siam. The main occupations of these Germans consisted of merchants, engineers and sailors. They faced internment together with their families once transferred to India. While the Siamese Government may have initiated this process, the British Government and the Government of India acted instantly, suggesting previous conversations about this process not recorded in the surviving archival documents.[81]

A series of structural factors therefore helped the migration of Germans to India during our period. In the case of the development of transportation, which aided, but did not cause, migration, when the steamship took over and the Suez Canal opened, this essentially acted as an enabling factor. Those Germans forced to internment camps in India during the First World War had absolutely no control over their fate. Religious belief acted as a key factor for missionary migration. Some of the narratives quoted above indicate the strength of this zeal, but also point to the importance of individual agency. While forced migration remained completely out of the hands of the Great War deportees, those who made their way as missionaries made their own decision to move.

We can see all of these factors as part of the globalisation of the nineteenth century in the range of ways suggested by Osterhammel in particular. Apart from the technological and transport factors, globalisation also operated through the spread of religious belief as Christianity became an increasingly global religion during this century as a result of the development of an evangelical zeal[82] which, in the German case, took the form of Pietism. Just as importantly, the power of empire becomes apparent in both the decisions taken to allow proselytisation in India in 1813 and 1833 and in the transportation which took place during the First World War.

Networks

Globalisation also reveals itself in the networks which have increasingly become an explanatory tool in mainstream migration theory as detailed in the latest edition of the classic text on *The Age of Migration*, which, while focusing upon the post-1945 period, helps our analysis. Castles, de Haas and Miller use the following description, which can serve as our starting point: 'Migrant networks can be defined as sets of inter-personal ties that connect migrants, former migrants and non-migrants in origin and destination areas through bonds of kinship, friendship, and shared community origin ... Migrant networks tend to decrease the economic, social and psychological costs of migration' partly because people have already made the journey to the country of destination and can therefore provide the links, help and information necessary to make the move.[83] The idea of networks also links with another aspect of globalisation, transnationalism, focusing upon the ways in which migrant groups interact with their land of origin, through a variety of means of communication, which also facilitates the migration process because of the information provided on the destination.[84]

Historians have increasingly adopted the network approach. Patrick Manning, in a study of migration in world history, has written that 'cross-community networks' which involve 'co-operation across distance and across boundaries of language and culture, facilitate the movement of migrants from one place to another'. Importantly, Manning identifies agents in the network in both the home and receiving society.[85] Klaus Bade, meanwhile, has written of the development of migration 'traditions', which evolve over time.[86] Among specific case studies, much attention has focused upon Irish migration networks over the last two centuries.[87]

From our own perspective, research has emerged on the evolution of networks in imperial migration. While the studies of population movement within the British Empire by Magee and Thompson and by Harper and Constantine have focused upon the traditional patterns of movement within the Empire, above all between Britain and the white Dominions, they have, nevertheless, utilised the concept of networks. Magee and Thompson make links with globalisation, families, charities and trade unions as facilitators of movement.[88] Interestingly, while Harper and Constantine have covered the traditionally studied routes of migration towards the White Dominions and have also examined settlement in Africa, as well as non-white migrants and settlers (which, nevertheless, have a significant historiography), they only overtly address networks when discussing migration towards Great Britain, even though they cover similar themes to Magee and Thompson.[89]

Scholars of the German diaspora have also adapted the concept of network migration, even though they may not have done so in an overt fashion. In particular the volume by Ulrike Kirchberger, on the way in which Germans proceeded to Britain and then on to other parts of the British Empire and the world beyond more generally, essentially deals with networks whether for missionaries, scientists, soldiers or transmigrants. In all cases particular connections brought them to Britain and then sent to them to the wider world.[90] Stefan Manz, in his study of the Germans in Glasgow, takes an approach which examines migration by focusing upon the evolution of particular occupational groups, demonstrating how links between the city, Great Britain and Germany helped this process to evolve.[91] An introductory essay to a volume on Germans in the British Empire by John R. Davis, Margrit Schulte Beerbühl and Stefan Manz pointed to the fact that non-British migration within the Empire 'includes transnational and truly global dimensions' which 'involve links that transcend and erode the boundaries of British domestic as well as imperial history'.[92] The essays in the volume essentially examine specific groups which emerged within the Empire.

The German migration to India lends itself to an analysis which uses network theory. While much research on contemporary movement uses such an analysis to break down and try to understand 'mass migration', it appears an obvious tool for understanding the movement of the small numbers of Germans to India. In particular, networks played a central role in the migration of missionaries and scholars and scientists to India, as the available information indicates.

All types of networks functioned together to transport missionaries to India including, above all, the individual groups concerned which provided the link between the geographical origins, which often focused upon a particular part of Germany for the different organisations, and the specific destination in India. Hartmut Tyrell has described the missionary bodies as independent sending institutions, pointing to their roles in bringing the individuals towards them and also developing a particular world view within them, creating a community and providing them with rules and regulations before finally sending them out to distinct destinations – a perspective also adopted by Jon Miller.[93]

The missionary organisations therefore played a number of roles. In the first place, they acted as the training centres which prepared those they would send out. The Basel Mission, for example, established its own educational activities from the early years of its history. The first school came into existence in August 1816 when it took in its first pupils, providing a set of rules. In addition, what would become known as the Missionshaus also opened shortly afterwards, essentially the training centre for missionaries. Men would remain here for between four and five years and would have to work between 16 and 17 hours per day on Mondays to Saturdays. They underwent a religious and intellectual training which created a full understanding of the Holy Scriptures. However, in view of the tasks ahead of them, they received a broader education which included languages and geography. In the early days of the Basel Mission, until the British Parliament allowed foreign missionary organisations to work in India in 1833, it had to work with the CMS, which meant that, at this stage, another network became involved in the process of sending those they trained abroad and which also meant that these early Basel employees received ordination from the Anglican Church, for whom they worked.[94]

Those trained by the Basel Mission left accounts of their education here. Weitbrecht spoke in glowing terms of his experience, which points to the sense of community created: 'The whole establishment, consisting of about sixty individuals, presents the beautiful picture of a *family*, living in the most unbroken harmony; humility, peace, and love reign there in a higher degree than the writer ever remembers to have witnessed elsewhere.'[95] On 14 August 1863, Christian Gotthilf Weigle stood before the door of the Basel mission house and would train there for four years before departing for India on 3 October 1867.[96] Samuel Hebich also spent time in the mission house in Basel, having previously served as an apprentice to his brother's business in Lübeck from the age of 14. During this time and a subsequent term spent working for a second firm – J. Brehns and Sons, following the completion of his apprenticeship which took him to St Petersburg, Sweden and Finland – he decided after a period of introspection on his religious vocation and simultaneously came into contact with the Lübeck Missionary Society. He entered the Basel mission house at the end of 1831, after previous correspondence. He underwent a three-year training period and sailed out to India in

1834.[97] Some of those who worked for the Basel Mission, including some of the early leading lights, followed a slightly different path into missionary work which did not involve the same formal period of study in Switzerland. For example, Hermann Mögling arrived at the mission house in Basel as a Tübingen University graduate, having already undergone seminary training from the second half of the 1820s, and would spend just one year there, studying Sanskrit, English and the history of the mission. After ordination in the Stiftskirche in Tübingen on 6 January 1836, he sailed to India via London at the end of March.[98]

Other missionary organisations also opened the same type of training establishment as the Basel Mission. Several short biographies of Hermannsburg employees tell of the time that they spent in the headquarters of this group in the north German town from which its name originates. They included Christian Kohlmeier, from the small town of Duingen, 115 kilometres south of Hamburg. The hagiographic account of him authored by Johann Wörrlein (who wrote all of the pamphlets considered here) tells of his first encounter with missionary work as a 15 year old when he heard the organisation's inspector speaking in Wilstedt near Bremen, just after the death of his father. 'That awoke in his heart the love of missionary work which became stronger and stronger and drove him to Hermannsburg five years later in 1872.' He then spent a further seven years there, including four in the mission house, before ordination in December 1879 and then setting out for India at the beginning of 1880.[99] Meanwhile, Ernst Jürgemeier, born in Heithöfen near Osnabrück in 1856, had, according to Wörrlein, already decided on a missionary life while at school. Wörrlein also claims that Jürgemeier's father had applied and obtained exemption for his son from military service so that in November 1882 he arrived in the mission house. 'Although learning did not come easily to him, he had already prepared himself, through diligence and faith, with very proficient knowledge. His friends in the mission house rated him very highly and grew very fond of him.' He left for India in 1888.[100] Finally, Paul Otto Petersen, born in Apenrade in Schleswig in 1844, developed his devotion to Christianity while serving as a caretaker in Herr Hilderbrandt's house in his home town, where the pious family directed him towards work in India. In 1871 he went to the mission house, sailing out four years later.[101] While these three accounts do not say much about the training and life once at Hermannsburg, the time spent there represented a key stepping stone for people who had already accepted their Christian calling.

The Leipzig Mission also established its own training seminar in 1854. Information on those who studied there suggests that they remained small in number, tying in with the fact that each organisation sent out a limited number of people either in total or in any particular year.[102]

For example, between 1891 and 1913 about five to six people finished the course every two years. Some did not go abroad straightaway but spent further time training in a type of internship ('Vikariat') or in learning English in England. Others had already undertaken theological training beforehand.[103]

As well as providing the training and standardisation necessary for the construction of a missionary, the networks also sent their employees to already established stations in India. While the risk of sailing to and living in India never disappeared, those who went out as missionaries had a delineated path opened up for them by the groups which employed them. The narratives of the spiritual awakening, training and the passage to India provide three parts of the process which brought Germans to their new place of work and residence, but they have also left information on the final stage in the form of their reception and early settlement, as a few examples illustrate. When Hermann Gundert landed in India in August 1836, he initially stayed with the London Missionary Society whose members then took him to a variety of sites which they ran.[104] Similarly, immediately upon landing in Calcutta, Weitbrecht met a whole series of friends from Europe. He then moved to Burdwan where he would start his missionary activity.[105] When the Leipzig-trained Alwin Gehring arrived in Madras in 1877, two of his colleagues boarded his ship and took him to the Leipzig mission house there. His network then accompanied him to Tranquebar, where other Leipzig missionaries helped him to integrate into his work and environment.[106] Similarly, when Georg Stosch landed in Madras on 12 October 1888: 'We raised our eyes to God and were greeted by the brothers who came to get us' who then took them to the mission house before proceeding to Tranquebar.[107] The Leipzig Mission, like its sister in Basel, also had a set of orders for those it employed, originating in 1847, in which it declared 'the word of God' lay at the basis of all of its activity, for the spread of which, at home and abroad, it would educate missionaries. At the centre lay the council, which payed for the transport of missionaries to India. Once there, they would travel straight to Tranquebar. During their first two years in India an older missionary would guide them and, at the end of the period, they would take an exam in Tamil.[108]

Many missionaries travelled in small groups, again facilitated by their networks, which further eased integration into the new work and environment. In his brief account of the work of Peter Lüchow in India, Johann Wörrlein pointed out that he emigrated with three other missionaries (including Kohlmeier) after ordination in December 1879. Wörrlein wrote that the older missionaries anticipated their arrival with 'great longing' because of the fact that several other Hermannsburg missionaries had recently departed.[109] Those sent out from Basel also often travelled as groups. Sometimes they went to the same station, while on other occasions they made their way to a variety of locations in India. Those in the former category included Johann Detzlinger, Johann Hiller and Georg Sutter, all of whom left on 25 July 1838 bound for Canara, although once they arrived they did not all work in the same station there. Two years later, Johann Michael Fritz and Johann Jakob Amman, who both departed on 18 February, worked in Canara and Malabar respectively.[110]

Women also went out to India, sometimes accompanying their husbands, but on other occasions to work in the country as single women, albeit using the same networks as men. The Basel Mission initially only accepted single male missionaries, but this changed during the course of the 1830s so that in 1837, Christian Blumhardt, the organisation's chief inspector, established a series of rules for married couples. In nineteenth-century Europe the extent of free choice involved in the decision of women to travel out as wives of Basel missionaries remained questionable, with parents, relatives and friends influencing the decision to emigrate. Nevertheless, many of these brides already had a religious disposition as they came from the families of ministers and missionaries.[111] For example, Johanna Werner, born in Fellbach in Württemberg in 1852, was the daughter of a Karl Friedrich Werner who had worked for the mission school in Basel and would then take over as parish priest in Fellbach (Württemberg). When he died in 1872 his family had to leave the vicarage and move to Unterweisach (Württemberg), where one of Johanna's brothers worked as the local pastor. Her passage to India really began when she received a letter from the recently widowed Basel missionary Gustav Ritter, stationed in Mukli and then Udipi, looking for a second wife to help him. Johanna felt excitement at opening the letter and discussed migration with her mother, who encouraged her to travel. She left Basel in September 1875 together with two other women and, two weeks after their arrival in India, they celebrated a triple marriage in Balmatha.[112] The experience of Paulina Bacmeister, who would marry Hermann Mögling, closely resembled that of Johanna Werner. Born in 1823 in Esslingen, just outside Stuttgart, she attended a Pietist school in nearby Korntal from the age of 15, subsequently becoming a teacher. In 1842, as in the case of Johanna Werner, a marriage proposal arrived in writing, in this case from Mögling's father via Gottfried Weigle. Also like Werner, she left Basel in 1842 with two other brides.[113] In total, it appears that 174 women travelled from Germany to India between the later 1830s and the eve of the First World War to marry Basel missionaries.[114]

As the century progressed, women increasingly migrated to India and other missionary destinations independently, at least from a husband or potential husband, but again in the service of one of the missionary societies who took them to their new home, either as 'sisters' or as teachers. One of the most independent of Leipzig Mission employees was Margarete Grote, born in Hary in Hanover in 1866 who originally worked as a teacher in Russia between 1885 and 1890. In 1891, the Leipzig Mission sent her to Tanjore where she served as superintendent of a school, after which she progressed to Madras to lead language studies. She actually left missionary service after meeting and marrying the German consul in Madras.[115] Lisa Streng spent her entire working life in the service of the Leipzig Mission. Born in Burgsalach in Middle Franconia in 1867, as the daughter of a minister (again confirming family continuity in religious service) she originally worked in several schools in Franconia, before volunteering for missionary work. The Leipzig Mission sent her to Coimbatore in Tamil Nadu in 1902, and she worked in various schools in South India after passing her Tamil exam in 1905, facing deportation in November 1915.[116] The Basel Mission, meanwhile, sent out 27 women from Germany (out of a total of 49) to work in its service in India between 1842 and the outbreak of the First World War. According to one source, all of these single women found employment as teachers for the Mission.[117]

Clearly, the missionary organisations acted as networks which took Germans in their service to India, offering the information which had become available as well as transportation. Once they arrived in their new country of residence, those missionaries already present guided them towards their new place of employment while, in the case of potential wives, they would meet their husbands – sometimes for the first time – already living in India.

As well as these missionary networks, two other pre-existing webs directed individuals towards overseas religious work. Place of birth played a key role, as general studies of nineteenth-century German emigration have demonstrated (Figure 2.2). For example, Stanley Nadel, in his book on German New York, traced the ways in which the origins of those who moved there changed as the nineteenth century progressed, so that Baden and Württemberg lost importance, while Prussia sent increasing numbers[118] – a picture mirrored in Great Britain[119] – essentially following the patterns of nineteenth-century German emigration.[120]

In the case of our missionaries, the picture does not change significantly during the course of the nineteenth century. What matters here is the fact that missionaries tended to travel abroad in the service of the grouping closest to them in geographical terms, as an examination of those who worked for the Basel, Leipzig and Hermannsburg organisations illustrates. As Table 2.1 demonstrates, the majority of those Germans sent out by the Basel Mission came from southern

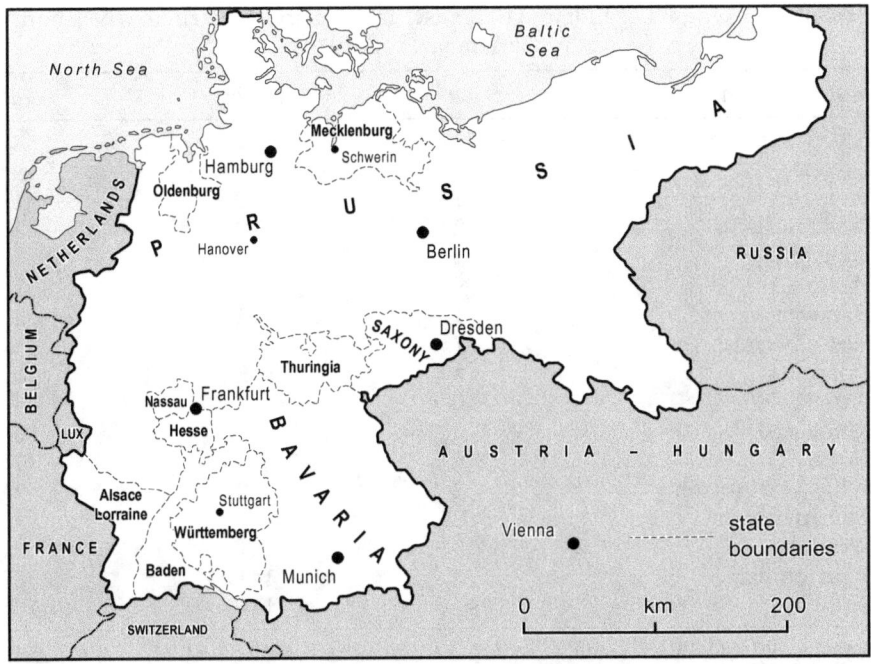

Figure 2.2 Map of the German Empire, 1871–1918

Germany, especially from nearby Württemberg and to a lesser extent Baden, while, further away, some also originated from Bavaria, Hesse-Nassau and Pfalz. Others, however, came from as far away as Prussia and East Friesland. Ultimately, one fact comes through clearly in Table 2.1: a large majority of those Germans sent out by the Basel Mission consisted of Württembergers. In the case of the overall figure, this stood at just over two-thirds (67.6 per cent). For men, the proportion remained slightly lower at 60 per cent, while for women it reached an even higher 80 per cent. The 58 from Baden accounted for just 12 per cent of the overall total, although a significant gender difference exists here, with 24 per cent of men originating here and just 10 per cent of women.

Table 2.2 indicates that the Leipzig missionaries also had distinct geographical origins. Most importantly, as in the case of Basel, most of those who went out from Leipzig originated either in the immediate locality or slightly further afield. Therefore, 44 per cent came from locations in Saxony. The vast majority of the rest came either from north Germany (East Friesland, Hanover, Pommerania, Schleswig-Holstein and Silesia) or from central Germany (Franconia and Thuringia).

Table 2.1 Origins of Indian-based Basel missionaries and their wives born in Germany, 1818–1914

State of birth	Men	Wives	Total
Baden	44	14	58
Bavaria	16	2	18
Bremen	1	0	1
East Friesland	2	0	2
Franconia	1	0	1
Hesse	9	2	11
Hanover	1	2	3
Hesse-Nassau	7	4	11
Palatine	8	2	10
Prussia	10	3	13
Rhineland	2	1	3
Saxony	9	3	12
Schleswig-Holstein	2	0	2
Thuringia	0	1	1
Westfalia	5	1	6
Württemberg	177	141	318
Total	294	176	470

Sources: BMA/Q-30.3,5, Gebietslisten, Indien, Männer 1; BMA/Q-30.3,5, Gebietslisten, Indien, Frauen.

Note: The geographical divisions used in the table match those in the documentation utilised by the archivist who listed the names and birthplaces of Germans sent out from Basel.

We can also briefly mention the short biographies of the Hermmansburg missionaries written by Wörrlein. Those born furthest away from Hermmansburg included Wörrlein himself, from Windsheim in middle Franconia – a considerable 474 kilometres away, together with Otto Petersen from Apenrade in Schleswig, now in Denmark (Aabenraa) – 284 kilometres away. The other two biographies point to Hermannsburg missionaries born closer to the home town of their organisation, including Christian Kohlmeier, born in Duingen (115 kilometres south) and Ernst Jürgenmeier from Heithöfen (162 kilometres to the west).[121]

While the small sample available on the Hermannsburg employees might prove inconclusive, it seems clear from the more copious information on those sent out from Basel and Leipzig that a direct relationship existed between place of birth and the missionary organisation for which individuals worked. The vast majority of those sent out from Basel came from Württemberg together with a notable minority from

Table 2.2 Major origins of Indian-based Leipzig missionaries sent to India before 1914

Place of origin	Total sent to India
Bavaria	4
East Friesland	3
Franconia	11
Hanover	7
Pommerania	11
Saxony	38
Schleswig-Holstein	2
Silesia	2
Thuringia	1
Württemberg	1
Other German locations	6
Total	86

Sources: Leipzig Missionswerk, Missionäre, Indien, www.lmw-mission.de/de/missionare--2-site-1.html, accessed 1 June 2015.

Note: The construction of this table involved an examination of the first 17 web pages of Leipzig missionaries sent out to India before the First World War. The table only utilises information for those born in Germany rather than others born in India (the children of already stationed missionaries), Sweden and other parts of Europe.

Baden, while a large minority of those who travelled with the Leipzig Mission came from the immediate surrounding areas of Saxony.

As well as focusing upon the relationship between locality and migration, network theorists also examine family. An excellent example of this factor playing a role, if we move forward a century and examine movement out of India and its diaspora, consists of South Asian migration towards Great Britain, where the standard pattern consisted of males progressing to the country during the later 1950s and 1960s followed by their wives and children during the 1970s.[122] We have already seen that a similar process operated among the German missionary migrants to India, where potential brides, usually from religious backgrounds, travelled to the country to marry husbands they had never met before, after consultation with their relatives. Further confirmation of the importance of family comes from an analysis of the ten German-born women for whom information on parental occupation survives, sent out by the Leipzig Mission before the First World War. In fact, five of them came from the family of a minister (Auguste Hensolt, Helene Frankel, Lina Streng, Elisabeth Schüler and Berta Hübener), while another four came from households headed by a teacher (Käthe Schmidt, Johanna and Aurelie Herget and Rosa Busch). The father of Emma Kerberg, however, worked as a brick manufacturer.[123] An examination of the men sent out by the Basel Mission to India reveals a different picture, with most coming from essentially artisan backgrounds, although they also included teachers, businessmen and theology students, confirming the findings of Jon Miller, who places migration against the background of 'pressures on the land caused by population growth and by the gradual industrial transformation of the land that was taking place in many parts of Europe' including Baden and Württemberg. Miller sees missionary work as an opportunity for 'upward mobility'.[124] In any case, there appears no obvious connection with a theological upbringing for the vast majority of Basel males.[125]

Family networks also reveal themselves in other ways. For example, the Leipzig Mission included one set of sisters (Johanna and Aurelie Herget), at least one set of brothers (Rudolf and Hiko Schomerus) and at least one father and son (Eduard and Martin Schäffer).[126] Basel sent out at least one set of brothers in the form of Carl and John Menge from Hanau in 1836 and 1840 respectively.[127] Sisters included Frieda and Wilhemina Geiner-Frohmmeyer from Württemberg (married in 1841 and 1842), Julie and Pauline Kittel-Eyth (1860 and 1861), Wilhelm-ine and Frederike Digel (1867 and 1871) and Luise and Lydia Stierlin (1883 and 1889), all of whom came from Württemberg. All travelled to marry and, in the case of Frieda and Wilhemina Geiner-Frohmmeyer and Julie and Pauline Kittel-Eyth, appear to have married men who were either brothers or cousins in view of the fact that they had the same surnames.[128]

The Basel Mission in India developed at least one truly diasporic family which lasted for decades in the form of the Gunderts. Hermann Gundert acted as the first link in the family chain. His daughter Marie became the second, and remained in India after the return of her father to Germany in 1859 because of ill-health. She married the missionary Charles Isenberg, who died, leaving her a widow. She returned home and married her second husband, Johannes Hesse, who had served in India for the Basel Mission between 1869 and 1873 but who would have to return home. This union would give birth to Hermann Hesse, who, while he did not serve as a missionary, developed a fascination with India.[129]

Network theory clearly plays a central role in explaining the migration of German missionaries to India in all sorts of ways. Does it also help to inform the movement of other groups? Ulrike Kirchberger has described 'a network of German scientists within the British Empire, often in close professional contact' who 'corresponded, exchanged botanical material and scientific literature, and referred to each others' works in their publications',[130] although she also offers a variety of other explanations for their presence in the Empire, including the fact that German universities developed a more advanced science than those in Britain and the fact that, for the indologists, better research opportunities existed in the Empire.[131] Meanwhile, Indra Sengupta has identified a network of scholars in Germany and Britain who helped to build up the collections of German university manuscripts from India.[132]

An examination of the foresters and a few scholars will illustrate these issues. Although Dietrich Brandis became the first major German figure to have had an impact on Indian forestry, other Germans already appear to have worked in this field. For example, in 1837, Dr Helfer wrote about the forests of Malabar.[133] Ultimately, Brandis secured his post in India through family connections as his marriage to Rachel, daughter of the Indian scholar and missionary Joshua Marshman, 'determined his career' because his wife's sister was married to General Sir Henry Havelock of the Indian Army, related to the Governor General of India, Lord Dalhousie. The marriage actually took place in 1854. The process of moving to India occurred after a post as Superintendent of the forest of the Pegu province of Burma became available. Rachel had previously corresponded with her father about finding a position for her husband in India. Marshman, in turn, wrote to Havelock as well as Dalhousie, who, after consulting with a botanist in India, offered Brandis this job. This did not equate to pure nepotism because Brandis's scientific training as a botanist also made him suitable for this first post in India.[134] Brandis played a significant role in the movement of William Schlich to a position in India because Professor Gustave Heyer, with whom Schlich studied forestry at Gießen University, recommended him, which resulted in an invitation to join the Forest Service of India from the India Office. When he landed in Calcutta in February 1867, he brought his colleague Berthold Ribbentrop with him.[135]

Networks played a determining role in the movement of German Indologists to India, as a few examples will illustrate. For example, after completing his PhD in Oriental Languages and Archaeology in Göttingen in 1858, Georg Bühler progressed to Paris to study Sanskrit manuscripts and then moved to England to look at further sources for three years, during which time he worked with Max Mueller in Oxford who helped him to secure two posts in India. He accepted the position of Professor of Oriental Languages at Elphinstone College in Bombay in 1863.[136] In 1866, Gustav Oppert moved to England at the instigation of Max Mueller. He secured a post in the Queen's Library at Windsor Castle and then began a career in India, where he initially moved to work in the Presidency College in Madras.[137] Friedrich Schrader, meanwhile, after training in Indology and researching into Buddhism, moved to London in the summer of 1905, where he was appointed to the position of Director of the Adyar Library in Madras.[138] These scholars resemble the early nineteenth-century missionaries who needed to move to London in order to develop the contacts necessary to take them to India, as Sengupta and Kirchberger have demonstrated.

Individual choice

Structural factors as well as networks played a central role in the elite migrations which took place from Germany to India in the century before the First World War. Migration theory tends to leave little room for individual agency.[139] While the reasons for migration from Germany to India in our period depend on the structural changes outlined above, some individuals do not appear to have links to any obvious network.

Thus, for example, Robert Vincent, whose path to becoming the Police President of Bombay involved giving up an apprenticeship as a businessman and then moving to Italy, where he joined Garibaldi's army. After capture and imprisonment, he sailed to England, but then became a sailor on a ship taking British soldiers to India and landed in Bombay.[140] The story of A. Anton, who became a musician in the army of Bengal, appears to lend itself even less to any of the explanations outlined above. The narrative of his 'experiences and adventures' begins on a 'dull rainy day' (2 June 1853) when he left the 'glorious scenes of our beloved fatherland' on a train bound for Trieste where he would board a boat for Alexandria.[141] After taking the overland route to Suez, he then boarded a ship to Aden and another to Bombay. As his narrative progresses, however, it appears that he may have had an invitation to join a military band in Wazīrābād in the Punjab, where he would remain for 18 months.[142] The other members of the orchestra, which he seems to have led, consisted of a combination of Indian Christians, Muslims and Hindus.[143]

While even this self-proclaimed adventurer also had some type of connection, which brought him to India, he did ultimately make the decision to move as an individual, as did those who worked for the major mission organisations. Although the evolution of nineteenth-century transport and the development of networks may have made the move to India easier, it still involved a considerable risk, perhaps indicated by the trauma of some of the separations which those who went to the East experienced. At the same time, while the majority of missionaries may not have died in India, disease remained a likelihood and death a strong possibility.[144] It seems tempting to view the most prominent German missionaries – such as Karl Graul or Carl Ochs from Dresden/Leipzig and Hebich, Mögling, or Gundert from Basel – as undertaking heroic journeys to a distant land in the earlier nineteenth century. The first volume of Graul's description of his travels begins with a bombastic account of the trip upon which he is about to embark yet, as this progresses, he utilises more matter of fact descriptions to convey the scenes he experiences.[145] Even the contemporary and more recent hagiographies give precise descriptions of the path which led the heroes of the text from, in the case of the Basel pioneers, Württemberg to the Malabar Coast.[146] Some of the travel accounts produced by missionaries later in the nineteenth century do not go into any detail about the way in which the individuals concerned finally came to make their decisions to travel to India,[147] although, like Graul, the narratives do not take a heroic perspective on their experiences.[148] Nevertheless, the mere writing and publication of these autobiographies stresses the importance of individual choice.

Although all migration ultimately involves a personal decision, a series of intervening factors helped to direct each individual towards the decision to move to India. At the structural level the development of the steam engine and the opening up of the Suez Canal made movement easier and quicker, although, as we have seen, missionaries in the earlier nineteenth century made the trip all the way around the Cape of Good Hope despite the dangers involved and the months needed for such a journey. Changing land patterns in Württemberg, for example, may also have helped to push individuals from this part of Germany towards the Basel Mission. In addition, a whole series of networks, whether local, familial or occupational, further played a role in the decision to emigrate. Those from religious families, at least in the case of women, appear to have had a tendency to become the wives of missionaries. At the same time, sets of brothers and sisters also migrated to India, while longer term family migration patterns also evolved, most clearly indicated by the Gundert-Hesses. German scholars in the nineteenth century utilised networks in order to secure academic positions, in this particular case in India, in the same way as their British contemporaries.[149] This leads us to the conclusion that, while individual choice always plays a role in the decision to migrate, the interplay of a variety of structural and intervening factors made this possibility more of a probability. Only in one case did individual choice play no role in the movement of Germans to India: the transportation from Africa and Siam during the First World War. In all of the other examples, structures, networks and individuals had a complex but decisive relationship.

On the other hand, we may therefore view German migrants to India as one of many groups who became increasingly mobile as a result of the types of globalisation described by Osterhammel, Conrad and Hobsbawm, fundamentally dependent upon the growth of empire although, in our case, they do not follow their own flag. The ease of transportation and European control of the world help to explain the movement of Germans. Those who moved to India as missionaries form part of a network who travelled not simply to India but, as Jon Miller and Wilhelm Schlatter detailed in the case of the Basel missionaries, to destinations throughout the world. The Germans in India form just one minor migratory stream in the explosion of global movement which evolved during the nineteenth century. Yet, as this chapter has demonstrated, each stream had unique features, with networks playing a central role. The highly educated elites covered here produced their own ego documents which allow us to establish the deeply personal nature of each decision to undertake intercontinental migration.

Notes

1. See, for example, Dudley Baines, *Emigration from Europe (1815–1930)* (Cambridge, 1995); Dirk Hoerder and Leslie Page Moch, eds, *European Migration: Global and Local Perspectives* (Boston, 1996); Charlotte Erickson, *Emigration from Europe, 1815–1914* (London, 1976); Terry Coleman, *Passage to America: A History of Emigrants From Great Britain and Ireland to America in the Mid-Nineteenth Century* (London, 1992); Philip Taylor, *The Distant Magnet: European Emigration to the USA* (London, 1971).
2. See, for example, Reinhard R. Doerries, 'German Transatlantic Migration from the Early Nineteenth Century to the Outbreak of World War II', in Klaus J. Bade, ed., *Population, Labour and Migration in 19th and 20th Century Germany* (Leamington Spa, 1987), pp. 115–34.
3. See, for example: Karen Racine and Beatriz G. Mamigonian, eds, *The Human Tradition in the Atlantic World, 1500–1850* (Plymouth, 2010); Martin Daunton and Rich Halpern, eds, *Empire and Others: British Encounters with Indigenous Peoples* (London, 1999).
4. Erickson's work on this theme is summarised in her collection of essays entitled *Leaving England: Essays on British Emigration in the Nineteenth Century* (London, 1994).
5. Marjory Harper and Stephen Constantine, *Migration and Empire* (Oxford, 2014).
6. Gary B. Magee and Andrew S. Thompson, *Empire and Globalisation: Networks of People, Goods and Capital, c1850–1914* (Cambridge, 2010).
7. Tanja Bueltmann, David T. Gleeson and Don MacRaild, eds, *Locating the English Diaspora, 1500–2010* (Liverpool, 2012).
8. Klaus J. Bade, *Migration in European History* (Oxford, 2003), pp. 117–29; F. Burgdorfer, 'Migration Across the Frontiers of Germany', in Walter F. Wilcox, ed., *International Migrations* (London, 1961 reprint), pp. 313–89. For specific case studies of Germans in newly acquired German colonies, see, for example: Klaus H. Rüdiger, *Die Namibia-Deutschen: Geschichte einer Nationalität im Werden* (Stuttgart, 1993); and Hermann Joseph Hiery, *Das Deutsche Reich in der Südsee: Eine Annäherung an die Erfahrungen verschiedener Kulturen* (Göttingen, 1995), pp. 213–42.
9. Erickson, *Leaving England*.
10. Eric Hobsbawm, *The Age of Empire, 1875–1914* (Harmondsworth, 1987), especially pp. 56–83 in the chapter entitled 'The Age of Empire'.
11. C. A. Bayly, *The Birth of the Modern World, 1780–1914* (Oxford, 2004).

12 Jürgen Osterhammel, *The Transformation of the World: A Global History of the Nineteenth Century* (Oxford, 2014).
13 Ibid., pp. 117–66.
14 Sebastian Conrad, *Globalization and the Nation in Imperial Germany* (Cambridge, 2010).
15 Dirk Hoerder, *Labor Migration in the Atlantic Economies: The European and North American Working Classes during the Period of Industrialization* (London, 1985); Bade, *Population, Labour and Migration*; Peter Marschalck, *Deustsche Überseewanderung im 19. Jahrhundert* (Stuttgart, 1973).
16 See especially: Fritz Joseephy, *Die deustche überseeische Auswanderung seit 1871* (Berlin, 1912); Eugen von, Philippovich, ed., *Auswanderung und Auswanderungspolitik in Deutschland* (Leipzig, 1892); Wilhelm Mönckmeier, *Die deutsche Überseeische Auswanderung* (Jena, 1912).
17 John E. Knodel, *The Decline of Fertility in Germany, 1871–1939* (Princeton, 1974), p. 32.
18 Panikos Panayi, *German Immigrants in Britain during the Nineteenth Century, 1815–1914* (Oxford, 1995), pp. 38–9.
19 See contributions to Bade, *Population, Labour and Migration*.
20 See the tables in Erickson, *Emigration from Europe*, pp. 28–9.
21 F. G. Huber, 'Auswanderung und Auswanderungspolitik im Königreich Württemberg', in Philippovich, *Auswanderung*, pp. 233–84.
22 See, for example, Rolf Engelsing, *Bremen als Auswandererhafen 1683–1880* (Bremen, 1961).
23 Panayi, *German Immigrants*, pp. 61–5; Ulrike Kirchberger, *Aspekte deutsch-britischer Expansion: Die Überseeinteressen der deutschen Migranten in Großbritannien in der Mitte des 19. Jahrhunderts* (Stuttgart, 1999), pp. 29–87; M. A. Jones, 'The Role of the United Kingdom in the Transatlantic Immigrant Trade, 1815–1875' (unpublished Oxford University PhD thesis, 1955).
24 Harper and Constantine, *Migration and Empire*, p. 300; David Arnold, *Technology and Medicine in Colonial India* (Cambridge, 2000), pp. 101–5.
25 Albrecht Frenz, *Hermann Gundert: Reise nach Malabar* (Ulm, 1998), pp. 29–169.
26 Mary Weitbrecht, *Memoir of the Rev. J. J. Weitbrecht: Compiled from his Journals and Letters by his Widow* (London, 1854), pp. 18–40.
27 J. Rhenius, *Memoir of the Reverend C. T. E. Rhenius, Comprising Extracts from his Journals and Correspondence, with Details of Missionary Proceedings in South India* (London, 1841), pp. 1–10.
28 Ibid., p. 10.
29 Ibid., pp. 10–13.
30 Ibid., p. 14.
31 Ibid., pp. 14–25.
32 Hermann Gundert, *Herrmann Mögling: Ein Missionsleben in der Mitte des 19. Jahrhunderts* (Stuttgart, 1882), pp. 91–104.
33 For a description of Suez in the middle of the nineteenth century, see J. Barthélemy Saint-Hilaire, *Egypt and the Suez Canal: A Narrative of Travels* (London, 1857). A more recent work is Valeska Huber, *Channelling Mobilities: Migration and Globalisation in the Suez Canal Region and Beyond, 1869–1914* (Cambridge, 2013).
34 Karl Graul, *Reise nach Ostindien über Palästina und Ägypten von Juli 1849 bis April 1853*, Vol. 1 (Leipzig, 1854), pp. 11–20.
35 Karl Heinrich Christian Plath, *Eine Reise nach Indien: Für kleine und große Leute beschrieben* (Berlin, 1880), pp. 1–39.
36 Georg Stosch, *Im fernen Indien: Eindrücke und Erfahrungen im Dienst der luth. Mission unter den Tamulen* (Berlin, 1896), pp. 1–13.
37 Alwin Gehring, *Erinnerungen aus dem Leben eines Tamulenmissionars* (Leipzig, 1906), pp. 1–4.
38 Jennifer M. Jenkins, 'Travelling to India in the 1850s: An Account by Fanny Würth-Leitner, One of Ferdinand Kittel's Travelling Companions', in William Madtha, Heidrun Becker, A. Murigeppa and H. M. Mahehshwari, eds, *A Dictionary with a*

Mission: Papers of the International Conference on the Occasion of the Centenary Celebrations of Kittel's Kannada-English Dictionary (Mangalore, 1998), p. 144.
39 Ibid., p. 146.
40 Ibid., p. 153.
41 Ibid., pp. 156–62.
42 Her early life can be traced in Marie Gundert Hesse, *Marie Hesse: Ein Lebensbild in Briefen und Tagebüchern* (Frankfurt am Main, 1977), pp. 12–35.
43 Ibid., p. 36.
44 Ibid., pp. 36–59.
45 Dagmar Konrad, *Missionsbräute: Pietistinnen des 19. Jahrhunderts in der Basler Mission* (Münster, 2001), p. 113.
46 *Dresdener Missions-Nachrichten*, 1843, pp. 25–9.
47 'Ankunft von fünf Missionarien in Ostindien', *Evangelische Heidenbote*, September 1840.
48 *Die Biene auf dem Missionsfelde*, May 1854.
49 AFST/LMW/II.31.1.18, Tagebuch Hermann Gäbler.
50 Conrad, *Globalization*, pp. 42–3.
51 Ernst Graf zu Reventlow, *Indien: Seine Bedeutung für Großbritannien, Deutschland und die Zukunft der Welt* (Berlin, 1917), pp. 77–8. For overall trade between individual Indian ports with Germany in the early twentieth century, see, for example: BA/R901/53195, 'Handelsberichte über das In- und Ausland, Bombay, Britisch-Ostindien, Handelsbericht des kaiserlichen Konsulats für das am. 31. März 1905 endende Rechnungsjahr'; BA/R901/5432, 'Handelsberichte über das Ausland, Bengalen, Handelsbericht des kaiserlichen Konsulats für das Jahr 1912'.
52 AA/R251730, Statement of Goods exported by Geo. A Jung + Co. Cochin per Barque 'Shim Lee', to Hamburg, 22 January 1881.
53 BA/R901/53081, Kaiserlich Deutsches Konsulat, Madras, 'Handelsbericht der Kaiserlichen Konsulates in Madras über Handel & Schiffahrt in der Präsidantschaft Madras im Jahre 1903/1904'.
54 BA/R901/53019, 'Verzeichniss der im Jahre 1900 im Hafen von Calcutta angelaufenden Schiffe der deutschen Handels-Marine'.
55 BA/R901/53018, 'Verzeichniss der im Jahre 1891 im Hafen von Calcutta angelaufenden Schiffe der deutschen Handels-Marine'.
56 BA/R901/13404, 'Berichte über Handel und Industrie, Handel und wirtschaftliche Verhältnisse Britisch Indiens', Berlin, den 29. September 1913.
57 AA/R140857, Kaiserlich Deutsches Konsulat, Cochin, Jahresbericht Cochin 1913.
58 Joachim Oesterheld and Günther Lothar, *Inder in Berlin* (Berlin, 1997), p. 9.
59 See AA/R251730.
60 A broad brush approach to nineteenth-century Christianity can be found in Sheridan Gilley and Brian Stanley, eds, *The Cambridge History of Chritianity*, Vol. 8, *World Christianities c.1815–c.1914* (Cambridge, 2006).
61 Jon Miller, *The Social Control of Religious Zeal: A Study of Organizational Contradictions* (New Brunswick, NJ, 1994), p. 12–13.
62 See, for example: Martin Brecht, 'Der Württemburgische Pietismus', in Martin Brecht and Klaus Deppermann, eds, *Der Pietismus im achtzehnten Jahrhundert* (Göttingen, 1995), pp. 225–95; and, more generally, Mary Fulbrook, *Piety and Politics: Religion and the Rise of Absolutism in England, Württemberg and Prussia* (Cambridge, 1983), pp. 130–52.
63 Judith Becker, '"Gehet hin in alle Welt": Sendungsbewustsein in der evangelischen Missionsbewegung der ersten Hälfte des 19. Jahrhunderts', *Evangelische Theologie*, vol. 72 (2012), p. 138.
64 Weitbrecht, *Memoir*, p. 12.
65 Ibid., p. 98.
66 Rhenius, *Memoir*, p. 29.
67 Perry Myers, 'The Ambivalence of a Spiritual Quest in India: Waldemar Bonsels's *Indienfahrt*', in Veronika Fuechtner and Mary Rhiel, eds, *Imagining Germany Imagining Asia: Essays in Asian-German Studies* (Rochester, NY, 2013), p. 131.

68 Gehring, *Erinnerungen*; Plath, *Eine Reise nach Indien*; Stosch, *Im fernen Indien*.
69 Stosch, ibid., p. 208.
70 See Chapter 1.
71 Andrew Porter, *Religion Versus Empire: British Protestant Missionaries and Overseas Expansion, 1700–1914* (Manchester, 2004), pp. 68–75.
72 Three volumes cover the internment of both locally based enemy aliens and those brought from further afield: Gerhard Fischer, *Enemy Aliens: Internment and the Homefront Experience in Australia, 1914–1920* (St Lucia, 1989); Panikos Panayi, *Prisoners of Britain: German Civilian and Combatant Internees during the First World War* (Manchester, 2012), pp. 39–77; and Andrew Francis, *'To Be Truly British We Must Be Anti-German': New Zealand, Enemy Aliens and the Great War Experience, 1914–1919* (Oxford, 2012), pp. 113–52. Internment in India receives fuller consideration in Chapter 6.
73 NA/FO383/46, A. W. Chitty to Secretary, Military, Department, India Office, 25 February 1915.
74 NA/FO383/46, American Consulate, Bombay to Deputy Secretary to the Government of Bombay, Political Department, 12 May 1915.
75 Daniel Steinbach, 'Power Majorities and Local Minorities: German and British Colonials in East Africa during the First World War', in Panikos Panayi, ed., *Germans as Minorities during the First World War: A Global Comparative Perspective* (Farnham, 2014), pp. 263–80.
76 NA/FO383/144, American Consulate General London to Prisoners of War Office, 8 May 1916.
77 Albert Achilles, *Erinnerungen aus meiner Kriegsgefangenschaft im Mixed-Transit-Camp Ahmednagar und Erholungslager Ramandrog in Indien während des ersten Weltkrieges 1914–1920* (Berlin, 1977), p. 7.
78 BA/MA/RM3/5375, p. 169; Steinbach, 'Power Majorities', p. 282.
79 NAI/Foreign and Political/WarB/March1918/551, Request of Certain German Prisoners of War Captured in East Africa and Interned in Ahmednagar to Return Home, Refused; NA/FO38/436, Enclosures to para 28 of General dispatch No 45, dated 24th May 1918.
80 NAI/Foreign and Political/ExternalB/September1921/353–424, List of Prisoners of War Who Were Transferred from Siam to India. The same list can be found in BL/IOR/L/MIL/7/18580.
81 Two sets of papers help to trace the entire process from July 1917 (but not before) until the following spring, in the form of: BL/IOR/L/MIL/7/18580, Internment in India of Enemy (German, Austrian) Aliens Deported from Siam; and NAI/Home/PoliticalB/March1918/194–246, Establishment of the Civil Camp of Sholapur for the Accommodation of Enemy Aliens from Siam.
82 This globalisation as a result of evangelisation during the nineteenth century is explored by Mark Hutchinson and John Wolffe, *A Short History of Global Evangelicalism* (Cambridge, 2012), pp. 15–145, which tackles the period from the 1790s to the outbreak of the First World War.
83 Stephen Castles, Hein de Haas and Mark J. Miller, *The Age of Migration: International Population Movements in the Modern World*, 5th Edition (Palgrave, 2013), p. 40.
84 Steven Vertovec, *Transnationalism* (Abingdon, 2009), pp. 13–20.
85 Patrick Manning, *Migration in World History* 2nd Edition (London, 2013), pp. 9–10.
86 Bade, *Migration in European History*, p. x.
87 See Donald Macraild and Enda Delaney, eds, *Irish Migration, Networks and Ethnic Identities since 1750* (London, 2007).
88 Magee and Thompson, *Empire and Globalisation*.
89 Harper and Constantine, *Migration and Empire*.
90 Kirchberger, *Aspekte deutsch-britischer Expansion*.
91 Stefan Manz, *Migranten und Internierte: Deutsche in Glasgow, 1864–1918* (Stuttgart, 2003), pp. 45–158.
92 Stefan Manz, Margrit Schulte Beerbühl and John R. Davis, 'Introduction: Germans in the British Empire', in Stefan Manz, Margrit Schulte Beerbühl and John R. Davis,

eds, *Transnational Networks: German Migrants in the British Empire, 1670–1914* (Leiden, 2012), p. 1.
93 Hartmut Tyrell, '"Organisierte Mission": Protestantische Missionsgesellschaften des "langen 19. Jahrhunderts"', in Klaus Korschorke, ed., *Etappen der Globalisierung in christentumsgeschichtlicher Perspektive* (Wiesbaden, 2012), pp. 255–71; Miller, *Social Control*.
94 Paul Eppler, *Geschichte der Basler Mission 1815–1899: Mit vier Kartenskizzen* (Basel, 1900), pp. 11–19. Wilhelm Schlatter and Hermann Witschi, *Geschichte der Basler Mission*, Vol. 1 (Basel, 1916), traces the evolution of education in Basel during the course of the nineteenth century.
95 Weitbrecht, *Memoir*, p. 10.
96 Christian Gotthilf Weigle, *Basler Missionar in Südmahratta* (Basel, 1879), pp. 18–22.
97 See, for example: Traugott Schölly, *Samuel Hebich: Der erste Sendbote der Basler Mission in Indien* (Basel, 1911), pp. 1–28; Johann Jakob Jaus, *Samuel Hebich: Ein Zeuge Jesu Christi aus der Heidenwelt* (Stuttgart, 1922), pp. 7–37; Samuel Hebich, *Züge aus dem Leben und Wirken des Missionars Samuel Hebich* (Elberfeld, 1864), pp. 3–8; Alfred Mathieson, *Hebich of India: A Passionate Soul-Winner* (Kilmarnock, 1936), pp. 9–31. Each of these follows the same basic narrative, utilising Hebich's own recollections.
98 Albrecht Frenz, *Eine Reise in die Religionen: Herrmann Mögling (1811–1881), Missionar und Sprachforscher in Indien, zum 200. Geburtstag* (Heidelberg, 2011), pp. 291–4; Hermann Gundert, *Herrmann Mögling: Ein Missionsleben in der Mitte des 19. Jahrhunderts* (Stuttgart, 1882), pp. 44–85.
99 Johann Wörrlein, *Christian Kohlmeier: Von 1888–1892 Missionar in Indien* (Hermannsburg, 1901), p. 4.
100 Johann Wörrlein, *Hermann Ernst Jügenmeier: Von 1888–1892 Missionar in Indien* (Hermannsburg, 1901), p. 4.
101 Johann Wörrlein, *Paul Otto Petersen: Von 1875 bis 1888 Missionar in Indien* (Hermannsburg, 1901), p. 3.
102 See Chapter 1.
103 Richard Handmann, *Die Evangelisch-lutherische Tamulen-Mission in der Zeit ihrer Neubegründung* (Leipzig, 1903), pp. 167–76; Paul Fleisch, *Hundert Jahre Lutherischer Mission* (Leipzig, 1936), pp. 25–7, 168–9.
104 Frenz, *Hermann Gundert*, pp. 186–206.
105 Weitbrecht, *Memoir*, pp. 39–61.
106 Gehring, *Erinnerungen*, pp. 6–64.
107 Stosch, *Im fernen Indien*, pp. 15–17.
108 *Missions-Ordnung: Zusammenstellung wichtiger Bestimmungen für die Missionare der Evangelisch-Lutherischen Mission in Indien* (Leipzig, 1908).
109 Johann Wörrlein, *Peter Wilhelm Heinrich Lüchow: Von 1880–1893 Missionar in Indien* (Hermannsburg, 1901), p. 3.
110 BMA/Q-30.3,5, Gebietslisten, Indien, Männer 1.
111 Konrad, *Missionsbräute*, pp. 29–78.
112 Rosemarie Gläsle, *Pauline und ihre Töchter: 'Missionsbräute' als lebenslange Weggefährtinnen Basler Missionare in Indien und China* (Erlangen, 2012), pp. 108–16.
113 Albrecht Frenz, *Texte aus dem Hinduismus übersetzt von Basler Missionaren* (Stuttgart, 2011), pp. 93–100.
114 BMA/Q-30.3,5, Gebietslisten, Indien, Frauen.
115 Leipziger Missionswerk, www.lmw-mission.de/de/missionar-125.html, 'Margarete Grote, geb.1866, gest.1937', accessed 1 June 2015.
116 Leipziger Missionswerk, www.lmw-mission.de/de/missionar-164.html, 'Lina Streng, geb.1867, gest.1946', accessed 1 June 2015.
117 BMA/Q-30.3,5, Gebietslisten, Indien, Schwestern.
118 Stanley Nadel, *Little Germany: Ethnicity, Religion, and Class in New York City, 1845–80* (Chicago, 1990), pp. 15–26.

119 Panayi, *German Immigrants*, pp. 42–61.
120 Erickson, *Emigration from Europe*, pp. 28–9.
121 Johann Wörrlein: *Vierzig Jahre in Indien: Erinnerungen eines alten Missionars* (Hermmansburg, 1913), p. 1; *Christian Kohlmeier*, p. 3; *Hermann Ernst Jügenmeier*, p. 4; *Paul Otto Petersen*, p. 3.
122 See, for example: Muhamad Anwar, *The Myth of Return: Pakistanis in Britain* (London, 1979), pp. 27–46; Pnina Werbner, *The Migration Process: Capital, Gifts and Offerings among British Pakistanis* (Oxford, 1990); Badr Dahya, 'Pakistanis in Britain: transients or settlers?', *Race*, vol. 14 (1973), pp. 243–8; Gurharpal Singh and Darshan Singh Tatla, *Sikhs in Britain: The Making of a Community* (London, 2006), pp. 31–8.
123 Leipzig Missionswerk, Geschichte, Missionare, Indien, www.lmw-mission.de/de/missionare--2-site-1.html, accessed 5 June 2015.
124 Miller, *Social Control*, pp. 45–6, 50–4.
125 BMA/Q-30.3,5, Gebietslisten, Indien, Männer 1.
126 Leipzig Missionswerk, Geschichte, Missionare, Indien, www.lmw-mission.de/de/missionare–2-site-1.html, accessed 5 June 2015. There is also a Max Schäffer but the relationship is not clear. This excludes missionaries with children born in India.
127 BMA/Q-30.3,5, Gebietslisten, Indien, Männer 1, p. 3.
128 BMA/Q-30.3,5, Gebietslisten, Indien, Frauen.
129 Albrecht Frenz, 'Dr. Hermann Gundert: A Biography', in Albrecht Frenz and Scaria Zacharia, eds, *Dr. Hermann Gundert and Malayalam Language* (Changanassery, 1993), pp. 128–9; Frau Adolf Hoffmann, *Sie reden noch: Sieben Lebensbilder aus der Missionsarbeit der Frau* (Basel, 1926), pp. 37–48; Hesse, *Marie Hesse*, pp. 74–256; Hermann and Adele Hesse, *Zum Gedächtnis useres Vaters* (Tübingen, 1930); Hermann Hesse, *Aus Indien* (Berlin, 1913); Vidhagiri Ganeshan, *Das Indienerlebins Hermann Hesses*, 2nd Edition (Bonn, 1980).
130 Ulriche Kirchberger, 'German scientists in the Indian Forest Service: A German contribution to the Raj?', *Journal of Imperial and Commonwealth History*, vol. 29 (2001), p. 10.
131 Ulriche Kirchberger, 'Deutsche Naturwissenschaftler im britischen Empire: Die Erforschung der außereuropäischen Welt im Spannungsfeld zwischen deutschem und britischem Imperialismus', *Historische Zeitschrift*, vol. 271 (2000), pp. 621–60.
132 Indra Sengupta, *From Salon to Discipline: State, University and Indology in Germany, 1821–1914* (Würzburg, 2005), pp. 135–40.
133 Indra Munshi Saldanha, 'Colonialism and professionalism: a German forester in India', *Environment and History*, vol. 2 (1996), p. 196. Richard Grove, *Green Imperialism* (Cambridge, 1995), pp. 380–473, does not mention any significant German contribution to forestry in India before 1857.
134 S. S. Negi, *Sir Dietrich Brandis: Father of Tropical Forestry* (Dehra Dun, 1991), pp. 1–8; Herbert Hesmer, *Leben und Werk von Dietrich Brandis, 1824–1907: Begründer der tropischen Forstwirtschaft, Förderer der forstlichen Entwicklung in den USA, Botaniker und Ökologe* (Opladen, 1975), pp. 1–12; Ajay S. Rawat, 'Brandis: The Father of Organized Forestry in India', in Ajay S. Rawat, ed., *Indian Forestry: A Perspective* (New Delhi, 1993), p. 85.
135 E. Mammen, M. S. Tomar and N. Parameswaran, 'A salute to William Schlich', *Indian Forester*, vol. 91 (1965), pp. 77–8.
136 M. Winternitz, *Georg Bühler und die Indologie* (Munich, 1898), pp. 3–5; Julius Jolly, *Georg Bühler, 1837–1898* (Strasbourg, 1899), pp. 1–2.
137 Valentina Stache-Rosen, *German Indologists: Biographies of Scholars in Indian Studies Writing in German* (New Delhi, 1981), p. 86.
138 Joachim Friedrich Sprockhoff, 'Friedrich Schrader zum Gedächtnis', *Zeitschrift der Deutschen Morgenländischen Gesellschaft*, vol. 113 (1963), pp. 1–2.
139 See, for example, Jan and Leo Lucassen, 'Migration, Migration History, History: Old Paradigms and New Perspectives', in Jan Lucassen and Leo Lucassen, *Migration, Migration History, History: Old Paradigms and New Perspectives* (Oxford, 2005),

pp. 9–38. Dirk Hoerder, *Cultures in Contact: World Migrations in the Second Millenium* (London, 2002), pp. 15–21, gives a nod in this direction. Oral history approaches inherently give individual choice centre stage, for which see, for example, Caroline B. Brettell and James F. Hollifield, 'Introduction: Migration Theory – Talking Across Disciplines' in Caroline B. Brettell and James F. Hollifield, eds, *Migration Theory: Talking Across Disciplines* (London, 2000), pp. 1–26.

140 Hans-Joachim Rehmer, 'Ein Mecklenburger – Polizeipräsident von Bombay', *Carolimium*, vol. 64 (2000), p. 25.
141 A. Anton, *Von Darmstadt nach Ostindien: Erlebnisse und Abenteuer eines Musikers auf der Reise durch Arabien nach Lahore: Die denkwürdigen Ereignisse der letzten Jahre* (Darmstadt, 1860), p. 4.
142 Ibid., p. 31.
143 Ibid., p. 42.
144 See Chapter 3.
145 Graul, *Reise nach Ostindien*, Vol. 1. See also Volumes 2 and 3.
146 For Hebich, see: Schölly, *Samuel Hebich*, pp. 1–28; Jaus, *Samuel Hebich*, pp. 7–37; Hebich, *Züge*, pp. 3–8; Mathieson, *Hebich of India*, pp. 9–31. For Mögling, see: Frenz, *Eine Reise in die Religionen*, pp. 291–4; Gundert, *Herrmann Mögling*, pp. 44–85. See also Gundert's account of his own journey as reconstructed in Frenz, ibid.
147 Good examples include: Plath, *Eine Reise nach Indien*; Gehring, *Erinnerungen*; E. R. Baierelein, *Unter den Palmen: Im Lande der Sonne* (Leipzig, 1890); Stosch, *Im fernen Indien*.
148 But Stosch, ibid., points to the fact that the decision to go to India in 1888 meant family sacrifice, as his wife stayed behind with three of their children while he took the two youngest with him.
149 Tamson Pietsch, *Empire of Scholars: Universities, Networks and the British Academic World, 1850–1939* (Manchester, 2013).

CHAPTER THREE

Everyday life

Following the passage to India, the elite Germans lived in a new environment to which some would gradually grow accustomed, although many would return to Europe earlier than anticipated. Some missionaries spent most of their lives in India, where they died, often prematurely, as a result of the contraction of a tropical disease. Those on research trips would spend a limited amount of time necessary to complete their work, although some academics and scholars, including those working in the development of Indian forestry, would spend much of their lives in the country.

These newcomers had varying experiences of Indian living conditions. The upper-class travellers, especially around the beginning of the twentieth century, encountered luxury, reminiscent of the British ruling classes. This contrasted with the missionaries living among Indians in the, nevertheless, racially hierarchical compounds which they had constructed, unprotected from many of the realities of the Indian environment. Most Germans who moved to India did so for the purpose of working, as revealed in detailed travelogues. They differed from their British counterparts, who (before 1858) P. J. Marshall divided into 'the soldiers in the barracks' and 'the officials, civil or military'.[1] The major activity of the Germans in India consisted of missionary work, which meant that the main task of these spiritual outsiders involved harvesting souls, whether this simply meant conversion, which usually involved indigenous intermediaries, or other forms of work such as teaching and healing. In addition, as illustrated especially by the case of Basel, the missionary societies also became involved in industrial employment. The labour they carried out may appear to contrast with the work of scholars, whose existence mirrored their European lives, but some of the most famous missionaries also carried out work which merits the description of scholarship.

This examination of the everyday lives of the Germans in India focuses upon the basic realties of their existence. The key themes consist of: arrival, travel and settlement; health, disease and death; housing; and work. As the narrative will demonstrate, while experiences may have differed between upper-class travellers and missionaries living in compounds, they remain those of an elite German grouping different from fellow German minorities employed in mainstream agricultural and industrial employment in the substantial communities which had evolved in, for example, Russia, the USA, Brazil or, on a smaller scale, Great Britain, although, within each of these cases, whether urban workers or rural settlers predominated, each also counted elite Germans.[2] At the same time, many of the experiences described here for the missionaries replicate themselves all over the globe. It is important to stress that the German missionary experience in India mirrors that of similar religious workers throughout the world during the nineteenth century, originating not just in Germany but also from other European states and the USA.

Arrival, travel and settlement

The passages to India which brought the missionaries, scholars and scientists to the country did not end in Bombay, Madras or Calcutta but continued for weeks, months or years after landing in these ports. The employment which these three groups carried out required them to lead a nomadic existence for at least some of their time in the country, whether carrying out research activities or searching for souls to convert. Most of those who settled in a particular location did so for only a short period of time, whether they consisted of missionaries moving from one station to another during the course of their service in India, and even moving backwards and forwards from Europe, or scholars who changed their posts after arrival. These activities may reflect a normal mobilities paradigm, involving people, ideas and goods, which social scientists have recognised as characterising the contemporary world,[3] but which may also represent historical normality and which historians more usually examine through the concept of globalisation.[4] Just as importantly when considering movement, we need to recognise that travel writing represents one of the oldest of literary genres. While, on the one hand, it may serve as a way in which writers identify and distinguish themselves from newly discovered environments, such writing also conveys the sense of excitement which new experiences bring, moving away from the norms of home,[5] which helps to explain the amount of information which survives on the travel of Germans within India, reflecting the patterns of British writing.[6]

The recollections start with descriptions of the journeys from the port of disembarkation to the initial destination whether, in the case of short-term visitors, it consisted of an intentional temporary stop or, for those remaining for an extended period, a longer sojourn. Before the arrival of the railways the newcomers travelled from their place of landing in various ways. Weitbrecht, after reaching Calcutta and meeting old acquaintances from Europe, initially proceeded to Burdwan, 101 kilometres further inland in Bengal 'in a little boat' to Chinsurah. From there, they 'proceeded by land, and the style of travelling, so totally new to me, quite amused me. Eight bearers are appointed to one palanquin, four of whom carry it on their shoulders in turn by means of poles affixed to the ends, and then exchange with the other four. They go about as quickly as bad post-horses.' In addition, 'one or more' men carried the luggage, 'which consists of square boxes, generally made of tin, and slung by cords fixed at the end of a bamboo, which is borne across the man's shoulder'. As journeys always occurred at night, the party also had a torch bearer which meant that 'one cannot have less than ten men. These change at intervals of six or eight miles, and we had forty individuals employed for each of us between Chinsurah and Burdwan, a distance of about forty miles.' Weitbrecht complained about the fact that he had to pay the men whenever they changed over, especially as this happened during the night and awoke him. He subsequently travelled towards Bancoorah on an elephant. Although he quickly returned to Calcutta, he took up his first post in Burdwan on 14 June and would remain here for ten years.[7] Accounts also exist of the initial arrival of some of the leading lights of the Basel Mission. When Hebich landed in Calicut on 13 October 1834, he actually spent his first days there in a tent 'situated on a hill near the town'. On 24 October, he 'sailed in a native boat for Mangalore, arriving on the 30th October. The journey which then took six days can now be done in almost as many hours.' He would remain there for a year.[8] When Mögling arrived off the Malabar coast in November 1836, the captain of his ship could not land at its intended destination of Kannanur but had to sail another five days northwards to reach Bombay, during which time he had an 'unbroken view of a magnificent, rich but unholy land'. After landing, his party 'stepped into the boat, in which four brown rowers waited for them'. He spent his first night in Bombay in the house of John Wilson of 'the Scottish Church', who had come on board to meet him, and would remain there for most of November, sailing subsequently to Mangalur, which he would reach on 6 December. Mögling would then begin to move inland from March, initially to Dharwar, which involved a boat to Goa and then an overland trip by foot. He would remain there for over a year.[9] When Graul landed in Bombay in December 1849, a German businessman from Kempten, Herr Zorn, greeted him and took him to 'the neighbouring fort' where he stayed in a

European-style house.[10] He remained in Bombay for two months and then sailed to Mangalore on the morning of 11 February 1850 on 'the *Dwarka*, a little steamer, which, at this time of year ran between Bombay and Colombo'.[11] After initially landing in Bombay and then Madras, A. Anton finally disembarked in Calcutta on 1 November 1853 where he stayed for five days in the Hotel Latour. He then travelled to Meerut 'in a so-called dackgarry, a small omnibus' drawn by horses, about 1,000 miles from Calcutta where he remained for 'nine days and nine nights'. He did not find this journey comfortable, partly because of space limitations and partly because the horses did not behave themselves. Part of his journey involved sailing along the Ganges and its tributaries. After reaching Meerut, he travelled to Wazīrābād in a palanquin, which required a similar level of manpower to that described by Weitbrecht.[12]

Not all of the arrivals of the 1830s had a constructed path ready for them. For instance, when the Basel-trained Johannes Lechler arrived in Madras on 9 June 1834, 'the question was whether I shall go to Tinnevelly or Manaveram or come to Madras ... The committee decided two days after my arrival that I shall go to my German brothers in Tinnevelly.'[13] Hermann Gundert, meanwhile, had initially lived in Madras in order to teach languages to the sons of Anton Groves, but they displayed no enthusiasm for this task which meant that Gundert soon moved away 'walked a lot, rode, let himself be carried or got into a carriage' for a 600-kilometre journey which took him to the area covered by the Tranquebar Mission.[14]

The expansion of the railways in India during the nineteenth century, as demonstrated by Ian Kerr,[15] made the journey to the first point of settlement easier for new arrivals. David Arnold has placed the expansion of the railways into the context of the development of science, technology and medicine in India from the establishment of the East India Company.[16] A series of narratives makes clear the importance of the railways. At the top of the social scale, the Kiel University Professor Paul Deussen stayed in Watson's Esplanade Hotel in the initial weeks after his arrival in November 1892, which 'counted as the first hotel in Bombay and is one of the largest, if not the largest, in the whole of India'.[17] Although he commented on the 'nice location, the comfortable furnishings and the delicious food, one cannot say that the stay in Watson's Hotel was particularly pleasant'. He continued:

> It was an endless coming and going; every week, when a new steam ship arrived from Europe the hotel was filled with noisy guests who disappeared a few days later to travel inland. There was an incessant trampling in the corridors, the slamming of doors, loud calls of 'boy' (as the English have named their servants) until midnight if not later.[18]

Deussen wrote about travelling through the streets of Bombay in a horse-drawn carriage. Here he met Venirâm, from the library of Elphinstone College, who would act as his guide.[19] For the journey into the Indian interior, which involved rail travel, Deussen boarded a train in Bombay – together with a 'tiffin basket' provided by his friends – bound for his next stop of Baroda, describing the Indian railways as 'sublimely organised'.[20]

The missionaries who arrived in the later nineteenth century also found themselves travelling on railways, even if they did not stay in quite the luxurious accommodation which Deussen used in Bombay. When Karl Plath landed in Bombay on 20 October 1877, 'brown servants' met his party and escorted them to a 'large Indian guest house' on four floors, which seemed comfortable, if not quite in the same class as Watson's, though Plath did not complain in the same way as Deussen. In any case, Plath only remained here for two days and then proceeded by train to Ghazipur, a distance of 1,631 kilometres.[21] When the Leipzig missionary Alwin Gehring arrived in Madras with his colleagues Johannes Kabis and Karl Pamperrien on 8 October 1877, they initially had to wait overnight in the port until a boat came to transport them ashore. They almost immediately made their way to Tranquebar, although they did not take the direct route because the South Indian Railway from Madras to Tuticors was still under construction, which meant that they had to take a more indirect route, the final part of which involved travelling in an oxcart.[22] Another Leipzig missionary, Hermann Gäbler, greeted by Gehring on his arrival in Madras on 26 September 1891, took a much more direct route after landing in Madras. On 30 September, he boarded a train bound for Vilupuram, which he reached within an hour, and began working the next day.[23]

The journey to India and the initial move towards the first place of settlement meant the beginning of an itinerant life for missionaries and scholars, whether this occurred in the short run in the search for converts and sources, or in the longer term, as members of both of these occupational groups rarely, if ever, spent their entire lives in India in one location. Furthermore, travel to and from Europe and India also became reality in many cases.

An article on 'Dangers during Mission Journeys in India' in the Basel publication *Der evangelische Heidenbote* from 1839 asserted that:

> The life of a missionary in the heathen world is always a wandering life ... The wanderings have a double purpose: firstly to bring the distant natives closer to the gospel so that, however, precise information can also be gathered about their moral and spiritual situation and about the means by which they can be helped.[24]

Twenty years later, the Basel Mission recorded that: 'Two great Missionary Tours have by the Lord's blessing been accomplished within the year' in both cases involving a team which combined European and native-born missionaries, catechists and scholars. The 'threefold object' of the second tour 'was to visit if possible the whole of the Canarese country with a good stock of Scriptures and Tracts for sale and distribution, to preach the Word wherever an opportunity might offer, and to ascertain from people of all classes what kind of books would be acceptable to them'.[25]

These trips could last for weeks or months. In 1870, two Basel missionaries based in Bettigherry 'made, together with the Catechists, a number of tours, travelling the one 60 and the other 45 days'.[26] In 1855, 21 years after his arrival in India, Hebich undertook a four-month journey which began on 7 May 1855 and ended in September and which took him from Cannanur deep into the interior as far as Bangalore, returning home on 1 September when he understandably declared 'Hallelujah'. During his journey he visited 21 different locations.[27]

These type of journeys represented normality for the leading lights of the German missions. Hebich had already made similar treks on several occasions during his previous 21 years in India.[28] Meanwhile, after his arrival in Madras in April 1836, Gundert spent much of the first three years of his life in India helping to establish, and touring the domains of, the Basel Mission in south-west India.[29] Mögling, meanwhile, made both short trips as well as longer journeys. The former included a trip from Dharwar to Hoobly in 1839,[30] while a much more substantial adventure occurred between 8 August and 8 November 1843, during which time he visited all of the stations in Canara.[31] The most monumental of all of the missionary descriptions came from Karl Graul, Director of the Leipzig Mission, whose journey lasted from 1849–53 and whose narrative involved not simply his observations and experiences in India but also information about the journey to and from Europe, resulting in five volumes of the most extraordinary detail.[32]

Nevertheless, as the extract from the *Evangelische Heidenbote* in 1839 makes clear, travelling from one mission station to another or between villages and towns in the search for converts constituted an important element of the everyday lives of missionaries. As in the case of the first arrival, the means and ease of transport changed as the century progressed. Johannes Leonberger, from Aldingen in Württemberg, who had arrived in India at the beginning of 1850,[33] published an article in the *Evangelische Heidenbote* of 1854 entitled 'How one Travels in India', after a 'long mission journey' of the previous year. This appears to have occurred on foot, but he took with him oxen who essentially acted as pack animals carrying two boxes which contained, in one case, clothes and books and, in the other, eating and cooking utensils as well as bread. His party consisted of 'two catechists from Bettigeri, as well as a cook, a servant with a stick [Lastochsen] and a policeman [Polizeidiener]'. On some parts of the journey they also needed the help of two others who had to carry 'a bed, a chair and a table'. He pointed out that as he travelled during the rainy season he had to sometimes wade through streams 2-feet deep. Although he led the oxen, he received help from another member of the party when crossing water. When they arrived in a new location, the policeman had to find 'wood, fire, water and milk' so that the cook could prepare breakfast. The 'ox servant [Ochsenknecht]' had to look after himself and the ox and to help find water. During the stay in individual villages, the catechists began to speak to locals. While this may have represented a good day, on some occasions they had difficulty securing the basics they needed for food and the continuation of their journey.[34] This vivid description of travelling from one village to another on foot found reflection in other recollections, even if they did not contain quite the same level of detail about the realities of walking through southern India.[35] Boats also proved useful to the missionaries travelling through the countryside searching for converts. Weitbrecht wrote a letter in which he described setting out with his colleague Timothy Sandys, of the CMS, at daybreak on 7 April 1831 in a rented boat. 'Our five rowers were Muslims' who 'sang Bengali songs'.[36] Meanwhile, when the Schlagintweit brothers made their trip through India in the 1850s, they utilised 20 camels with 11 drivers and six porters, as well as horses, although in some parts of the Himalayas which they climbed they became completely dependent on porters because animals could not climb that high.[37]

The arrival of railways made travelling within India easier and quicker but still allowed scope for missionaries and scholars to paint vivid pictures, as evidenced in Gehring's account of his years of learning and wandering as a missionary among the Tamils.[38] After leaving Bombay, Paul Deussen's research trip took him to Peshawar and then further on to the Himalayas, Calcutta, Madras and then back to Bombay and Ceylon for a return trip to Brindisi.[39] The Königsberg Professor of Comparative Linguistics, Richard Garbe, travelled to India in September 1885 where he spent one and a half years visiting a series of locations[40] including Bombay, Benares, the Himalayas and Ceylon. He recalled leaving Bombay at 8 one evening in late October when he headed towards cooler districts further north on a night train which passed through Baroda, 'through green fields and woodlands in the fertile Gujerat'. He described Ahmenabad and another train which took him on a 24-hour journey to Jeypur. A further ten-hour rail journey away lay 'the Indian imperial city' of Calcutta. There then followed a seven-and-a-half hour journey to Agra on 6 November, 'the Hindu New Year'.[41] Garbe then spent a year studying in Benares,[42] during which time he took express trains to visit Calcutta, which took 19 hours.[43] When he finally left Benares for the Himalayas, he travelled in the most comfortable way writing that 'Indian railway carriages offered an unsurpassable luxury' which resembled the cabin on a ship and included a bathroom and a dressing room, screened by windows of blue glass and blinds.[44]

These extracts from the travel sketches of Garbe point to two important realities about the lives of Germans who travelled to India during the nineteenth century, illustrating the fact that the mobilities paradigm applies to virtually all of the groups under consideration. First, they rarely stayed in any particular place for any length of time. Second, few spent the majority of their lives in India, often returning because of illness. In many cases, they travelled backwards and forwards between Europe and Asia on several occasions.

This type of mobile life applied not simply to the scholars but also to the missionaries. Edmund Baierlein perhaps provides an extreme example of the level of movement which could take place. Born in Zirke in Posen in 1819, he had already spent time working for the Leipzig Mission in Michigan in the late 1840s and early 1850s. He landed in Madras in December 1853 and, in the following year, found himself stationed in Sadras, 42 miles to the south, after receiving instructions from Leipzig. In 1856 he had to take a break in the 'blue mountains' to the west because of sunstroke, but returned by the end of the year. In 1857 he moved to Cuddalore, 102 kilometres south of Sadras, but then briefly transferred to Tranquebar, before returning at the end of the year. He left for Germany in 1860 and arrived there in January 1861, where he remained until the end of the following year. He departed again in August 1862 and travelled via Jerusalem, which he had always wanted to visit, arriving in Madras in November 1862 and returning to Cuddalore, where he seems to have established the new station of Chidambaram, 57 kilometres further south (Figure 3.1). In 1870, his wife had to return home, and he followed in 1871, making his way back to India for the third time at the end of 1872 and opening a new station in Bangalore. He appears to have returned home in 1886 and retired in the following year after 40 years serving the Leipzig Mission, of which 33 (excluding the two returns home) involved working in India.[45]

Baierlein's life finds reflection in other Leipzig case studies. Heinrich Beisenherz, who spent 42 years in India, first arrived in 1870 as a 26 year old and worked in eight different locations, which included one visit home.[46] Hermann Beythan arrived as a 26 year old in February

Figure 3.1 A missionary preaching in the temple city of Chidambaram

1902, and spent time in five different locations before returning after just seven years in 1909 to study medicine which would allow him to work in missionary service in another vocation.[47] Gustav Hermann Gäbler reached Madras in September 1891 and would work in Coimbatore, Wiruttsalom, Madras (two spells), Tiruvallar, Tranquebar and Villuparam, returning home three times between 1891 and 1916 and finally facing deportation in early 1916 after a spell as an internee.[48] Like Baierlein, other Leipzig missionaries spent only part of their global lives abroad in India, including Ernst David Appelt who arrived in Tranquebar in 1845, returned to Germany on holiday in 1849 and then went on to become pastor of the German community in Dutton in Australia.[49]

Christoph Gäbler has identified 130 missionaries sent out from Leipzig between 1841 and 1915, including 100 German men and women born in Europe. The spells which these Germans spent in India varied greatly, with some remaining for just one year as well as four for over 40 years, although the longest serving of all European Leipzig missionaries were Swedish-born Carl Sandegren (48 years: 1869–1917) and David Bexell (56 years: 1887–1933). The deportations of Germans from India during the First World had an impact on these time spans, as they ended potentially longer careers.[50] Many missionaries died in India as a result of diseases they contracted, while others would have returned home and died in Germany.[51] Such life stories find reflection in those who worked for the Basel Mission.[52]

As Table 3.1 demonstrates, 44 per cent of German missionaries from Leipzig spent less than ten years in the country, while 24 per cent spent 10–20 years and 20 per cent spent 21–30. Clearly, there exists a reverse relationship between the length of time spent in India and the number of people who remained there. This finds explanation in death in India and in the deportations of the First World War. Similar patterns reveal themselves with regard to Basel in the case of both the missionaries and their wives, who essentially followed their husbands. Interestingly, women who worked independently of husbands for Basel spent less time in India than males working for either Leipzig or Basel. Of the 28 German-born Basel females who went to India between 1842 and the outbreak of the Great War, only four stayed for more than ten years.[53] A similar picture evolves for Leipzig women due to a combination of returning home as a result of sickness and the consequences of the Great War.[54]

Academics also spent itinerant lives in India. This would clearly apply to those making research trips to the country, which could mean journeys of thousands of miles. The Schlagintweits began in Bombay, moved to Madras, 'Central India', then south towards Ceylon, back to the Ganges and Bengal, then toward Agra and Delhi and then further north towards the Punjab and Assam, after which they progressed to the Himalayas.[55] Garbe made a journey which also went from the Himalayas to Ceylon during which time he visited tourist attractions, libraries and scholars, a path which also applies to Deussen.[56] The biologist Oscar Kauffmann, meanwhile, made an equally extensive

Table 3.1 Time spent by German-born Leipzig missionaries in India

Years Spent in India	Entered India 1841–59	Entered India 1861–79	Entered India 1881–99	Entered India, 1901–14	Total
Under 10	8	9	9	18	44
10–20	2	5	8	9	24
21–30	1	7	9	3	20
31–40	3	3	1	0	7
Over 40	2	2	1	0	5
Total	1	25	28	30	100

Source: www.gaebler.info/india/leipziger_indienmissionare-1.htm, Gaebler Info und Genealogie, Liste der IndienmissionarInnen der Leipziger Mission, accessed 15 June 2015.

journey at the start of the twentieth century, on this occasion concentrating on the natural environment, especially animals but also humans and plants.[57] Two leading Roman Catholic missionaries made similar vast geographical trips, resembling that of Graul in the middle of the nineteenth century, in which they travelled throughout the country and recorded their experiences and perceptions.[58]

While most of these scholars essentially passed through India, in visits which could take over a year, other German academics settled in the country although, once again, movement remained part of their lives. The experience of Georg Bühler resembles some of the missionaries. He took up his post as Professor of Oriental Languages at Elphinstone College in Bombay in 1863 and made research trips further south between 1866 and 1869. In 1868 he took up a new position as Educational Inspector in Gujurat and Officer in charge of the search for Indian manuscripts, which meant that he had responsibility for reforming primary and secondary schools, although his research also continued. An accident in 1869 meant that he had to return to Europe for recuperation for a year, but he travelled back in the following decade, during which time he continued with both his administrative role and academic research. He ultimately had to leave India in 1880 because of ill health, but took up a chair in Vienna.[59] Bühler's former student, Alois Anton Führer, an ordained priest as well as a trained academic, initially took up a post as a Sanskrit teacher in the Jesuit College in Bombay in the late 1870s, during which time he travelled to London and Germany carrying out research and networking. In 1885 he became Curator of Lucknow Provincial Museum and, later in the same year, started working for the Archaeological Survey of India, which ensured that his travels continued.[60]

Führer's life epitomised that of other Germans who moved to India during the nineteenth century. Few would have spent their entire careers in the country, either because of the nature of missionary and academic life or because they had to return home due to sickness. Even those who did spend extended periods in the country either moved around because of the nature of their work or had to make short-term journeys to Europe in order to recuperate from the illnesses they had contracted.

Health, disease and death

Remaining healthy became one of the central challenges for the Germans in India. Many returned home prematurely, while disease resulted in the early deaths of others. Philip Curtin's *Death by Migration* took a pioneering approach to the consequences of European exposure to tropical diseases during the nineteenth century by comparing the death rates of European troops who stayed at home with those moving into the tropics. In the case of British soldiers, a significantly higher death rate existed among those who went to India due to exposure to new diseases which they had not experienced in childhood, especially malaria and cholera. By the early twentieth century, the European death rate in India had declined as a result of a revolution in hygiene and tropical medicine, to almost the same level as that in Europe.[61] David Arnold's account of the spread of Western medicine in India has focused both upon its impact upon Europeans but also on the way in which it spread to wider Indian society, especially in the fight against smallpox, cholera and plague.[62] As he has shown elsewhere, Western medicine did not simply impact upon British India but also upon the territories taken over by all of the expanding nineteenth-century empires, initially to save European lives, but increasingly as a demonstration of the power of imperial rulers along with political, military and technical control.[63]

Providing an accurate quantitative picture of the health of the Germans in India proves difficult because of the absence of consistent and reliable information, even on the missionaries, despite the fact that birth and death dates and places of death exist for those sent out from Basel[64] (but not for all of those who worked from Leipzig).[65] Nevertheless, some statistical and much qualitative material points to the perception of India as a site of disease. Illness could result in short-term sickness, returning home, either for good or for recuperation purposes, or death.

The journey of the epidemiologist Robert Koch to study cholera in Bombay in 1883 and the plague in the same city 13 years later points to an official German recognition of the importance of India as one site of disease, together with Africa, where he also travelled.[66] At the same time, sojourners in India devoted attention to the diseased people they encountered. For example, the Roman Catholic missionary Severin Noti included a series of appendices to the letters he published after visiting India at the start of the twentieth century, including one on the plague, focusing upon Bombay (Figure 3.2).[67] Similarly, Oscar Kauffman wrote that, while he stayed in Bombay in 1907, '200 people lost their lives daily to the Black Death'.[68] The missionary press also focused upon the plight of Indians suffering from both disease and hunger.[69] Missionary organisations paid much attention to the health of the population with whom they worked. Basel, for example, sent out nine doctors to a hospital in Betgeri, including two Germans.[70]

In 1913, a Dr Fisch produced a report on the health of the Basel missionaries in India, which appears to cover the entire period of activity here as he claimed that 82 'brothers and sisters' had died, of which the 'tropical climate' accounted for 62, including as many as 51 perishing from typhus, or 10 per cent of all the Indian missionaries. The drinking

Figure 3.2 Plague and cholera in Bombay, 1910

of infected water, often from uncovered wells, played the largest role in these deaths. Fisch put forward a series of ways in which to reduce mortality as a result of typhus, including: drinking only boiled water and milk; eating only cooked fruit and vegetables; and avoiding wells near rubbish tips. While typhus may have caused more deaths than any other disease among the Basel missionaries, malaria led to larger numbers of people falling ill: 94 in all or 14.6 per cent of all those serving in India. Dysentery, meanwhile, with similar causes to typhus, led to 46 cases of illness and seven deaths, either directly or indirectly.[71] The Hermannsburg Mission lost a total of 16 people from the families who worked for it in India between 1876 and 1880, which led to the introduction of a system of recuperation periods in Europe.[72] Dagmar Konrad has written that 'sickness and death were the daily companions of men and women in the missionary countries'[73] beginning with the lengthy sea journey.[74]

A certificate from the Deutsches Institut für ärtzliche Mission in Tübingen in October 1912, following an examination of the Leipzig missionary Fritz Bauer who had travelled to the country in 1903, indicates the types of afflictions faced in India and their consequences. In 1903, Bauer suffered from typhus and malaria that lasted for six weeks, with malarial fever returning on several other occasions. He further had boils and acne, especially on his legs, and also had a sensitivity towards the sun's rays. The certificate stated that 'Mr Bauer gives the impression of somebody who is worn out' and concluded that he 'suffers from anaemia, liver and spleen enlargement'. The doctor who carried out the examination 'advised him to recuperate for three months',[75] although he appears to have returned to India shortly afterwards.[76]

If some of those who became ill soldiered on in India, others returned home either temporarily or for good, while many perished, as several life stories indicate. Ludwig Bernhard Ehregott Schmid who worked for the CMS, had a relatively mild illness in October 1818, as he recorded in his diary, as a result of 'the very unhealthy air. I was tormented by a violent headache with fever and other symptoms of an approaching serious sickness', which put him out of action for a short spell.[77] August Mylius, who initially went out as a Leipzig missionary but then worked for Hermannsburg, suffered from a range of ailments in his first spell in the late 1840s, including headaches and sunstroke whose consequences led him to return home after a period on the coast failed to cure him.[78] Most famously, Gundert had to travel back to Germany in 1859 because of sickness after falling ill with diarrhoea which had developed into dysentery in the previous spring, despite the fact that he had remained in relatively good health in India for over two decades other than 'a prolonged bronchitis from 1849–52 and at times slight haemorrhoids during this period'. His intestinal illness continued after his return home.[79]

Unlike Gundert, Weitbrecht and members of his family paid the ultimate price for service in India, as his life story in the country attests. For example, one Sunday evening in June 1834 he 'wrote of a severe pain on my chest, which rapidly increased, and became so violent, that in the course of an hour I could scarcely breathe'. An English doctor 'lost no time in opening a vein, and I was relieved by spurious bleeding and by the medicines which he administered'. The doctor told him that 'too great exertion' caused the attack, although Weitbrecht also blamed the climate and 'the effects of sin'.[80] The following year he was 'laid quite aside by inflammation of the membranes of the brain, caused by exposure to the sun'.[81] In February 1836 he was 'laid aside by a lingering attack of remittent fever'.[82] Weitrbecht and his wife also experienced the loss of two young children while in India.[83] Ultimately, he died in Calcutta 1852 as a result of contracting cholera.[84]

Weitbrecht's death in India finds reflection in other life stories of missionaries and their wives. Mathilde Gräter actually died in Trieste from dysentery on 10 October 1872 on her way home from India; the disease first manifested itself three days after she left Bombay on 21 August. In September 1872, Friederike Digel died in Mangalur less than a year after she had landed in India.[85] In fact, she seems to have been the sister of Luise Stahl, who perished in Mangalore on 7 December 1870. Luise's husband described how on 31 October of that year 'she got up in a tired state and could not even eat rice and pepper water'. They then went out and on the way back she developed a headache and cold hands; when they arrived home her hands and head had become very hot. For the rest of the week she experienced variations in temperature and further headaches. After visiting a doctor on 6 November her condition improved, but she developed diarrhoea two days later, which, together with fever, did not disappear during the whole of November. Her condition continued to deteriorate until she died.[86] Those Hermannsburg missionaries who perished in India included Paul Petersen, who contracted cholera at the beginning of February 1888 and died shortly after this,[87] and Peter Lüchow, who died in May 1893 after suffering for several months with a fever.[88]

Missionaries therefore routinely became subject to disease. Many returned home simply to recover and then make their way back in order to continue with the vocation they had chosen, while others returned to Europe too exhausted and sick to contemplate making another 5,000-mile journey which could take weeks or months. Hundreds lost their lives for the cause in which they believed, as did their wives and children. While the advancement of medicine and hygiene by the end of the nineteenth century may have lessened the death rate, sickness remained a fact of everyday life.

Housing

Missionaries would have experienced the realities of life in India to a greater extent than other Germans, such as researchers and businessmen, because of the areas in which they lived, away from any obvious type of luxury even though they created residences within compounds which, to some extent, insulated them from the outside world. While the housing there proved superior to that of the indigenous population, it remained below the comfort of some of the top Indian hotels described by travellers and academics.

When missionaries reached a standstill, they resided in the stations which emerged throughout the country. When Andreas Köhler arrived in the Basel mission station in Keti in June 1873, he found himself living in one of the two accommodation blocks built for missionaries and their wives,[89] reflecting the type of lodgings established in these missionary stations not only in India but also in other locations. In fact, in many cases the missionaries lived in the mission house, which dominated the stations established by missionaries of all denominations throughout the world. Within the individual rooms the Europeans tried to recreate an ordered existence, separate from that of the indigenous population, in which the wife played a central role.[90]

Clearly, the construction of accommodation for the missionaries became a major development upon which they commented, whether it meant that they lived within the mission house or in lodgings outside it within the compound. Charles Rhenius, who worked for the CMS in the 1820s, mentioned in his diary on 22 July 1830 that 'we laid the foundations both of the chapel and the bungalow'.[91] Meanwhile, the Reverend William James Deerr, who worked for the same group, complained about the fact that 'the house now in building will not admit of two families' in the station where he lived.[92] A letter published in the *Magazin Neueste Geschichte* in 1829, written by Wilhelm Dürr from Culna, displayed excitement with new accommodation: 'I am reporting to you with delight that our bungalow (Indian home) is now ready and the fact that we have moved in. We feel so happy, as only a person on this earth can, because our prospects in this city seem very encouraging.'[93] Before the building of such homes, the missionaries had to live in other types of accommodation, as recalled by the Basel-trained Johannes Lehner in 1834 shortly after arriving in Mangalore. 'The house we have rented is on a hill outside the town and, because of its healthy and odourless situation is especially suitable for the beginning of our work.'[94] A similar sense of excitement to that expressed by Dürr appears in a description of the opening of the Leipzig mission house in Cuddalore in 1870: 'Here we bring you dear friends of the mission, a new picture from our mission field; we feature the dwellings of our missionaries in Cuddalore.' The description focused on the amount of time taken to build this accommodation (over a decade) and the features which included a 'pretty tower'.[95]

In 1894, the Gossner Mission published a volume about its work in India which included details of the various stations and the accommodation used by its European workers. The 'oldest mission house' had opened in Ranchi in 1845 and acted as a multipurpose building where the missionaries lived and where teaching took place (Figure 3.3). The 'newest mission house', still under construction in Chakrdharpur, would have a temporary dwelling house until an 'authentic bungalow' was constructed. Meanwhile, the first accommodation in Govindpur appeared in 1850 built by the hand of missionary Conrad, who also constructed a well here. When his successor, Didlaukies, arrived with his family, followed by other 'East Prussian Lithuanians', the quality of the living space in the mission house had reached high standards and included 'a big, airy vernada'. On the right-hand side of

Figure 3.3 The first Gossner mission house in Ranchi

the house lay a study. The house also contained a reception and guest room to cater for visiting missionaries. The bathroom included bathtubs but not a shower. The pictures on the wall featured 'religious stories' or 'relatives in the homeland'. The furniture 'was made from cane'. Personal possessions included a harmonium and a piano. The kitchen lay in a separate building.[96] Clearly, by the end of the nineteenth century the missionaries had constructed European-style homes built for comfort, which reflected those which they had left behind, but which made allowances for local conditions.

Missionaries who wrote about their accommodation at this time generally appreciated where they lived as they moved into already existing quarters, unlike those at the beginning of the nineteenth century who displayed great excitement once their new homes became habitable, both because they created some sort of permanence, despite the itinerant nature of their lives, but also because of the fact that the missionaries could move into familiar and relatively comfortable European-style surroundings. The narrative constructed by the long-serving Leipzig employee Alwin Gehring about the various homes in which he lived in a series of locations has a series of features. When he moved to Kumbakonam, he actually recalled the 'dangers' he experienced which included snakes, scorpions and a cyclone which visited him after the construction of new accommodation in 1880. His fondest memory here consisted of the birth of his first child, which cemented the sense of domesticity, although shortly after this event he had to move on to a posting in Burma.[97] The dangers upon which Gehring comments frightened other European visitors. When Margarete Grote arrived in Madras in December 1891 she claimed that she initially stayed in a room with few windows but with numerous large doors, which allowed a limited amount of sunlight. In addition 'rats, squirrels, bats and innumerable creeping, buzzing creatures live in my room and are very lively at night'. Grote also commented on the dampness and humidity which resulted in an ever-present mould.[98]

Despite the desire to recreate the type of domesticity characteristic of Europe, the missionaries could not escape from the realities of their geographical situation, whether in terms of wildlife, sickness or climate, even after they had moved into the established mission stations. After leaving Watson's in Bombay, Paul Deussen painted a basically positive picture of the accommodation in which he resided during the rest of his 1892–3 research trip. Due to 'health considerations' his party invariably decamped in 'the first class hotel of a locality'. He continued:

> Indeed this was often the only hotel and many locations, such as Ujjain, Gaya and others had absolutely no hotel. In these cases the government maintained lodgings, called a dak bungalow ... in which one had a right to a room with a bed for one rupee, on condition that one had to vacate the room if a newcomer arrived and claimed the room. As a rule, one was the only guest in the small house. The furnishing of the room was completely primitive, the beds, as a rule, free of insects.[99]

Despite the problems encountered upon first arriving in India, especially by the missionaries, the various elite German groups made attempts to reconstruct the type of housing in which they had resided in Europe. This involved the addition of new elements such as verandas, while most Europeans resided in bungalows. Ultimately, the accommodation aimed to separate the newcomers from the indigenous population in an attempt to create European communities, but some elements such as insects, climate and disease remained.

Work

As an elite group, the Germans in nineteenth-century India also carried out work reflecting their position on the social scale. The contact which they had with the indigenous populations tended to involve them having a position of superiority, especially in the case of missionaries. Researchers, whether scientists or indologists, held professional positions.

The type of work which the missionaries carried out divides into a series of categories, broadly defined as preaching, administrating, teaching, healing, researching and providing industrial work. The conversion of non-Christians and their gathering into congregations became the central aim of the German missionary organisations, as outlined prominently in the set of rules which they established. The second of the founding principles of the Leipzig Mission stated that missionaries did not simply go into the 'heathen world' to 'win' 'individuals' for the gospel but also 'to gather those that have been won into congregations of the Evangelical Lutheran confession'.[100]

The initial preaching necessary to achieve this aim operated on a variety of levels and involved not simply the Germans and other Europeans, but also the intervention of local-born catechists, a process which the Tranquebar Mission had established during the eighteenth century.[101] Nevertheless, those born in Europe also played a role in 'spreading the word', especially as part of their training involved learning local languages. Numerous accounts illustrate the realities of the conversion process. The German-born CMS employee Charles Benjamin Leupolt pointed out that while Europeans did not venture out by themselves, 'we preach in the streets, by the river-side, and in the cold season we itinerate, going from village to village to make known the glad tidings of salvation'. Leupolt pointed out that in 'our preaching we make use of parables to arrest the attention of our hearers, and to illustrate truth more easily than merely by plain language'.[102]

Weitbrecht, who initially worked in Bengal, 'accustomed himself, from the first, to do his best in speaking to the people without an interpreter, and thus he gained confidence and freedom of expression ... but sometimes he was almost overcome by a sense of his deficiency in the language', which, however, did not prevent him from baptising those willing to submit themselves to this process.[103] Gundert left details of the type of activities he undertook during 'an exploratory tour in the western valley of Chittoor on the Palmaner road' in September 1837 accompanied by two Indians. On the morning of 9 September, Gundert and his colleagues sat down under a large tree. 'Immediately people came, and were most interested in what they heard. They also understood me very well, which was a great comfort to me, as in many cases I had been frightened by people's excuses for not hearing.'[104] Despite a presence in India since 1834, Hebich still carried out preaching at a Hindu religious festival in Taliparambu 25 years later which involved both speaking and singing in 'Malayalam verse a German melody from our Indian songbook'.[105] Towards the end of the nineteenth century,

Georg Stosch gave an account of his experiences of attempted conversions with a native-born catechist in a village of 'pariahs' who initially asked for money, to which Stosch replied, 'We can only preach to you the kingdom of heaven', which reduced interest.[106]

While this type of indifference, and even hostility,[107] became part of the everyday experiences of the missionaries, they clearly had success in view of the growth of their mission stations, which allowed many of them to reduce their wandering activities. During his final two years working for the Basel Mission in India, Gundert appears to have led an itinerant lifestyle no different from that of the 1830s in its intensity – although by this time he devoted much of his time to administrating the work of his organisation here, which involved meeting a wide range of individuals from both his own group, either as individuals or at conferences, as well as government administrators, those practising Hinduism and Islam and prospective and actual converts, which meant that he still held services and carried out baptisms.[108] This combination of activities characterised the lives of many of the longstanding senior missionaries.[109]

Baptism formed a central part of the activities of missionaries, as indicated by the birth of the Basel-led parish in Anandapur. It appears to have first come into existence as a result of a 'christening festival' in April 1857 involving 130 souls, with further baptisms occurring during the years which followed, including some carried out by Mögling. As these conversions took place, the first buildings appeared including a church, while Mögling gave lessons in carrying out baptisms.[110] Once these mission stations became settled, the trained priests from Europe clearly made the church central to their activities. In 1865, a group describing itself as the 'German Lutheran Mission' outlined its activities in the various substations in its centre in Tirhoot. In Moriaro, 'divine service' took place twice on Sunday. In Muzaffarpur, a total of 29 baptisms had taken place, together with two marriages and the burial of three adults and four children. Some of the congregations here counted only a handful of people.[111] This contrasts with some of the stations of the Gossner Kohls Mission, which, according to one account, could attract as many as 2,000 people on feast days.[112] The same source presented a scene on a Sunday morning when people made the journey to hear a service, which had meant sleeping overnight in the compound. The ringing of the bells resulted in a colourful scene as people moved towards the church where they willingly sang hymns. The language used in the service reflected that used by the congregation, which usually consisted of a Kohls dialect.[113] The Sunday evening service could also prove popular, on one occasion attracting as many as 1,800 people, although this (probably significantly exaggerated figure) would include not simply those who had undergone confirmation and baptism, but also those who had not – and, in any case, the author points out that this took place on 'a great feast day'.[114]

Such figures represent estimates, but those referring to education, using classroom registers, prove more accurate. If preaching stood at the centre of the solar system of missionary activity, this centre had two suns for both Roman Catholics[115] and Lutherans because of the importance of teaching. This acted as a way of bringing children into Lutheran Christianity, as preparation for conversion, but also served as the leading charitable activity. 'Among the most important branches of the mission is the spread of Christian education.'[116] This statement, referring to the Gossner Mission, found reflection elsewhere. Julius Richter, following a visit to inspect German missionary activity in north India, wrote that: 'Of the branches of the missionary establishments which present themselves to study for an observer, the missionary school activity is the most splendid and the one which catches the eye.' He asserted that the 1891 Indian census listed 541 higher mission schools with 55,148 pupils. He also pointed to the different types of schools which emerged, including not just high schools but also colleges and seminaries.[117]

The Basel Mission began to develop schools from its early days of independent activity in India. The first opened in Mangalore in 1836 with just four pupils, followed two years later by the first English school in the same location.[118] By 1841, a total of 80 boys had received educational instruction in Mangalore. Some stayed as boarders, while others paid day visits. The school cared for both the spiritual and material wellbeing of its pupils, providing not only education but also meals. While Mögling held responsibility for the English school together with Gottfried Weigle, Georg Sutter looked after the missionary school.[119] As the century progressed, educational activity in Mangalore developed further with a focus not only on boys but also girls' education, as well as the establishment of a Catechsist Seminary in 1840 which would evolve into the Karnataka Theological College.[120] This type of pattern expanded to other areas administered by the Basel Mission including Coorg, which had an English school in Merkara from 1855, in this case actually employing an Englishman by the name of Lewis, although the Durlach (in Karlsruhe)-born Christian Richter soon took over the running of this establishment. A central school also emerged in Merkara, which counted over 100 pupils divided into four classes by the middle of the 1860s teaching a wide range of subjects. Expansion of education by Basel also took place into the surrounding countryside in Coorg.[121]

The Gossner Mission developed a similar range of educational activity. By 1874, it had opened 16 schools teaching 439 boys and 151 girls.

Some of the teachers consisted of Indians educated in seminary classes.[122] Some schools existed in mission stations while others evolved in villages, which totalled 15 and 61 respectively in 1894. The largest boys' school in Ranchi counted 260 pupils, while schools for girls also existed, together with a seminary.[123] The Breklum Mission devised a similar system and by 1914 it taught 1,913 children.[124]

The Leipzig Mission continued educational activity originally established in Tranquebar in the eighteenth century, which meant that Cordes focused upon it from the start, establishing a seminary as early as 1842. By the outbreak of the First World War, Leipzig had responsibility for 242 primary and high schools as well as a seminary in Tranquebar and industrial schools which taught children trades. In 1910, the organisation educated 6,745 boys and 2,546 girls. The German teachers included Helene Frankel, who led the elementary school in Tanjore at the start of the twentieth century.[125]

As well as focusing upon education with the perceived benefit of bringing children into Christianity, most of the missionary organisations also devoted attention to women, which often meant the establishment of specific bodies for their assistance and education. As early as 1841, the Basel Mission had made a call to the 'Christian Women of Germany and Switzerland' to assist with the 'education of the female sex in India', which, mirroring the European views of Indian women during this period in which missionaries played a prominent role,[126] began with descriptions of the 'situaiton of the female sex in India' which focused upon childhood, domestic life, the burning of widows and the consequences of Indian attitudes towards women and girls. The pamphlet called for the establishment of a 'German Women's Society for Female Education in the Heathen World' for the purpose of educating girls, which would necessitate the sending out of German women to help in this process. There followed the global Basel Women's Mission Committee, which, although initially led by the mission inspector of the time Wilhelm Hoffmann, worked in the interests of women and increasingly came under the control of female missionaries, even though this process took much of the nineteenth and early twentieth centuries.[127]

Similar narratives to Hoffman's written on the position of Indian women followed during the course of the nineteenth century, including one by O. Gründler of the Frauen-Verein für christliche Bildung des weiblichen Geschlechts im Morgenlande, which examined 'The Misery of Women in India' and looked at its roots as well as the position of girls, women within marriage, widows and the development of work among women by all missions there during the course of the nineteenth century.[128] A 1902 pamphlet by Johann Wörrlein justified the existence of a special Hermannsburg Mission group to help women by again pointing to the 'misery' of their lives, but also asserting that only 1,200 women worked as missionaries to help females in India, which, as the country counted 150 million women, meant that each one had responsibility for over 100,000 women, and, like Hoffmann 60 years earlier, called for more volunteers.[129] This grouping actually seems to have employed a limited number of women over the following decades, but those who did work for it included Martha Drewes, Elise Kastens and Anna Marie Meyberg, who lived in India when the Great War broke out.[130] Meyberg, employed in Tirupati, recalled that, even before the beginning of the conflict, 'dark clouds gathered on the horizon' as early as February when the plague arrived, leading to emigration: 'many streets were completely empty and cordoned off by the police'. The mission lost many of its pupils to the disease, although it did not spread to the entire town which meant that the mission could continue its work. As an indication of the type of hands-on work which the Hermannssburg sisters carried out, Meyberg told the story of a widow she saw sitting outside her own house looking 'deeply unhappy'. After some hesitation Meyberg went to the widow's doorstep and asked her about the cause of her unhappiness and discovered that she had lost all of her children. Meyberg claimed that she persuaded the old woman to accept the word she preached. Meyberg also presented the story of a similar conversion of another women 'who we often visited during her serious illness'. Meyberg asserted that during 1913 'we had, above all else, attempted to win over schoolgirls' by 'finding entry into new houses' and that, despite resistance, persistence meant that the number of homes in which the mission had success had increased from 80 to 120. Meyberg further wrote of saving 'the poorest amongst the daughters of India, the temple girls'.[131]

The specially constituted women's subgroups, while they carried out similar work to that of the overall mission, had the specific aim of utilising German women to speak directly to Indian women and girls, as recognised by Alwin Gehring when describing Leipzig missionary activity in the 'Tamil land', pointing to the fact that European females worked with Indian women, 'the so called bible sisters'.[132] Like the other missionary bodies, Leipzig developed its own women's mission, which increasingly formalised its activities as the First World War approached.[133]

Healing became an important aspect of missionary work, as David Hardiman has recognised in his study of missionary activity among the Bhils of western India.[134] However, according to Eva Bell, 'Christian medical work began as an after-thought' for the Basel Mission.[135] Bell identifies Eugen Liebendoerfer from Leutkirch in Württemberg as the pioneer in this area, as he arrived in Nettur in 1875 and realised the need to become a doctor after experiencing an accident on a river resulting in 80 casualties, which led him to return to Basel to study medicine. He then proceeded to Calicut in 1886 where he opened a clinic, followed by a hospital in 1892, while in the following year he took charge of a 'Leprarorium'. The Calicut hospital would subsequently expand. The Basel missionaries then developed similar activities in Betegeri and Mangalore.[136] Hospitals became part of a welfare activity which evolved during the course of the late nineteenth and early twentieth centuries and included, for example, a Catholic-run facility for deaf children in Bombay as well another for orphans in the same city which began in the 1850s and in which German missionaries played a significant role.[137]

In an attempt to spread their influence, the Basel missionaries in particular did not simply focus upon the spiritual and welfare needs of the Indians with whom they came into contact but also impacted upon their economic activity, initially by focusing upon agriculture but then by moving towards the introduction of industry. The background for the evolution of such enterprise may lie in Protestant ideology, which not only wanted to convert Indians but also wished to modernise them and turn them away from idleness. At the same time, once conversion took place, those who had adopted Christianity found themselves outside the employment-based caste system, which meant that they needed to take up a new economic activity.[138] Initially, Basel looked at the possibility of training people to repair watches and to work in the printing press, as well becoming involved in weaving, establishing an Industrial Commission in 1846. In 1854, the Commission became a separate department with its own finances and sent for Gottlob Pfleiderer to run this body.[139] Over the following decades, industrial activity focused upon two areas in particular in the form of weaving and tile making. By 1913, the Basel Mission ran seven weaving establishments and seven tile factories employing 20,000 members of its congregation, together with another 1,000 non-Christians, meaning that it had become the largest industrial employer in South Canara and Malabar. The profit it made allowed it to cover 25 per cent of the annual expenses of the Basel Mission in India.[140] By this time, the industrial and commercial activity had clearly become established on a highly professional basis as further evidenced by the emergence of the Basel Mission Trading Company, which had direct access to European stock exchanges.[141] Those who came from Germany had a range of roles to play in the evolution of this industrial enterprise, whether as supervisors in the factories or as administrators in the overall running of the industrial activity, most of whom had undergone the basic missionary training in Basel.[142]

EVERYDAY LIFE

In addition to industrial work, missionaries also played a leading role in scholarship and, as we have seen, their activity in this area overlapped with that of the indologists. This interest began from the early eighteenth century with the pioneering activities of Bartholomäus Ziegenbalg almost immediately after his arrival in Tranquebar in 1706[143] but also, for example, those of Benjamin Schultze later in the century, as Heike Liebau has acknowledged.[144] During the nineteenth century, German missionaries carried out research on a range of subjects. Some simply wrote general studies of what they observed, which, however, could take up hundreds of pages. A good example is *Das Kurgland und die evangelische Mission in Kurg*, written by the Basel missionary Hermann Mögling together with V. D. M. Weitbrecht (described as 'Sekretär' on the title page). The book actually devotes just 81 from 334 pages (in part 3) to the evangelical mission in this area, which Weitbrecht wrote. Mögling produced the background narrative. Part one tackled the land (which included observations on plants, climate and landscape) and the people (including family and religion) while the second part described the history of the area.[145] Another Basel missionary, Christan Irion, in his volume on *Malabar und die Missionsstation Talatscheri*, spent about a quarter of his book providing background on the land, the people, their religion and their caste, after which he described the growth of Basel activity there.[146] Similarly, the Leipzig missionary Edmund Baierlein wrote an account of the Tamils and missionary work among them, in which 95 of 242 pages covered the way of life of the local population including their agriculture, literature, 'domestic life' and religion.[147] While such narratives contain an element of scene setting before an account of the way in which missionaries made a difference to local inhabitants, the descriptions of land, people and religion demonstrate an empirical approach based upon reading, observation and knowledge.

Apart from the type of geographical descriptions produced by Mögling and Irion, missionaries became well versed and essentially embedded in the areas in which they lived, which meant that their researches did not simply focus on detailed descriptions of these locations, but also on a variety of aspects of these environments and cultures. A full understanding of such activities needs to appreciate the academic background and training of some missionaries. Mögling, together with Gundert and Gotffried Weigle, had all studied at Tübingen, while another Basel missionary, Ferdinand Kittel (although he did not receive a university education), obtained a PhD from Tübingen after he returned to Germany in 1892 'for his contributions to Dravidology'. The focus of Gundert and Kittel on language partly comes from their Lutheran background, which demanded the translation of the scriptures into local languages,[148] although previous Roman Catholic missionaries had already carried out linguistic work in south India. Nevertheless, the German missionaries of the nineteenth century could tap into 'effective printing technology and publishing systems' in contrast to their predecessors.[149] Gundert's work in the Malayalam language had a series of aspects to it. He initially composed hymns in 1840, by which time he had already begun working on a Malayalam grammar published in 1860, followed by *A Malayalam and English Dictionary*, which appeared in 1872.[150] Kittel published a similar range of works to Gundert, although he concentrated on the Kannada language, spoken in Karnataka where he settled, producing a grammar eventually issued in 1903. His other work focused upon the study of Hinduism as well as local music.[151] Another Basel-trained missionary, Karl Gottlieb Pfander, who made his way to Agra via central Asia, specialised in the study of Islam. Once in Agra he became involved in theological disputes with Islamic scholars.[152]

Missionaries from other groups also carried out scholarship in India. Andreas Nehring has examined the work of those from Leipzig in his monumental study on *Orientalismus und Mission* which looks at the range of activities in which those from Leipzig became involved, especially the deconstruction of Hinduism and caste, the study of the environment in the areas in which they lived and the translation of Tamil texts into English. As the title of his book suggests, Nehring sees the efforts of the Leipzig missionaries as part of an Orientalist project.[153] While Joseph Bara, in his study of the Gossner and Jesuit missionaries in Chotanagpur, rejects the idea that evangelists and colonialists became interlinked even though they had some aims in common, he nevertheless asserts that to 'pave the way for the acceptance of Christianity by the Indians, the missionary groups concentrated on demolition of' their 'faith structure', which they could only accomplish by first studying and understanding it, mirroring the perspective of Nehring. The Gossner missionaries, like their German brethren from other organisations, developed this understanding by living among the Mundas and Uraons, who they nevertheless described as 'savages', 'bears' and 'wolves'.[154] Klaus Roeber listed ten ways in which the Gossner missionaries appropriated and culturally transferred knowledge, including through research on language and literature, ethnology and geography and economics but also through the building of schools.[155]

While the missionaries may have studied the cultures in which they lived with the ultimate aim of unlocking them as a way of allowing the penetration of Christianity, this represents a simplification of their experiences in view not only of the commitment of many of them – such as Gundert, Mögling and Baierlein – to the areas in which they lived, but also because it denies the long-term impact of their research.[156]

The German scholars and scientists who moved to India during the course of the nineteenth century became involved in a similar range of activities to their missionary compatriots, including research, teaching and administrative activities characteristic of any university work, as the examples of Georg Bühler and his student Alois Anton Führer illustrate.[157] Friedrich Otto Schrader, born in Hamburg in 1876, studied philosophy, indology and languages at several universities between 1897 and 1902, during which time he wrote a doctorate on Buddhism. After moving to London, he secured a position as Director of the Adyar Library in Madras. Once he took up his new post, he studied a variety of south Indian languages including Tamil, Telugu, Canarese and Malayalam, as well as undertaking extensive tours to South India and Ceylon and then to the north as far as Kashmir in order to acquire manuscripts for his library. He also compiled a large descriptive catalogue of Sanskrit manuscripts in the Adyar Library. While incarcerated in Ahmednagar during the First World War, Schrader learnt Tibetan and Siamese.[158] Several Germans worked at Poona College near Bombay, including Martin Haug who became Superintendent of Sanskrit studies here. Apart from travelling to Gujurat to collect manuscripts which would eventually find their way to Munich after Haug took up a chair in Sanskrit there, he published and translated work which fitted into the trajectory of his career both before and after his Indian sojourn. Franz Kielhorn, born in Osnabrück in 1840, succeeded Haug as Superintendent of Sanskrit studies in Poona and then became Principal of the college. He worked with Georg Bühler on the 'Bombay Sanskrit Series' and searched for manuscripts in western India. He published several collections of primary sources while in India, as well as a *Sanskrit Grammar*. The efforts of Bühler, Haug and Kielhorn played a central role in the preservation of Sanskrit texts.[159]

Although the Schlagintweit brothers published their experiences of their travels in India and the Himalayas during the middle of the 1850s in several volumes which covered not simply their scientific work but also their impressions of the landscape and the people they encountered,[160] the core of their work, which consisted of conducting a magnetic survey of India, meant that they travelled through the country and beyond into the Himalayas. The actual itinerary of the Indian part of the survey involved two different journeys, with Adolphe leaving Bombay on 5 November 1854 and travelling to Madras via Poona 'from where geological excursions in different parts of the Dekkan in the direction of Sholapoor, to Saigruh, Poorundbur, were made'. Hermann and Robert left Bombay on 30 December and joined Adolphe in Poona on 3 January, but they then took different routes to Madras after Bellary, completing their journeys by February. They made observations in six different magnetic stations (Bombay, Mahabelashwar, Poona, Kulladghee, Bellary and Madras) using 'the smaller universal magnetometer'. In addition, they gathered a wide range of materials including 'a large set of all the different waters from wells, springs and rivers we found on our way', all of which they arranged for transportation to Europe. They also put together books 'containing the detailed geological and topographical observations and the two sets of maps and landscape drawings ... deposited in the Surveyor General's Office, Calcutta'.[161] The brothers then proceeded to Calcutta, from where they moved north on the second part of their journey towards the Himalayas, again splitting into two parties. They took measurements in at least ten different locations and also carried barometers with them. They were able 'to determine the elevation above the sea of 350 to 400 places'.[162]

Dietrich Brandis probably had a greater impact upon India than any other German in the nineteenth century. While the overwhelming majority of his compatriots constituted elites, Brandis had the most significant influence on the country because of the seniority of his position as the leading civil servant in the management of the vast forests of India between 1864 and 1883. His job had various aspects to it. In the first place, he travelled to the areas of forestry for which he held responsibility, especially when he took up his position, visiting Oudh and Bussahir in the Central Provinces. He would subsequently go to Assam, the North West Provinces, the Punjab and southern India. Those scholars who have written about Brandis essentially see him as the father of forestry in India. He played a large role in the passage of several pieces of legislation, especially the Indian Forest Acts of 1865 and 1878 which had the management and preservation of Indian woodlands as their central aim. He also advocated the establishment and preservation of trees near villages. His influence came from the fact that he carried out research and wrote about the forests he observed, which eventually led to the publication of a 767-page volume on *Indian Trees* after he retired. He also initiated a scheme for the selection and training of civil servants to work in the Indian Forest Service.[163] The German successors of Brandis as Inspector General of forests in India, Sir William Schlich and Berthold Ribbentrop, essentially continued his work. Schlich only held the position for two years between 1883 and 1885 but he had already spent time serving as conservator of forests in Burma, Sind and then the Punjab, having arrived in India in 1867. In the intervening years he had played a significant role in the development of education for foresters and had also helped to establish the *Indian Forester*.[164] Berthold Ribbentrop held the top job from 1885–1900.

Like Brandis, he toured extensively and also increased the income of the Forestry Department, as well as further improving recruitment to the forestry service and management of the forests.[165] At the end of his spell in office, he published a large survey of *Forestry in British India* in which he not only covered the different types of woodlands which existed in his domains, including alpine, deciduous and dry, but also outlined forest administration and its history and forest laws.[166]

Survival and success

The German elites who settled in nineteenth-century India faced a series of problems, despite the networks which paved their way to their new environment. In view of the employment networks which brought most of them to the country, they would pursue a delineated career path which might involve some type of routine. However, routine did not usually greet them. The missionaries carried out a variety of tasks, from preaching and teaching through to healing and researching. Similarly, the scholars and scientists had interesting working lives.

One factor that characterised all of the Germans in nineteenth-century India was mobility. This is partly due to the fact that a large percentage consisted of temporary visitors who could, however, remain for periods lasting from months – in the case of scholars on research trips – to decades, for those academics who secured posts or for missionaries. Just as importantly, few of the Germans lived a sedentary existence once in India. Movement within the country represented everyday life for both missionaries and scholars. This entailed travelling from one depository of manuscripts to another or, in the case of missionaries, a wandering existence in an attempt to secure conversions. At the same time, few of the Germans who settled in India stayed in any one location for any length of time. The example of Alwin Gehring, who transferred from one station to another while working for the Leipzig Mission, proves typical.

The greatest problem facing the Germans who travelled to nineteenth-century India was the environment. Many commented on the weather and wildlife. Above all, they had to face tropical diseases. Some, like Gundert, would succumb and return to Europe for good, having spent over 20 years in the country. Others needed to move backwards and forwards: while Brandis may have served as Chief Inspector of forests in India for two decades, he returned to Europe through 1865–7 and 1871–4, largely for health reasons.[167] Numerous others perished to sickness, especially typhus, although the numbers who died as a result of illness declined as the century progressed and medical and hygiene knowledge increased.

Ultimately, whatever length of time they spent in India, most of the Germans constituted professional elites. They had moved to the country for the purposes of employment in life-defining occupations, whether, for example, this consisted of academic work or the missionary vocation. In the case of the latter it provided the absolute centre of their existence for which, in many cases, they sacrificed their lives.

These German elites reflected the lives of their contemporaries who made their way to locations throughout the globe during the nineteenth century. Markus Denzel's collection of essays on the subject contains accounts of all of the groups considered in this chapter in a variety of locations including, for example: Hessian refugees who made their way to North America during the nineteenth century,[168] reflecting the movement of such individuals throughout Europe in this period;[169] businessmen, researchers and travellers in Latin America as identified by Michael Zeuske;[170] and German Jewish bankers in Paris.[171] Bankers, both Jewish and Gentile and originating in a variety of European locations, became global figures during the nineteenth century, as Stanley Chapman documented in his research on the rise of merchant banking.[172] The most famous of these global banking families included the Speyers, originating in Frankfurt and also developing branches in London and New York during the nineteenth century.[173] A series of scholars have demonstrated the development of global German merchant networks during the eighteenth and nineteenth centuries.[174] The lives of German missionaries find reflection in the experiences of their brethren, both German and non-German, throughout the world during the nineteenth century: India provides just one example. Those scholars who have written about the evolution of German missionary activity during the course of the nineteenth century have stressed the fact that India became just one area of concentration, illustrated especially by the five-volume history of the Basel Mission produced by Wilhelm Schlatter and Hermann Witschi, the first three volumes of which – written solely by Schlatter – concentrate purely on the century leading up to the outbreak of the First World War.[175] The sophisticated type of activity which evolved in India also developed in the other major areas of concentration in which Basel became active, especially in China[176] and the Gold Coast.[177] In addition, Basel also worked on a smaller scale in other areas including Borneo,[178] Togo, Cameroon and Liberia[179] and, in the earlier nineteenth century, southern Russia.[180] Basel, of course, provides just one example of global missionary activity during the nineteenth century, stressed – in the German case – by the two-volume account by Wilhelm Oehler.[181] Whether scholars, businessmen, missionaries or travellers, India reflected the global lives of thousands of other elite German migrants.

Notes

1. P. J. Marshall, 'British Society in India under the East India Company', *Modern Asian Studies*, vol. 31 (1997), p. 92.
2. Gerd Stricker, ed., *Deutsche Geschichte im Osten Europas: Rußland* (Berlin, 1997); Dittmar Dahlmann and Ralph Tuchtenhagen, eds, *Zwischen Reform und Revolution: Die Deutschen an der Wolga 1860–1917* (Essen, 1994); Victor Dönninghaus, *Die Deutschen in der Moskauer Gesellschaft: Symbiose und Konflikte (1494–1941)* (Munich, 2002); Stanley Nadel, *Little Germany: Ethnicity, Religion, and Class in New York City, 1845–80* (Chicago, 1990), pp. 62–90; Walter D. Kamphoefner, *The Westfalians: From Germany to Missouri* (Princeton, NJ, 1987); Frederick C. Luebke, *Germans in Brazil: A Comparative History of Cultural Conflict During World War I* (Baton Rouge, LO, 1987); Panikos Panayi, *German Immigrants in Britain during the Nineteenth Century, 1815–1914* (Oxford, 1995).
3. As an introduction, see, for example, John Urry, *Sociology Beyond Societies: Mobilities for the Twenty-First Century* (London, 2000); John Urry and Margaret Grieco, *Mobilities: New Perspectives on Transport and Society* (Farnham, 2011); John Urry and Anthony Elliot, *Mobile Lives* (London, 2010); and Thomas Bitchnell and Javier Caletrio, eds, *Elite Mobilities* (London, 2012).
4. See Dirk Hoerder, *Cultures in Contact: World Migrations in the Second Millenium* (London, 2002), who does not, however, overtly engage with the mobilities paradigm. Valeska Huber, *Channelling Mobilities: Migration and Globalisation in the Suez Canal Region and Beyond, 1869–1914* (Cambridge, 2013), deals more overtly with the Suez Canal using the mobilities concept as it proved fundamental for the passage of both people and goods. Gary B. Magee and Andrew S. Thompson, *Empire and Globalisation: Networks of People, Goods and Capital, c1850–1914* (Cambridge, 2010), examine the movement of both goods and people. More traditionally, Klaus J. Bade placed long-distance German migration during the nineteenth century into the context of movement within German borders, for which see contributions to his edited *Population, Labour and Migration in 19th and 20th Century Germany* (Leamington Spa, 1987). See also Jürgen Osterhammel, *The Transformation of the World: A Global History of the Nineteenth Century* (Oxford, 2014), pp. 117–66.
5. See, for example, Casey Blanton, *Travel Writing: The Self and the World* (London, 2002); and Tim Youngs, ed., *The Cambridge Introduction to Travel Writing* (Cambridge, 2013). The relationship between the self and the observed receives more attention in Chapter 5.
6. See, for example, Indira Ghose, *Memsahibs Abroad: Writings by Women Travellers in Nineteenth Century India* (Oxford, 1998).
7. Mary Weitbrecht, *Memoir of the Rev. J. J. Weitbrecht: Compiled from his Journals and Letters by his Widow* (London, 1854), pp. 42–3, 44, 54.
8. Alfred Mathieson, *Hebich of India: A Passionate Soul-Winner* (Kilmarnock, 1936), pp. 35–41.
9. Albrecht Frenz, *Eine Reise in die Religionen: Herrmann Mögling (1811–1881), Missionar und Sprachforscher in Indien, zum 200. Geburtstag* (Heidelberg, 2011), pp. 297–303; Hermann Gundert, *Herrmann Mögling: Ein Missionsleben in der Mitte des 19. Jahrhunderts* (Stuttgart, 1882), pp. 98–110.
10. Karl Graul, *Reise nach Ostindien über Palästina und Ägypten von Juli 1849 bis April 1853*, Vol. 1 (Leipzig, 1854), p. 22.
11. Ibid., p. 165.
12. A. Anton, *Von Darmstadt nach Ostindien: Erlebnisse und Abenteuer eines Musikers auf der Reise durch Arabien nach Lahore: Die denkwürdigen Ereignisse der letzten Jahre* (Darmstadt, 1860), pp. 26–31.
13. *Der evangelische Heidenbote*, 1 March 1835.
14. Albrecht Frenz, 'Hermann Gundert: A Biography', in Albrecht Frenz and Scaria Zacharia, eds, *Dr. Hermann Gundert and Malayalam Language* (Changanassery, 1993), pp. 69–72.
15. Ian J. Kerr, *Building the Railways of the Raj* (New Delhi, 1995).

16 David Arnold, *Science, Technology and Medicine in Colonial India* (Cambridge, 2000), pp. 105–13, 211–13.
17 Paul Deussen, *Erinnerungen an Indien* (Leipzig, 1904), p. 19.
18 Ibid., p. 27.
19 Ibid., pp. 29, 31–5.
20 Ibid., pp. 44–5.
21 Karl Heinrich Christian Plath, *Eine Reise nach Indien: Für kleine und große Leute beschrieben* (Berlin, 1880), pp. 45–9.
22 Alwin Gehring, *Erinnerungen aus dem Leben eines Tamulenmissionars* (Leipzig, 1906), pp. 6–16.
23 AFST/LMW/II.31.1.18, Tagebuch Hermann Gäbler.
24 *Der Evangelische Heidenbote*, 1839, p. 23.
25 Basel German Evangelical Missionary Society, *Report of the Basel German Evangelical Missionary Society. Forty-Fourth Year. 1859. Twentieth Report of the German Evangelical Mission in South-Western India* (Mangalore, 1860), p. 21.
26 Basel German Evangelical Missionary Society, *Report of the Basel German Evangelical Missionary Society for 1870. Twenty-First Report of the German Evangelical Mission in South-Western India* (Mangalore, 1871), p. 39.
27 *Magazin für die neueste Geschichte der evangelischen Missions- und Bibelgesellschaften*, 1856, pp. 88–90.
28 See, for example: ibid., 1841, pp. 271–81; *Evangelische Heidenbote*, 1836, pp. 91–2.
29 Albrecht Frenz, *Hermann Gundert: Reise nach Malabar* (Ulm, 1998), pp. 146–350.
30 *Magazin für die neueste Geschichte der evangelischen Missions- und Bibelgesellschaften*, 1839, pp. 486–507.
31 Gundert, *Herrmann Mögling*, pp. 177–84; *Evangelische Heidenbote*, 1844, pp. 47–50, 70–4.
32 Karl Graul, *Reise nach Ostindien über Palästina und Egypten von Juli 1849 bis April 1853* (Leipzig, 1854–6).
33 BMA/Q-30.3,5, Gebietslisten, Indien, Männer 1, entry 312.
34 *Evangelische Heidenbote*, 1854, pp. 69–70.
35 See, for example, ibid., 15 June 1830, pp. 45–6.
36 Ibid., 1 February 1832, p. 9.
37 Hermann von Schlagintweit Sakülünski, *Reisen in Indien und Hochasien: Eine Darstellung der Landschaft, der Cultur und Sitten der Bewohner, in Verbindung mit klimatischen und geologischen Verhältnissen Basirt auf die Resultate der wissenschaftlichen Mission von Hermann, Adolph und Robert von Schlagintweit ausgeführt in den Jahren 1854–1858*, Vol. 1 (Jena, 1869), pp. 78–86; Helga Alcock, *The Schlagintweit Brothers: Achievements in High Asia* (Totnes, 1981).
38 Gehring, *Erinnerungen*, pp. 25–68.
39 Deussen, *Erinnerungen*.
40 Valentina Stache-Rosen, *German Indologists: Biographies of Scholars in Indian Studies Writing in German* (New Delhi, 1981), p. 69.
41 Richard Garbe, *Indische Reiseskizzen* (Berlin, 1889), pp. 43–59.
42 Ibid., pp. 75–123.
43 Ibid., p. 128.
44 Ibid., p. 153.
45 E. R. Baierlein, *Unter den Palmen im Lande der Sonne* (Leipzig, 1890); AFST/LMW/II.31.1.3., Pfr. Raimund Baierlein; www.lmw-mission.de/de/missionar-9.html, Leipziger Missionswerk, Eduard Raimund Baierlein, accessed 15 June 2015.
46 AFST/LMW/II.31.1.8, Pfr. Heinrich Beisenherz.
47 AFST/LMW/II.31.1.10, Pfr. Hermann Beythan; www.lmw-mission.de/de/missionar-157.html, Leipziger Missionswerk Hermann Beythan, accessed 15 June 2015.
48 AFST/LMW/II.31.1.18, Pfr. Gustav Hermann Gäbler; www.lmw-mission.de/de/missionar-124.html, Leipziger Missionswerk, Gustav Hermann Gäbler, accessed 15 June 2015.

EVERYDAY LIFE

49 AFST/LMW/II.31.1.2, Pfr. Ernst David Appelt; www.lmw-mission.de/de/missionar-61.html, Ernst David Appelt, accessed 15 June 2015; www.gaebler.info/india/leipziger_indienmissionare-1.htm, Gaebler Info und Genealogie, Liste der IndienmissionarInnen der Leipziger Mission, accessed 15 June 2015.
50 www.gaebler.info/india/leipziger_indienmissionare-1.htm, Gaebler Info und Genealogie, Liste der IndienmissionarInnen der Leipziger Mission, accessed 15 June 2015.
51 For death and return, see pp. 83–7 below.
52 BMA/Q-30.3,5, Gebietslisten, Indien, Männer 1. Within this reference, the tables on Schwestern and Frauen do not provide information on the range of places which women worked.
53 BMA/Q-30.3,5, Gebietslisten, Indien, Schwestern.
54 See the brief biographies of Margarete Grote, Else Frey, Auguste Hensolt, Helene Frankel, Lina Streng, Elisabeth Schüler, Berta Hübner, Käthe Schmidt, Aurelie Herget, Rosa Busch, Emma Karberg and Johanna Herget in www.lmw-mission.de/de/missionare.html, accessed 15 June 2015.
55 Schlagintweit Sakülünski, *Reisen in Indien*, Vol. 1. The subsequent volumes deal with the Himalayas.
56 Garbe, *Indische Reiseskizzen*; Deussen, *Erinnerungen an Indien*.
57 Oscar Kauffmann, *Aus Indiens Dschungeln: Erlebnisse und Forschungen*, two volumes (Leipzig, 1911).
58 Severin Noti, *Aus Indien: Reisebriefe eines Missionärs* (Einsiedeln, 1908); Joseph Dahlmann, *Indische Fahrten*, two volumes (Freiburg im Breisgau, 1908).
59 M. Winternitz, *Georg Bühler und die Indologie* (Munich, 1898); Julius Jolly, *Georg Bühler, 1837–1898* (Strasbourg, 1899), pp. 2–8; Stache-Rosen, *German Indologists*, p. 88.
60 Andrew Huxley, 'Dr Führer's Wanderjahre: the early career of a Victorian archaeologist', *Journal of the Royal Asiatic Society of Great Britain and Ireland*, Series 3, vol. 20 (2010), pp. 489–502.
61 Philp D. Curtin, *Death by Migration: Europe's Encounter with the Tropical World in the Nineteenth Century* (Cambridge, 1989).
62 David Arnold, *Colonizing the Body: State Medicine and Epidemic Disease in Nineteenth-century India* (London, 1993).
63 David Arnold, 'Introduction: Disease, Medicine and Empire', in David Arnold, ed., *Imperial Medicine and Indigenous Societies* (Manchester, 1988), pp. 1–26.
64 See the files in BMA/Q-30.3,5. Significantly, the tables do not list cause of death.
65 The information available on individual missionaries in www.lmw-mission.de/de/missionare.html, does not always even provide details on place and date of death and rarely on the cause of death. The same applies to the Personalakten of the Leipzig missionaries in the Archiv der Frankeschen Stiftung.
66 Robert Koch, *Reiseberichte über Rinderpest, Bubonenpest in Indien und Afrika, Tsetse- oder Surrakrankheit, Texasfieber, tropische Malaria, Schwarzwasserfieber* (Berlin, 1898), pp. 1–3; Benhard Möllers, *Robert Koch: Persönlichkeit und Lebenswerk* (Hannover, 1950), pp. 140–7; Wolfgang Genschorek, *Robert Koch* (Leipzig, 1975), pp. 154–64; Georg Gaffky, Richard Pfeiffer, Georg Sticker and Adolf Dieudonné, *Bericht über die Thätigkeit der zur Erforschung der Pest i. J. 1897 nach Indien entsandten Kommission* (Berlin, 1899). Koch also travelled to other tropical locations during both of his journeys.
67 Noti, *Aus Indien*, pp. 321–37.
68 Kauffmann, *Aus Indiens Dschungeln*, Vol. 1, p. 6.
69 See, for example, articles on hunger in *Der evangelische Heidenbote*, March 1855 and April 1877, and on cholera in the April 1877 edition.
70 BMA/Q-30.3,5, Gebietslisten, Indien, Ärtzte.
71 BMA/C-10.07.10, Dr. med. Fisch betr. Gesundheitsverhältnisse der indischen Missions Geschwister vom 10.6.1913.

72 Joachim Lüdemann, *August Mylius (1819–1887): Lutherische Missionarsexistenz in Tamilnadu und Andhra Pradesh* (London, 2003), pp. 450–61.
73 Dagmar Konrad, *Missionsbräute: Pietistinnen des 19. Jahrhunderts in der Basler Mission* (Münster, 2001), p. 327.
74 Ibid., p. 329.
75 AFST/LMW/ II.31.1.4, Deutsches Institut für ärtzliche Mission, Aerztliches Zeugnis, 30. Okt. 1912.
76 www.lmw-mission.de/de/missionar-162.html, Leipziger Missionswerk, Friedrich Bauer, accessed 18 June 2015.
77 UB/CRL/SC/CMS/B/OMS/C I2 O217, Ludwig Bernhard Ehregott Schmid, Journal from September 1818 to September 1819.
78 Lüdemann, *August Mylius*, pp. 178–84.
79 Frenz, 'Hermann Gundert', pp. 128–9.
80 Weitbrecht, *Memoir*, pp. 104–5.
81 Ibid., p. 132.
82 Ibid., p. 144.
83 Ibid., pp. 168–9, 364–5.
84 Ibid., pp. 545–9.
85 *Der evangelische Heidenbote*, 1872, pp. 148–50.
86 Ibid., March 1871.
87 Johann Wörrlein, *Paul Otto Petersen: Von 1875 bis 1888 Missionar in Indien* (Hermannsburg, 1901), pp. 17–19.
88 Johann Wörrlein, *Peter Wilhelm Heinrich Lüchow: Von 1875 bis 1888 Missionar in Indien* (Hermannsburg, 1901), pp. 14–15.
89 Willi Bidermann, *Missionar in den Blauen Bergen: Andreas Köhlers Weg nach Indien* (Bietigheim-Bissingen, 1997), pp. 96–9.
90 Konrad, *Missionsbräute*, pp. 258–325.
91 J. Rhenius, Memoir of C. T. E. Rhenius, *Comprising Extracts from His Journals and Correspondence, with Details of Missionary Proceedings in South India* (London, 1841), p. 329.
92 UB/CRL/SC/CMS/B/OMS/CI1O88, letter of 23 February 1825.
93 *Magazin Neueste Geschichte*, 1829, p. 641.
94 *Magazin Neueste Geschichte*, 1 September 1835.
95 *Evangelisch-lutherisches Missionsblatt*, 1870, p. 240.
96 H. Kausch and F. Hahn, *50 Bilder aus der Gossnerschen Kols-Mission mit erläuterndem Text und Karte* (Berlin, 1894), pp. 33–40.
97 Gehring, *Erinnerungen*, pp. 66–8.
98 AFST/LMW/II.31.1.131, undated and unsourced newspaper article entitled 'Aus Indien'.
99 Deussen, *Erinnerungen*, p. 19.
100 *Missions-Ordnung: Zusammenstellung wichtiger Bestimmungen für die Missionare der Evangelisch-Lutherischen Mission in Indien* (Leipzig, 1908), p. 5. For Breklum, see Otto Waack, *Indische Kirche und Indien-Mission*, Vol. 1, *Die Geschichte der Jeypore-Kirche und der Breklumer Mission (1876–1914)* (Erlangen, 1994), pp. 279–8.
101 See especially, Heike Liebau, *Cultural Encounters in India: The Local Co-workers of the Tranquebar Mission, 18th to 19th Centuries* (New Delhi, 2013). Indian catechists receive more attention in Chapter 4.
102 Charles Benjamin Leupolt, *Further Recollections of an Indian Missionary* (London, 1884), pp. 60–1.
103 Weitbrecht, *Memoir*, pp. 63–4, 65.
104 Albrecht Frenz, ed., *Hermann Gundert, Tagebuch aus Malabar, 1837–1859* (Stuttgart, 1983), pp. 3–6.
105 *Evangelisches Missions-Magazin*, 1860, p. 128.
106 Georg Stosch, *Im fernen Indien: Eindrücke und Erfahrungen im Dienst der luth. Mission unter den Tamulen* (Berlin, 1896), pp. 72–3.
107 See Chapter 5.
108 Frenz, *Hermann Gundert, Tagebuch*, pp. 351–98.

109 See, for example, Weitbrecht, *Memoir*.
110 H. Mögling and V. D. M. Weitbrecht, *Das Kurgland und die evangelische Mission in Kurg* (Basel, 1866), pp. 301–9.
111 German Lutheran Mission (Tirhut, India), *The Twenty Sixth Annual Report of the German Mission in Tirhoot* (Muzaffarpur, 1866).
112 L. Nottrott, *Die Gossner'sche Mission unter den Kolhs: Bilder aus dem Missionsleben* (Halle, 1874), pp. 273.
113 Ibid., pp. 275, 276.
114 Ibid., p. 280.
115 For an introduction to Roman Catholic educational activity, see Chapter 1.
116 Kausch, *50 Bilder*, p. 71.
117 Julius Richter, *Nordindische Missionsfahrten: Erzählungen und Schilderungen von einer Missions-Studienreise durch Ostindien* (Gütersloh, 1903), p. 295.
118 'Basel Mission Work in India: A Chronology', in Godwin Shiri, ed., *Wholeness in Christ: The Legacy of the Basel Mission in India* (Mangalore, 1985), p. 78; C. Stolz, *Die Basler Mission in Indien: Zugleich als Festschrift zum 50 jährigen Jubiläum der Kanara-Mission* (Basel 1884), p. 28.
119 *Magazin für die neueste Geschichte der evangelischen Missions- und Bibelgesellschaften*, 1841, pp. 255–70.
120 S. D. L. Alagodi, 'The Basel Mission in Mangalore: Historical and Social Context', in Reinhardt Wendt, ed., *An Indian to the Indians? On the Initial Failure and the Posthumous Success of the Missionary Ferdinand Kittel (1832–1903)* (Wiesbaden, 2006), pp. 152–4.
121 Mögling and Weitbrecht, *Das Kurgland*, pp. 270–82.
122 Nottrott, *Die Gossner'sche Mission*, pp. 295–6.
123 Kausch and Kahn, *50 Bilder*, pp. 71–80.
124 Waack, *Indische Kirche*, pp. 451–3.
125 AFST/LMW/II.31.1.129, Missionslehrerin Helene Frenkel 1873–1955; *Zweiundneunzigster Jahresbericht der Evangelisch-lutherischen Mission zu Leipzig* (Leipzig, 1911), p. 35; D. Paul, *Die Leipziger Mission Daheim und Draussen* (Leipzig, 1914), pp. 156–73; Richard Handmann, *Die Evangelisch-lutherische Tamulen-Mission in der Zeit ihrer Neubegründung* (Leipzig, 1903), pp. 377–89.
126 See, for example, Mary A. Procida, *Married to the Empire: Gender, Politics and Imperialism in India, 1883–1947* (Manchester, 2002), pp. 165–89; Padma Anagol, 'Indian Christian Women and Indian Feminism', in Clare Midgely, ed., *Gender and Imperialism* (Manchester, 1998), pp. 79–103.
127 Wilhelm Hoffmann, *Die Erziehung des weiblichen Geschlechts in Indien: Ein Aufruf an die christlichen Frauen Deutschlands* (Stuttgart, 1841); Waltraud Haas, *Erlitten und Erstritten: Der Befreiungsweg von Frauen in der Basler Mission 1816–1966* (Basel, 1994), pp. 26–66; BMA/C-10.02.17, Luise Saladin, 'Die Entwicklung der Frauenmission in Indien', 2 March 1940; *Neunzigster Jahresbericht der evangelischen Missions-Gesellschaft zu Basel auf 1. Juli 1905* (Basel, 1905), pp. 50–61.
128 O. Gründler, *Frauenelend und Frauenmission in Indien* (Berlin, 1895).
129 Johann Wörrlein, *Ist in Indien eine besondere Frauenmission nötig?* (Hermannsburg, 1902).
130 Georg Haccius, *Die letzten Erlebnisse unserer indischen Schwestern* (Hermannsburg, 1916).
131 Ibid., pp. 16–17.
132 Alwin Gehring, *Das Tamulenland, seine Bewohner und die Mission* (Leipzig, 1927).
133 AFST/LMW/II.31.11.3, Frauensmissionsconferenz der Deustchen u. Schwedischen Diozese in Kodaikanal am 5. Juni 1913.
134 See, for example, David Hardiman, *Missionaries and Their Medicine: A Christian Modernity for Tribal India* (Manchester, 2008).
135 Eva Bell, 'Medical Work of the Basel Mission in India', in Shiri, *Wholeness in Christ*, p. 238.
136 Ibid., pp. 238–57.

137 *Echo aus Indien*, March, September 1913.
138 Henry S. Wilson, 'Basel Mission's industrial enterprise in South Kanara and its impact between 1834 and 1914', *Indian Church History Review*, vol. 14 (1980), pp. 92–4; Rudolf H. Fischer, 'Mission and Modernisation: The Basel Mission Factories as Agencies of Social Change (1850–1914)', in Shiri, *Wholeness in Christ*, pp. 200–3; Jaiprakash Raghaviah, *Basel Mission Industries in Malabar and South Canara, 1834–1914: A Study of its Social and Economic Impact* (New Delhi, 1990), pp. 5–10.
139 Wilson, ibid., pp. 95–9; Hermann Pfleiderer, *Gottlob Pfleiderer: Der erste Basler Missionskaufmann in Indien* (Stuttgart, 1929), pp. 11–29.
140 Fischer, 'Mission and Modernisation', p. 200.
141 Raghaviah, *Basel Mission Industries*, pp. 37–8; Gustav Adolf Wanner, *Die Basler Handels-Gesellschaft A.G., 1859–1959* (Basel, 1959).
142 Ibid., p. 38; Fischer, 'Mission and Modernisation', p. 204; German Evangelical Mission, *The Fifteenth Report of the German Evangelical Mission on the Western Coast of India* (Mangalore, 1855), pp. 20–1; Basel German Evangelical Missionary, *Report of the Basel German Evangelical Mission in South-Western India for 1870* (Mangalore, 1871), p. 31.
143 See Chapter 1.
144 Heike Liebau, 'Deutsche Missionare als Indienforscher: Benjamin Schultze – Ausnahme oder Regel', *Archiv für Kulturgeschichte*, vol. 76 (1994), pp. 111–33.
145 Mögling and Weitbrecht, *Das Kurgland*.
146 Christan Irion, *Malabar und die Missionsstation Talatscheri* (Basel, 1864).
147 Edmund Raimund Baierlein, *The Land of the Tamulians and its Missions* (Madras, 1875). See the deconstruction of this work in Andreas Nehring, 'Missionsstrategie und Forschungsdrang: Anmerkungen zu Mission und Wissenschaft in Südindien im 19. Jahrhundert', in Heike Liebau, Andreas Nehring and Brigitte Klosterberg, eds, *Mission und Forschung: Translokale Wissensproduktion zwischen Indien und Europa im 18. und 19. Jahrhundert* (Halle, 2010), pp. 21–31.
148 Scaria Zacharia, 'Tuebingen Heritage as Reflected in the Dictionaries of Gundert and Kittel', in William Madtha, Heidrun Becker, A. Murigeppa and H. M. Mahehshwari, eds, *A Dictionary with a Mission: Papers of the International Conference on the Occasion of the Centenary Celebrations of Kittel's Kannada-English Dictionary* (Mangalore, 1998), pp. 9–17.
149 Hans-Juergen Findeis, 'Language – Religion – Mission: Some Reflections on the Contribution of Missionaries to Indian Languages in the Context of Mission History', in ibid., p. 223.
150 Frenz, 'Hermann Gundert', pp. 94–7; Scaria Zacharia, 'Dr. Hermann Gundert and Malayalam Language: The Context of Understanding', in Albrehct Frenz and Scaria Zacharia, eds, *Dr. Hermann Gundert and Malayalam Language* (Changanassery, 1993), pp. 15–43.
151 See contributions to Wendt, *An Indian to the Indians?*
152 Christoph Friedrich Eppler, *Karl Gottlieb Pfander: Ein Zeuge der Wahrheit unter den Bekennern des Islam* (Basel, 1888), pp. 1–3, 122–38.
153 Andreas Nehring, *Orientalismus und Mission: Die Repräsentation der tamulischen Gesellschaft und Religion durch Leipziger Missionare 1840–1940* (Wiesbaden, 2003).
154 Joseph Bara, 'Unlocking Tribal Knowledge to the World: German Missionaries in Chotangapur, East India (c.1850–1930) ', in Ulrich van der Heyden und Andreas Feldtkeller, eds, *Missionsgeschichte als Geschichte der Globalisierung von Wissen: Transkulturelle Wissensaneignung und -vermittlung durch christliche Missionare in Afrika und Asien im 17., 18. und 19. Jahrhundert* (Stuttgart, 2012), pp. 55–65.
155 Klaus Roeber, 'Missionare der Gossner Mission als Forscher und Wissenschaftler', in ibid., p. 341.
156 See for example: Findeis, 'Language'; Wendt, *An Indian to the Indians?*; and the contributions of Srinivasa Havanur, Kuttamath K. N. Kurup and Uliyar P. Upadhyaya to Shiri, *Wholeness in Christ*.

157 See p. 83.
158 Joachim Friedrich Sprockhoff, 'Friedrich Otto Schrader zum Gedächtnis', *Zeitschrift der Deutschen Morgenländischen Gesellschaft*, vol. 113 (1963), pp. 1–3.
159 Stache-Rosen, *German Indologists*, pp. 73–4, 94–5; Donald Clay Johnson, 'German influences on the development of research libraries in nineteenth century Bombay', *Journal of Library History*, vol. 21 (1986), pp. 215–27.
160 Hermann von Schlagintweit Sakülünski, *Reisen in Indien und Hochasien Basirt auf die Resultate der wissenschaftlichen Mission von H, A und R von Schlagintweit ausgefuhrt in den Jahren 1854–1858*, three volumes (Leipzig, 1869–80); Emil Schlagintweit, *Indien in Wort und Bild*, two volumes (Leipzig, 1880–1).
161 Adolphe and Robert Schlagintweit, *Report on the Proceedings of the Officers Engaged in the Magnetic Survey of India* (Madras, 1855).
162 Adolphe and Robert Schlagintweit, *Report upon the progress of the Magnetic Survey of India, and of the researches connected with it in the Himalaya Mountains, from April to October 1855* (Agra, 1856).
163 S. S. Negi, *Sir Dietrich Brandis: Father of Tropical Forestry* (Dehra Dun, 1991); Herbert Hesmer, *Leben und Werk von Dietrich Brandis, 1824–1907: Begründer der tropischen Forstwirtschaft, Förderer der forstlichen Entwicklung in den USA, Botaniker und Ökologe* (Opladen, 1975), pp. 70–281; Ajay S. Rawat, 'Brandis: The Father of Organized Forestry in India', in Ajay S. Rawat, ed., *Indian Forestry: A Perspective* (New Delhi, 1993), pp. 88–100; Ramachandra Guha, 'Dietrich Brandis: A Vision Revisited and Reaffirmed', in Mark Poffenberger and Betsy McGean, eds, *Village Voices, Forest Choices: Joint Forest Management in India* (Oxford, 1996), pp. 86–94; Indra Munshi Saldanha, 'Colonialism and professionalism: a German forester in India', *Environment and History*, vol. 2 (1996), pp. 195–219; Dietrich Brandis, *Indian Trees; An Account of Trees, Shrubs, Woody Climbers, Bamboos and Palms Indigenous or Commonly Cultivated in the British Indian Empire* (London, 1906).
164 'Dr William Schlich', *Indian Forester*, vol. 15 (1889), pp. 47–51; E. Mammen, M. S. Tomar and N. Parameswaran, 'A salute to William Schlich', *Indian Forester*, vol. 91 (1965), pp. 77–82.
165 'The retirement of Mr Ribbentrop, C.I.E', *Indian Forester*, vol. 26 (1900), pp. 614–16.
166 Berthold Ribbentrop, *Forestry in British India* (Calcutta, 1900).
167 Hesmer, *Leben und Werk von Dietrich Brandis*, pp. 70–281.
168 Eckhart G. Franz, 'Freiheit jenseits des Meeres: Hessische Polit-Emigration nach Übersee im 19. Jahrhundert', in Markus A. Denzel, ed., *Deutsche Eliten in Übersee (16. bis frühes 20. Jahrhundert)* (St Katharinen, 2006), pp. 85–93.
169 Christine Lattek, *Revolutionary Refugees: German Socialism in Britain, 1840–1860* (London, 2006); Hans-Ulrich Thamer, 'Flucht und Exil: "Demagogen" und Revolutionäre', in Klaus J. Bade, ed., *Deutsche im Ausland – Fremde in Deutschland: Migration in Geschichte und Gegenwart* (Munich, 1992), pp. 242–9.
170 Michael Zeuske, 'Deutsche als Eliten in Lateinamerika (19. Jahrhundert): Regionen, Typen, Netzwerke und paradigmatische Lebensgeschichten', in Denzel, *Deutsche Eliten*, pp. 173–206
171 Dieter Brötel, 'Die deutsche "Kolonie" in Paris: Imperiale Aktivitäten jüdisch-deutscher Bankiers, 1860–1880', in ibid., pp. 319–60.
172 Stanley D. Chapman, *The Rise of Merchant Banking* (London, 1984).
173 Antony Lentin, *Banker, Traitor, Scapegoat, Spy? The Troublesome Case of Sir Edgar Speyer* (London, 2013), pp. 2–3.
174 See the following contributions to Andreas Gestrich and Margrit Schulte Beerbühl, eds, *Cosmopolitan Networks in Commerce and Society 1660–1914* (London, 2011): Margrit Schulte Beerbühl and Klaus Weber, 'From Westphalia to the Caribbean: Networks of German Textile Merchants in the Eighteenth Century', pp. 53–98; Bradley B. Naranch, 'Between Cosmopolitanism and German Colonialism: Nineteenth-Century Hanseatic Networks in Emerging Tropical Markets', pp. 99–132; and Monika Poettinger, 'German Entrepreneurial Networks and the Industrialization of Milan', pp. 249–92.

175 Wilhelm Schlatter and Hermann Witschi, *Geschichte der Basler Mission*, five volumes (Basel, 1916–70).
176 Wilhelm Schlatter, *Geschichte der Basler Mission*, Vol. 2 (Basel, 1916), pp. 271–407.
177 Wilhelm Schlatter, *Geschichte der Basler Mission*, Vol. 3 (Basel, 1916), pp. 19–195.
178 Schlatter, *Geschichte*, Vol. 2, pp. 408–21.
179 Schlatter, *Geschichte*, Vol. 3, pp. 1–16, 199–221.
180 Wilhelm Schlatter, *Geschichte der Basler Mission*, Vol. 1 (Basel, 1916), pp. 93–119.
181 Wilhelm Oehler, *Geschichte der deutschen evangelischen Mission*, two volumes (Baden-Baden, 1949–51).

CHAPTER FOUR

Community

In his study of the construction of German communities abroad, influenced by nationalist organisations in the newly created German Empire in the decades leading up to the First World War, Stefan Manz focused upon a series of characteristics which went towards the development of these communities. Three elements in particular, led from the German imperial centre, characterised the urban German diaspora communities which existed by 1914: branches of the German Navy League; a Protestant church; and a German school.[1]

Using these three elements in particular, the Germans in India would not appear to have developed the type of community which characterised, for example, Russia,[2] the USA,[3] Canada[4] and Brazil,[5] where some of the most substantial settlements had developed, or other parts of the globe where smaller groupings had emerged including, for example, Argentina,[6] Australia,[7] Chile[8] and Great Britain.[9] In these locations with significant German settlements a rich ethnicity emerged revolving around religion, politics, trade union activity and high and low culture. Some German commentators who made their way to India during the course of the nineteenth century identified the semblance of a German community, although the organisations concerned with constructing the German diaspora tended to disregard the Germans in India.

Rather than constructing communities and identities in which allegiance to the fatherland became the central tenet, the main loyalty of the missionaries lay to their Protestant (or Roman Catholic) God. While the establishment of churches played a large role in the emergence of a German community in urban environments in other parts of the world, as demonstrated by Manz,[10] religion remained central for missionaries who squarely focused upon constructing a community based upon Christianity. This meant building self-standing mission stations, with their own housing, schools and other institutions. The communities which emerged functioned through the institutions which they established, which meant interaction with indigenous Indians and, especially in the case of the early Basel missionaries, their British brethren. While relationships between the Basel missionaries and other Europeans operated upon an equal footing, interaction with Indians partially worked on the basis of a racial hierarchy, with Germans at the top. However, the missionaries had to co-operate with Indians as intermediaries for the purpose of carrying out further conversions, as Heike Liebau carefully demonstrated in the case of the Tranquebar Mission.[11] Within the emerging religious communities of mixed ethnicity, German identity survived. One indication of this was the development of German families over several generations so that some of those recognised as German actually had an Indian birthplace. At the same time, the German missionaries used their native language in most correspondence, as well as in many of their publications, especially magazines, annual reports, centenary publications or long-term histories of German missionary activity in India published for fundraising purposes in the German and Swiss homeland.

Unlike most of the secular German groupings, the German centre made little effort to politicise the missionary communities, probably because of their size and diverse nature, although some of the organisations which tried to construct a global German diaspora certainly claimed the German missionaries as part of this global network. Only with the outbreak of the First World War did the missionaries become truly German because the British authorities, working from London-based perceptions, turned them into enemies.

Secular German communities

Despite the small numbers of Germans who lived in India in the century before the First World War, some of their countrymen who travelled here commented on their presence. Graul pointed to the recent establishment of 'a pair of Germans, one a Bavarian and the other Swiss, as businessmen in Bombay'. He also mentioned a German Jewish jeweller and suggested that: 'The German businessmen in East India come mostly from Switzerland and Hamburg. There were ten in Calcutta at the time.'[12]

By the beginning of the twentieth century, something resembling a German community had actually evolved in Bombay, as several commentators noted. The 1909 'travel impressions' of Count Hans von Koenigsmarck included a chapter on the 'German Indian Colony', although it amounted to only one individual in the form of a tailor called Armin Muller who complained about his income and the fact that his wife had left him. The rest of Koenigsmarck's brief chapter focused on highly tangential historical German connections with India and did not suggest any real community.[13] Hermann Dalton similarly met just two Germans in Bombay a decade earlier, probably from Pomerania, while visiting the Royal Alfred Sailors Home which, he claimed, housed 18,000 sailors per year. Once again, like Graul and Koenigsmarck, Dalton gives no sense of a genuine German community in Bombay.[14] A decade before Dalton's travels, Richard Garbe mentioned that, two days after arriving in Bombay, he received 'a friendly invitation from Mr Heinrich' to spend time 'in German company in the villa – or in Indian parlance – in the bungalow of my agreeable compatriot' who took him for a walk along the Malabar Coast.[15]

By the beginning of the twentieth century, both the German consulates and those organisations concerned with the German diaspora had become interested in the presence of Germans in India and in the concept of a German community in the country. The most detailed examination came from the Allgemeiner Deutscher Schulverein zur Erhaltung des Deutschtums im Auslande,[16] which published an account of the activities of Germans abroad in the decade leading up to the First World War. Its 1906 *Handbuch des Deutschtums im Auslande* provided an introduction to the activities of German organisations throughout the world. It devoted three pages to 'Vorderindien', including Ceylon and Burma. The description included a table which claimed that 1,696 Germans lived in India in 1901, which it divided into provinces, including 658 in Bombay, 359 in Bengal and 239 in Madras. The publication asserted that: 'Larger German colonies are present only in Bombay and Calcutta.' The narrative claimed that in 1904 about 100 Germans lived in Bombay, including Austrians and Swiss who made up about a third of the 'Deutscher Verein' there. The *Handbuch* saw even more signs of German cultural life in Calcutta, with a 'thriving German colony' consisting of a club and a branch of the German Navy League which counted 19 members, according to Stefan Manz. The *Handbuch* also identified a German Evangelical Seaman's Mission in Calcutta, another element of German diasporic activity as Christiaan Engberts has identified in Antwerp and Rotterdam. This had connections with the Gossner Mission which, from 1902, organised services for the seamen who spent time in this city, although these only appear to have taken place once every two to three months with limited attendance – counting, for example, 23 people at one service right before Christmas 1908 and just six on 9 August 1909. The *Handbuch* claimed that only 14 Germans lived in Madras but that they regularly met in a club. It then went on to list individual Germans who lived throughout India. A section on German missions described activity in this field, although the same subheading also included a description of German commercial activity in India.

After a section on Ceylon, the article concluded with a list of German consulates.[17]

A couple of other articles from nationalistic publications of this period briefly touch upon the Germans in India. Alfred Geiser's *Deutsches Reich und Volk* groups them together in a category of 'Germans in South Asia', which, in one paragraph, briefly gives numbers in cities from Tehran to Manila and includes Bombay and Madras.[18] Meanwhile, an article by Alfred Wirth on 'Germanity [Deutschtum] in Asia' (stretching from Turkey to Siberia to China and all places in between) in a journal entitled *Deutsche Erde,* appears to repeat some of the information provided by the *Handbuch des Deutschtums im Auslande* although Wirth also claimed that 'I have further met watchmakers, bakers and landlords in Murree, Rawalpindi and Simla'.[19] Another article concerned with the German diaspora published in the early 1920s and looking back to the immediate pre-War period, contained under a page of information on the Germans in India (half of which focused upon the consequences of the First World War), which simply gave a brief outline of facts and figures regarding Germans in urban locations and the number of missionaries in the country.[20]

By the early twentieth century, the German foreign office and consulates in India became interested in German community. A newspaper article in a foreign office file written by Katharine Zitelmann carried the title of 'German Schools and German Life Abroad' with the subtitle of 'Impressions from a World Tour'. Although this contains much the same information as the piece in the *Handbuch des Deutschtums im Auslande,* Zitelmann describes some of the individual Germans she met and their attitude towards their homeland. In Benares she 'found a German architect in a distinguished position in English employment' who moved to India when he was 'very young' and 'became an English citizen a long time ago' but 'was extremely amiable towards me and did not deny his nationality'. She also met the 'cotton exporter and carpet manufacturer' Weylandt in Agra 'whose hospitality towards travelling compatriots is famous. I was also granted an evening to spend in his beautiful home. His house is operated in a very German way. I was thus surprised to learn that he is also an English citizen', although he appears to have changed his nationality for tactical reasons connected with his marriage and the fact that he lived hundreds of miles from the nearest German consul. Weylandt had several children, most of whom also had British nationality.[21]

By 1911, the Germans in Bombay appear to have developed a community life similar to that which existed in larger German settlements throughout the world, despite the small numbers who lived here. The organisations which had come into existence included: a branch of the

COMMUNITY

German Navy League;[22] a German Benevolent Society for the Support of Needy Germans, which had recently gathered enough funding to come into existence; a German reading circle, which had just inherited 'two large book donations worth approximately 1,000 Marks'; and a singing group [Liederkranz], which had recently overcome financial difficulties and which included imperial citizens and 'other German speakers, namely Swiss'. The last of these groups celebrated the Kaiser's birthday, another key German diasporic activity of this period, although it aimed to create a 'real German club, to which Swiss, Austrians etc, could have entry as exceptional members without voting rights'. Despite the fact that the new society counted only 60 members, it had gathered 20,000 Marks in a very short time. 'The visit of His Imperial Highness the Crown Prince and the long stay of the large cruiser "Gneisau" in the port of Bombay had a very favourable influence upon the Germans in Bombay.'[23] During his stay in Bombay, which lasted from 14–16 December 1910, the Crown Prince hosted a 'garden festival' for the 'German colony' in the villa of the consul. 'All Germans who attended – about a hundred – were introduced to the Crown Prince and he spoke with each individual for a few minutes.'[24] The visit clearly had a galvanising influence upon the Germans of Bombay (Figure 4.1). A couple of years before this, a letter to the Kaiser on 30 September 1908, anticipating a possible visit on the *Seeadler*, advised against such a course of action: 'The Germans of Bombay have unfortunately been

Figure 4.1 The German Crown Prince in Bombay, December 1910

divided into 2 camps for many years. On one side stands the consul and a small number of Germans while on the other the longest resident Germans and their entourage of employees and naturalised Englishmen.' The origins of this division appear to lie in a dispute over the celebration of the Kaiser's birthday in the 'German-Swiss Club', in which the consul 'tactlessly' became involved.[25]

The Germans in India therefore developed the type of secular ethnicity which characterised the diaspora in other parts of the world, at least in Bombay, but on a much smaller scale. The numbers involved did not allow the evolution of the sophisticated ethnic life which included newspapers and trade unions characteristic of London, Buenos Aires or New York, for example.[26] As the discussion above makes clear, while two branches of the Navy League may have emerged in India by the outbreak of the First World War, they counted just a handful of members. Germans in Madras actually joined the organisation as individuals because not enough of them lived there to sustain a branch.[27] In addition, no German schools emerged in the urban locations where Germans found themselves because they did not count enough German children. Churches aimed purely at Germans could also not develop as the maximum potential congregation stood at just 100 souls in Calcutta and Bombay. Those bodies which emerged reflected the class backgrounds of the settlers in the form of the nationalistic Navy League and *Vereine*. Clearly, no space existed for trade unions from the point of view of political persuasion, numbers and the nature of employment.

The article written by Katharine Zitelmann points to the fact that some of the Germans lived as individuals amongst Indians and Britons. Such people sometimes decided to take out British nationality, a situation reflected in Bombay. At the same time, German communities also emerged in the wider sense to include Austrians and Swiss reflecting, for instance, the situation in Italy, which also counted small numbers of Germans.[28] This raises the question in the Indian case of the extent to which Germans became assimilated into wider 'European' society. One of the clearest indications of this lies in the fact that some of the early missionaries worked for the English-based CMS, while intermarriage became common.[29] At the same time, several of the German travellers in India wrote of a European society which appeared to include their compatriots. When Graul visited Bombay he outlined the 'non-Indian population' there,[30] which included Parsis, Jews and the handful of Germans he met, the last of whom appeared to form part of the 'pure blooded Europeans – mostly civil servants, military personnel and businessmen'.[31] Meanwhile, Garbe described European society in India as consisting of 'the English officers and civil servants, the German merchants and the missionaries',[32] although most of his chapter on

'The Life of Europeans in India'[33] does not distinguish between different nationalities and essentially refers to the British. The Schlagintweit descriptions of Europeans in Bombay also worked along the same assumptions.[34]

Historians of European society in India have paid little attention to Germans, presumably because their numbers make them too small to identify. David Arnold does not mention Germans, although he includes reference to other Europeans including Italians and French people.[35] Other accounts (some now rather dated), generally written by non-academics, overtly focus upon British society with little engagement with the concept of Europeans.[36] Fischer-Tiné's study of *Low and Licentious Europeans* does make some reference to Germans, but not to other groups and focuses overwhelmingly on Britons.[37] This reflects numerical reality and would also help to explain Elizabeth Buettner's use of the term Europeans. Her *Empire Families*, however, identifies one German in the form of the nanny used by Annette Beveridge who would offer an example of somebody who had become completely assimilated into English (or European society).[38]

Those Germans living in India and not working for the missions therefore essentially had two options open to them when it came to the maintenance of their German identity. First, they could basically assimilate into British society to the extent that they changed their nationality. This seemed inevitable for those living as isolated German individuals in a particular town, although Herr Weylandt in Agra tried to maintain something of his roots by the way in which he ran his house. Second, they could attempt to maintain their identity by gathering together with other Germans (as well as Austrians and Swiss), although such activity remained a pale imitation of the larger German communities in cities dotted throughout the world and even of the activities which took place in the German missionary stations, essentially because of numbers.

Whatever interaction the Germans in India may have had with wider European (i.e. British) society,[39] it seems clear that a distinct, if tiny, secular German community had evolved and become politicised by the outbreak of the First World War – as Stefan Manz has demonstrated – like their brethren in much larger German communities in other parts of the world, making this group a small cog in the machine of global German diasporic consciousness.

German missionary families

The family created an important sense of community for many German missionaries, reflecting the situation of fellow evangelists in other parts of the world. Emily J. Manktelow has described missionary families as 'the building blocks of an enterprise that spanned the globe in the nineteenth (and twentieth) century' in her recent British-centred study of this subject. She describes families as 'an integral component of the missionary enterprise, both as active agents on the global stage and as a force within the enterprise that shaped understandings and theories of mission itself'. She also speaks of 'missionary dynasties'.[40] More generally, Elizabeth Buettner has described 'the integral role of family practices in the reproduction of imperial rule and its personnel', offering a new perspective on the British in India.[41]

The Basel Mission's first inspector, Christian Blumhardt, believed that single males could best carry out the work of bringing the Gospel to 'the heathen' by sacrificing their lives entirely to the Lord, but this remained a complex problem for Basel because of the desire of so many of its missionaries to get married and the fact that many already had wives before they left Europe. In 1837 the Mission therefore formulated a set of rules regarding marriage which, most importantly, accepted wives on the condition that work remained at the centre of the missionary's life.[42] Waltraud Haas has viewed the attitude towards marriage as part of the process of marginalising women which characterised the male-centred Basel Mission and its leaders. She argues that this view lasted throughout our period, despite the fact that women increasingly played a role both as wives and self-standing employees.[43]

The Leipzig Mission does not appear to have regarded women as a problem in quite the same way as Basel did in its early days, but it did not regard marriage as a formality, trying to control the partners of its agents. The 1908 Leipzig regulations stated that: 'Although the wife of the missionary is not directly involved in missionary work, it is of the utmost importance for missionary work that she has the spiritual, mental and physical suitability to act as a capable helper for her husband in the work, privations and dangers of missionary life.' An 'inappropriate choice' could 'weaken' the ability of the missionary to carry out his work. Marriage, therefore, did not remain a 'mere private matter' which meant that those desiring to make such a move needed to receive approval from the Mission. The regulations also pointed to a preference for marriage to take place after arrival in India and 'under no circumstances before the passing of the Tamil exams'.[44] The Basel Mission instituted similar controls. When Andreas Köhler obtained permission to marry Emilie Layer, the daughter and sister of missionaries, he did so on condition that he continued to work in Keti and that he did not request more substantial accommodation, although in this case the marriage did not go ahead because of his untimely death.[45] Köhler's earlier nineteenth-century predecessor, the Basel-trained but

CMS-employed John Weitbrecht, knew exactly the role of his wife when writing to her father immediately after their marriage in Calcutta: 'I must send your dear circle a few lines, to assure you of my high regard for you, and of my gratitude towards our heavenly Father, who, in His wise and kind providence has sent your beloved M. from a distant land to Bengal to become my wife. One more fitted to be a real helpmeet to me in my glorious work, and to make me happy amidst all the trials of my arduous work could not be given.'[46]

While the German missionary societies might have eventually regarded marriage as a building block of their work, their desire to control the choice of wife pointed to a mistrust of romantic attachment, which might undermine the organisation's investment in training its employees in both Europe and India. This also suggests a mistrust of women per se, although we should remember that both Leipzig and Basel employed single women, especially as teachers. The Leipzig ordinances also point to the reason why many wives came from religious families.[47] Ultimately – as Haas suggests – in a nineteenth-century context, men remained at the centre of missionary activity, serving God first and having to choose the right kind of wife.

Despite (or because of) the severe Pietistic controls over marriage, many of the missionaries led happy lives once they found the correct wife even though, in many cases, they first met each other when the wife arrived in India and married shortly thereafter.[48] Despite the sacrifices which the women had made in leaving their families behind in Europe and the trials and tribulations they would face once in India, one account of the Gossner Mission implied a relatively luxurious existence: 'Many conscientious German housewives could hardly conceive that the wife of an Indian missionary neither cooks by herself nor helps with the washing.' While some chose to carry out housework out of thrift, every family had its own cook and a 'washer (dobi, a Hindu caste)'.[49] Nevertheless, the same account told the story of a woman betrothed to a missionary who died before she arrived in Calcutta. Although she subsequently married another missionary and gave birth to two children, they all perished.[50]

While the death of children remained normal both in India and Europe during the nineteenth century, many of the offspring of missionary marriages not only grew to adulthood but also, in some cases, moved into missionary work, creating the type of dynasties described by Manktelow. Rosmarie Gläsle has written of missionary daughters of the second, third and fourth generation. Those in the second generation included Debora Johanna Hoch Pfleiderer born in Mangalore in 1860 and marrying another missionary here, Mark Hoch, after his arrival in 1881. Gläsle counts their daughter Hanni Richter-Hoch, born in

Mangalore in 1884 as a missionary daughter of the third generation of this particular family. Finally Hanni Richter-Hoch married Theodor Samuel Ritter, another missionary, and gave birth to Mathilde Elise Gläsle-Ritter in Puttur in India in 1911 – who became a children's nurse (and would not face deportation during the Great War because she did not have German nationality), married another missionary, Hermann Gläsle, and is described by Rosmarie Gläsle as a mission bride of the fourth generation. The longevity of this missionary family in India seems remarkable, essentially beginning in 1854 when Gottlob Pfleiderer arrived in the country as the first businessman to work for the Basel Mission, followed five years later by his first wife Johanna Pfleiderer-Werner who married him instantly upon landing, and lasting until 1934 when Mathilde Elise Gläsle-Ritter travelled to China.[51]

Many other 'first generation' missionaries had children who moved into the same vocation. Richard Handmann, who spent 25 years in India working for Leipzig between 1862 and 1887, fathered two sons who moved into the same field.[52] Heinrich Paul Handmann, born in Trichinopoly in 1869, went back to Germany to study theology in Leipzig and Erlangen and then moved to the missionary seminar, returning to India in May 1894 for ordination but dying just six months later in Porayar.[53] Richard's second son, Otto Richard Handmann, lived a far longer life, born in Porayar in 1875 and dying in 1956. In between he returned to Germany to study theology in Erlangen, Greifswald and Leipzig, taking up a position as a vicar in Ispringen (Baden) and then progressing to the Leipzig missionary training seminar and returning for ordination in India in 1900, where he remained until deportation in 1916.[54] Meanwhile, another Leipzig missionary, Karl Pamperrien, who spent time in India from 1877–1920,[55] fathered two daughters who worked for Leipzig in India. Maria, born in Tanjore in 1881, worked as a teacher in several locations until deportation in 1915.[56] However, her elder sister, Martha, born in Tanjore in 1880, did not have the same dedication to missionary work. She took an administrative post in the Madura Diocese in 1904, but left missionary service in 1906.[57]

While families may have stood at the centre of the missionary communities which emerged, a minority of the children of the 'first generation' would have followed in the footsteps of their parents. Johannes Uffmann, born on 29 December 1878 in Purulia, the son of the Gossner missionary, Heinrich Uffmann, provides a good example. Johannes visited the imperial German Consulate in 1910 about his lapsed German nationality, having previously worked as a German government inspector in German East Africa. By 1910 he found employment as assistant manager of the Amandpur Timber and Trading Company of Caltutta, servicing its branch in Camp Dooroop, '75 English miles' from Lohardaga.[58]

Children remained at the centre of the German missionary families, whether or not they followed in the footsteps of their parents, which meant that their schooling became a key concern, as in the case of British children, whether or not they had missionary parents. In some cases, this meant that children returned home to Europe, as Manktelow has demonstrated in the case of those born to British parents, but some education certainly took place in India.[59] Once again, the missionary organisations took an interest such that the 1908 Leipzig ordinances contained a paragraph on 'The Education of Children' stating, in its opening clause, that responsibility 'lies in the first instance with the missionaries themselves'. While the regulations spoke of paying for children's education in Europe and also providing the costs for those who wished to sail to Germany when they reached adulthood, they do not mention any official educational provision in India, which presumably meant that most of the children would have experienced private tuition in view of the relatively small numbers who would have found themselves in any particular mission station.[60] The annual reports of the Basel Mission give an indication of the number of children likely to have found themselves in India. In 1905, the station with the largest number of adults from Europe, Mangalore, counted 22. Thirteen of these were married, but the 1905 annual report does not state the number of children there, which could not have totalled more than a few dozen at most. Meanwhile, the smaller stations at Utakamand and Kotageri each counted only one couple,[61] which would have made private schooling the only available form of education.

One solution to the isolation of these children away from others of German origin lay in the establishment of schools aimed at the offspring of the missionaries, which proved problematic.[62] In 1909, the Hermmansburg and Leipzig Missions developed an idea for the opening of a school in Kodaikanal for the education of children between the ages of 6 and 12. One Hermannsburg and two Leipzig missionaries therefore launched an appeal initially aimed at all missionaries but asking them to contact others who might have an interest. The appeal argued the school as desirable from the point of view of parents, mothers, the missionary occupations, the children and Christian education. Although primarily aimed at the children of missionaries, the proposed school would also educate 'eventually some children of German businessman etc. in India'. Those behind the project chose Kodaikanal because of its elevated and healthy position with a 'totally unique climate' in a wooded environment with eucalyptus trees and good transport links.

But, despite the professional marketing of the proposed school, it never seems to have materialised.[63]

German families may have played a central role in the missionary experience in India but, as with all else when considering the Germans here, we need to remember that they remained diasporic families. While, on the one hand, we can point to the lineage drawn up by Rosmarie Gläsle, many other families, of which the Gundert-Hesse's provide an excellent example, counted members scattered throughout Europe and India. Diaspora functions not simply on a national scale but also on a family level with members learning to deal with the inevitable separation, as Elizabeth Buettner has demonstrated in her study of British families in India.[64]

German missionary communities

Families helped to maintain German identities in India, especially in cases where both partners were German. While missionary organisations certainly constructed community, in which religion and an element of racial hierarchy played a role, to what extent did they form outposts of *Deutschtum*, as German nationalist writers claimed at the beginning of the twentieth century?

One way of answering this question involves analysing the origins of those who lived in missionary stations. While most Basel Mission employees originated in Württemberg, and while a large minority of those working for Leipzig came from Saxony,[65] these types of local origins do not preclude the development of German communities in the diaspora before the foundation of the German nation state in 1871. Regional-based German identities emerging from emigration from particular parts of Germany became the norm before nationalist organisations started claiming Germans abroad as part of the new German nation state. These emerged into a more unified German community as the Great War approached, helped by the fact that post-1870 migrants had already developed German consciousness before emigration, as Stanley Nadel demonstrated in his study of the Germans of New York.[66]

The Basel Mission had an especially complicated German identity. While the majority of its missionaries came from Württemburg, the second largest group originated from Switzerland, resulting in the type of multinational German identity found in Bombay at the start of the twentieth century. This situation would have emerged in the individual Basel mission stations counting a few European missionaries each. For example, the largest stations in Mangalore in 1845 housed the following: Johannes Ammann from Schaffhausen in Switzerland; Adam Bührer (Lohn, Switzerland); Christian and Frieda Greiner (Württemburg); Johann

Metz (Württemburg); Hermann Mögling (Württemburg); Georg and Julia Sutter (Baden); Christian and Pauline Weigle (Württemburg).[67] Forty years later, out of the 16 'European employees' working in Mangalore, nine came from Württemburg (including Stuttgart), one from Westfalia, one from Heilbronn, one from Bavaria, two from Switzerland, while two had birthplaces in India, as indicated by Table 4.1.[68]

German became the main language of communication of the Basel missionaries. The extent to which individuals used German dialects proves difficult to establish. In the case of the Mangalore station in 1885, for example, the Württemburgers probably spoke Swabian, the historic language of this region,[69] although they would have used a more standardised form of German to have communicated with Heinrich Altenmüller from Westfalia and the two Swiss employees. The use of German becomes more apparent by examining the documentation produced by all of the German-based missionary organisations. All of the regular magazines appeared, without exception, in this language, whichever organisation published them.[70] Similarly, the annual reports almost always used German (with a few exceptions in English and French issued by the Basel Mission from the 1850s to the 1870s) as did

Table 4.1 Origins of Basel Mission employees working in Mangalore in 1885

Name	Origin
Altenmüller, Heinrich	Möllenkotten, Westfalia
Dietz, Elisabeth	Württemburg
Dietz, Ernst	Heilbronn
Digel, Thomas	Neuffen, Württemburg
Franke, Johannes	Oberurbach, Württemburg
Funk, Johannes	Wüstenroth, Württemburg
Gräter, Benignus	Hall, Württemburg
Hauri, Rudolf	Hirschtal, Switzerland
Hirner, Gottlob	Böblingen, Württemburg
Hoch, Markus	Mangalore
Krapf, Johannes	Mattweil, Switzwerland
Layer, Johannes	Dharwar, Karnataka
Männer, August	Ansbach, Bavaria
Pfleiderer, Karl	Waiblingen, Württemburg
Staib, Ferdinand	Stuttgart
Stierlen, Friedrich	Wain, Württemburg

Sources: *Siebenzigster Jahresbericht der Evangelischen Missionsgesellschaft zu Basel auf 1. Juli 1885* (Basel, 1885), p. xvii; BMA/Q-30.3,5, Gebietslisten, Indien, Männer 1.

retrospective accounts and histories either of missionary work in general in India or of the activities of individual organisations over a specific time period. Virtually all of the missionaries wrote their own personal accounts in German, with the exception of those who worked for British missionary groups in the earlier nineteenth century.[71] Such publications needed to appear in German so that a German-speaking public in Europe would be inspired by the stories within them to financially contribute towards the work of the missions.[72] The annual reports often came with a list of donors and the sums which they contributed,[73] which, in the case of those Basel reports which appeared in English, included Britons.[74] The primary language of communication for German missionaries among themselves and with those who read their publications in Europe consisted of standardised German.

Nevertheless, a list of publications issued by the Basel Mission in south-western India in 1859 helps to establish the multilingual nature of missionary work. It points to two 'German monthly periodicals' in the form of *Der Evangelische Heidenbote* and the *Evangelisches Missions-Magazin*, together with several books on missionary work and 'a great variety of German tracts on Missionary Subjects, and collections of cheap prints, representing missionary scenes'. Interestingly, the list counts 12 publications in French, perhaps aimed at French speakers in Switzerland. They include annual reports and specific accounts of mission work. There then follow details of over 60 publications in English. These mainly consist of tracts, biblical stories translated into English, presumably for the purpose of use in schools, but also include Canarese grammar books.[75] A Basel report a decade later provides a statistical breakdown of the books printed and sold by the Mangalore 'Book and Tract Depository and Printing Press' which included 35,389 'religious books and tracts, including almanacs' in the following languages: 18,747 in Canarese; 15,754 in Malayalam; 653 in Tulu; 167 in English; and 68 in 'English and Canarese'. In addition, it sold 337 New Testaments in Tulu and Malayalam and 14,188 schoolbooks: 5,922 in Canarese; 8,217 in Malayalan; and 49 in English.[76] This simply confirms the multilingualism of the German missionaries. While they may have communicated with each other in German (or some type of German dialect) and also published their activities to supporters in Germany and Switzerland primarily in German, they used local languages as well as English to communicate with potential converts and pupils.

Most of them used English for the purpose of communicating with English authorities and missionaries and because they also carried out some educational instruction in English. At the same time, they also needed to master the languages of the locality in which they lived for the purpose of preaching and teaching. Returning to their status as elite migrants, those who worked in the mission stations consisted of multilingual cosmopolitans who had mastered at least three languages.

But what does this discussion about language reveal about German community? On the one hand, it suggests that the mission stations operated as outposts of German language use. In linguistic terms, the assumptions of the early twentieth-century nationalists make sense, not only because of the means of communication between missionaries here but also because of the diasporic nature of the groups. They remained in contact with the homeland (even though, in the case of the Basel headquarters, this lay in Switzerland) through both family correspondence and the publications issued to illustrate activity in the mission field, whether in India or any other part of the world. The fact that the mission employees used more than one language does not distinguish them from other generally accepted outposts of *Deutschtum* in the sense that immigrants usually adopted the language of the country in which they settled, especially through subsequent generations, although this happened more rapidly in some areas than others.[77] Peter Rosenberg and Harald Weydt demonstrated the complexity of German language use in Russia in the late nineteenth and early twentieth centuries involving bilingualism and the use of dialects from the areas in Franconia where the Germans originated, as well as the incorporation of Russian words.[78] In the case of the German missionaries in India, the use of English and local languages became essential, otherwise the mission stations could not carry out their tasks.

The primary aim of these stations was spreading Christianity. They formed part of the German diaspora because those leading them consisted of Germans (with some Swiss) offering a Lutheran Christianity, in the same way as English-based missions offered Anglicanism[79] or the Welsh Calvinistic Methodists' Foreign Missionary Society offered an alternative to Anglicanism, as Andrew J. May has demonstrated in the case of north-east India.[80] They therefore differ from the German urban settlements, even though Lutheranism and the establishment of a German church remained at the heart of many of these communities, as demonstrated by Stefan Manz but also by Frederick C. Luebke in the case of the USA. Luebke claimed that Germans in America during the nineteenth century 'identified themselves first of all as Catholics, Lutherans, Evangelicals, Mennonites, or Methodists, and only secondly (sometimes only inadvertently) as Germans'.[81] The mission stations clearly did not develop the whole gamut of ethnic organisations that the more secular settlements did because of their entirely religious focus. They also ultimately remained immune from the proselytising German diasporic nationalism of the late nineteenth and early twentieth centuries.

A closer examination of the main elements of the mission stations will help to further illustrate their nature, weighing up the relative importance of German and religious identity. The compounds in which the missionaries lived had evolved gradually during the course of the nineteenth century. A pictorial account published by the Basel Mission in 1860 tried to give a flavour of the types of locations in which the organisation operated. Much of this narrative actually focused upon the exotic landscape as well as providing local histories and descriptions of how Basel became involved in particular locations. A beautiful line drawing of the mission station in Kety in present-day Tamil Nadu came with a description of the few buildings present, which consisted, in the foreground, of 'the assembly hall of the native Christians and the homes of the two missionaries (Figure 4.2). The house located at the highest point on the right is newly built and contains the house of a third missionary and the sanatorium for sick Basel missionaries in East India. To the left in the foreground at the foot of the mountain lies the village of Kaity [sic].'[82] This points to the size of the smaller Basel mission stations, in this case next to a village. It does not seem to have included a church, with services presumably taking place in the assembly hall. The statistics provided by the 1860 Basel annual report listed '16 communicants', '3 non-communicants', '17 children', '12 Christian Day Scholars' and '8 vernacular schools' with 92 pupils,

Figure 4.2 The Basel mission house in Kety

pointing to the fact that gaining school pupils proved easier than conversions, although many parents remained indifferent partly because they saw 'no pecuniary advantage in learning' and partly because of 'their dread of the influence of the Christian books read by the children'.[83] The number of pupils reached just 24 in 1875.[84] Alwin Gehring worked for the Leipzig Mission in a station of a similar size to Kety located in Pudukotei, which included 'a mass of fruit trees especially mango and tamarind' together with 'bamboo bushes, which were not only nice to look at, but also provided material for the chapel and the school buildings'. Gehring stated that the school, which catered for only 12 pupils, existed 'in name only'. He claimed that the small number of Christians had to live in the mission garden because the local population would not rent them houses. 'Our poor chapel found itself within the town, wedged between the houses and the heathen.'[85]

Kety and Pudukotei provide examples of small mission stations in southern India located in a tropical rural idyll in the eyes of the missionaries. One account of Gossner mission stations from 1874 described them 'simply' as 'the living quarters of the missionaries and the place where the main church and main school of a missionary district lies'. They are 'the lanterns from which the light shines out into the heathen darkness'. This particular account believed that stations benefitted by being located in an important administrative centre, as in the case of Ranchi, Purulia (Figure 4.3) and Chaybassa.[86]

The Gossner Mission certainly built some impressive churches in these larger stations, although those in the smaller locations remained much more modest.[87] Ranchi, the headquarters of the Gossner Mission, provides an example of a station at the opposite end of the scale to Kety. A rather nationalistic report from 1899 by Hermann Dalton commented not only on the church there but also on the schools, which he claimed incorporated the entire age range from the most junior ages to the equivalent of German gymnasiums, which meant that school buildings formed an important feature.[88]

The Basel, Leipzig[89] and Breklum[90] missions also constructed similarly large stations. One of the most significant centres of Basel activity lay in Managalore. As early as 1845 it claimed 374 individuals. This figure included not just the Tulu parish (with 135) and the Tamil equivalent (15) but also four schools (including a seminary) with a total of 161 pupils and seven catechists and school teachers, to which the statistical breakdown also added the parish of Kadike, which meant another 56 people.[91] The Mangalore station became ever more sophisticated as the century progressed. In fact, by 1890, it operated in three locations in the city. The first of these, in the centre of Nireschwalla, had three compounds, with the largest of these housing the bookshop, warehouse,

Figure 4.3 The Gossner church in Purulia

school and missionary accommodation. The smaller compound here included '3 homes for native Christians, 1 catechist house and 1 schoolhouse'. The second area of Mangalore in which Basel operated lay near the 'upper bazar' and again divided into three sections, including a two-storey home, school buildings, an English school, accommodation for catechists and a girls' school. Finally, Balmattha, 'on a hill at the eastern end of the city', also included a missionary and catechist house as well as a seminary and a parish school.[92] The Managlore station also became involved in industrial activity, with a weaving unit and a book press.[93] By the middle of the 1880s, the number of people working for the Basel Mission in Mangalore had increased to 69, including 29 Europeans (15 men and 14 women) and 40 natives, including nine catechists, 12 Christian male teachers, eight Christian female teachers and seven 'heathen teachers and assistants'.[94]

At the same time as Lutheran activity evolved, the German Jesuits also spread their influence – although they often prove difficult to distinguish from other Europeans in multinational Roman Catholicism, making any idea of German identity highly problematic. Nevertheless, several German publications focused upon their activities – even though they worked with their co-religionists from other European states – based in two areas in particular, in Poona near Bombay and

Gujarat, although German Catholics also worked in Sind, Dhawar and Kathari.[95] Poona proved especially international, although in 1914 a total of 95 from 123 of the Jesuits were German subjects, 'the rest being Swiss, Luxemburgers and American citizens'. These, together with '37 secular priests and about 138 nuns', served a 'Catholic population in the Bombay-Poona Mission ... reckoned at about 42,000'.[96] It does seem that, in some cases, some concentration of Germans took place in particular mission stations which mirrored those set up by other denominations. For example, a station emerged in the village of Kendel in Maratha where the missionaries initially stayed in tents, although in 1879 a chapel and living quarters opened, followed by an 'emergency chapel and accommodation for the poor' in nearby Malan. 'In the year 1879 207 heathen were christened in the villages of Large and Small Kendel, Malan, Khelde, Pathre, Nimburi, Amulner and Gonegaon.' Seven German fathers actually worked in the Kendel station during its first six years of existence, although it appears that native priests took over there because the Germans succumbed to disease and climate.[97] This development indicates the multinational nature of Jesuit activity but also points to a level of equality between natives and Germans. This internationalism also becomes clear in Gujarat, run by German Jesuits from 1858 but employing native-born priests in the stations established there in the decades which followed.[98] The multi-ethnic nature of the Catholic missions, parishes and schools raises questions over the German nature of Catholic activity to an even greater extent than in the case of the Lutheran missions. This assignation partly came from the persecution which resulted from the First World War, when the Indian authorities interned Catholic Jesuits who possessed German nationality and therefore imposed a national identity upon them. This in turn led to the appearance of two major publications which came to their defence.[99] Although *Die katholischen Missionen*, a German publication examining Roman Catholic missionary work throughout the world, had appeared from 1894, it did not concern itself purely with the activities of those with German origins and neither did the purely Indian-focused *Echo aus Indien*, which ran 1912–14. At the same time, German Catholics took the lead in some of the work carried out in India, especially in the opening of schools and colleges.[100] Catholic missionary activity remained even more multi-ethnic than that of Protestants.

Before reaching any final conclusions about the German nature of Roman Catholic and Lutheran missionary activity, a statistical snapshot from the late nineteenth and early twentieth centuries offers some further perspectives on this issue. So far, much of the discussion has focused upon the Germans themselves rather than those with whom they interacted. The figures gathered together for the propaganda produced for German speakers in Europe focused especially upon the size of the congregations which had developed in the wider world. We can extrapolate these from annual reports. In 1910, for example, the Leipzig Mission employed 56 Europeans in India consisting of a mixture of missionaries, female teachers, doctors and nurses. In addition, it listed 29 natives who worked for it, all described as country preachers, together with 69 catechists. The same report mentioned 40 stations, including eight controlled by the 'Swedish diocese'. It claimed a 'soul count' which ranged from 54 in Panrutti to 2,155 in Pandur, giving an Indian total of 21,981. None of the stations counted more than a handful of employees. Furthermore, the same report mentioned 290 schools and claimed to educate 8,695 boys and 3,045 girls with a significant percentage of the pupils described as 'not Christian' (6,573 boys and 1,664 girls).[101] An examination of Basel would point to a similar picture,[102] while Breklum carried out activity on a smaller scale.[103] The Gossner Mission, meanwhile, claimed 91,468 people by 1910 as a result of its work among the Kols.[104]

What do these statistics tell us about *Deutschtum* in India? What relationship exists between the European missionaries and the congregations they established? The tens or hundreds of thousands of Indians whom the missions claimed seem a long way from the few hundred Germans who lay at their heart. The idea that the wider congregations formed German communities appears absurd. Those Germans who lay at their centre would have had little contact with the mass of Indians which the European headquarters claimed in their statistics, certainly in the case of the Gossner Mission. On the other hand, it seems feasible that, for example, the 18 missionaries and their 15 wives in Mangalore could collectively know all of the 2,124 parishioners claimed in 1895, although to these we also need to add 1,077 schoolchildren.[105] Broken down in this way into individual mission stations, there appears the possibility of direct contact. Even so, this does not take us any further in our analysis of the German nature of the mission stations.

Ultimately, we can suggest that they remained German at heart because their headquarters lay in German-speaking Europe and because of the fact that their core employees consisted of Germans. While they did not constitute beacons of *Deutschtum* in the political sense which the early twentieth-century nationalists claimed, they played the same game of empire building as the European states which expanded during the course of the nineteenth century. The production of maps, the claiming of particular areas of India by individual missions, together with the assertion that tens of thousands of people somehow belonged to the missions – almost in a sense of owing some sort of allegiance – mirrors the game played by the great powers. This discourse becomes clear not simply in the annual reports which the missions issued, together with lists of the numbers and mission stations which they claimed, but also in some of the broader publications they issued. *Umschau auf dem Gebiete der evangelisch-lutherischen Mission in Ostindien*, put together by the leading Leipzig missionary Richard Handmann, which comes with two maps, precisely illustrates this process.[106] As does the atlas of Basel missionary activity by the inspector of the time, the Stuttgart-born Joseph Josenhans, which covers the power of the Basel Mission throughout the world.[107] Numerous volumes constructed narratives which began by outlining the condition of an area over which a particular mission took control before the mission arrived, partly for the purpose of suggesting its primitive nature, and then proceeded to describe the growth of the mission stations.[108] This game also operated on a national basis, focusing not simply upon those areas of India controlled by German missions but the entire range of missions which existed in the country, implying that while the British may have had political control, they did not have spiritual authority.[109]

German racial or multiracial religious communities?

We might therefore view the mission stations as playing the role of the hill stations in British political control as demonstrated by Judith T. Kenny,[110] at least in German missionary discourse. They remained islands of *Deutschtum* (albeit on a tiny scale, counting a handful of people) and exercised control over a vast expanse of territory. However, like British imperial control, these stations could only function if they utilised natives as active agents in a similar way to state structures and trading companies.[111] While these types of relationships meant that Europeans exercised control at the top of the scale, they could not function without the use of Indians. On the one hand the missions might appear to operate as a racial hierarchy, yet, on the other they also suggest multi-ethnicity, especially when Indians worked as pastors.

Heike Liebau has written the seminal study on the role of Indians in the growth of German missionary enterprise with her study on the Tranquebar Mission. She recognises the difficulty of categorising the nature of these relationships when she states that 'missionary work always proved to be a complex, often long-lasting and direct encounter between representatives of different religions and cultures in the process of which new social and religious values and norms were negotiated'. She asserts that we should not view the Indians as 'passive ... servants' but as actors in the process of negotiation between the missionaries and natives.[112] Both Liebau and Henriette Bugge, focusing on the activities of French and Danish missionaries in the Tamil speaking area of South Arcot, recognise the different roles fulfilled by Indians, which essentially follow the categorisations constructed by the mission groups of the time, including country priets, catechists and schoolmasters – although by the end of the nineteenth century, as Jeffrey Cox has recognised in his study of British and American missionaries in the Punjab, the organisations had also begun to use native women. Bugge has written that while the missionaries in her study spent some of their time 'on sermons and baptism ... they were also administrators, handling the money which came from the home board, supervising the building of churches and schools, and employing and educating numerous native-born intermediaries between the mission and the congregation'. Although Liebau, Bugge and Cox do not dismiss racial hierarchies, their perspective on missionary work recognises some element of equality, if only for practical purposes.[113]

Other studies of missionary work in India focus more upon the role of racism and orientalism in the relationship between Europeans and Indians, reflecting the wider racial lens with which Europeans viewed India and its people.[114] They stress the distinction made by the missionaries about those with whom they came into contact,[115] with Andreas Nehring providing perhaps the most notable German-based example of this approach in his study of the Leipzig Mission.[116]

We are not concerned at this stage with offering a full deconstruction of the interethnic interaction and the role of racism in the encounter of Germans with India,[117] but rather with establishing whether racial hierarchy or ethnic equality characterised the way in which the German missionaries viewed their converts, parishioners and Indian co-workers. In one obvious way a hierarchy existed, which becomes clear in any examination of the statistical material compiled by any of the missionary groups. For example, the Basel Mission report of 1855 contains a table of its activities which, moving from left to right, reveals both ethnic and gendered hierarchies. Under a heading of 'European Agency' come 'Brethren' followed by 'Sisters'. There then follows a column for catechists and then another main heading for schoolmasters, divided into Christians and heathens.[118] This categorisation would continue in subsequent reports until the end of the nineteenth century with the mission also dividing schoolchildren into Christians and heathens.[119] The Leipzig Mission utilised a similar categorisation. The 1910 annual report, for example, divided its mission workers into Europeans, who totalled 56 in 1910, with males listed first (24) followed by female teachers (seven), those working for the Swedish diocese (13) and those on leave in the 'homeland'. There then follows a list of 29 native workers in India. A separate table uses a ten-point hierarchy as follows:

missionaries; female mission teachers; native pastors; candidates; catechists and catechist helpers; evangelists; bible women; parish elders; and lower church servants. Interestingly, this report divided pupils into 'Lutheran Christians, other Christians, and non-Christians', with the gender hierarchy remaining.[120] Finally, the Breklum groupings operated in the following way: European brothers and sisters (men followed by women); catechists; and teachers (Christian male and female and heathen). Schoolchildren came under the headings of Christian and heathen male and female.[121]

These tables produced by three of the major missionary organisations clearly operated upon a gendered and age hierarchy with males preceding females followed by boys and girls. At the same time, the ethnic/racial hierarchy becomes clear. Europeans always came first even though, in the case of Leipzig (as well as Gossner), Indians could serve a pastors. Belief also played a role with Lutheran Christians at the top followed by other Christians with non-believers at the bottom. As Liebau has established, this hierarchy had a long history.[122]

What does the work carried out by natives and their relationship with and perception by Europeans say about the ethnic and racial hierarchy? A 1914 list of 44 Indian 'mission servants' who worked for the Leipzig station in Pandur included four catechists, five assistant catechists and 28 teachers. The list also gives their length of service. While some had only worked for the Mission for a few years, the assistant catechists V. A. Paul and N. S. David had served it for 35 and 36 years respectively, while six others had found employment for over 20 years. The average period of service for the 39 individuals for whom we have length of employment stood at almost ten years. Like Europeans, many Indians devoted their lives to missionary work. The list also came with comments against each name, most of which generally praised the work of the 'mission servants' with the phrase 'good teacher' appearing on several occasions. Others did not receive such positive praise. Two received the description of demonstrating intent but 'little success'.[123] As in the case of the European servants of the missions, the natives also had to follow a set of rules, as indicated by the 25-page document with 83 clauses printed by the Leipzig Mission in 1906.[124]

Along with teachers, the most significant role played by Indians consisted of catechists, essentially the bridges between the European missionaries and those they wished to convert. The 29 Indian employees of Leipzig in 1910, for example, served this role despite their description as *Landprediger*.[125] In 1875, the Basel Mission counted 164 native employees including 95 teachers and 49 catechists. One account of the Gossner Mission described the catechists as 'national helpers in the truest sense of the word'. While they had received a basic education, they obtained further training from the missionaries and needed to pass an exam, and still others engaged fully with ethical issues. Although some worked in fixed locations, others carried out tasks which involved travel, whether this meant preaching, baptising or visiting the sick. When travelling:

> Clothed with the national chadder over which they wear a light, white jacket, shoes on naked feet and with a long bamboo stick in hand they set out either alone or in twos over mountain and valley through wild forests and gushing rivers in order to bring peace. On their shoulder they carry a linen bag which contains a spiritual tool: the bible, together with individual books from the bible, several catechisms and the volume in which they have written comprehensible questions and answers to the main teachings provided by the missionaries. And so they move from one location to another holding conversations everywhere and propagating through speech the gospel. As natives, who have previously lived mostly in heathen darkness, they understand the best places to meet.[126]

Apart from the Christian imperialist language which this extract uses, its other main characteristic is the fact that it places the catechists in their own landscape, which would clearly have given them an advantage over Europeans, as they worked amongst the people from whom they had originated. Patras provides an example of a Gossner catechist. Born as a 'heathen' he had to 'earn his bread' from an early age. 'He had already learnt to read and write as a heathen.' He originally worked for 'social-political agitators' but met 'missionary Lorbeer, who busied him as a cow hand in the construction of the Lohardagga station. He did so well here, however, and demonstrated such an aptitude to work for the parish that he was hired as a catechist in 1873.'[127] Tandvaran Pilley, who took the Christian name of Stephan, began his path towards Christianity and becoming a catechist for the Basel Mission in Myavaram after attending English school, where he first came across the scriptures, and despite strong opposition from his aunt who, however, subsequently also converted to Christianity.[128] Basel developed an organised way of training catechists from the middle of the nineteenth century, involving classes and concluding with preaching tours.[129]

It seems clear that Indians also became pastors, not simply in Roman Catholicism but also for the Basel and Leipzig Mission and, especially, for Gossner. In 1855, one member of the catechist class in Mangalore displayed such promise that 'at the request of the Home Committee' he was 'sent to Europe in order to be further instructed in our Missionary College at Basel'.[130] In fact, he followed in the footsteps of Anandrao Kaundinya who underwent conversion in 1843, travelled to Basel, became ordained in Leonberg in 1851 and then returned to work as a missionary in Mangalore.[131] By the beginning of the twentieth century,

Leipzig had also begun to employ Indians as pastors. For example, N. Dēwasagājam took over responsibility for the small community in Rājapuram having previously held charge over Purselbākum. His successor there consisted of C. Pākiam.[132] But it appears that the Gossner Mission had the most trust in native-born pastors. By 1894, it employed 18 Indians in this position, with some parishes experiencing several generations of leadership by Indian clerics (Figure 4.4).[133] They included Paulus Remo, who came from 'an affluent, reputable heathen family in Jargo. Over twelve years ago he turned to Christianity after reading the New Testament. From that time onwards he led the Jargo parish until the year 1866 when brother Onasch', presumably a German, took over responsibility, suggesting a genuine equality between Europeans and Indians (Figure 4.5).[134]

While relatively small numbers of natives became pastors, they played a more significant role as teachers, both men and women. In January 1865, for example, when the Basel Mission in India employed 48 brethren and 31 sisters, it also utilised the services of 61 'catechists and schoolmasters', five 'native schoolmistresses' and 19 'heathen schoolmasters'.[135] Meanwhile, in 1910, when Leipzig counted 56 European missionaries and 29 country preachers in India, the number of native male teachers

Figure 4.4 Gossner Mission parish elders, catechists and clergymen

Figure 4.5 Indian Gossner Mission pastors

stood at 415, together with 115 females, teaching a total of 6,745 boys and 2,546 girls,[136] pointing to their importance in education and to the fact that they worked in a wide range of locations incorporating not solely the mission station but also the villages within each parish.[137]

In 1912, Mauelmedu Mathusamy wrote a 'short history' of his life for the Leipzig Mission. Born in 1863 to Christian peasant parents in Vaiyolagam near Pudukkottai, Richard Handmann baptised him in the following year. He then underwent an education which lasted from primary school through to the seminary. He continued his studies in 1887 and took up a school teaching post in Travancore in the same year, where he remained until 1892. He then moved to teach in the Leipzig seminary in India. In this particular case, educational work acted as a stepping stone on the path towards ordination and work as a pastor.[138] Despite the tone of his life history as a biblical parable, all was not well in the world of Leipzig teachers. In September 1902, 14 of them sent a printed memorial written in reverential terms but, nevertheless, complaining about their rates of pay.[139]

While some level of equality may have existed in the operation of the mission, the missionaries adapted local practices, used by both higher castes and the British, in utilising servants,[140] as explained by Alwin Gehring. 'Because of the strictly caste controlled labour division as well as the climatic conditions, the household of a European necessitates a considerable number of servants.'[141] The Gossner mission house in Govindpur, for example, remained habitable because 'all of the larger rooms have a powerful fan (pantah), on the ceiling, which is pulled with a string by a coolie outside on the veranda'.[142] Gehring constructed a servant hierarchy, at the bottom of which stood the 'boy', who had to help with a variety of tasks. Above him stood 'an ox or horse servant and a gardener'. Others helped with cooking. While this may have suggested that missionary wives had little to do, Gehring pointed out that, on the contrary, they led the household and had the task of maintaining order. Gehring also addressed the religious and ethical issues raised by the Christian employment of servants and pointed to fact that the missionaries tended to hire 'Christian pariahs' who would have positive experiences of 'education' and 'cleanliness' in the German missionary household and stood 'higher than the heathen pariahs'. Gehring argued that those Indian servants who worked for Leipzig missionaries were treated in a Christian manner.[143]

German communities?

The German-led parishes and the use of servants seems a long way from the German communities sought out by those nationalists trying to incorporate the Germans in India into the German diaspora at the beginning of the twentieth century. But both the use of servants and the Christian leadership confirm the position of the Germans in India as elites. As the nineteenth century progresses, so does their position as managers, directing operations from the mission station, with much work carried out on the ground by Indians.

Several salient points have emerged about German communities in India in the century leading up to the Great War. First, the type of concentrations which emerged in the states where Germans counted significant numbers could not materialise in India because of the small numbers who lived here. The only place where this really occurred was Bombay just before the outbreak of war. Even there, the organisations which emerged remained pale imitations of those which developed in other parts of the world, and could only function if they included Austrians and Swiss. As Katharine Zitelmann revealed, some Germans continued the traditions of their homeland in the domestic sphere even though they had taken up British nationality.

The issue of the missionary groups as German raises some complex problems. On the one hand, they clearly have Germans at their heart. They provide leadership, whether through initially establishing the mission stations and surrounding parishes or subsequently administering them. They might form part of the de facto German diaspora of the early twentieth century but their primary allegiance lies with Christianity, albeit of a Lutheran variety, and never to the newly formed German nation state which emerged from 1871. Apart from the nature of their religion, their *Deutschtum* also exists in their language use.

But language offers a way into the multi-ethnic nature of the German missionaries who had to master both English and Indian languages in order to carry out their work. In this sense they resemble more conventional diasporas who also need at least some handle on local languages wherever they settle. But interethnic interaction remains central to the work of the missionary in a way that it does not for the employment-focused and geographically concentrated working-class German migrants of the nineteenth century. Germans in Chicago in the second half of the nineteenth century, for example, founded a whole series of ethnic organisations aimed primarily at the preservation of German culture, encompassing work, education and politics.[144]

German-led missionary communities therefore remained multi-ethnic by nature: otherwise they could not function. They also remained hierarchical because of the fact that Germans established and subsequently led them. Indians could enter into the inner echelons of the hierarchical structure through training, and as the nineteenth century progressed they increasingly took up positions as pastors. But, even then, the tables produced in the Basel and Leipzig annual reports did not dispense with ethnic hierarchies.

German community therefore exists in India before the First World War, but it remains different from that found in the mass settlements in other parts of the world. While nationalism played a role in the final years of peace, the main driving force remained Lutheranism, which led to the development of complex ethnic relationships. The missionaries only finally become German when the Government of India labelled them as such after the outbreak of the Great War.

Notes

1. Stefan Manz, *Constructing a German Diaspora: The 'Greater German Empire', 1871–1914* (London, 2014).
2. See, for example: Gerd Stricker, ed., *Deutsche Geschichte im Osten Europas: Rußland* (Berlin, 1997); Dittmar Dahlmann and Ralph Tuchtenhagen, eds, *Zwischen Reform und Revolution: Die Deutschen an der Wolga 1860–1917* (Essen,1994); and Victor Dönninghaus, *Die Deutschen in der Moskauer Gesellschaft: Symbiose und Konflikte (1494–1941)* (Munich, 2002).
3. See, for example: Stanley Nadel, *Little Germany: Ethnicity, Religion, and Class in New York City, 1845–80* (Chicago, IL, 1990); Frederick C. Luebke, *Germans in the New World: Essays in the History of Immigration* (Chicago, IL, 1990).
4. Gerhard P. Bassler, edited and translated by Heinz Lehmann, *The German Canadians, 1750–1937* (St John's, Newfoundland, 1986).

5   Frederick C. Luebke, *Germans in Brazil: A Comparative History of Cultural Conflict during World War I* (Baton Rouge, LO, 1987).
6   Ronald C. Newton, *German Buenos Aires, 1900–1933: Social Change and Cultural Crisis* (London, 1977).
7   Jürgen Tampke, *The Germans in Australia* (Cambridge, 2006).
8   Katharina Tietze de Soto, *Deutsche Einwanderung in die chilenische Provinz Concepción 1870–1930* (Frankfurt, 1999).
9   Panikos Panayi, *German Immigrants in Britain during the Nineteenth Century, 1815–1914* (Oxford, 1995).
10 Manz, *Constructing a German Diaspora*, pp. 176–215.
11 Heike Liebau, *Cultural Encounters in India: The Local Co-workers of the Tranquebar Mission, 18th to 19th Centuries* (New Delhi, 2013).
12 Karl Graul, *Reise nach Ostindien über Palästina und Egypten von Juli 1849 bis April 1853*, Part 3, *Die Westküste Indiens* (Leipzig, 1854), pp. 104, 326, note 43.
13 Hans von Koenigsmarck, *Die Engländer in Indien: Reiseeindrücke* (Berlin, 1909), pp. 58–61.
14 Hermann Dalton, *Indische Reisebriefe* (Gütersloh, 1899), p. 350.
15 Richard Garbe, *Indische Reiseskizzen* (Berlin, 1889), p. 36.
16 For more on this group, see Gerhard Weidenfeller, *VDA, Verein für das Deutschtum im Ausland: Allgemeiner Deutscher Schulverein (1881–1918): Ein Beitrag zur Geschichte des deutschen Nationalismus und Imperialismus im Kaiserreich* (Bern, 1976).
17 Allgemeiner Deutscher Schulverein zur Erhaltung des Deutschtums im Auslande, ed., *Handbuch des Deutschtums im Auslande, nebst einem Adressbuch der deutschen Auslandschulen, zwei Kartenbeilagen und fünf Kartenskizzen* (Berlin, 1906), pp. 213–16; Manz, *Constructing a German Diaspora*, p. 115. For services in Calcutta, see EZA 5/3132 including: Hagemann to Evangelischen Kirchenausschuß, 6 November, 1909; and Bericht des Missionars P. O. Hertzenberg über Arbeit unter den Deutschen in Calcutta, 12 January 1909. For more on the importance of German seamen's homes, see Christiaan Engberts, 'The rise of associational activity: early twentieth century German sailors' homes and schools in Antwerp and Rotterdam', *Immigrants and Minorities*, vol. 32 (2014), pp. 293–314.
18 Alfred Geiser, *Deutsches Reich und Volk: Ein nationales Handbuch* (Munich, 1910), p. 560.
19 Alfred Wirth, 'Das Deutschtum in Asien', *Deutsche Erde*, vol. 1 (1902), p. 138.
20 Friedrich Wilhelm Mohr and Walter von Hauff, *Deutsche im Ausland* (Breslau, 1923), pp. 262–3.
21 AA/R62397, extract from *Tägliche Rundschau*, 11 November 1904.
22 Manz, *Constructing a German Diaspora*, p. 116.
23 AA/R1480884, Kaiserlich Deutsches Konsulat, Bombay to Reichskanzler Dr Bethmann Hollweg, 15 February 1911. For celebrations of the Kaiser's birthday, see Manz, ibid., pp. 198–200.
24 Oscar Bongard, *Die Reise des Deutschen Kronprinzen durch Ceylon und Indien* (Berlin, 1911), p. 64.
25 AA/R1480884, Meurer an seine Majestät den Kaiser Berlin, 30 September 1908.
26 See, respectively: Panayi, *German Immigrants*, pp. 145–99; Newton, *German Buenos Aires*, pp. 3–31; Nadel, *Little Germany*, pp. 91–162.
27 Manz, *Constructing a German Diaspora*, p. 115.
28 Daniela Luigia Caglioti, *Vita parallele: Una minoranza protestante nell'Italia dell'Ottocento* (Bologna, 2006).
29 For intermarriage, see Chapter 5.
30 'Die nichtindische Bevölkerung Bombays', in Graul, *Westküste Indiens*, pp. 90–104.
31 Ibid., p. 102.
32 Garbe, *Indische Reiseskizzen*, p. 239.
33 Ibid., pp. 205–54.

34 Hermann von Schlagintweit-Sakülünski, *Reisen in Indien und Hochasien Basirt auf die Resultate der wissenschaftlichen Mission von H, A und R von Schlagintweit ausgefuhrt in den Jahren 1854–1858*, Volume 1, *Indien* (Jena, 1869), pp. 43–6; Emil Schlagintweit, *Indien in Wort und Bild*, Vol. 1 (Leipzig, 1880), pp. 16–18.
35 David Arnold, 'The white town of Calcutta under the rule of East India Company', *Modern Asian Studies*, vol. 34 (2000), pp. 307–31.
36 See, for example: Michael Edwardes, *Bound to Exile: The Victorians in India* (London, 1969); Dennis Kincaid, *British Social Life in India, 1608–1937* (London, 1973); and David Gilmour, *The Ruling Caste: Imperial Lives in the Victorian Raj* (London, 2005).
37 Harald Fischer-Tiné, *Low and Licentious Europeans: Race, Class and 'White Subalternity' in Colonial India* (Hyderabad, 2009).
38 Elizabeth Buettner, *Empire Families: Britons and Imperial India* (Oxford, 2004), p. 54. See also Elizabeth Buettner, 'Problematic spaces, problematic races: defining Europeans in late colonial India', *Women's History Review*, vol. 9 (2000), pp. 277–98, which mentions some hostility towards non-British Europeans, but the term overwhelmingly refers to those of British ancestry. Satoshi Mizutani, *The Meaning of White: Race, Class, and the 'Domiciled Community' in British India 1858–1930* (Oxford, 2011), also essentially refers to the British, emphasising their numerical dominance.
39 See Chapter 5.
40 Emily J. Manktelow, *Missionary Families: Race, Gender and Generation on the Spiritual Frontier* (Manchester, 2013), pp. 2, 208, 210.
41 Buettner, *Empire Families*, p. 2.
42 Waltraud Haas, *Erlitten und Erstritten: Der Befreiungsweg von Frauen in der Basler Mission 1816–1966* (Basel, 1994), pp. 21–6.
43 Ibid., pp. 26–55.
44 *Missions-Ordnung: Zusammenstellung wichtiger Bestimmungen für die Missionare der Evangelisch-Lutherischen Mission in Indien* (Leipzig, 1908), pp. 12–13.
45 Willi Bidermann, *Missionar in den Blauen Bergen: Andreas Köhlers Weg nach Indien* (Bietigheim-Bissingen, 1997), pp. 129–32.
46 Mary Weitbrecht, *Memoir of the Rev. J. J. Weitbrecht: Compiled from his Journals and Letters by his Widow* (London, 1854), p. 101.
47 As discussed in Chapter 2.
48 Dagmar Konrad, *Missionsbräute: Pietistinnen des 19. Jahrhunderts in der Basler Mission* (Münster, 2001), pp. 161–90.
49 L. Nottrott, *Die Gossner'sche Mission unter den Kolhs: Bilder aus dem Missionsleben* (Halle, 1874), p. 311.
50 Ibid., pp. 316–18.
51 Rosmarie Gläsle, *Pauline und ihre Töchter: 'Missionsbräute' als lebenslange Weggefährtinnen Basler Missionare in Indien und China* (Erlangen, 2012), pp. 45–249.
52 www.lmw-mission.de/de/missionar-82.html, Leipziger Missionswerk, Richard Handmann, accessed 17 July 2015.
53 www.lmw-mission.de/de/missionar-133.html, Leipziger Missionswerk, Heinrich Paul Handmann, accessed 17 July 2015.
54 www.lmw-mission.de/de/missionar-148.html, Leipziger Missionswerk, Otto Richard Handmann, accessed 17 July 2015.
55 www.lmw-mission.de/de/missionar-142.html, Leipziger Missionswerk, Karl Pamperrien, accessed 17 July 2015.
56 www.lmw-mission.de/de/missionar-169.html, Leipziger Missionswerk, Maria Pamperrien, accessed 17 July 2015.
57 www.lmw-mission.de/de/missionar-170.html, Leipziger Missionswerk, Martha Pamperrien, accessed 17 July 2015.
58 AA/R140879, Kaiserlich Deutsches Generalkonsulat für Britisch Indien und die Kolonie Ceylon an dem Reichskanzler, Staatsminister Dr. von Bethmann Hollweg, 22 June 1910.

59 Manktelow, *Missionary Families*, pp. 100–7, 113–22. See also: Buettner, *Empire Families*, pp. 72–109, 146–87; and Marie Gundert Hesse, *Marie Hesse: Ein Lebensbild in Briefen und Tagebüchern* (Frankfurt am Main, 1977), pp. 19–35.
60 *Missions-Ordnung*, pp. 17–18.
61 *Neunzigster Jahresbericht der Evangelischen Missions-Gesellschaft zu Basel auf 1. Juli 1905* (Basel, 1905), pp. 104–5.
62 Manktelow, *Missionary Families*, pp. 100–7, describes British attempts.
63 AA/R62397, Kaiserlich Deutsches Generalkonsulat für Britisch Indien und die Kolonie Ceylon an dem Reichskanzler, Staatsminister Dr. von Bethmann Hollweg, 6 September 1909; AFST/LMW/II.31.1.188, Aufruf zur Gruendung einer deutschen Schule (besonders fuer Missionskinder) in Kodaikanal, Mitte August 1909.
64 Buettner, *Empire Families*, pp. 110–45.
65 See Tables 2.1 and 2.2.
66 Nadel, *Little Germany*, pp. 155–62.
67 *Magazin für die neueste Geschichte der evangelischen Missions- und Bibelgesellschaften*, Viertes Quartalheft, 1845, p. 21; BMA/Q-30.3,5, Gebietslisten, Indien, Männer 1; BMA/Q-30.3,5, Gebietslisten, Indien, Frauen.
68 Fourteen of the males working here were married, but it has not proved possible to establish the origins of their wives.
69 As an introduction to Swabian, see, for example, Charles V. J. Russ, 'Swabian', in Russ, ed., *The Dialects of Modern German: A Linguistic Survey* (Abingdon, 2013), pp. 337–63.
70 See the full list of these in the Bibliography.
71 The most obvious examples here are: Karl Benjamin Leupolt, *Further Recollections of an Indian Missionary* (London, 1884); and Weitbrecht, *Memoir*. The latter, however, also includes translations made by his wife, Mary.
72 Julia Ulrike Mack, *Menschenbilder: Anthropologische Konzepte und stereotype Vorstellungen vom Menschen in der Publizistik der Basler Mission 1816–1914* (Zurich, 2014).
73 See, for example, *Vierundvierzigster Jahresbericht der evangelischen Missionsgesellschaft zu Basel auf 1. Juli 1859* (Basel, 1859), pp. 137–52.
74 See, for example, German Evangelical Mission, *The Fifteenth Report of the German Evangelical Mission on the Western Coast of India* (Mangalore, 1855), pp. 58–64.
75 Basel German Evangelical Missionary Society, *Report of the Basel German Evangelical Missionary Society. Forty-Fourth Year. 1859. Twentieth Report of the German Evangelical Mission in South-Western India* (Mangalore, 1860), pp. 8–10.
76 Basel German Evangelical Missionary, *Report of the Basel German Evangelical Mission in South-Western India for 1870* (Mangalore, 1871), pp. 28–9.
77 See the discussion in Luebke, *Germans in Brazil*, pp. 57–8.
78 Peter Rosenberg and Harald Weydt, 'Sprachen und Sprachgemeinschaft der Wolgadeutschen', in Dahlmann and Tuchtenhagen, *Zwischen Reform und Revolution*, pp. 306–46.
79 For a broad-brush approach, see Bernard Palmer, *Imperial Vineyard: The Anglican Church in India under the Raj from the Mutiny to Partition* (Lewes, 1999).
80 Andrew J. May, *Welsh Missionaries and British Imperialism: The Empire of Clouds in North-East India* (Manchester, 2012).
81 Manz, *Constructing a German Diaspora*, pp. 176–226; Frederick. C. Luebke, *Bonds of Loyalty: German Americans and World War I* (De Kalb, IL, 1974), pp. 34–5.
82 Evangelische Missions-Gesellschaft, *Album der Basler Mission: Bilder aus Indien* (Basel, 1860).
83 Basel German Evangelical Missionary Society, *Report of the Basel German Evangelical Missionary Society. Forty-Fourth Year*, pp. 56–9.
84 *Sechzigster Jahresbericht der evangelischen Missionsgesellschaft zu Basel auf 1. Juli 1875* (Basel, 1875), p. xxxiii.
85 Alwin Gehring, *Erinnerungen aus dem Leben eines Tamulenmissionars* (Leipzig, 1906), p. 97.
86 Nottrott, *Die Gossner'sche Mission unter den Kolhs*, p. 271.

87 H. Kausch and F. Kahn, *50 Bilder aus der Gossnerschen Kols-Mission mit erläuterndem Text und Karte* (Berlin, 1894), pp. 51–66.
88 Dalton, *Indische Reisebriefe*, pp. 141–2.
89 For an indication of the scale of Leipzig activity and a description of the stations which this group ran, see, for example: E. R. Baierlein, *Die evangelische lutherische Mission in Ostindien* (Leipzig, 1874), pp. 182–237; Richard Handmann, *Umschau auf dem Gebiete der evangelisch-lutherischen Mission in Ostindien* (Leipzig, 1888), pp. 9–53; Richard Handmann, *Die Evangelisch-lutherische Tamulen-Mission in der Zeit ihrer Neubegründung* (Leipzig, 1903), pp. 185–286; and *Evangelisches-Lutherisches Missionsblatt*, 15 July 1875, pp. 210–52.
90 For Breklum activity and mission stations, see: *Bericht über die Arbeit der Schleswig-Holsteinischen Evangelisch Lutherischen Missionsgesellschaft für die Zeit vom 1. April 1900 bis dahin 1901* (Breklum, 1901); Otto Waack, *Indische Kirche und Indien-Mission*, Vol. 1, *Die Geschichte der Jeypore-Kirche und der Breklumer Mission (1876–1914)* (Erlangen, 1994).
91 *Magazin für die neueste Geschichte der evangelischen Missions- und Bibelgesellschaften*, Viertes Quartalheft, 1845, p. 96.
92 Evangelische Missionsgesellschaft (Basel), *Verzeichnis der Basler Missions-Stationen in Indien: Mit Bezeichnung der Eigentumsverhältnisse* (Basel, 1888–91), pp. 3–4. For a brief history of the Mangalore station, see K. Hartenstein, *Das Werden einer jungen Kirche im Osten: 100 Jahre Basler Missionsarbeit in Indien* (Stuttgart, 1935), pp. 58–74.
93 Hartenstein, ibid., p. 72; Jaiprakash Raghaviah, *Basel Mission Industries in Malabar and South Canara, 1834–1914: A Study of its Social and Economic Impact* (New Delhi, 1990).
94 *Siebenzigster Jahresbericht der Evangelischen Missionsgesellschaft zu Basel auf 1. Juli 1885* (Basel, 1885), p. xxxviii.
95 See: Alfons Väth, *Die deutschen Jesuiten in Indien: Geschichte der Mission von Bombay-Puna* (Regensburg, 1920); and P. Beda Kleinschmidt, *Auslanddeutschtum und Kirche: Ein Hand- und Nachschlagebuch auf Geschichtlich-Statistischer Grundlage*, Vol. 2. *Die Auslandeutschen in Übersee* (Münster, 1930), pp. 230–7.
96 Ernest R. Hull, *The German Jesuit Fathers of Bombay: By an Englishman Who Knows Them* (Bombay, 1915), pp. 30–1.
97 Väth, *Die deutschen Jesuiten*, p. 122.
98 Ibid., pp. 199–206; 'Die Mission der deutschen Jesuiten in Guzerat', in *Die katholischen Missionen*, 1903–4, pp. 34–9, 56–62.
99 Väth, *Die deutschen Jesuiten*; Hull, *German Jesuit Fathers*.
100 Hull, ibid., pp. 21–6.
101 *Zweiundneunzigster Jahesbericht der Evanglische-lutherischen zu Leipzig, umfassend den Zeitraum vom 1. Januar bis 31. Dezember 1910* (Leipzig, 1911), pp. 26–35.
102 See, for example, *Achtzigster Jahresbericht der Evangelischen Missionsgesellschaft zu Basel auf 1. Juli 1895* (Basel, 1895). Basel employed slightly more Europeans relative to the size of congregations.
103 *Bericht über die Arbeit der Schleswig-Holsteinischen Evangelisch Lutherischen Missionsgesellschaft*.
104 *Jahresbericht des Stettiner Hilfsvereins für die Goßnersche Mission für das Jahr 1910* (Stettin, 1911).
105 *Achtzigster Jahresbericht der Evangelischen Missionsgesellschaft zu Basel*.
106 Handmann, *Umschau*.
107 Joseph Josenhans, *Atlas der evangelischen Missions-Gesellschaft zu Basel* (Basel, 1857).
108 See, for example: H. Mögling and C. Weitbrecht, *Das Kurgland und die evangelische Mission in Kurg* (Basel, 1866); E. R. Baierlein, *The Land of the Tamulians and its Missions* (Madras, 1875); Handmann, *Die Evangelisch-lutherische Tamulen-Mission*.
109 See, for example: Reinhold Grundemann, *Kleine Missions-Geographie und -Statistik zur Darstellung des Standes der evangelischen Mission am Schluss des*

COMMUNITY

     19. Jahrhunderts (Stuttgart, 1901); Julius Richter, *A History of Missions in India* (Edinburgh, 1908). More recently, Jeffrey Cox, *The British Missionary Enterprise Since 1700* (London, 2008), views the efforts of British groups as exercises in institution building.
110 Judith T. Kenny, 'Climate, race, and imperial authority: the symbolic landscape of the British hill station in India', *Annals of the Association of American Geographers*, vol. 85 (1995), pp. 694–714.
111 See, for example, C. A. Bayly, *Indian Society and the Making of the British Empire* (Cambridge, 1988).
112 Liebau, *Cultural Encounters*, p. 6.
113 Heike Liebau, 'Country Priests, Catechists and Schoolmasters as Cultural, Religious and Social Middlemen in the Context of the Tranquebar Mission', in Robert Eric Frykenberg and Alaine M. Low, eds, *Christians and Missionaries in India: Cross-Cultural Communication since 1500, with Special Reference to Caste, Conversion and Colonialism* (Grand Rapids, MI, 2003), pp. 70–92; Jeffrey Cox, *Imperial Fault Lines: Christianity and Colonial Power in India* (Stanford, CA, 2002), pp. 87–115; Henriette Bugge, *Mission and Tamil Society: Social and Religious Change in South India (1840–1900)* (Richmond, 1994), p. 79.
114 See, for example: Kenneth Ballhalchet, *Race, Sex and Class under the Raj: Imperial Attitudes and Policies and their Critics, 1793–1905* (London, 1980); Thomas R. Metcalf, *Ideologies of the Raj* (Cambridge, 1998); Mizutani, *Meaning of White*.
115 Esme Cleall, *Missionary Discourse: Negotiating Otherness in the British Empire, 1840–1900* (Basingstoke, 2012).
116 Andreas Nehring, *Orientalismus und Mission: Die Repräsentation der tamulischen Gesellschaft und Religion durch Leipziger Missionare 1840–1940* (Wiesbaden, 2003).
117 This is the function of Chapter 5.
118 German Evangelical Mission, *Fifteenth Report*, p. 56.
119 *Achtzigster Jahresbericht der Evangelischen Missionsgesellschaft zu Basel*.
120 *Zweiundneunzigster Jahresbericht der Evanglische-lutherischen zu Leipzig*, pp. 26–35.
121 *Bericht über die Arbeit der Schleswig-Holsteinischen Evangelisch Lutherischen Missionsgesellschaft*, pp. 42–3.
122 Liebau, *Cultural Encounters*, pp. 177–268.
123 AFST/LMW/II.31.1.183, Missionsdiener der Station Pandur, 27 August 1914.
124 AFST/LMW/II.31.1.187, 'Dienstordnung fuer die eingeborener Arbeiter im Dienst der Leipziger Mission', c. 1906.
125 *Zweiundneunzigster Jahresbericht der Evanglische-lutherischen zu Leipzig*, p. 29.
126 Nottrott, *Die Gossner'sche Mission unter den Kolhs*, p. 332.
127 Kausch and Kahn, *50 Bilder*, p. 87.
128 *Der Evangelische Heidenbote*, 1 and 15 July 1833.
129 German Evangelical Mission, *Fifteenth Report*, p. 18.
130 Ibid.
131 Mrinalini Sebastian: 'Localised Cosmopolitanism and Globalosed Faith: Echoes of "Native" Voices in Eighteenth and Nineteenth Century Missionary Documents', in Judith Becker, ed., *European Missions in Contact Zones: Transformation Through Interaction in a (Post-)Colonial World* (Göttingen, 2015), pp. 61–3; 'The Scholar Missionaries of the Basel Mission in Southwestern India: Language, Identity, and Knowledge in Flux, in Heather Sharkey, ed., *Cultural Conversions: Unexpected Consequences of Christian Missionary Encounters in the Middle East, Africa and South Asia* (Syracuse, NY, 2013), pp. 183–92.
132 *Zweiundneunzigster Jahesbericht der Evanglische-lutherischen zu Leipzig*, p. 43.
133 Kausch and Kahn, *50 Bilder*, pp. 85–6.
134 Nottrott, *Die Gossner'sche Mission unter den Kohls*, p. 336.
135 Basel German Evangelical Missionary, *Report of the Basel German Evangelical Missionary Society. Forty-Ninth Year. 1864. Twenty Fifth Report of the German Evangelical Mission in South-Western India* (Mangalore, 1865), pp. 7–8.

136 *Zweiundneunzigster Jahesbericht der Evanglische-lutherischen zu Leipzig*, pp. 26–9, 35.
137 Nottrott, *Die Gossner'sche Mission unter den Kohls*, p. 330; Kausch and Kahn, *50 Bilder*, pp. 83–4.
138 AFST/LMW/II.31.11.14, 'A Short History of the Life of Mathusamy, Mauelmedu', 15 April 1912.
139 AFST/LMW/II.31.11.14,'A Memorial to the Venerable Church Council, Leipzig Evangelical Lutheran Mission, Tranquebar', 4 September 1902.
140 See, for example, Fae Dussort, ' "Strictly Legal Means": Assault, Abuse and the Limits of Acceptable Behaviour in the Servant/Employer Relationship in Metropole and Colony 1850–1890', in Victoria K. Haskins and Claire Lowrie, eds, *Colonization and Domestic Service: Historical and Contemporary Perspectives* (Abingdon, 2015), pp. 153–71; Nupur Chaudhuri, 'Memsahibs and their servants in nineteenth century India', *Women's History Review*, vol. 3 (1994), pp. 549–62.
141 Alwin Gehring, *Das Tamulenland, seine Bewohner und die Mission* (Leipzig, 1927), p. 58.
142 Kausch and Kahn, *50 Bilder*, p. 40.
143 Gehring, *Das Tamulenland*, pp. 58–60.
144 See contributions to Hartmut Keil and John B Jentz, eds, *German Workers in Industrial Chicago, 1850–1910: A Comparative Perspective* (DeKalb, IL, 1983).

CHAPTER FIVE

Interethnic perceptions and interactions

Racism, orientalism, Christianity and contact

The German religious communities which emerged in India during the nineteenth century point to the complex relationships which existed between the migrants from Europe and indigenous people. On the one hand, some type of racial hierarchy appears to have operated in which the Germans (and other Europeans) remained at the top, with indigenous people constituting the lower echelons of the racial pyramid – even though Indians could move towards the higher layers of German Christianity in India, especially if they became pastors.

This description suggests a one-way process in which only Indians underwent change. However, Judith Becker has suggested that the experience of missionaries living in India meant that transformation took place for both immigrants and long-term settlers leading to a third way, in which, for example, new forms of Christianity and personal identities would emerge. Becker's monumental study, based upon years of archival research, focuses upon the activity of the Basel Mission in south India and demonstrates interaction and change in a variety of ways, including within the lives of individual missionaries preaching, teaching and writing.[1] Becker has utilised these ideas to bring together a series of scholars in an edited book which demonstrates that the type of transformations which she studied occurred throughout the world.[2] A collection edited by Heather Sharkey has examined the 'unexpected consequences' of 'cultural conversion' in the Middle East, Africa and South Asia.[3]

If we move beyond the missionary perspective, one of the most obvious ways in which this transformation took place involved interethnic relationships which, as both contemporaries[4] and subsequent scholars have indicated,[5] had become normal in the Indian environment beginning with Portuguese settlement, if not quite as normal as in the case of New Zealand.⁶ While such unions took place between Europeans and Indians, they also occurred, perhaps more regularly, between different European groups. While transformation may have taken place as a result of interethnic interaction between Europeans and Indians, as well as between Europeans from different parts of the continent, 'entanglement' also occurred, as Kris Manjapra stressed in his study of the relationship between Germany and India. Although he focused upon the intellectual sphere, he also examined the 'German Servants of the British Raj', focusing upon those who worked as scientists and scholars at the height of the Empire.[7]

Entanglement or transformation points to the fact that some sort of pre-existing positions existed which subsequently underwent change. Clearly, one of these positions was religion. Christianity and Hinduism form the starting points in the case of any spiritual transformation, resulting in conversion on the Hindu side and acceptance of some of the norms of Indian life on the other. This type of crossover indicates a positive example of the consequences of religious contact. However, indigenous religion and those who practised it usually rejected Christianity, indicated most clearly by the limited inroads which Christianity made in India, despite the master narratives constructed by missionaries about their activities there. Initially at least, the discourse of the German missionaries in their numerous publications about India rejected and even ridiculed Hinduism and Islam.

This points to a negative perception among the missionaries and other Germans who found themselves in nineteenth- and early twentieth-century India. While Andreas Nehring's study of the activities of the Leipzig Mission in the country details Orientalist research, it also accepts exchange and input from Tamil society.[8] Any examination of German orientalism and India has to overcome the hurdle of German indology or the serious study of Indian languages and history which involved both academics and missionaries. As in the rest of this volume, the discussion here will not engage with the academic findings of those scholars who never visited India, but will instead focus upon Orientalist perceptions of those who travelled to the country, including academics. Orientalist here, following Said, refers to the belief that certain traits characterise the peoples of the East, in this case Indians.[9]

Such perceptions also merit the description of racist, evolving as they do in the racial hierarchical society of British India, which Satoshi Mizutani has explored to demonstrate that the white ruling elites marginalised poor and mixed-race Britons,[10] fed by the preconceptions which those who travelled to India carried with them about the people they encountered.[11] Any preconceptions which already existed often became strengthened by the boundaries which the imperial state solidified during the course of the nineteenth century.[12]

The perspectives of Christianity, orientalism and racism,[13] which determine European views and actions in India, led to the development of a series of perceptions which the Germans in India, whether short-term visitors or longer term residents, perpetuated. The observers focused upon a series of aspects of Indian life including: the nature of Hinduism (especially in the case of missionaries); the position of women; and the prevalence of poverty and disease. However, many travelogues devoted positive attention to the Indian landscape, although descriptions of cityscapes often contained negative language focusing upon poverty and disease.

While Germans may form part of the European elite in India, they distinguished themselves not simply from Indians but also from the British, with whom they developed a generally positive relationship before 1914 which facilitated the crossing of boundaries. Against the background of diplomatic and imperial rivalry as the First World War approached, some travelogues focused upon British control of India.[14] For much of the nineteenth century, however, Germans worked in harmony with British elites who controlled India. With the arrival of the first Germans working for the CMS, marriage with Britons, as well as other Europeans, became normal, reinforcing the idea of a European, rather than purely British, white society.

Marriage between Germans and Indians, including mixed race 'Eurasians', however, remained rarer. Despite this, the types of perceptions which existed among newly arrived Germans in India softened after years of contact with either the British or the Indian population, although some of those who simply passed through may not have undergone transformation.

Indian landscapes

Both travellers and longer term residents devoted time to the Indian landscape, where three perspectives reveal themselves. Many descriptions focused upon the wonder of India, the exotic landscape, taking a romantic yet perhaps Orientalist view, concentrating upon uniqueness. At the same time, more matter of fact descriptions also emerged, especially from academics and more seasoned travellers. Finally, especially in the case of missionaries, a description of the landscape acted as a precursor for sketches of local populations, religion and, therefore, the necessity for conversions.

One of the most gushingly positive portrayals of the Indian landscape came from Emil Schlagintweit who, at the beginning of the first volume of his *Indien in Wort und Bild*, wrote:

> In the Indian Empire virtually every natural development is represented, every type of scenery can be found; there is scarcely another country of such great proportions, of such rich contrasts. From the plains of the Ganges and the Indus, made fertile by mighty rivers and bathed in brilliant sunshine, the Himalayan mountains, incorporating the highest peak on earth, soar upwards covered in eternal snow; from the rainless deserts and undulating steppes in the west there follow in the interior of the peninsula fertile plateaus, the ridges of the bordering mountains covered in impenetrable forests; at the ocean's edge river deltas cultivate in a remarkably lush way the desire of any planter.

Schlagintweit's introductory description continued for several further pages, zooming in on particular areas and on the plant and animal world, with 'the tiger', 'the elephant' and the 'holy cow' receiving special attention, as do snakes, accompanied by orientalist images (Figure 5.1).[15] The rest of Schlagitweit's work becomes more focused and 'scientific' in the same way as the accounts produced after his tour of India with his brothers in the 1850s.

Otto Ehlers displayed the same level of enthusiasm as Emil Schlagintweit about his journey to India in 1890, describing it as 'a dream come true'. One of his chapters focused upon an elephant hunt which took place near the Brahmaputra River,[16] pointing to an age when big game hunting had become part of a chivalrous code, as evidenced by the fact that the German crown prince had shot a tiger when he made his visit to India in 1910.[17]

Other accounts focused upon particular locations. The German missionary Hermann Dalton, following his visit in the late 1890s, spoke particularly positively (reflecting the accounts of other Germans and Europeans) of the foothills of the Himalayas, in his case Darjeeling: 'How wonderful it is here upon high in the elevated health spa of the Himalayas.' Part of the enthusiasm for this region lay in the fact that Dalton, like other travellers, arrived here after enduring the heat below, in his case 'the boiler of Calcutta'.[18]

Although many of the missionary accounts of landscapes play a scene-setting role for the descriptions of the activities which follow their arrival, some of them appreciate the environment for its own sake. The 1860 *Album der Basler Mission*, with the subtitle of *Bilder aus Indien*, both describes the Basel mission stations in southern India and contains narratives focusing upon both natural and manmade phenomena. Those in the former category include the Kateri waterfall, which one could reach by travelling south from Kety 'on a path laid out for

Figure 5.1 A classic Orientalist image

pedestrians and riders' which progressed 'over the back of a hill to a small marshy plain which leads to several winding valleys'.[19] While Alwin Gehring also produced a fairly standard missionary account of the landscape of the land of the Tamils, its inhabitants and the activities of missionaries – which began with a 'geographical' section[20] – his memoirs revealed a keen eye for detail, which included perceptive and appreciative observations of landscape. For example, he described the area north of Kumbakonam, where he lived with his wife, as 'the bread basket of south India' with 'the greatest fertility. The soil does not simply count as among the best in India, but also qualifies itself especially for rice cultivation.' To the south he painted a picture of a completely different landscape which had 'the character of a jungle'. More than virtually any other German missionary, Gehring developed a deep appreciation of the environment in which he found himself, indicating the extent to which he had become accustomed and almost rooted within it, meaning his narrative remained relatively free of orientalist language.[21]

Among the various German descriptions of life in India from our period, Waldemar Bonsels' semi-fictional *Indienfahrt* has attracted the most attention.[22] Bonsels had worked for the commercial arm of the Basel Mission but left his position because he viewed this as the driving force behind much of the activity of the Mission, which he regarded as unchristian. Both his account of the reason for his resignation[23] and his *Indienfahrt* demonstrate a deep appreciation of nature. The former viewed India as 'a sad and glorious land. One could describe Malabar, the coastal strip of western India, as a Paradise.'[24] The *Indienfahrt* outlines a variety of landscapes, including coast, swamp, jungle and mountain.[25] Bonsel's volume has given rise to a variety of interpretations. Perry Myers has written of 'the ambivalence of a spiritual quest'[26] in which any positive outlook towards India needs balancing against 'nature's relentless severity' and 'the maliciousness of British colonial power'.[27] Vidhagiri Ganeshan has come to similar conclusions, while also pointing to Bonsels' fascination with 'nature' and the 'animal world'.[28]

Ganeshan has also pointed to the fact that the most famous of German literary figures to have written about India in the early twentieth century – Hermann Hesse – did not actually visit the country, despite the title of his 1913 volume *Aus Indien*, meaning that a full circle did not quite occur as he did not return to the land beloved of his grandfather, Hermann Gundert. In fact, using the German nomenclature for India in which Vorderindien means India while Hinterindien refers to the Far East (outside Japan and China), Hesse sailed to Singapore and Indonesia via the Suez Canal. He did, however, visit Ceylon. His volume contains rich and romantic descriptions of the landscapes which he visited, pointing to a move away from religion which had motivated his grandfather to a fascination with nature by the early twentieth century.[29]

German academics approached the natural environment in a more scientific sense. For example, the Indian foresters Brandis and Ribbentrop categorised and mapped the trees and forests of India.[30] While the short reports by the Schlagintweits on their magnetic survey also remained essentially scientific,[31] we have already seen the enthusiasm demonstrated for the natural environment in Emil Schlagintweit's *Indien in Wort und Bild*. The earlier fuller three-volume account of the work connected with the magnetic surveys,[32] in which the first volume of 589 pages focused upon India before the journey to the Himalayas, offers a variety of perspectives. On the one hand, it contains scientific descriptions of vegetation, categorising trees by their Latin names[33] as well as providing equally scientific geological descriptions elsewhere.[34] However, the account also covers the totality of experiences and observations, offering intelligent comments on all manner of issues from the urban landscape of Bombay and Calcutta, through the forms of transport in Bengal and Hindustan, climatic conditions in Assam and the peoples of India as observed by the Schlagintweits. They provide the most detailed German observations of India, of a primarily scientific nature, from the nineteenth century.

A few other scientific or pseudo-scientific travelogues also merit attention. The subtitle of Oscar Kauffmann's two-volume *Aus Indiens Dschungeln*, 'experiences and researches', points to Kauffmann as an academic, although he provides little information about himself and does not mention an academic affiliation. Despite the title of the work, it does not focus upon Indian jungles but a recollection of his experiences of a journey which he seems to have undertaken from 1906–9 and which took him over much of India from Cochin, through the central provinces, to Kashmir and Assam. One of the most remarkable aspects of this work consists of the number of photographs it contains, especially of Indian people throughout the country, although it also includes some pictures of landscapes, together with several incorporating the obligatory hunting theme of the early twentieth century. On the one hand Kaufmann takes an orientalist perspective, marvelling at the uniqueness of some of the sights he witnesses. Yet some of the photographs of Indians demonstrate a genuine humanity, revealing people carrying out their everyday lives in their home environment (Figure 5.2).[35]

We can also point to two other accounts of journeys to India. The first of these involved the leading German biologist Ernst Haeckel, who travelled to the country in 1881 and then on to Ceylon, where he spent most of his time. His narrative resembles that of the Schlagintweits in the sense that it consists of both scientific and observational themes.[36]

Figure 5.2 A sympathetic image of two Indian girls

Finally, the lesser known account written by Oscar Flex differed from many of those quoted above because he lived in India, where he learnt Urdu and Hindi and worked on tea plantations – eventually reaching a senior managerial position with an English tea firm.[37] While his account focused especially upon his own personal experiences, he had an appreciation of the environment in which he worked. His introductory chapter, on land and people, provided a sketchy account of Assam. However, his descriptions of the landscape in which he worked demonstrated an appreciation and attention to detail similar to that of Alwin Gehring whom he resembles in the sense that he had become essentially assimilated into his surroundings.[38]

Many of the accounts of landscape cited so far reveal an acceptance of its intrinsic value. While some missionaries shared this appreciation, large-scale narratives often used physical descriptions as prologues for the arrival of a particular mission group. Some of the descriptions remained matter of fact, others had some appreciation of the landscape, while still others displayed the most overt of orientalist and patronising language.

The CMS employee, John Weitbrecht, provides an early example of this last approach in his *Protestant Missions in Bengal*. The first chapter ('On the Character of the Country, and the Moral Condition of the Inhabitants of India') examined the character of Indians and their food, furniture and dress. The opening platitudinous sentence ran: 'That wide and thickly populated country in the south of Asia, which we call India, is bounded by the Indus on the west, and the Buramputer on the east, and is one of the most interesting countries which has ever attracted the attention of the western nations, either in ancient or modern times.' At the heart of this statement lies the relationship between India and Europe, central to the missionary narrative, especially as Weitbrecht then proceeds to describe the arrival of Europeans from Alexander the Great, through Vasco de Gama to the East India Company. Several pages of overtly racist language follow in which Weitbrecht describes the characteristics of the 'Hindoos' focusing upon their appearance and their religion. For example 'the Hindoo husbandsman is far less laborious and persevering than the English peasant', although Weitbrecht explained this through the fertility of the 'tropical climate'. The description of nature remained matter of fact: 'Bengal abounds in fruit-trees of various kinds: of these the best known are the mangoe, the pine-apple, the citron, orange, and pomalo, the palm, the tamarind, cocoa-nut, plantain, and pomegranate-trees.' There then follows an account of the seasons, paying particular attention to extremes and differences from Europe. Ultimately, this volume has little appreciation of Indian nature and reveals little of the scientific method which characterised serious missionary researchers such as Gundert. Weitbrecht's belief in Christianity left space for little else.[39]

Other books about missionary activity in India devoted an even smaller proportion of their narrative towards nature and the landscape, with even less elaboration.[40] A volume which resembles Weitbrecht's, although written 30 years later, consists of the translated *Land of the Tamulians and its Missions* by the Leipzig missionary Edmund Baierlien.[41] As recognised by Andreas Nehring,[42] the opening line of this volume proves particularly interesting. 'The world had already attained a respectable age, before it knew anything of the land of the Tamulians.' Knowledge of the area in the West grew with the arrival of 'a weak and delicate man' in the form of Bartholomäus Ziegenbalg. 'Since his time this distant land has been brought nearer home, and now the land of the Tamulians is known in every quarter of the globe.'[43] Nehring uses this passage as an introduction to a discussion of the value of missionary research activities.[44] But it puts forward a Christian imperialist attitude where the key message is the irrelevance of the history of the Tamils before Ziegenbalg discovered it. The pages which follow use standard geographic descriptions of trees, animals, weather and landscape,[45] which include the sentence: 'Although not exactly beautiful, still it is a greatly favoured country.'[46]

We can conclude this section on missionaries and landscape by referring to three contrasting books. First, a general study by Julius Richter on German missionary work in south India which, reflecting the nature of the other volumes which Richter wrote, remains factual. Despite some colourful chapter headings when describing Basel activity, such as 'In the Blue Mountains' and 'In the Land of Palms and Pepper', he does not provide much elaboration in the text which follows.[47] Hermann Mögling together with V. D. M. Weitbrecht produced a hefty tome on the activities of the Basel Mission in Coorg, in which Mögling had played a large role, containing much information on land, people and history before moving on to describe the evangelical mission there. The sections on the land, while largely matter of fact, outlining staple crops, nevertheless contained an appreciation of the beauty of the natural environment, dividing it up into areas dominated by hills, water, and forest.[48] Finally, the Breklum missionary Ernst Gloyer wrote a volume on Jeypur, where his organisation worked, which focused simply on the area itself including geographical features, plants and animals before moving on to people, languages and religion, but contained nothing about the activities of the mission.[49]

Landscape formed a key part of German understanding of India, partly explained by the central role which observation of the natural environment plays in all travel writing. While some of our observers showed an appreciation of the landscape which bordered on romanticism, others either described it in a cursory fashion or simply used it as a scene-setting tool before the arrival of missionaries.

'The heathen'

German proselytisers in India concerned themselves primarily with religion, especially Hinduism. The research which some missionaries carried out demonstrates a readiness to understand indigenous religion. However, much of the language used to describe Hinduism abounds in orientalist and imperialist language. Some recent scholarship, in an overall critique of orientalist discourse, has seen Western commentators as responsible for developing Hinduism into one belief system.[50] While some German and other Western scholarship may have helped in understanding the nature of this indigenous set of Indian beliefs,[51] German and other missionaries constantly used the phrases 'heathen' and 'heathenism' to describe the nature of religion in both India and other parts of the world. They served both a 'descriptive and pejorative' function according to Nehring, who dates their use in the Leizpig Indian environment back to Ziegenbalg.[52] Writing on the utilisation of the terms by the Basel Mission, Julia Mack traces their use back to antiquity and links them with concepts such as barbarity.[53] Heathen and heathenism became part of the everyday discourse of nineteenth-century missionaries. Indeed, one of the main journals published by the Basel Mission carried the title of *Der evangelische Heidenbote*.

The missionaries did not focus solely upon Hinduism but also looked at the other belief systems in India. When recalling his life in India, CMS employee Charles Benjamin Leupolt wrote about both 'Mohammedans' and 'Hindus'. When writing about the former, he especially focused upon 'miracles and prophecies', which he dismissed, while describing Hinduism in just 11 pages.[54] Karl Gottlieb Pfander particularly focused upon Islam,[55] while Baierlein, for example, also devoted attention to Buddhism.[56]

Rather than providing a complete deconstruction of the views of German missionaries towards Indian religions, especially Hindu practices, it seems more productive to focus upon the key perceptions in their writing. In his observations on Bengal, Weitbrecht wrote a chapter 'On the Idolatrous Ceremonies of the Hindoos'. Here he focused upon 'the idol temples: these are, generally speaking, not such splendid edifices as our churches. Shiva's mundir, or temple, is a regular square building, surmounted by a dome or arched roof. The room in which the idol is placed, is not generally more than ten or twelve feet square.' He contrasted the smaller buildings in villages with the 'splendid pieces of architecture' in cities such as Benares. He also contrasted the services there with those in a church, for 'the passions are never raised to heaven' as 'the daily worship ... is performed by the solitary priest, with all the dullness, carelessness and insipidity, necessarily connected with a service in a strange tongue, repeated before an idol made of cold stone'. These 'idols of stone and metal' also attracted the wrath of Weitbrecht, focusing especially upon what he viewed as the immorality of Hindu worship, a theme taken up elsewhere.[57] For example, a 1905 article claimed that: 'Immorality belongs to the worst fruits of Hinduism. The service with its worship of the despicable lingam, with its crude immoral literature and with the institute of the temple dancers, that has been named the bubo of the Indian people, is a hotbed of immorality.' The author blamed this for the numbers of 'fallen women' found especially in the large cities.[58] The Leipzig missionary Reinhold Grundemann linked Hindu worship with 'superstitions fear of ghosts, soothsaying, fortune-telling and magic'.[59] An article in *Der evangelische Heidenbote* even claimed the existence of devil worshippers.[60]

As well as the worship of idols and the immorality which the missionaries viewed as inherent in Hinduism, they also inevitably focused upon polytheism as a central contrast with Christianity.[61] An article on the 'Festival of the Gods in Taliparambu' in Kerala pointed to the fact that 33 deities were celebrated with 'very old songs'. Basel missionaries had visited this event on 15 occasions by 1860, as they saw it as an opportunity to secure converts.[62] Another article from 1912 described a festival in the village of Hara which had two high points: 'the sacrifice of a buffalo' and a fight involving elephants.[63]

Hindu festivals therefore attracted particular attention from missionaries. As in the case of Taliparambu, one of the main reasons for visiting them lay in the fact that they provided potential converts.[64] Missionaries also focused upon bazaars, both because of the numbers of people who visited them and because of their activity and colour. An 1897 article stated: 'When we, who know India, say the word bazaar, we are transposed to a place of colourful life and movement, which in diversity and originality one could only find in wonderful India.' This represents one of the 'Pictures from a North Indian Town', with the other two consisting of the Hindu temples and the mosques, described in a relatively non-judgemental manner.[65] A more detailed account of 'Pictures from South Indian Everyday Life' painted by the Basel missionary Samuel Limbach included a description of the bazaar, as well as focusing upon the rhythm of work and daily routine, without any particular focus upon religion.[66]

Apart from the attention devoted to the nature of belief in terms of services and practice, the other key theme which attracted the attention of both religious and secular Germans in India consisted of caste. For the Leipzig missionaries in particular this issue, and whether those converted could continue to hold on to their caste identities, caused much conflict.[67] Graul summarised the way in which Leipzig should deal with the question. Although the organisation 'fully acknowledges that Caste ... is as *it now exists among the heathen*, not a merely civil but also religious institution' this type of social stratification 'is totally opposed to the word and spirit of the Gospel'. Graul asserted that 'the holding of Caste *in the Native Churches* is essentially different from the holding of Caste among the heathen' because 'the indiscriminate partaking of the same cup at the Lord's table necessarily involves the *breaking of Caste*' as does the introduction of the 'Holy Scripture, which expressly declares the common origin of the whole human race'. Graul believed that caste would disappear over time through education and the evolution of a national church.[68]

Many religious observers shared Graul's rejection of caste as an unacceptable system of controlling society. Weitbrecht described it 'the curse of the haughty Brahmin' which created an 'intolerable burden' for 'the despised Sudra, or the servile caste' whose 'allotted task was to perform every kind of menial labour for their nobler-born brethren, both at home and in the field'. The Brahmins, according to Weibtrecht, believed that: 'What God has appointed ... we cannot alter. So holy and unchangeable is this institution of castes, in the eyes of the people, and so firm is the belief of the Hindoo as to the appointment being of Divine authority, that a transition from one caste to the other is absolutely impossible.' However, Weitbrecht further asserted that 'castes have been considerably intermixed with each other' in 'modern times'.[69] Half a century later, the Leipzig missionary Georg Stosch asserted that: 'The incomprehensible things about India include caste. Nobody can understand India without understanding the issue of caste.' Stosch also pointed out that: 'The missionary encounters the question of caste daily wherever he comes and goes' and that it hindered the spread of Christianity. Viewing the issue through a Christian European perspective, he claimed that 'India's caste system in its present situation had few defenders and many denouncers'. Stosch wrote of its responsibility for 'all injustice and inhumanity'. He especially criticised what he saw as the haughtiness of the Brahmins. 'The Christian feeling of the Europeans finds it especially disconcerting that the individual castes do not eat with each other and that the higher castes do not eat with Europeans.' Stosch further scolded the caste system because 'the practice of compassion is simply confined to people of the same caste', which meant that giving to the poor only happened at weddings and funerals. Consequently, 'Christianity has no mightier enemy in India than caste'.[70]

While Weitbrecht and Stosch focused upon the evils of caste, other missionary narratives took an approach similar to Emil Schlagintweit, who, following the scientific method which characterised his other work and that of his brothers, outlined the different caste groups which existed and the numbers which each of them counted in the various regions which he visited, for which he put together tables.[71] Gehring recognised the importance of caste in Indian life, without condemning it in the same way as Weitbrecht and Stosch, and then gave a brief history of its evolution and an outline of stratification according to employment.[72] Similarly, when describing activity in the Basel mission station in Talatscheri, Christian Irion essentially produced an outline of the different caste groups there, which, in his categorisation, included 'forest dwellers', 'slave castes' and the 'najadis'. He described the najadis as the 'last of the 72 castes' who lived through begging and 'could not approach any of the better inhabitants'.[73] This reflected the Christian concern for the lowest castes or 'pariahs', 'excluded through the laws of man from every position in the society of their fatherland, robbed of all privileges, which the other classes of inhabitants enjoy'.[74]

The question of women

Missionaries also devoted attention to what they saw as the downtrodden position of women in India, reflecting a longlasting concern of European settlers and observers.[75] An account by the Gossner missionary Helene Lorbeer, published in 1911, summarised the key concerns of German and other European missionaries. Her narrative evolved from visiting Indian women in their homes. First, using orientalist and sensual language, she entered a 'senana', where she met and spoke to a young Muslim woman resembling 'a fairy princess from one thousand and one nights'. Apart from commenting upon her attire, Lorbeer also focused on the paleness of the woman's skin. Lorbeer concluded that she came from a high caste and also spoke to her about the fact that she had not seen her mother and sister for a long time. In another house, 'The women, mother, daughter and daughter in law, were dreadfully shy and sad, seemed unused to laughing, even to speaking.' Lorbeer also wrote about an 18-year-old widow with whom she had spoken and claimed that 23 million widows lived in India, partly caused by child marriages. They all had an 'emptiness in their heart' and some would have preferred death because of their position in society, especially when they found themselves living with their mother-in-law because of the superior position of the son in the family home.[76]

Lorbeer's pamphlet essentially brings out the key concerns of Germans and other Europeans on the Indian women's question, focusing upon sexuality and second-class status. One of the most disturbing sexist and Orientalist German books about women in India came from the pen of the ship doctor Erwin Rosenberger, who visited brothels in Bombay between 1908 and 1914. Rosenberger focused upon the 'flesh girls' and 'pleasure girls' with whom he came into contact in Bombay who included not just Indians but also Japanese and European women. One chapter of his book, on 'The Hindu Girls', gives a guiltless account of the fact that the 'Hindu-Girl' he had 'visited' in a 'house of pleasure' was 'very young', before then comparing the merits of these Hindu girls with Japanese and Syrian women.[77] Such approaches to the exploitation of women clearly contrast with those put forward by missionaries. For example, Anna Lucas, in her account of the activities of the Gossner Mission, focused upon 'India's Temple Girls', presented by their parents as a gift because they would, through their actions, 'secure material and perpetual goods from the Gods'. However, once they left their parents they became 'the property of the priests', implying sexual abuse and a connection with 'girl trafficking'.[78]

For missionaries, sexual exploitation formed one aspect of the second-class status of Indian women, which began at birth. While Gehring wrote that the 'birth of a girl is not greeted as a joyful event',[79] another account by O. Gründler asserted that the parents regarded it as 'bad luck and punishment', although 'motherly love quickly wins'.[80] Gründler stated that the 'roots of the misery' of women 'lay in the teachings about reincarnation' whereby the 'sick, cripples, women and non-believers' had committed 'earlier sins'.[81] When writing about matrimony, Gründler focused upon the fact that the parents in law controlled the household into which the new bride moved.[82] He also described the unenviable fate of the Indian widow: 'To the Hindu an unmarried female being is an abomination. A woman without a man does not even have the right to exist; if her husband is no more, she herself is also no more.'[83] Missionary magazines particularly concerned themselves with widow burning (which took place into the twentieth century despite the abolition of sati in 1829).[84] Gründler summed up the views of German missionaries on the position of women in India when he quoted an 'eye witness' who stated: 'The daughters of India are unwelcome at birth, remain without education in their childhood, become slaves through marriage, are cursed as widows and die unlamented.'[85]

Urban landscapes

Together with observations about the countryside which they encountered, Germans in India spent time in big cities, which led to numerous and detailed commentaries about these urban environments on any manner of subjects, from the nature of the population, especially when it demonstrated ethnic diversity, to the style of housing. Many observers spent at least some time in Bombay, as well as travelling to the Himalayas. Benares became another key stop, as recognised by Aurélie Choné.[86] Writers visited Benares as the spiritual homeland of India and Hinduism. But some tourists, such as Richard Garbe, became contemptuous of their new environment, which, in the case of Garbe, Kaushik Bagchi, explains through an orientalist outlook.[87] Some Germans did not like the urban environment of Benares because of difficulties navigating narrow streets, while others felt repulsed by the Ganges.[88] More especially, as Choné asserts, 'Hindus and Europeans did not hold the same understanding of "holy".'[89] Positive perceptions of Benares also emerged from some travelogues, especially of the architecture, for example, [90] while the Roman Catholic missionary Joseph Dahlmann admired the devotion of pilgrims.[91] Detlef Bracker, the superintendent of the Breklum Mission, wrote one of the most positive accounts not only of Benares but of religious buildings in several other locations following a visit he made just before the outbreak of the First World War, using not only enthusiastic language but also providing photographs of both Hindu buildings and those who practised the religion.[92]

Observers of Indian cities, as well as of more rural environments, also focused upon disease and hunger.[93] For example, while in Bombay in 1907, Oscar Kauffmann experienced an outbreak of the plague which meant that '200 people lost their lives' to the disease on a daily basis. While Kauffmann essentially partakes in an exercise in body counting,[94] the missionaries constructed more heartfelt narratives on the plight of the people among whom they lived. An article from *Der evangelische Heidenbote* of March 1855 stated that: 'In recent months we have seen with heavy heart in the whole of the middle highland of south India a general famine and starvation until finally, at the beginning of September, the rains finally arrived almost two months late to relieve the land and people.' The long article which followed went into detail about the consequences of the famine. Two decades later, the April 1877 edition of *Der evangelische Heidenbote* carried stories about both hunger in south Mahattra and cholera in Calicut.

Perceptions of the British

German writers in India also paid great attention to the British, whether because they encountered them in everyday life or because they passed comment on the rulers of the country. Perry Myers has identified three key, yet contradictory, perceptions of Britons put forward by German writers at the end of the nineteenth century: an admiration for British rule; British ignorance of the cultural treasures of India; and a belief that Germany would provide a better rule because of a greater understanding of the Indian environment.[95]

In fact, Germans in India wrote about the British presence in the country throughout the nineteenth century because of the necessity of interaction. Graul's major narrative, for instance, devoted attention to both the British missionary organisations with which he came into contact and the British Government and its officials. While in Bombay, for example, he focused upon: British laws and their relationship with already existing legislation, especially with regard to religion; the complaints of Indians against British rule; and British institutions in the city. He also met prominent British missionaries and described the activities of the Scottish Mission here.[96] He concentrated on similar subjects when he progressed to Madras.[97] Other religious commentators, such as Christian Irion when writing about Talatscheri, commented on the establishment of British rule as part of a history of India.[98]

Later in the nineteenth and into the twentieth century, as Myers suggests, German writers focused more specifically upon British rule in India, as revealed in the orientalist perspective of Paulus Cassel who travelled from the Nile to the Ganges. He admired the British as global travellers who had conquered the world, including the whole of India, with 'the sword'. Nevertheless, anticipating some of the writers examined by Myers, Cassel pointed to the role of Germans in the study of India and to Indo-Germanic ties.[99] A few years after Cassel, Garbe offered a less impressionistic account of English rule in India in which he analysed the military as having a closer relationship with the civil service than in the German case. He also commented on the 'prevailing overall order and security' which he put down to the civil service. However, he believed that two factors played a central role in British control of India in the form of 'the servile nature of the Hindus' and 'the intense repulsion which the individual Indian races felt against each other' which prevented the evolution of a unified national feeling.[100]

On the eve of the First World War, two books appeared dealing with the British in India. The first of these by Georg Wegener, a Berlin geography professor who accompanied the German princes on their visit to India in 1910, spent most of its 44 pages essentially outlining the landscape, climate, history and demography of the country and then moved on to analyse the problems faced by the British authorities in the last 19 pages. The approach remains purely academic, meaning an absence of any overt personal impressions.[101] The second immediate pre-War volume did not focus simply upon British rule despite its title of 'the English in India', as its subtitle, travel impressions, provides a better understanding of its content although – as a soldier – the author,

Hans von Koenigsmarck, devotes much attention to the most important strategic positions, including chapters on the north-west frontier and the Khyber pass. In fact, much of the narrative outlines discussions with senior figures in the British military and civil administration. This essentially superficial book concluded with: 'Die englischen Frauen in Indien for ever'.[102]

Everyday interaction between Germans and Indians

German impressions of India therefore encompass a broad and complex panorama in which the academic, religious or other background of the observer played a major role. While missionaries tried to understand the nature of Hinduism, many of the narratives which emerged displayed an abhorrence of some its practices, above all idolatry, the caste system and the position of women. Despite the (admittedly hierarchical) Christian communities which they constructed, the missionaries did not abandon their disdain for 'the heathen', as revealed in some of the memoirs written after their return to Germany. If interaction involves a crossing of borders, Indians carried out much of the travelling within their homeland in a religious sense by sacrificing their belief.

Missionaries, by necessity, had the greatest level of interaction with Indians, usually involving intermediaries. While many of the other employment groups may have had more dealings with the British than with Indians, they could not function in their everyday existence without some interaction with the latter. The range of attitudes expressed by Germans towards Indians varied from the clearly humane to the downright racist and orientalist. But even when natives did receive good treatment from Germans, this often operated in a racial hierarchy which characterised the missionary structures.[103] As Germans formed a (minor part) of the 'white race',[104] they often adopted the same racist ideas and practices and remained at the top of the racial pyramid, guaranteed by their position as educated elites. While some of the long-term German residents of India (whether missionaries or not) may have developed empathy for those with whom they worked, those who spent shorter periods in the country had less chance to break down boundaries.

The tea planter and plantation superintendent Oscar Flex offers some interesting insights into the racial position of a professional German in the middle of the nineteenth century. On the one hand, he appears to have become integrated into Indian society, at least to the extent that he learnt to converse in Hindi. When he met his first set of employees, as assistant to 'Mr Oldham' in a plantation in Tingamonar, he promised, to those who could speak Hindi, that he would treat them in a just way and hoped that he would not have to institute a 'strict discipline' because of their 'obedience and diligence'. For those who could not speak Hindi, a translator repeated his words in Assamese.[105] Upon his arrival in Tingamonar he also had a conversation with an Englishman called Perton based on a 'four year intimate coexistence with the natives', which Flex had experienced, in which he suggested that an unequal relationship existed between Europeans and Indians that would change if Europeans put themselves in the position of Indians, which would involve 'a study of their languages and customs'.[106] Perton dismissed this view with the retort: 'I am a tea planter and not a linguist.'[107] Despite Flex's empathy and interaction with Indians, he ultimately falls into the European elite, with Indian servants assisting him.[108]

The Kiel Professor Paul Deussen also displayed empathy towards the Indians with whom he came into contact during his visit in 1892. He spoke positively about his first 'travel attendant' Lalu because of his servility, the fact that he knew his place in the caste system and the fact that he attended to Deussen's every need without complaint.[109] Deussen also described Venirám 'the young, 25 year old scholar, who was the perfect example of an Indian Pandit. He knew absolutely nothing about Europe and European things. The English language ... was completely unknown to him' to the extent that he could not read European script. 'Like all adult Indians, he was married, but had left his wife and children behind in his home village and came to Bombay in order to earn his scholarly livelihood at Elphinstone College by collating manuscripts and drawing up catalogues.' Deussen even tells us that Venirám's father had given up all his worldly possessions and moved to Benares. Like his father, Venirám lived a strict religious life reflected in his prayers, dress and food. While Deussen may appear to construct an Indian stereotype, his language remains non-judgemental. From his own point of view, he found Venirám an excellent colleague and guide while in Bombay, arriving at his hotel early in the morning and conversing with him in Sanskrit.[110] When he subsequently met a group of professors at the Sanskrit College in Jeypur, Deussen regarded them as equals – although he commented on their curiosity about his caste.[111] He also interacted with Indian professors in Benares on an equal basis,[112] and wrote of Indians as friends.[113] Other German professors who visited India spoke with equal humanity about the Indians with whom they came into contact so that, for example, Franz Reuleaux wrote several pages on the position of the 'punkawalla' during his stay in Calcutta.[114]

The German consulate in this city treated its servants with decency, although they regularly asked for pay rises – usually received favourably. In 1907, the consulate employed six servants consisting of: two ushers; a doorman; a waiter; a sweeper; and a water carrier. All received a salary increase in April of that year because of a rise in the price of rice.[115] Some of the Indian employees had worked for the Consulate for a significant amount of time. For example, Tarapado Choudhury, who served as a clerk, entered employment in 1892 and still worked for the Calcutta Consulate in 1913.[116] Meanwhile, Apurla Kumar had entered service in 1902 and in 1908 asked for a pay rise to bring him towards the salary of Choudhury.[117]

Despite cordial relations between Indians and Germans, they operated on the basis of the social stratification which existed in India. Deussen could speak to Indian academics as equals but clearly his servants retained their status. But in all of his relationships this particular professor, while playing his role as such, did not display contempt for those Indians with whom he came into contact. This contrasts with Garbe, although his negativity aimed at colonial society in general rather than simply Indian servants. He described 'conversations with servants displaying an unbelievably naïve character', which he also applied to discussions between Europeans and traders. He essentially referred to the patronising way in which Europeans spoke to Indians but also to the readiness with which Indians played the subservient role. 'When one is first in India, one is surprised by the self-assured demeanour of Europeans and the devotion with which the natives respect them.'[118] Garbe did not believe in the idea that Europeans could socialise with 'higher class Indians' on an equal footing. Garbe blamed this on caste and the fact that a 'westerner' would not display his 'innermost feelings'.[119] Garbe also commented upon the racial nature of Indian society, which meant an aloofness towards those of mixed race.[120] Garbe's comments may reflect the reality of colonial life, but they reveal his own prejudices against both Indians and resident Europeans.[121]

Missionaries had the most direct contact with Indians because of the nature of their vocation. Indeed, Judith Becker has written about the development of a 'contact religiosity'. She examines the arrival of Europeans with preconceived ideas which became broken down once they made contact with Indians, resulting essentially in a softening of the position of both sides towards each other, meaning that the missionaries abandoned some of their orientalism so that the religious breakthrough could take place. Becker indicates the way in which the contact occurred and identifies the mission strategies, which included sermons and conversations, which then led to the evolution of schools and the type of bureaucracy which would develop as the nineteenth century progressed.[122] Becker identifies three of the founding fathers of the Basel Mission in India – Hebich, Mögling and Gundert – as pioneers of this form of contact religion.[123] Becker also focuses upon friendships which developed between Germans and Indians, pointing to the fact that 'Hermann Anandrao Kaundinya became Hermann Mögling's best friend and closest confidant in India following the death of his stepbrother Gottfried Weigle'.[124] Fundamental to the breakthrough was missionaries learning local dialects. While, on the one hand, this may simply have had a utilitarian purpose, it also allowed the missionaries a profound insight into the cultures with which they came into contact, especially for those who carried out grammatical work on Indian languages.[125]

Becker's perspective moves away from, and further develops, that of Heike Liebau, who focused more heavily upon the Indians who worked for the Tranquebar Mission. Mrinalini Sebastian has even written about the evolution of 'localised cosmopolitanism' in missionary 'contact zones', referring to the way in which new cultural practices evolved,[126] which contrasts with the position taken by Monica Juneja, who questioned the extent to which boundaries broke down.[127]

Reinhardt Wendt has stressed the role of publications and speeches in conversion.[128] By the outbreak of the First World War, both the Basel and Leipzig missionaries had drawn up 'manuals' to help their missionaries.[129] The pamphlet written for the Basel Mission by Johannes Hesse devoted much attention to the theological issues encountered in the Indian environment, about which any preacher would need some knowledge to supplement that of his own belief, arguing for a reasoned, rather than arrogant and aggressive, approach.[130] Hesse's pamphlet concluded with a list of 27 'interjections and questions' to expect when preaching which he claimed to have heard 'countless times'. 'By believing in Jesus does one get buffalo, oxen and clothes? What is in it for us if we convert ... Here is a cripple; if Jesus makes him healthy we will believe ... If the Christians have no Gods, why do they then build a temple?'[131] Other sources also provided details of preaching. The 1871 Basel report of activity in south India summed it up in this succinct manner:

> Preaching to the Heathen is carried in one form or another in all stations, although there are only few Missionaries set apart for this purpose, the majority having either congregations or schools as their primary duty and employing also a good number of Catechists for those purposes; and if in a station like Mangalore the congregation is very large and the schools give much work, much time does not remain for bazaar-preaching and itinerating. But missionaries with small congregations like Dharwar, Gooledgood, Chombala, Kaity, &c. can spare much time for itinerating, whilst Calicut, Cannanore, Honore have each one or two Missionaries and a number of catechists whose chief duty is preaching to the heathen. The different characters of people and districts and stations necessitate

a variety of methods in carrying out the work, preaching either in the bazaar, or visiting from house or from village to village or going to markets and heathen festivals, where a great number of people gather.[132]

Baierlein, in common with other missionaries, used poetic and evocative language to turn preaching into an almost heroic experience, where the speaker ventured into a hostile religious and climatic environment. He painted a picture of a missionary stepping out 'at midday, as the shadows begin to become longer and the heat is no longer rising ... guided by a Catechist, through the streets of the heathen world. The heat is dreadful and no wind makes it more bearable in the narrow streets.' The missionary then tries to enter into conversation with people without success and greets others on their doorstep. These events take place on the day of a religious procession and, while the missionary has little success on this occasion, he would return to the same spot in future.[133] Another publication by Johannes Hesse mentions the work of 'missionary Ahrens' who gave a lecture 'under a shady tree very close to a weekly market', where a 'mission tent stood', to 'thirty or forty' listeners.[134] These evocative pictures of lone preachers attempting to attract converts appeared regularly in the pages of the Basel *Evangelische Heidenbote*, often written by the speakers.[135] Three of the leading Basel pioneering missionaries – Hebich, Mögling and Gundert – also kept a record of their activities, while, in the case of Hebich in particular the series of hagiographies about him constructed the same heroic images of preaching.[136] Albrecht Frenz has described Mögling as developing into 'an Indian guru, a role cherished in India since time immemorial'.[137]

As some of the extracts above suggest, the sermons preached by missionaries to audiences of all sizes formed the first step in the conversion process. Some individuals listened to several sermons and made efforts to come into contact with those they had heard. Wilhelm Hansenwandel claimed that in April 1875 'so many heathens visited me in order to ask questions and receive instruction about the Christian religion, that I rarely ever preached in the Bazar', although many of those who visited lost interest once 'they took a look at their sinful lives'.[138] This type of initial interest followed by a change of mind finds reflection elsewhere. Jakob Jaus's biography of Hebich describes a 'festival' in a 'fishing village' in 1846 at a time of cholera, where Hebich spoke 'full of fervour', stating: 'I have already preached Jesus, who is the resurrection and life, from one house to another, for nearly three years, and now you sit before your dead Gods. God will punish you.' Hebich had actually helped families suffering from cholera. 'Some individuals allowed themselves to be baptised because of the fear and need in their hearts. But few of them remained true.'[139] Sickness acted as a catalyst for conversion on other occasions, as in the case of a father who visited the Dharwar Mission, run by Basel. 'He was instructed in the word of God and has conducted himself satisfactorily. His wife also showed, during a serious illness, that the word of God had not been without influence on her heart. In December last the family was baptized.'[140]

These extracts demonstrate that the process from preaching to baptism remained long and complicated and often needed some intervening factor such as sickness. The overwhelming majority of Indians either rejected or ridiculed the preachers.[141] Gundert realised the difficulties involved shortly after arriving in 1836, when another missionary told him about 'the black side of the Tamils and their conversion: their weaknesses, their money grabbing, the ability of the families to stick together, mendacity, ingratitude, hypocrisy, etc.' However, Gundert believed that a missionary 'must go deep, if he wants to preach to the heathens as brothers'.[142] The depth and commitment required comes through in Gundert's diary entries in his early years in India.[143]

The Basel Mission published two pamphlets celebrating the conversion of higher caste Hindus during the 1880s. One of these focused upon Jakob Ramawarma, the son of the Maharaja of Tripumtura, born in 1814. Ramawarma lost his parents in 1828, came into contact with Christianity in the early 1830s and underwent baptism in 1835. Ramawarma eventually became ordained in Kannanur in a ceremony attended by Gundert and Irion.[144] The second Brahmin conversion involved Ragappaja, who made an appearance at the mission house in Basrur in July 1882, where he met the missionary Ludwig Gengnagel, with whom he wanted to discuss the Gospel as his brother had come into contact with it after purchasing 'good words' at a Hindu festival. Gengnagel's pamphlet describes Ragappaja's process of conversion, which involved much discussion of the scriptures, in great detail.[145]

Germans and Britons

Interaction between Germans and Indians remained complex and involved the use of intermediaries during the process of conversion. While missionaries measured their success through the size of their congregations, they also regularly wrote about the constant hostility which they experienced.[146] As well an interacting with Indians, the Germans also had to work with the British.

German missionary organisations closely co-operated with British groupings. Paul Jenkins has described the relationship between the CMS and the Basel Mission as 'an early experiment in inter-European co-operation'.[147] The employment of Basel-trained missionaries by the CMS in the earlier nineteenth century followed an agreement in

1818, whereby Basel would provide a fixed number of missionaries and the CMS would help with their education. This co-operation operated on a global level[148] and, on a broader basis, culminated in the World Missionary Conference in Edinburgh in 1910.[149] In the Indian environment, a National Christian Council came into existence in 1914, evolving from efforts at co-operation between all of the Christian groupings from the middle of the nineteenth century, leading initially to a National Missionary Council. Three conferences had already taken place between 1855 and 1859 in Calcutta, Benares and Nilagiri.[150] In 1897, Anglican, Lutheran, Congregationalist, Baptist and Methodist missionaries established the South India Missionary Association in order to allow consultation and united action. There followed the fourth All India Missionary Conference in 1902. German groupings became part of the National Christian Council from its inception, although its first major task involved picking up the pieces of German missionary work following the outbreak of war.[151] Apart from the fact that German missionaries, most famously Rhenius and Weitbrecht, worked for English organisations in the earlier nineteenth century, some of the most prominent Germans initially gravitated towards the British groupings which already existed in India while also seeking out other Germans and making attempts to expand the activities of the groups they represented, as the examples of both Gundert and Graul indicate.[152]

Conflict also arose between German and British missionaries. In the case of those working for the CMS, both linguistic and ecclesiastical issues led to disputes during the 1820s and 1830s. The most dramatic of these involved Rhenius and the CMS and led to the boarding up of his church in Tirunelveli.[153] Missionary organisations, including those from Germany, also engaged in 'sheep stealing' of already converted Christians from other denominations, not just from Roman Catholics, but also from Protestant groups, continuing a centuries old tradition in India.[154] In southern India, territorial disputes arose in the areas originally controlled by the Tranquebar Mission in the eighteenth century as British and American groups moved in.[155]

A complex mix of relationships also developed between secular Germans and Britons. Those employed in an almost entirely British environment essentially became part of broader European society. A. Anton, for example, following the Indian Mutiny, could write in a diary entry of 18 September 1857: 'Delhi has been taken, hurrah for old England.'[156] Similarly, while Oscar Flex may have questioned the attitudes of the Englishmen with whom he worked, he formed part of European society, even though it remained overwhelmingly British in its composition.[157]

The aristocratic Hans von Koenigsmarck became completely integrated into the upper echelons of British society when he visited India shortly before the outbreak of the First World War, meeting some of the leading figures in the country.[158] Similarly, just as he had interacted positively with Indians, Paul Deussen also enjoyed the company of Britons. For example, he made a journey to Fort Jamrud in the Khyber Pass, where he met Colonel Warburton, who 'received us in a very friendly manner in his office'.[159] When he proceeded to Amritsar he enjoyed a 'very pleasant conversation' while having dinner in a bungalow, especially with 'a Mr Summers' who 'subsequently introduced himself as a Member of Parliament'. Deussen developed a friendship with Summers and met him later in Delhi and Lucknow.[160] He also became friends with a Mrs Davidson, whom he met both in the Himalayas and in Bombay.[161] In the latter, he visited the Cosmopolitan Club, gave a lecture to the Asiatic Society and was looked after by Professor Peterson.[162] Both Koenigsmarck and Deussen clearly had well-developed social skills which allowed them to ease into British high society in India, in contrast to the more critical and misanthropic Garbe who wrote about his experiences in India in a negative manner. Garbe's volume contains an entire chapter on the life of Europeans in India using impersonal language with no named individuals.[163]

Interethnic relationships

Garbe's chapter contains reference to 'Eurasians or East Indians' with an 'olive colour' excluded from the inner echelons of European society. He gives an example of a woman with a European father and an Indian mother who described the prejudice she faced.[164] Other German observers also commented upon people of mixed ethnic heritage. The missionary Johannes Hoffmann, for example, quoting the 1911 census, pointed to the presence of 90,000 'half-castes' (*Mischlinge*), which he did not marginalise to the same extent as Garbe, adding them to the 170,000 Europeans.[165] Graul had identified them as 'half European' and distinguished between the 'Indo-Portuguese' and the 'Indo-Britons'.[166]

In fact, interethnic relationships in India characterised the history of Europeans from the arrival of the Portuguese in the sixteenth century.[167] However, as Graul and Garbe recognised, and as later confirmed by Mizutani, Eurasians faced marginalisation in British India. Mizutani points out that the reason for this lay both in a fear of miscegenation and in their relative poverty.[168] Esme Cleall, meanwhile, in her study of missionary attitudes in the colonial environment, has pointed to the fact that: 'All missionary sexuality was expected to occur within marriage' and that 'like other colonial thinkers, missionaries continued to find "mixed race" relationships unacceptable over the course of the nineteenth century and the difference of Indians and Africans was thought to be self-evident'.[169] Cleall's logic therefore suggests that Christian principles could not overcome the racism inherent in imperialism.[170] As the statistics below suggest, marriages between Germans and Indians, whether missionaries or not, rarely took place – although sex certainly did, as confirmed by Dr Rosenberger, even though in his case it involved payment. However, a handful of Germans did marry Indians, some of whom have left a trace of their lives. The main reason why marriages between German missionaries and Indians remained rare may have had as much to do with the control which the missionary organisations exercised, acting as marriage bureaus to ensure that the people it had invested in training secured unions with equally religious women, [171] as it had to do with racism. Cleall's perspective contradicts that put forward by Judith Becker, as well as Heather Sharkey, who view the missionary experience as a way of breaking down barriers.

In order to come to conclusions, we need to provide statistical data about marriage, available from several sources. Most German missionaries married other Germans, which was inevitable because of the control which, for example, Basel and Leipzig exercised. On the other hand, Paul Jenkins has pointed out that 'about half of the marriages' of CMS employees from 'the European mainland', overwhelmingly Germans, 'were concluded with English women and half with women from the German-speaking world'.[172] Jenkins' assertion refers to continental Europeans sent throughout the globe, but Table 5.1 points to a similar picture for those who went to India. The figures encompass all wives, including those cases where the first and even second died. Marrying an English wife therefore became just as normal as finding a German one. Those in the former category included Weitbrecht, who actually married the widow of an English missionary, T. K. Higgs, in 1834.[173] Weitbrecht's memoirs, compiled by his widow after his death, stated:

Table 5.1 Nationality of the wives of German-born missionaries employed by the Church Missionary Society

Nationality	British	German	Other European	Not given	Indian	Not married	Total
Total	24	23	2	4	1	5	59
Percentage	40.7	39	3.4	6.8	1.7	8.4	100

Source: Church Missionary Society, *Register of Missionaries, Clerical, Lay, & Female, and Native Clergy, from 1804 to 1904* (London, 1904), pp. 1–152.

'The lady to whom he became engaged had been prepared by a peculiar course of Providential discipline to take an active part in missionary work, and had already enjoyed some little experience of it practically.'[174] This suggests some type of arranged marriage, and it seems the CMS had some control over unions in the same way as Basel and Leipzig. When William James Deerr wanted to marry Mary White he wrote to the CMS about his decision but also asked if his future wife could run her own schools.[175] Table 5.1 also points to the marriage of one German-born missionary to an Indian. The couple concerned consist of Christian Bomwetsch, born in Schorndorf in Württemberg in 1820 and trained at the Basel Seminary and CMS College. Bomwetsch spent most of his time in education at Santipore and nearby Calcutta, where he must have met his wife, 'Mani Mukhta Biswas, a Native Teacher in the Central School, Calcutta', whom he married in 1856.[176] However, CMS employees tended to form unions either with English or German women. The one case which involved marriage to an Indian resembles the marriage of Weitbrecht and Deerr in the sense that in both instances wives worked for the mission, suggesting that, for Bomwetsch and Biswas, social status and religious belief trumped race.

However, in the case of Leipzig and Basel, marriage even with other Europeans remained unusual in view of the control exercised over unions and the fact that both communities operated in more German environments than those which the CMS-employed Germans encountered. Leipzig records remain patchy when it comes to marriage details, but a sample of 13 personal files which give details of partners reveals that all married other Germans. In fact, they often chose people from the same area, suggesting that marriage or betrothal occurred before emigration. Thus, Ernst David Appelt from Margorin in Posen married Emilie Zibell from Samocin in Posen, although this union occurred in India. Similarly, Baierlein married fellow Posener Barbara Zielenzig, while Arthur Fehlberg from Carwitz married another Pommeranian in the form of Henriette Falbe from Stettin in India. Finally, Richard Fröhlich from Hanover married Mathilde August from Brunswick in India.[177]

An examination of the unions of German-born males who worked for Basel shows that the overwhelming majority of them married other German women, or at least women with German names, again largely explained by the control over this issue which the Mission exercised. Some of these may have consisted of Swiss women, but the 'Gebietslisten' compiled by the Basel Mission archive identified only three wives as born in Switzerland. The German names could also include women born in India to missionary parents. While some of the marriages to women with British-sounding names in Table 5.2 repeat those in Table 5.1, a few occured in the late nineteenth and early twentieth centuries.

Table 5.2 Ethnicity of the wives of German-born missionaries employed by the Basel Mission, 1820–1918

Nationality	German	British	Swiss	Other European	Indian	Total
Total	265	27	3	4	4	303
Percentage	87.5	8.9	1.0	1.3	1.3	100

Source: BMA/Q-30.3,5, Gebietslisten, Indien, Männer 1.

For example, Gottlob Engel from Württemberg married Agnes Brown,[178] while Robert Büchner from Erfurt married Marie Stork in 1901 and Friedrich Hernecken took Mary Stokes as his wife in 1899.[179] We might speculate that these women may have worked for British or US missions, but no evidence supports this assertion.

Table 5.2 also indicates that four Germans married Indians, despite the claim by Catherine Stenzl that 'in the Basel Mission the differences between Indians and Europeans were seldom forgotten and a strict separation was maintained: marriages between Europeans and people of other races were not allowed'.[180] The 12 marriage rules drawn up by Christian Blumhardt in 1837 did not make any overt reference to race.[181] The four Indo-German marriages in Table 5.2 include the already mentioned Bomwetsch,[182] but the other three require further analysis. In 1836, Johann Lechler from Münklingen in Württemberg married 'a lady in Madras', which seems too vague to allow any conclusions about ethnicity and might refer to a British, Indian or German woman.[183] Of more certainty, and probably one of only two genuine marriages between Germans and Indians, Johannes Haller from Aldingen in Württemberg took 'Anna Mercia Pereira (Indien)', perhaps a woman brought up as a Roman Catholic, as his wife in 1858.[184]

The final interethnic union contained in the Gebietlisten leads us to the most celebrated nineteenth-century marriage between a German and an Indian. In 1903, Wilhelm Heckelmann from Neesbach in Hesse Nassau married 'E. Kaundinya Indien'.[185] Emilie is the daughter of the most famous mixed-race partner in the form of Anandrao Kaundinya. Kaundinya was also the father of R. Kaundinya who worked as a planter in German East Africa.[186] Born to a Brahmin family in Mangalore in 1825, Anandrao Kaundinya became a Christian in 1844 after falling sick and reading the scriptures. In fact, Kaundinya already had an Indian wife, Lakshmi, whom he initially appears to have deserted when travelling to Europe for training in Basel. Upon his return he persuaded her to convert, but she died shortly afterwards, which devastated him. He considered taking a native Indian woman for his wife, but caste became an issue. His mentor Hermann Mögling therefore found a suitable

German woman for him, Marie Reinhardt. This contrasts with the objection to the marriage of Johannes Zimmermann on the Gold Coast to a black woman from the West Indies. While the grounds for the objection may lie in the fact that he did not obtain permission to marry, in contrast to Kaudinya's union, racism played a part, as the Basel Mission committee forbade Zimmermann from returning to Germany where he would lose his citizenship rights.[187]

Any conclusions about marriage and ethnicity among German missionaries in India need to consider the control which the mission organisations exercised over all aspects of the lives of those they had invested time and money in training, including the choice of wife. However, in view of the tiny minority of Germans who chose Indian wives, racism must have played a role. In this sense, missionaries fell into the white racial elites who controlled India although, in view of the presence of 'Eurasians' in the country, the German missionaries appear even more ethnically exclusivist in their marriage patterns than the rest of the white population. Kaundinya's exception occurred because of the support of Mögling. Marrying Englishwomen maintained racial boundaries – even though this type of union remained unusual, except in the case of the CMS – again pointing to the control of the missions.

What about the rest of the German population in India? As Dr Rosenberger makes clear, interracial sex clearly took place. The women he visited included Indians, Japanese and Germans.[188] However, more long-term relationships also developed as revealed in lists of 'hostile aliens ... remaining' in India after general deportation had taken place in 1915–16. The information on 55 mostly mixed marriages involving Germans summarised in Table 5.3 proves especially useful. The two purely German unions do not reflect reality as most of those who had faced repatriation would have retained German nationality unaffected by a foreign partner and we can assume that most Germans in India married other Germans. As in the case of the missionaries, the main alternative consisted of Britons, again pointing to the fact that they counted by far the largest available European population and to the fact that race influenced decisions, especially bearing in mind the fact that four from five marriages involved Germans and Europeans or Americans. As an indication of the level of integration of Germans into British society we can point to Mrs Will, the 'British wife of a German prisoner of war who himself was born of a German father and British mother'. The other Europeans consist of one Armenian, one Swede, one Swiss and one Greek. The Eurasians included Mrs Minnie Volandt (married to a prisoner of war) who did not speak German and 'has never left Bombay in her life, except to visit her interned husband at Ahmednagar'. The other non-Europeans consist of a Syrian, a South

Table 5.3 Ethnicity of marriage partners exempted from internment in India in 1916

Nationality	German German	German British	German Eurasian	German Indian	German US	German other European	German other non-European	Total
Total	2	37	5	4	2	4	4	58
Percentage	3.5	63.7	8.5	6.9	3.6	6.9	6.9	100

Source: IOR/L/MIL/7/18565, List of hostile aliens now remaining in India owing to their being exempted from repatriation, 1916.

African, the 'half-breed (French-African) wife of a German' and the 'half-breed Mauritian wife of a German, who was naturalised in British India in 1910'. It seems as though four Indian women married German men, although the list does not provide details of their ethnicity, stating simply 'born in India'.[189] These statistics confirm the fact that, as with missionaries, racial boundaries generally remained intact, although those not connected with religion appear to have participated in more interethnic sex and marriage.

Hostility towards German missionaries

Once the First World War broke out, Germans would face the type of hostility from British society and government in India which they experienced in other parts of the British Empire. Before this time, they had become integrated into European society in the country, indicated most clearly by the normality of marriage to the British, even though distinct German identity – both religious and secular – had evolved by 1914. Marriage statistics also point to the distance which existed between Germans and Indians, despite the development of congregations in which both worked together but within which a racial hierarchy existed with German managers at the top.

Although the missionary propagandists pointed to the size of congregations to indicate the level of success of their efforts in India and elsewhere, in reality they converted only a tiny percentage of the Indian population, even in the areas where they located their mission stations. While they celebrated their successes, they experienced daily ridicule and insult, which could turn violent.

James Deerr painted a picture of a typical scene in 1835:

> We went together into the great bazaar and addressed some of the people standing idle with these words. Come, we shall teach you the way of salvation! To which one of them replied how do you know that we have not the way of salvation? Because you worship sticks and stones. God is a spirit and his true worship is in spirit and in truth. A considerable number of people collected and listened with great attention, till at last a very common looking chap abused our young man, prattling a good deal without knowing himself what he meant, and when he was interrogated, he said: I mean to say that I shall not worship Jesus Christ.[190]

A Basel annual report from 1870 similarly asserted that: 'Willingness to hear the word is generally not met with very frequently, though there are also many encouraging signs ... Open opposition and violence are however disappearing more and more, though it is rather indifference which comes instead of it.' The same report mentioned the fact that

'Mr Metz', who had worked for seven months in one particular district where he felt he had made some progress, found that one of the 'headmen' had 'warned people against me'.[191] Meanwhile, Gehring mentioned the fact that: 'Together with the evangelists, I have preached to the heathen in and near Trichinopoli when it did not always go peacefully and smoothly. The closer to an idol's temple, the more fanatical were the heathens.' On one occasion:

> We stood near a clock tower on the side of the street which led to the cliffs. A great mass of people had gathered around us. Scarcely had I begun to speak to them, when a naughty boy began to cry 'hui, hui'. That was the signal for a general uproar. There was incessant whistling, screaming and howling which prevented further lecturing. Those behind pushed closer and closer. Some pulled my cassock from behind and I immediately saw that nothing could be done.

They therefore escaped towards their church.[192] In 1890, *Der Evangelische Heidenbote* carried an article on 'The hatred of the Name Jesus in India', written by Thomas Digel who worked in North Canara and who claimed that in recent years daily and weekly newspapers, which 'inculcate the people with hatred against Christ and Christianity', had 'shot up like mushrooms on an oak tree'.[193] But the missionaries and the organisations which employed them viewed hostility as an occupational hazard[194] which did not stop them from preaching. Gottlieb Pfander became the German missionary with the reputation for some of the most aggressive preaching and disputation in public places, concentrating in Moslem areas (having mastered his knowledge of Islamic scripts) not only in British India but also elsewhere in the Middle East.[195] As well as the type of public resistance in the streets described by Deerr and Gehring, those trying to convert could also face hostility from the families of individuals who wanted to embrace Christianity, most famously in the case of Kaundinya.[196]

The extracts above point to the threat of violence, which could percolate to the surface. Judith Becker has pointed to the fact that Basel missionaries regularly reported violence, which she asserts helped to 'exoticise' the reports they wrote, providing several examples from the 1840s.[197] Gundert reported on the violence carried out by the Mappila Muslims in Malabar during the 1840s, although it did not focus upon the missionaries.[198] However, attacks against Basel buildings occurred in the 1850s. For example, in 1856 both the recently built missionary home and the church in Udapi faced destruction as a result of arson, although the fires do not seem to have resulted in any injuries.[199]

The Indian Mutiny of the following year, motivated by anti-British including anti-Christian feeling,[200] impacted upon missionaries. Most of the Germans viewed the events of 1857 from a distance, as the rebellion remained concentrated in northern India. Baierlein's memoirs contained a chapter on the rebellion, which occurred when he lived in Kudelur, describing events which happened further north but also pointing to the fear which they caused in the European population of the city.[201] This feeling of unease also surfaced in Tranquebar, where rumours circulated in August 1857 about an imminent uprising in the south.[202] The German missionary publications also carried stories of the events in northern India using terrified and indignant language,[203] while one article listed the death of seven missionaries (none of them German) working for a variety of organisations, as well as the scale of damage to buildings which resulted.[204] Baierlein actually wrote one of the most evocative articles, again from a distance, in which he spoke of 'bloody and gruesome scenes' and 'the screams of murdered men, women and children'.[205] One piece from 1859 asserted that, although 'the whole of the south remained calm and still' in 1857 hostility had begun to spread against Christianity.[206]

While most Germans remained distant from the violence of 1857 and simply experienced fear, others lived much closer to the epicentre. They included A. Anton, who worked for a British Army band in the Punjab and therefore received news of the military consequences of the uprising. In fact, the house of his brother, who lived in Umballa 'as the band master of the ninth Lancers ... was burnt down'.[207] He also described a scene on 30 July. 'A fanatical Hindu ran towards me with a raised sword with the call ... our brothers have risen ... I quickly got dressed, armed myself and ran outside' where 'bullets flew over my head'.[208] He continued to 'sleep with sword and weapons of all sorts and surrounded by dogs' for six months.[209] The other major narrative of the mutiny written by a German came from Charles Leupolt, who worked for the CMS in Benares. His description remained more matter of fact than Anton's and he experienced no violence. While he remained in the city, other missionaries and their families, as well as his daughter, fled to Secrole.[210] Leupolt asserted that missionaries 'had nothing to fear from the mutineers. Some were murdered along with other Europeans, but none were singled out.'[211] However, letters written by Leupoldt and his daughter Martha in the summer of 1857 did not have such a calm tone as they described the events happening around them.[212] Another CMS missionary, Frederic Edward Schneider, lived in Agra in the summer and autumn of 1857, and described the fear which reigned in the city as well as relief following the arrival of British troops.[213]

While Leupoldt escaped any direct physical violence, the Gossner mission stations experienced it at closer quarters following the uprising in Chota Nagpur from the end of July. This first impacted on the station at Hazaribagh from where the only missionary, Henry Batsch, had fled to Calcutta. Meanwhile, the Ranchi missionaries also escaped to Calcutta, where they had initially travelled but then returned. The mutineers reached Ranchi on 2 August and destroyed all European buildings, including those of the mission station. Converted Christians also suffered persecution. The missionaries described the scenes of destruction on their return, although the station soon got back on its feet.[214]

Prejudice and interaction

While the German missionaries became caught up in the violence of the Indian Mutiny, they did not constitute its main focus and none appear to have experienced direct violence, either because they remained distant from the epicentre of events or because they fled. However, German missionaries faced direct hostility in the century before the First World War, which we should not find surprising given the fact that they travelled around India trying to persuade people to give up their ancestral religion. In some cases this animosity would result in violence, although ridicule surfaced more regularly. While conversions took place after an often lengthy process in which intermediaries played a central role, the German missionaries only had an impact in the stations which they established. Most Indians, even in the areas in which they became concentrated, ultimately ignored them.

Conversion proved the clearest symbol of interethnic interaction, indicating a break through the barriers between Germans and Indians. As the narrative above has indicated, these barriers involved much prejudice in which missionaries focused especially upon what they viewed as the faults of Hinduism, above all the worship of false Gods and caste. Other Germans critiqued the position of Indian women. While landscapes generally elicited positive reactions from travelling and resident Germans, cityscapes often gave rise to negative images by focusing on issues such as disease. Barriers with the British remained lower than those with Indians, although some emerged, especially by the early twentieth century, demonstrating envy about British control.

The cultural encounter was easier when it involved Germans and Britons than Germans and Indians. While German communities, especially revolving around religion, existed in nineteenth-century India, some indicators point to the absorption of Germans into wider British or European society. Intermarriage became normal, at least amongst those working for the CMS as well as for Britons not connected to missionary organisations. On the other hand, the control exercised over choice of partner by Leipzig and Basel made marriage with anyone other than another German unusual.

The cultural encounter with Indians remained much more hierarchical. Working within the structures of British rule, the Germans controlled any type of relationship with Indians, above all in the missionary sphere. Although little evidence surfaces of literally 'going native', those Germans who spent much of their lives in the country would have become integrated into their surroundings, even if they still remained at the top of the religious hierarchy they had established. Reading the experiences of Gehring, Gundert or Mögling reveals a deep appreciation of the environment in which they lived and the people with whom they interacted. Clearly, the main type of conversion consisted of baptism, which involved Indians taking on the religion of Europeans. While admiration for Buddhism had developed within Germany during the second half of the nineteenth century, little evidence exists of Germans abandoning Christianity for this belief.[215] If the ultimate form of integration consists of intermarriage, this rarely happened – even among secular Germans.

While initial prejudices often broke down, especially in the understanding which many missionaries developed of their new environment and in cultural conversion through religion, limits existed to the extent to which transformation occurred. The case of Kaundinya and his Indo-German children provide the ultimate symbol of the breakdown of barriers, but they also point to the difficulties involved, in the form of the resistance from his family. Such unions remained rare. Sex was different. The greater regularity of unions between Britons and Germans points to the lower barriers of the two groups as well as the way in which Germans formed part of wider European society in India, despite their small numbers within it.

Notes

1 Judith Becker, *Conversio Im Wandel: Basler Missionare Zwischen Europa und Sudindien und die Ausbildung einer Kontaktreligiosität, 1834–1860* (Göttingen, 2015). This work receives further attention later.
2 Judith Becker, ed., *European Missions in Contact Zones: Transformation through Interaction in a (Post-) Colonial World* (Göttingen, 2015).
3 Heather Sharkey, ed., *Cultural Conversions: Unexpected Consequences of Christian Missionary Encounters in the Middle East, Africa and South Asia* (Syracuse, NY, 2013). These ideas receive further attention later.
4 Hermann von Schlagintweit-Sakülünski, *Reisen in Indien und Hochasien Basirt auf die Resultate der wissenschaftlichen Mission von H, A und R von Schlagintweit ausgefuhrt in den Jahren 1854–1858*, Vol. 1, *Indien* (Jena, 1869), p. 47; Karl Graul, *Reise in Ostindien von December 1849 bis Oktober 1852*, Vol. 1, *Bombay, das Tulu-Land, Malajalam, die Nilagiris* (Leipzig, 1854), pp. 100–2.
5 See, for example: Adrian Carton, *Mixed-race and Modernity in Colonial India: Changing Concepts of Hybridity across Empires* (London, 2012); William Dalrymple, *White Mughals: Love and Betrayal in 18th-Century India* (London, 2004).

6 Damon Iremina Salesa, *Racial Crossings: Race, Intermarriage and the Victorian British Empire* (Oxford, 2011).
7 Kris Manjapra, *Age of Entanglement: German and Indian Intellectuals across Empire* (London, 2014), pp. 17–36. See also Chapter 2.
8 Andreas Nehring, *Orientalismus und Mission: Die Repräsentation der tamulischen Gesellschaft und Religion durch Leipziger Missionare 1840–1940* (Wiesbaden, 2003).
9 Edward Said, *Orientalism* (London, 2003 reprint), pp. 31–49.
10 Satoshi Mizutani, *The Meaning of White: Race, Class, and the 'Domiciled Community' in British India 1858–1930* (Oxford, 2011).
11 Christine Bolt, *Victorian Attitudes to Race* (London, 1971), pp. 157–205.
12 Thomas R. Metcalf, *Ideologies of the Raj* (Cambridge, 1998).
13 Julia Ulrike Mack, *Menschenbilder: Anthropologische Konzepte und stereotype Vorstellungen vom Menschen in der Publizistik der Basler Mission 1816–1914* (Zurich, 2014), utilises such concepts but not in an overt sense, preferring, as the title suggests, to use the idea of 'anthropological concepts' and 'stereotypical perceptions' in her study of the publicity material issued by the Basel Mission.
14 Perry Myers, 'German Travellers to India at the Fin-de-Siècle and their Ambivalent View of the Raj', in Joanne Miyang Cho, Eric Kurlander and Douglas T. McGetchin, eds, *Transcultural Encounters between Germany and India: Kindred Spirits in the Nineteenth and Twentieth Centuries* (London, 2014), pp. 84–98.
15 Emil Schlagintweit, *Indien in Wort und Bild*, Vol. 1 (Leipzig, 1880), pp. 1–11.
16 Otto Ehlers, *An indischen Fürstenhöfen* (Berlin, 1894).
17 Oscar Bongard, *Die Reise des Deutschen Kronprinzen durch Ceylon und Indien* (Berlin, 1911), pp. 79–92. For an introduction to hunting and imperialism, see John M. MacKenzie, *The Empire of Nature: History, Conservation and British Imperialism* (Manchester, 1988), which includes a chapter (7) on 'The Imperial Hunt in India'.
18 Hermann Dalton, *Indische Reisebriefe* (Gütersloh, 1899), p. 91. Other enthusiastic accounts of the Himalayan region include: Paul Deussen, *Erinnerungen an Indien* (Leipzig, 1904), pp. 162–74; Max Zimmer, *Unsere Reise durch Indien, Java u. Ceylon im Jahre 1910* (Baden-Baden, 1911), pp. 155–6; and Richard Garbe, *Indische Reiseskizzen* (Berlin, 1889), pp. 159–60.
19 Evangelische Missions-Gesellschaft, *Album der Basler Mission: Bilder aus Indien* (Basel, 1860).
20 Alwin Gehring, *Das Tamulenland, seine Bewohner und die Mission* (Leipzig, 1927).
21 Alwin Gehring, *Erinnerungen aus dem Leben eines Tamulenmissionars* (Leipzig, 1906), pp. 59–60.
22 Waldemar Bonsels, *Indienfahrt* (originally 1912; Norderstedt, 2008). Truth and fiction in this work has received analysis from Kamal Karnick, 'Warheit und Dichtung in Bonsels "Indienfart"', in Rose-Marie Bonsels, ed., *Indien als Faszination: Stimmen zur 'Indienfahrt' von Waldemar Bonsels* (Wiesbaden, 1990) pp. 13–93.
23 Waldemar Bonsels, *Mein Austritt aus der Baseler Missions-Industrie und seine Gründe: Ein offener Brief an die Baseler Missions-Gemeinde in Württemberg und der Schweiz* (München-Schwabing, 1904).
24 Ibid., pp. 4–5.
25 Bonsels, *Indienfahrt*.
26 Perry Myers, 'The Ambivalence of a Spiritual Quest in India: Waldemar Bonsels's Indienfahrt', in Veronika Fuechtner and Mary Rhiel, eds, *Imagining Germany Imagining Asia: Essays in Asian-German Studies* (Rochester, NY, 2013), pp. 131–53.
27 Ibid., p. 151.
28 Vidhagiri Ganeshan, *Das Indienbild deutscher Dichter um 1900: Dauthendey, Bonsels, Mauthner, Gjellerup, Hermann Keyserling und Stefan Zweig: Ein Kapitel deutsch-indischer Geistesbeziehungen im frühen 20. Jahrhundert* (Bonn, 1975), pp. 138–61.
29 Vidhagiri Ganeshan, *Das Indienerlebnis Hermann Hesses*, 2nd Edition (Bonn, 1980); Hermann Hesse, *Aus Indien* (Berlin, 1913); Hermann Hesse, *Autobiographical Writings* (London, 1973), pp. 58–75.

INTERETHNIC PERCEPTIONS AND INTERACTIONS

30 Berthold Ribbentrop, *Forestry in British India* (Calcutta, 1900); Dietrich Brandis, *Indian Trees: An Account of Trees, Shrubs, Woody Climbers, Bamboos and Palms Indigenous or Commonly Cultivated in the British Indian Empire* (London, 1906). John Augustus Voelcker, *Report on the Improvement of Indian Agriculture* (London, 1893) falls into a similar category to these two volumes.
31 Adolphe and Robert Schlagintweit, *Report on the Proceedings of the Officers Engaged in the Magnetic Survey of India* (Madras, 1855); *Report upon the Progress of the Magnetic Survey of India, and of the Researches Connected with it in the Himalaya Mountains, from April to October 1855* (Agra, 1856).
32 Hermann von Schlagintweit-Sakülünski, *Reisen in Indien und Hochasien Basirt auf die Resultate der wissenschaftlichen Mission von H, A und R von Schlagintweit ausgefuhrt in den Jahren 1854–1858*, three volumes (Leipzig, 1869–80).
33 Hermann von Schlagintweit-Sakülünski, *Reisen in Indien und Hochasien Basirt auf die Resultate der wissenschaftlichen Mission von H, A und R von Schlagintweit ausgefuhrt in den Jahren 1854–1858*, Vol. 1, *Indien* (Jena, 1869), pp. 69–77.
34 Ibid., pp. 141–8.
35 Oscar Kauffmann, *Aus Indiens Dschungeln: Erlebnisse und Forschungen*, two volumes (Leipzig, 1911).
36 Ernst Haeckel, *Indische Reisebriefe* (Berlin, 1883).
37 Oscar Flex, *Pflanzerleben in Indien: Kulturgeschichtliche Bilder aus Assam* (Berlin, 1873).
38 For examples of Flex's appreciation of the natural environment, see, for example, ibid., pp. 12–13, 132–3, 172–4.
39 J. J. Weitbrecht, *Protestant Missions in Bengal Illustrated: Being the Substance of a Course of Lectures Delivered on Indian Missions* (London, 1844), pp. 1–22.
40 See, for example, K. Kühnle, *Die Arbeitsstätten der Basler Mission in Indien, China, Goldküste und Kamerun: Mit Übersichtskarte und Stationsbildern* (Basel, 1896), pp. 5–6; Christian Irion, *Malabar und die Missionsstation Talatscheri* (Basel, 1864), pp. 1–5.
41 E. R. Baierlien, *The Land of the Tamulians and its Missions* (Madras, 1875).
42 Andreas Nehring, 'Missionsstrategie und Forschungsdrang: Anmerkungen zu Mission und Wissenschaft in Südindien im 19. Jahrhundert', in Heike Liebau, Andreas Nehring and Brigitte Klosterberg, eds, *Mission und Forschung: Translokale Wissensproduktion zwischen Indien und Europa im 18. und 19. Jahrhundert* (Halle, 2010), pp. 21–31.
43 Baierlien, *The Land of the Tamulians*, p. 1.
44 Nehring, 'Missionsstrategie'.
45 Baierlien, *The Land of the Tamulians*, pp. 1–16.
46 Ibid., p. 14.
47 Julius Richter, *Die deutsche Mission in Südindien: Erzählungen und Schilderungen von einer Missions-Studienreise durch Ostindien* (Gütersloh, 1902).
48 Hermann Mögling and V. D. M. Weitbrecht, *Das Kurgland und die evangelische Mission in Kurg* (Basel, 1866).
49 E. Gloyer, *Jeypur, das Haupt-Arbeitsfeld der Schleswig-Holsteinischen evangelisch-lutherischen Missionsgesellschaft zu Breklum auf der Ostküste Vorderindiens* (Breklum, 1901).
50 See, for example, Richard King, *Orientalism and Religion: Postcolonial Theory, India and the Mystic East* (Abingdon, 1999); Nehring, *Orientalismus und Mission*, pp. 242–82; Brian K. Pennington, *Was Hinduism Invented? Britons, Indians, and the Colonial Construction of Religion* (Oxford, 2007).
51 See the highly critical Vishwa Adluri and Joydeep Bagchee, *The Nay Science: A History of German Indology* (Oxford, 2014).
52 Nehring, *Orientalismus und Mission*, pp. 244–8.
53 Mack, *Menschenbilder*, pp. 108–9.
54 Charles Benjamin Leupolt, *Further Recollections of an Indian Missionary* (London, 1884), pp. 20–42.
55 Christoph Friedrich Eppler, *Karl Gottlieb Pfander: Ein Zeuge der Wahrheit unter den Bekennern des Islam* (Basel, 1888), pp. 122–38.

56 Edmund Raimund Baierlein, *Die Ev.-luth. Mission in Ostindien* (Leipzig, 1874), pp. 43–58. See also the German admiration for Buddhism outlined in Perry Myers, *German Visions of India, 1871–1918: Commandeering the Holy Ganges during the Kaiserreich* (Basingstoke, 2013).
57 Weitbrecht, *Protestant Missions in Bengal*, pp. 102–9.
58 *Evangelisches Missions-Magazin*, 1905, pp. 505–6.
59 Reinhold Grundemann, *Missions-Studien und Kritiken in Verbindung mit einer Reise nach Indien* (Gütersloh, 1894), p. 38.
60 *Der evangelische Heidenbote*, 1847, p. 56.
61 See, for example, Baierlein, *Die Ev.-luth. Mission in Ostindien*, pp. 59–74.
62 *Evangelisches Missions-Magazin*, 1860, pp. 115–47.
63 *Beiblatt zur Allgemeinen Missions=Zeitschrift*, 1912, pp. 85–93.
64 Karl Heinrich Christian Plath, *Eine Reise nach Indien: Für kleine und große Leute beschrieben* (Berlin, 1880), pp. 65–74.
65 *Beiblatt zur Allgemeinen Missions=Zeitschrift*, 1897, pp. 1–11.
66 S. Limbach, *Bilder aus dem Südindischen Volksleben* (Basel, 1893).
67 Richard Handmann, *Die Evangelisch-lutherische Tamulen-Mission in der Zeit ihrer Neubegründung* (Leipzig, 1903), pp. 302–47; Nehring, *Orientalismus und Mission*, pp. 102–23.
68 Karl Graul, *Explanations Concerning the Principles of the Leipzig Missionary Society, with Regard to the Caste Question* (Madras, 1851), pp. 1–2.
69 Weitbrecht, *Protestant Missions in Bengal*, pp. 68–70.
70 Georg Stosch, *Im fernen Indien: Eindrücke und Erfahrungen im Dienst der luth. Mission unter den Tamulen* (Berlin, 1896), pp. 157–75.
71 Emil Schlagintweit, 'Ostindische Kaste in der Gegenwart', *Zeitschrift der Deutschen Morgenländische Gesellschaft*, vol. 33 (1879), pp. 549–607.
72 Gehring, *Das Tamulenland*, pp. 10–28.
73 Irion, *Malabar*, pp. 7–23.
74 *Evangelisch-lutherisches Missionsblatt*, November 1857, pp. 331–2.
75 As an introduction, see, for example, Indrani Sen, *Women and Empire: Representation in the Writing of British India (1858–1900)* (Hyderabad, 2002), pp. 39–70.
76 Helene Lorbeer, *Frauenleben und Frauenelend am heiligen Ganges* (Berlin, 1911).
77 Erwin Rosenberger, *In indischen Liebesgassen: Aus dem Tagebuch eines Schiffsarztes* (Vienna, 1924).
78 Anna Lucas, *Die Deutschen in Indien* (Bordelsholm, 1925), pp. 129–30.
79 Gehring, *Das Tamulenland*, p. 35.
80 O. Gründler, *Frauenelend und Frauenmission in Indien* (Berlin, 1895), p. 9.
81 Ibid., p. 7.
82 Ibid., p. 13.
83 Ibid., p. 21.
84 For accounts of widow burning, see: *Die Biene auf dem Missionsfelde*, July 1844, p. 53; *Evangelisches Missions-Magazin*, 1914, p. 128. For more on this subject and European attitudes towards this practice, see Andrea Major, *Sovereignty and Social Reform in India: British Colonialism and the Campaign against Sati, 1830–1860* (London, 2011).
85 Gründler, *Frauenelend*, p. 25.
86 Aurélie Choné, 'Die Stadt des Lichts, eine für den Fremden unsichtbare Stadt? Probleme der Wahrnehmungsperspektive von Benares in deutschsprachigen Indienreiseschriften (1880–1930)', in Manfred Durzak, ed., *Bilder Indiens in der deutschen Literatur* (Frankfurt, 2011), pp. 41–54.
87 Kaushik Bagchi, 'An Orientalist in the Orient: Richard Garbe's Indian journey, 1885–1886', *Journal of World History*, vol. 14 (2003), pp. 309–12.
88 Choné, 'Die Stadt des Lichts', pp. 43–4.
89 Ibid., p. 45.
90 As an indication, see: Franz Reuleaux, *Eine Reise quer durch Indien im Jahre 1881: Erinnerungsblätter* (Berlin, 1884), pp. 97–102.
91 Joseph Dahlmann, *Indische Fahrten*, Vol. 1 (Freiburg im Breisgau, 1908), p. 233.

92 Detlef Bracker, *Burgen der Finsternis in Indien* (Breklum, 1916).
93 Esme Cleall, *Missionary Discourse: Negotiating Otherness in the British Empire, 1840–1900* (Basingstoke, 2012), pp. 79–97, discusses missionary perceptions of sickness.
94 Kauffmann, *Aus Indiens Dschungeln*, pp. 6–7.
95 Myers, 'German Travellers to India'.
96 Graul, *Bombay*, pp. 32, 104–18, 151–5.
97 Karl Graul, *Reise in Ostindien von December 1849 bis Oktober 1852*, Vol. 3, *Der Süden Ostindiens und Ceylon*, Part 2 (Leipzig, 1856), pp. 106, 108–9, 133–5.
98 Irion, *Malabar*, pp. 31–8.
99 Paulus Cassel, *Vom Nil zum Ganges: Wanderungen in die orientalische Welt* (Berlin, 1880), pp. 244–7.
100 Garbe, *Indische Reiseskizzen*, pp. 245.
101 Georg Wegener, *Das heutige Indien: Grundlagen und Probleme der britisch-indischen Herrschaft* (Berlin, 1912).
102 Hans Von Koenigsmarck, *Die Engländer in Indien: Reiseeindrücke* (Berlin, 1909).
103 See Chapter 4.
104 Mizutani, *The Meaning of White*.
105 Flex, *Pflanzerleben in Indien*, p. 76.
106 Ibid., p. 71.
107 Ibid., p. 72.
108 See, for example, ibid., p. 65.
109 Deussen, *Erinnerungen*, p. 25.
110 Ibid., pp. 32–3.
111 Ibid., pp. 73–4.
112 Ibid., pp. 137–42.
113 Ibid., pp. 168–9.
114 Reuleaux, *Eine Reise quer durch Indien*, pp. 35–7.
115 AA/R140877, Kaiserlich Deutsches Generalkonsulat to Reichskanzler Fürsten von Bülow, 15 April 1907.
116 AA/R140879, Tarapado Choudhury to Imperial German Consul General, 14 July 1913.
117 AA/R140878, Apurla Kumar to Imperial German Consul, 6 January 1908.
118 Garbe, *Indische Reiseskizzen*, pp. 227–32.
119 Ibid, p. 236.
120 Ibid., p. 241.
121 For further analysis, see Bagchi, 'An Orientalist in the Orient'.
122 Becker, *Conversio im Wandel*, pp. 164–77, 663–82.
123 Becker, *Conversio im Wandel*, pp. 154–64.
124 Ibid., p. 618.
125 See Chapters 3 and 4 for missionaries and language.
126 Mrinalini Sebastian, 'Localised Cosmopolitanism and Globalised Faith: Echoes of "Native" Voices in Eighteenth- and Nineteenth-Century Missionary Documents', in Becker, *European Missions in Contact Zones*, pp. 48–64.
127 Monica Juneja, 'Mission und Begegnung: Gestaltung und Grenzen eines kommunikativen Raumes', in Monica Juneja and Margrit Pernau, eds, *Religion und Grenzen in Indien und Deutschland: Auf dem Weg zu einer transnationalen Historiographie* (Göttingen, 2008), pp. 123–44.
128 Reinhardt Wendt, ' "Reden" und "Schreiben" in den Evangelisationsstrategien von Basler Missionaren und Jesuiten in Südwestindien und im südlichen Mindanao im 19. Jahrhundert', in Reinhard Wendt, ed., *Wege durch Babylon: Missionare, Sprachstudien und interkulturelle Kommunikation* (Tübingen, 1998), pp. 131–79.
129 L. Schomerus, 'Mittel und Wege zur Erlösung im indischen Heidentum nach Theorie und Praxis', in D. Paul, ed., *Die Leipziger Mission daheim und draussen* (Leipzig, 1914), pp. 113–35; Johannes Hesse, *Die Heidenpredigt in Indien* (Basel, 1883), p. 3.
130 Hesse, ibid., pp. 12–13, 38–44.

131 Ibid., pp. 45–8.
132 Basel German Evangelical Missionary, *Report of the Basel German Evangelical Mission in South-Western India for 1870* (Mangalore, 1871), p. 22.
133 Baierlein, *Die Ev.-luth. Mission in Ostindien*, pp. 257–63.
134 Johannes Hesse, *Die Heiden und Wir: 220 Geschichten und Beispiele aus der Heidenmission* (Calw, 1906), p. 277.
135 See, for example, *Evangelische Heidenbote*: June 1828, pp. 35–6; November 1836, pp. 91–2; July 1846, pp. 49–52.
136 For Hebich, see, for example: Samuel Hebich, *Züge aus dem Leben und Wirken des Missionars Samuel Hebich* (Elberfeld, 1864), pp. 17–43; Hermann Gundert and H. Mögling, *The Life of Samuel Hebich: By Two of His Fellow-Labourers* (originally London, 1876; Memphis, TN, 2012), pp. 33–6; Alfred Mathieson, *Hebich of India: A Passionate Soul-Winner* (Kilmarnock, 1936), pp. 118–26; Traugott Schölly, *Samuel Hebich: Der erste Sendbote der Basler Mission in Indien* (Basel, 1911), pp. 89–96; George N. Thomssen, *Samuel Hebich of India: A Master Fisher of Men*, 2nd Edition (Mangalore, 1915), pp. 164–75. For Mögling, see Hermann Gundert, *Herrmann Mögling: Ein Missionsleben in der Mitte des 19. Jahrhunderts* (Calw, 1882), pp. 150–6. For Gundert, see, for example: Hermann Gundert, *Aus dem Briefnachlass von Hermann Gundert* (Stuttgart, 1907). Much on Gundert can also be gleaned from the three volumes put together by Albrecht Frenz: *Hermann Gundert, Tagebuch aus Malabar, 1837–1859* (Stuttgart, 1983); *Hermann Gundert: Schriften und Berichte aus Malabar* (Stuttgart, 1983); and *Hermann Gundert: Reise nach Malabar* (Ulm, 1998).
137 Albrecht Frenz, *Eine Reise in die Religionen: Herrmann Mögling (1811–1881), Missionar und Sprachforscher in Indien, zum 200. Geburtstag* (Heidelberg, 2011), p. 322.
138 *Der evangelische Heidenbote*, 1876, p. 11.
139 Johann Jakob Jaus, *Samuel Hebich: Ein Zeuge Jesu Christi aus der Heidenwelt* (Stuttgart, 1922), p. 61.
140 German Evangelical Mission, *The Fifteenth Report of the German Evangelical Mission on the Western Coast of India* (Mangalore, 1855), pp. 9–10.
141 See later in the chapter.
142 Gundert, *Briefnachlass*, p. 366.
143 Frenz, *Gundert Tagebuch*, pp. 3–48.
144 Jakob Ramawarma, *Der indische Fürstensohn Jakob Ramawarma: Erstling der Malabar-Prediger* (Basel, 1880).
145 Ludwig Gengnagel, *Sieg des Evangeliums in einem Brahmanen-Herzen* (Basel, 1883).
146 See later in the chapter.
147 Paul Jenkins, 'The Church Missionary Society and the Basel Mission: An Early Experiment in Indo-European Cooperation', in Kevin Ward and Brian Stanley, eds, *The Church Mission Society and World Christianity, 1799–1999* (Richmond, 2000), pp. 43–63.
148 Jenkins, 'Church Missionary Society', pp. 57–8.
149 Brian Stanley, *The World Missionary Conference, Edinburgh 1910* (Grand Rapids, MI, 2009).
150 *Evangelisches Missions-Magazin*, 1859, pp. 114–16.
151 K. Baago, *A History of the National Christian Council of India, 1914–1964* (Nagpur, 1965), pp. 4–5, 15, 23.
152 Frenz, *Reise nach Malabar*, pp. 186–219; Graul, *Bombay*, pp. 31–3.
153 Jenkins, 'Church Missionary Society', pp. 59–61.
154 See, for example: Michael Bergunder, 'Proselytismus in der Geschitche des Indischen Christentums: Eine Ökumenische Bestandsaufnahme', in Ulrich van der Heyden and Jürgen Becker, eds, *Mission und Gewalt: Der Umgang christlicher Missionen mit Gewalt und die Ausbreitung des Christentums in Afrika und Asien in der Zeit von 1792 bis 1918/19* (Stuttgart, 2000), pp. 371–84; and C. S. Mohanavelu, 'Karl Graul's Efforts to Promote Evangelical Lutheran Mission in Tamil Nadu, 1844–1864', in idem., pp. 386–96.

155 Handmann, *Die Evangelisch-lutherische Tamulen-Mission*, pp. 286–302.
156 A. Anton, *Von Darmstadt nach Ostindien: Erlebnisse und Abenteuer eines Musikers auf der Reise durch Arabien nach Lahore: Die denkwürdigen Ereignisse der letzten Jahre* (Darmstadt, 1860), p. 62.
157 Flex, *Pflanzerleben in Indien*.
158 Koenigsmarck, *Die Engländer in Indien*.
159 Deussen, *Erinnerungen*, p. 91
160 Ibid., p. 101.
161 Ibid., p. 173.
162 Ibid., pp. 204–8. The text of his lecture can be found on pp. 239–51.
163 Garbe, *Indische Reiseskizzen*, pp. 205–54.
164 Ibid., pp. 341–2.
165 Johannes B. Hoffmann, *37 Jahre Missionär in Indien: Tröstliche Erfahrungen beim Naturvolk der Mundas: Der Misserfolg in der Missionierung höherer Kasten und seine Ursachen* (Innsbruck, 1923), p. 34.
166 Graul, *Bombay*, pp. 100–2.
167 Carton, *Mixed-Race and Modernity*.
168 Mizutani, *The Meaning of White*, p. 78. See also: Christopher J. Hawes, *Poor Relations: The Making of a Eurasian Community in British India, 1773–1833* (Richmond, 1996); and Allen D. Grimshaw, 'The Anglo-Indian community: the integration of a marginal group', *Journal of Asian Studies*, vol. 18 (1959), pp. 227–40.
169 Cleall, *Missionary Discourse*, pp. 68–9.
170 See the classic and sweeping Victor Kiernan, *The Lords of Human Kind: European Attitudes to Other Cultures in the Imperial Age* (Harmondsworth, 1972).
171 See Chapter 2 and 4.
172 Jenkins, 'Church Missionary Society', pp. 48–9.
173 Church Missionary Society, *Register of Missionaries, Clerical, Lay, & Female, and Native Clergy, from 1804 to 1904* (London, 1904), p. 29.
174 Mary Weitbrecht, *Memoir of the Rev. J. J. Weitbrecht: Compiled from his Journals and Letters by his Widow* (London, 1854), p. 100.
175 UB/CRL/SC/CMS/B/OMS/CI1O88, Letter from James Deerr, 23 February 1825.
176 Church Missionary Society, *Register of Missionaries, Clerical, Lay, & Female, and Native Clergy*, p. 66.
177 This analysis has used the following personal files from the AFST/LMW: II. 31.1.2., Ernst David Appelt; II. 31.1.3., Raimund Baierlein; II. 31.1.7., Dietrich Bergstedt; II. 31.1.8., Heinrich Beisenherz; II.31.1.11, Ernst Brutzer; II. 31.1. 13, Julius Döderlein; II.31.1.15, Matthäus Ellwein; II. 31.1. 16, Arthur Fehlberg; II. 31.1.18., Gustav Hermann Gäbler; II. 31.1.21., Richard Frölich; II.31.1.28, Gustav-Theodor Göttsching; II.31.1.30, Carl-Ernst Grahl; II. 31.1.31, Johannes Große.
178 The year of marriage is not given, but Engel emigrated in 1892.
179 These are entries 1316, 1290 and 1291 respectively in BMA/Q-30.3,5, Gebietslisten, Indien, Männer 1.
180 Catherine Stenzl, 'Racial Stereotypes in the Construction of the Other and the Identification of the Self: The Basel Mission and its Industries in India ca. 1884', in Martin Tamcke and Gladson Jathanna, eds, *Construction of the Other, Identification of the Self: German Mission in India* (Vienna, 2012), p. 46.
181 As printed in Dagmar Konrad, *Missionsbräute: Pietistinnen des 19. Jahrhunderts in der Basler Mission* (Münster, 2001), p. 34.
182 BMA/Q-30.3,5, Gebietslisten, Indien, Männer 1, 252.
183 Ibid., 114.
184 Ibid., 392.
185 Ibid., 1522.
186 R. Kaundinya, *Erinnerungen aus meinen Pflanzerjahren in Deutsch-Ost-Afrika* (Leipzig, 1918).
187 Wilhelm Schlatter, *Geschichte der Basler Mission*, Vol. 3., *Die Geschichte der Basler Mission in Afrika* (Basel, 1916), p. 51; Jon Miller, *The Social Control of Religious Zeal: A Study of Organizational Contradictions* (New Brunswick, NJ,

1994), pp. 134–5; Stenzl, 'Racial Stereotypes', pp. 46–7; Mrinalini Sebastian, 'The Scholar-Missionaries of the Basel Mission in Southwest India: Language, Identity and Knowledge in Flux', in Sharkey, *Cultural Conversions*, pp. 183–95; J. Jayakiran Sebastian, 'The baptism of death: reading the life and death of Lakshmi Kundinya', *Mission Studies*, vol. 28 (2011), pp. 26–53; Albrecht Frenz, *Freiheit hat Gesicht. Anadapur – eine Begegnung zwischen Kodagu und Baden-Württemberg. Pauline Franziska Mögling, Herrmann Anandrao Kaundinya, Herrmann Friedrich Mögling – Stephanas Somaya Almanda, Otto Kaufmann. Briefe, Berichte und Bilder versehen mit Einleitung, biografischen Skizzen und Anhang* (Stuttgart, 2003), pp. 41–56.
188 Rosenberger, *In indischen Liebesgassen*.
189 See IOR/L/MIL/7/18565, List of hostile aliens now remaining in India owing to their being exempted from repatriation, 1916.
190 UB/CRL/SC/CMS/B/OMS/ CI1O88, 'Extracts from my Journal', 10 April 1835.
191 Basel German Evangelical Missionary, *Report of the Basel German Evangelical Mission in South-Western India for 1870*, pp. 22–3.
192 Gehring, *Erinnerungen*, p. 147.
193 *Der Evangelische Heidenbote*, November 1890.
194 Hesse, *Die Heidenpredigt*.
195 Eppler, *Karl Gottlieb Pfander*, pp. 122–38; Christine Schirrmacher, *Mit den Waffen des Gegners: Christlich-muslimische Kontroversen im 19. und 20. Jahrhundert* (Berlin, 1992), pp. 43–53; Avril A. Powell, *Muslims and Missionaries in Pre-Mutiny India* (Richmond, 1993), pp. 132–57.
196 Sebastian, 'Scholar-Missionaries', pp. 187–8; Sebastian, 'Baptism of death', pp. 27–8.
197 Becker, *'Conversio im Wandel'*, pp. 317–19.
198 Albrecht Frenz, 'Berichte über Aufstände der Mappilas in Hermann Gunderts Briefen und in seinem Tagebuch', in van der Heyden and Becker, *Mission und Gewalt*, pp. 385–96.
199 *Der evangelische Heidenbote*, June 1856.
200 See Saul David, *The Indian Mutiny* (London, 2002); Biswamoy Pati, ed., *The 1857 Rebellion* (Oxford, 2007); Eric Stokes, *The Peasant Armed: The Indian Rebellion of 1857* (Oxford, 1986); and R. Mukherjee, ' "Satan let loose upon Earth": the Kanpur Massacres in India in the Revolt of 1857', *Past and Present*, no. 128 (1990), pp. 92–116.
201 E. R., Baierlein, *Unter den Palmen im Lande der Sonne* (Leipzig, 1890), pp. 84–118.
202 *Evangelisches Lutherisches Missionsblatt*, January 1858, p. 4.
203 See, for example: ibid., October 1857, pp. 311–13; *Der evangelische Heidenbote*, 1857, pp. 97–9.
204 *Evangelisches Missions-Magazin*, 1858, pp. 111–12.
205 *Der evangelische Heidenbote*, January 1858, p. 5.
206 *Evangelisches Missions-Magazin*, 1859, p. 227.
207 Anton, *Von Darmstadt nach Ostindien*, p. 50.
208 Ibid., p. 51.
209 Ibid., p. 63.
210 Leupolt, *Further Recollections*, pp. 351–71.
211 Ibid., p. 350.
212 *Der evangelische Heidenbote*, September 1857, pp. 74–9, December 1857, pp. 103–9.
213 UB/CRL/SC/CMS/B/OMS/CI10256, Frederic Edward Schneider to H. Venn, 10 November 1857.
214 B. H. Mather, 'The Gossner Mission to Chota Nagpur 1845–1875: A Crisis in Lutheran-Anglican Missionary Policy' (University of Durham MA Thesis, 1967), pp. 196–201; Eyre Chatterton, *The Story of Fifty Years' Mission Work in Chota Nagpur* (London, 1901), pp. 8–10; *Evangelisches Missions-Magazin*, 1858, p. 111; *Die Biene auf dem Missionsfelde*, November 1857, pp. 81–8, December 1857, pp. 89–92.
215 Myers, *German Visions*.

CHAPTER SIX

The impact of the Great War

The Germans become German

In the century leading up to the First World War, the German elites in India had an undeveloped idea of their national identity, which in most cases, and especially for those working for missionary organisations, remained subconscious. For these religious proselytisers, the basis of their identity remained their belief in a Lutheran or Roman Catholic Messiah. Germanness reveals itself most clearly in language use and (for Lutherans) choice of marriage partners. If German community developed, it revolved around Lutheranism. Missionaries did not fit easily into the German diaspora with which many nationalist writers tried to associate them after 1870. Apart from their primarily religious affiliation, the necessity of interaction with Indians and Britons made them different from some of the large and concentrated German communities in Russia and Brazil, for example. If the missionaries in India had a tenuous connection with their German homeland, other long-term German residents had an even more dubious relationship with the land they had left behind. Some lived as individuals in locations away from their countrymen and developed a British-based European identity, which could mean marrying a British woman or taking up British citizenship. For much of the century before 1914, German identity and community in India remained an illusory concept either because of the greater importance of religion for many of the Germans who lived in the country or because the non-religious migrants essentially moved into British society.

Government records in the India Office Library, the British National Archives and the National Archives of India make virtually no reference to Germans before 1914: they did not exist in the official mind. The outbreak of the First World War completely transformed this situation. Germans in India became highly visible to the imperial authorities for the first time, despite their minuscule numbers in the overall population of India, which meant that they faced the type of persecution which characterised the experience of minorities throughout the globe during the First World War.[1] The clearest indication of their sudden visibility lies in the mass of official archival documents which have survived detailing their experiences during the Great War.[2] While they may not have experienced the kind of murderous persecution faced, for example, by those caught up in the collapse of the Ottoman Empire in particular,[3] the small numbers of Germans who lived in India expertly publicised their experiences of interment and subsequent deportation. For the first time the Germans in India became clearly German because the imperial authorities assigned this nationality to them.

Despite their small numbers, their plight during the Great War resembles that of their brethren throughout the world, who faced a combination of nationalist and xenophobic public opinion, official restrictions, property confiscation, internment and deportation. Although this persecution became a global phenomenon,[4] the British Empire perfected the internment and ethnic cleansing of Germans on a global scale. The largely integrated German communities of Britain,[5] Australia,[6] Canada,[7] New Zealand[8] and South Africa[9] faced official and unofficial Germanophobia which gripped the British Empire. Despite the tiny numbers of Germans in India compared with the larger communities in other parts of the Empire, internment camps would emerge there as part of an imperial system of incarceration.[10]

The plight of the Germans in India during the First World War, which involved their identification as such by the British State, therefore needs to be understood against the background of the fact that all parts of the Empire played a role in the conflict, whether in terms of contributing manpower or resources.[11] While the historiography of India tends to ignore the Great War,[12] the role of Indian soldiers has received attention, especially in the last decades.[13] Shortly after the conclusion of peace, the Government of India published an account of the country's contribution to the Great War, pointing out that it sent 943,344 people (552,311 combatants and 391,033 non-combatants) to a series of fronts across the world.[14] Much later, Dewitt Ellinwood and S. D. Prahan pointed to the fact that 'whenever Britain was at war, India, in some sense, was also at war'.[15] Judith Brown has provided perhaps the most concise account of the impact of War on India, concluding that 'the colonial relationship appeared to hold firm' despite the nervousness which led to the Montagu Declaration of 1917 and its promise of elements of home rule. 'The Indian Empire successfully met the challenge of war. It defended itself and sent massive supplies overseas to meet the physical demands made on it by the metropolitan country.'[16] Brown mentions economic distress due to the War[17] and points to the fact that the 'European element' in the country 'was suddenly and drastically reduced' because troops and members of the Indian Civil Service travelled to Europe to participate in the armed struggle.[18]

Despite the reduction of personnel, the Government of India embarked upon a system of controlling the Germans in its midst, which utilised an efficient bureaucracy. Mirroring the situation elsewhere in the British Empire, the authorities marginalised, persecuted and eventually eliminated the Germans, a process which involved a series of steps. In the first place, legislation confirmed their enemy status. Second, measures closed down German businesses and missionary organisations. Third, most German males, and some women and children, experienced internment. Finally, the Germans faced deportation, meaning an end to a continuous presence since the arrival of Ziegenbalg in 1706, although the German-based missionary organisations survived as not all employees were of German birth.

Germanophobia

In most parts of the world in which the Germans faced persecution during the First World War, especially in countries which had democratic systems, public opinion acted as a driving force for the measures which governments introduced. Hostility could manifest itself through the written word, demonstrations and riots, which peaked in the spring and summer of 1915 following the sinking of the *Lusitania*. In view of the small numbers of Britons living in India, the type of mass Germanophobic hysteria which had characterised states such as Britain, the USA, Russia, Brazil and Australia would not surface on the same scale.[19]

In fact, however mild the reaction of British society in India, powerful negative views did surface. This partly manifested itself in the press, as newspapers played a role in unifying the British World during the Great War.[20] An article in the *Madras Mail* from 17 July 1915 provides an indication of the views of some sections of British society in India, tying in with ideas perpetuated in Britain.[21] The piece claimed that for 'many days past we have been receiving letters from our readers' regarding 'the subject of alien enemies still at large in India', which indicated that 'the public is deeply stirred by this matter'. The article tackled the views of British missionaries who had expressed concern about the treatment of their German brethren 'but we ventured to say that some of our correspondents are disquieting themselves unnecessarily. The piety of this or that German Missionary are irrelevant. We have to deal with German Missionaries as Germans, and not as Missionaries.'[22] This final sentence confirms the labelling and transformation of the

German missionaries in India into Germans. British public opinion in the country had determined this. Some newspapers, including those which had an overtly Christian background, had also turned against the Germans in India to the extent of constructing them into a racial group. Thus the *Christian Patriot* of 11 September 1915 described the Germans as African in origin. 'They came to Europe as a people of barbaric conquerors and destroyed a higher civilization.'[23]

As well as newspapers, the European Association preached Germanophobia. This group had come into existence in the early 1880s in order 'to watch over and protect the interests of Europeans in India and others associated with them by community of sympathies and interests'.[24] By the outbreak of War in 1914, it counted 11 branches and 2,931 members, which actually increased to 3,308 shortly afterwards. If it ever had any German or other non-British European supporters before 1914, these quickly disappeared. The 62 council members listed in its 1915 annual report have obviously British names, with the exception of E. A. Wernicke of the Darjeeling branch.[25] Its main concern following the outbreak of War consisted of 'the question of the abuse of privileges accorded to Germans residing in Calcutta and the leniency with which they were being treated by the Government, also the danger of such persons being at large'.[26] Tactics included sending letters to the Government of India complaining about what it viewed as the leniency of the authorities towards the treatment of Germans – whether in terms of failure to implement wholesale internment or the fact that some German businesses remained open despite the passage of enemy trading legislation. The European Association also focused upon missionaries, repeating the assertions put forward in the *Madras Mail* article.[27] A long letter dated 12 June 1915 and addressed to 'The Secretary to Government of India, Home Department' summed up many of the concerns about and prejudices against Germans, stressing their potential as spies and saboteurs if they remained at liberty.[28] The organisation also focused upon individuals which it viewed as threatening or in any sense disloyal, again reflecting the situation in Britain and elsewhere.[29] For example, the group focused upon 'the retention of Herr Büchner as His Excellency the Viceroy's Bandmaster'. His 'continued employment ... has aroused' the 'indignation' of 'His Majesty's Loyal Subjects in India'.[30] In fact, this issue reached the House of Commons, where Austen Chamberlain, the Secretary of State for India, declared that the 'selection of a bandmaster is a matter for the Viceroy alone, and I should not think of interfering in such a matter'. In any case, Büchner 'is a naturalised British subject in India, where he has resided for twenty-one years' and 'either has retired or is on the eve of retirement'.[31] Chamberlain had fielded a question about this issue a year earlier, in July 1915, which also included reference to a 'German band conductor of the Governor of Bengal' who faced internment as early as October 1914.[32]

Individuals also preached the type of Germanophobia put forward by both the press and the European Association. Colonel Harry Ross of the Indian Army complained about the reluctance of the government to introduce internment despite the fact, for example, that 'German missionaries of the Basel Mission had in several cases shown themselves anti-British if not in some cases preaching sedition'.[33] German missionaries also reported on the hostility they faced in India. The Basel employee Jakob Maue recalled the negative articles which appeared in the British Indian press, especially following European battles such as the Marne. As in Europe, the Kaiser attracted particular attention. Maue reported one newspaper article calling for Germans to 'be thrown out' of 'every human society', particularly in association with 'atrocities' carried out by the Germans in Belgium, France and Russia.[34]

Christian brotherhood?

The article in the *Madras Mail* had dismissed the 'anxiety' of British missionaries regarding the treatment of their German brethren,[35] pointing to the fact that a sense of Christian solidarity existed among British religious workers – although not enough to stand up to either a Germanophobic British public opinion or, more importantly, the might of the Government of India implementing important measures against Germans.

Religious organisations which made efforts to assist German missionaries included the recently formed National Christian Council. It both gathered funding and defended German missionaries against accusations of treachery and anti-British and pro-German sentiments. At a meeting in Matheran in November 1915, it passed a resolution 'not without discussion' dissociating itself 'from those imputations of ulterior political motives which have been so freely made against the German missionaries'.[36] Other organisations, working with this body, undertook similar actions. By the end of August 1914, 48 members of the South India District Committee of the London Missionary Society signed a letter to 'the German Missionaries working in South India' which assured them 'of our hearty sympathy with you in the trying position in which you are placed by the present war'. The signatories accepted that 'you and we are loyal to our own countries' but 'earnestly hope and pray that' the war 'may soon come to an end'. The letter continued:

> We wish to assure you that the war can in no way diminish the admiration which we feel for you our fellow-missionaries, and for the splendid work

for which God has used you in the Indian Empire, from the days of Ziegenbalg until now.

We earnestly trust that no political events will ever be allowed to weaken the ties of mutual sympathy which exist between the missionaries of all nationalities now working in India ...

And we further hope that in the financial stress caused by the war, a stress which in considerable measure we share with you, it will be possible for you to preserve from permanent loss the large amount of organised work which you have built up in the past, and which has been a means of blessing to this country.[37]

A similar letter expressed a 'desire in the midst of this painful strife to extend on behalf of the Standing Committee of the Conference of British Missionary Societies the hand of brotherly sympathy and Christian fellowship'.[38]

The body that appears to have made the most significant efforts on behalf of the German missionaries was the Madras Representative Council of Missions. In a letter to 'the German Missionaries in India' dated Christmas Day 1914, this group asserted: 'We have made representations to Government in the matter of your educational work, have communicated with the World's Missionary Conference Continuation Committee with a view to securing financial help, and have raised a considerable sum for cases of more urgent need.'[39] The letter also commented upon requests 'asking us to approach Government with a view to getting some modification of the internment order as far as German missionaries are concerned' but asserted that 'it is impossible for us, however deeply we feel with you, to interfere with Government in measures which they have thought necessary to take, or in any way to put obstacles in the way of their discharging their responsibilities for the safety of the diverse communities under their rule'. In what seems tantamount to a defence of government policy, the letter asserts that internment 'is directed against you not as missionaries but as loyal subjects of a Government with which we are at present unfortunately at war'. Although 'wholeheartedly loyal to our own government' the Council looked to 'our common allegiance to the Lord Jesus Christ as something deeper and stronger than the sincere and fervent patriotism which for some time is dividing the nations to which we respectively belong'.[40] Another letter followed in September 1915, suggesting shock at the developments which had taken place in the meantime. 'We have been distressed at the manifestations of bitterness in the public press.' While again expressing sympathy with the position of German missionaries, this particular letter came closer to criticising the British Government without actually doing so, as 'we are not at liberty to make any statement regarding the reasons which have led to the steps which Government has taken'.[41]

This type of expression of brotherly love, without open criticism of the actions of the Government of India, found reflection in the pages of *Harvest Field*, subtitled 'A Magazine Devoted to the Interests of Missionary Work in the Indian Empire'. The idea of loving thine enemy certainly surfaced in many pieces.[42] At the beginning of 1915, an editorial criticised the policy of internment because 'the men and women arrested and interned ... are working chiefly if not exclusively for the benefit of the people, and ... cannot possibly communicate with their fellow countrymen in Germany'. The piece asked that individuals should not be 'treated as criminals, that husbands be not separated from wives and children'. The editorial requested that the authorities allow missionaries 'to return to their stations'.[43] However, by August 1915 an article by Bernard Lucas on 'The Position of German Missionaries' asserted that: 'On the question of internment the missionary body, I think, must trust the Government entirely ... They are in a much better position to know what the political situation demands.' If this 'necessitates the internment of the German missionaries, we ought unreservedly to acquiesce in it, while deeply regretting the injury to the work which will ensue, and fully sympathising with our German brethren'. Lucas regarded the 'demand for the exclusion of German missionaries from India after the war is over' as 'an entirely different matter' because their main duty consisted of serving Christ rather than 'sowing the seeds of sedition in the British Empire'. But the piece continued that 'it is incumbent on the part of every German who claims to be treated as an honourable enemy to repudiate deeds' such as the sinking of the *Lusitania*, atrocities in Belgium and the use of poisonous gas 'as infamous'. However, Lucas concluded by asking for understanding and sympathy.[44]

The British missions therefore took a contradictory position towards their German brethren in India during the war. On the one hand they professed (what appear platitudinous displays of) Christian love and brotherhood. While they sometimes questioned government policy, they generally acquiesced, either because their Christianity could not conquer their patriotism or because they could ultimately do little other than offer some financial help and sympathy in the face of the global persecution of Germans by the British Empire.

The legal exclusion of Germans

The first manifestation of this persecution in India consisted of the labelling and legal exclusion of the Germans as a result of the introduction of a series of measures mirroring the picture elsewhere in the British Empire, especially Great Britain but also, for example, Australia and New Zealand.[45] In Great Britain, the government introduced the Aliens Restriction Act on 5 August 1914, the day after the declaration of War, controlling all aspects of the lives of aliens and also allowing further changes through the introduction of Orders in Council. In India, the government worked with both existing legislation as well as introducing new measures dealing specifically with foreigners.[46]

The main pre-War measure used to control outsiders in India, the Foreigners Act of 1864, underwent a series of amendments, implementing tighter control over the movement of Germans in India. It continued to define a foreigner as 'a person not being either a natural-born subject of His Majesty ... or a Native of British India'. The first four sections of the Act allowed the Governor-General to exclude and detain individual aliens and also 'place on any person as to whom a question shall arise the onus of proving that he is not a foreigner'. While the Act had 25 sections, only the first four operated until the outbreak of war. This changed from August 1914 following a notification by the *Gazette of India* on 8 August. Most importantly, sections 6 and 7 'require every foreigner to report in writing on his arrival in India with particulars as to his name, nationality and destination'.[47] In fact, as early as 4 August, and separate from the amendments to the Foreigners Act, 'the registration of all Germans and Austrians at defended ports was ordered to be effected, and on the 8th idem the registration of persons of these nationalities was made general throughout the country. At the same time, all were placed under police surveillance.' Meanwhile, on 12 August, 'the exemption enjoyed by Germans and Austrians under the Arms Act was cancelled and their disarmament was ordered',[48] meaning that they had to surrender any items held under licence.[49]

On 20 August, there followed the key piece of wartime alien legislation in the form of the Foreigners Ordinance. Most importantly, this meant that the Governor-General could 'prohibit, or regulate and restrict in such manner as he thinks fit, the entry of foreigners into British India and their departure from British India' and also 'regulate and restrict in such manner as he thinks fit the liberty of foreigners residing in British India'.[50] On 22 August, 'these powers were delegated to the military authorities with reference to' Germans and Austrians of military age, which, from 7 October stood at 17–45 for Germans. This provided the legislative basis for the introduction of internment,[51] as did clauses which determined that foreigners could only reside in particular parts of India.

The Ordinance also controlled the routes and ports which foreigners could use to enter or leave India.[52] By the end of August, these ports consisted of Calcutta, Madras and Rangoon.[53] The Ingress into India Ordinance 1914, which followed on 5 September, could prohibit the entry of foreigners.[54] Thus, 'adult male Germans and Austrians of combatant ages, whether members of crew or passengers, entering British Indian ports in neutral vessels, should be taken off the vessels and detained and dealt with in the same manner as other Germans and Austrians already in India'.[55]

A further amendment to the Foreigners Act of 1864 took place in the spring of 1915, which granted the full rights of British subjects to those who had become naturalised and also strengthened the ability of 'local officers' with regard to provisions 'by which a foreigner could be placed under restraint'.[56] The Foreigners (Amendment) Act 1915 and the Foreigners Ordinance did not solve the problem of women who took the nationality of their husbands following marriage. However, in September 1915 the Government of India decided that British women married to Germans would retain their foreigner status while unnaturalised German women married to Britons would remain foreigners.[57]

Questions arose as to whether the Government of India had an obligation to provide financial assistance to those Germans who remained at liberty. Initially, it seems as if missionaries gained some support, as evidenced by the grant obtained by the Gossner Mission. However, by 21 May 1915, the India Office in London had decided that 'the discontinuance of support of alien enemy missionaries from Provincial or local funds should henceforth be the general policy'.[58]

Some personal narratives described the consequences of the legislation during the early stages of the War. Else Gaebler, married to the Leipzig missionary Gustav Gaebler, lived in Madras at the beginning of August 1914. 'Everywhere, amongst browns and whites, great excitement ruled' and Germans soon attracted the label of enemies. 'Until now we had never had anything to do with the police, but now policemen were our daily guests.'[59] Meanwhile, on 3 August, the German Consul in Calcutta sent a telegram to the Kols Mission in Ranchi requesting army reservists to proceed to Bombay following the German declaration of war on Russia. In fact, 200–300 reservists had already registered with the Calcutta Consulate between 31 July and 2 August and had all gathered in the German Club on 4 August with a view to returning home, but the local police had become aware of this development and removed them to Darjeeling. On 5 August, news reached the Gossner missionaries about the British declaration of war on Germany, which made them enemies overnight. Although they initially continued with their work, the introduction of the Foreigners Ordinance meant that they had to register with the police. Indian policemen also watched them, which some resented, largely because the Indians carried their jobs out thoroughly – meaning looking through windows and examinations of papers – pointing to a racist feeling that natives had got the upper hand.[60] Missionaries tended to remain free for longer than other Germans.[61] Liberty, however, remained limited as restrictions came into operation which necessitated a license for travel.[62] Those missionaries not facing internment remained under parole, which meant that they signed an agreement 'not to undertake anything against the English government and not to influence the natives'.[63]

Trading with the enemy

As well as dealing with individuals, the Government of India introduced measures to tackle the presence of German organisations in the country, encompassing both businesses and missionary bodies. Mirroring legislation passed in both Great Britain, other parts of the Empire, as well as outside the British imperial sphere,[64] the Government of India quickly implemented mesaures to deal with the perceived threat of enemy businesses, supported by British trading interests in India – which saw the opportunity to take over German-owned companies – as well as by the European Association, whose members would have included British businessmen.[65] The Indian Tea Association wished to take over all liquidated German firms.[66] Immediately after the outbreak of war, a series of British newspapers in India also devoted attention to what they viewed as the threat posed by German businesses and their employees.[67] Nevertheless, some regional administrations in India questioned the desirability of eliminating German business interests.[68]

The Foreigners Ordinances and the Trading with the Enemy laws dealt with German firms in India. While the former focused primarily upon individuals, the latter tackled companies, although the two sets of measures interlinked and supported each other. The Foreigners Ordinance of 14 October 1914 stated that 'foreigners residing or being in British India, shall be prohibited from carrying on trade or business or from dealing with any property' while the Hostile Foreigners (Trading) Order of 14 November 1914 forbade foreigners from economic activity in British India except under license, meaning that those companies refused permission would face liquidation while their assets would fall into the hands of the Custodian of Enemy Property in India, confirmed by subsequent legislation including the Enemy Trading (Winding Up) Order of July 1916. The Trading with the Enemy measures passed at the beginning of the war, meanwhile, concentrated upon prohibiting business with the German Empire, which initially excluded German firms 'established in neutral or British Territory', although this changed with the passage of Trading with the Enemy legislation later in the War to include German firms in any enemy controlled territory.[69] By the end of the War, the Custodian of Enemy Property in India appears to have sold all enemy property except that which repatriated prisoners of war could physically take with them.[70]

Those companies which received a license to trade under the Hostile Foreigners (Trading) Order included the Continental Tyre and Rubber Company with headquarters in Hanover but with branches in Bombay, Calcutta and Rangoon, run by Berthold Rosenthal under the supervision of the Controller of Hostile Trading Concerns. But the license issued on 15 January 1915 simply lasted until 14 February and essentially aimed at supervising the activities of the firm in India, which had to 'dispose of the whole of their stock in trade and realise all outstanding debts and credits' by the latter date.[71] Over 20 companies received similar licenses simply aimed at facilitating the winding up process in early 1915, while another five firms had to close down immediately.[72]

Several Germans appealed against the decision to close down their firms, claiming special circumstances which should allow them to stay in business; in some cases, such as that of G. von Berckfeldt, sending out letters while interned. Berckfeldt objected to the closure of his business on several grounds, including his nationality, because 'I have been released from allegiance to Germany over 28 years ago and have further been admitted a European British subject by the High Court at Calcutta, in proof of which I hold documents'.[73] Theodor Westmann of Wutow, Gutmmann and Co., based in Calcutta, while born in Germany in 1860, had become naturalised in 1906. Similarly, his business partner, Jaques Wutow, had also taken out naturalisation in 1894. Nevertheless, their business faced liquidation.[74]

As the War progressed, increasing suspicion in both India and beyond fell on to missionary organisations. In August 1914, misgiving arose about 'a secret German publication on the working of German schools in foreign countries' which led to a thorough investigation into the nature of missionary preaching and teaching in India, raising suspicion, for example, that 'the Jesuits in Bombay are Germans' and 'have considerable influence and possibly teach from a pro-German aspect'. Meanwhile, 'Ernst Petzholtz of Berlin' wrote 'to Dr. Johannes Stosch of the Gossner Lutheran Mission, Ranchi, giving exaggerated accounts of German victories and requesting the mission to publish the truth regarding this and the peaceful intentions of Germany'. Similarly, while 'members of the Basel Mission in Mangalore and elsewhere' were 'possibly of Swiss nationality' they 'identify themselves completely with the cause of Germany'.[75] By the end of 1914, the Government of India tried to establish the number of Germans and Austrians employed by missionary societies by contacting the regional governments.[76] At the conclusion of the enquiry, the Home Department of the Indian Government came to the conclusion that 'since hostilities have commenced there has been evidence in certain quarters of the existence of feelings of enmity, and restrictive measures have had to be adopted'. Furthermore, 'it is undoubted that the promotion of a world-wide educational policy was one of the means of furthering its influence definitely held in view by the German Empire'. Consequently, the Government of India decided that 'it is not proper that local Governments should continue during the war to subsidise institutions directed by members of nations with whom hostilities are in progress', even if this resulted in 'the stoppage of the work done'.[77] These moves followed the peak in Germanophobia within the British Empire after the sinking of the *Lusitania* and 'other outrages',[78] leading to the decision to break up the missions because it is 'impossible to believe that the conclusion of the war will leave anything but a legacy of acute racial antagonism which will remain for many years'.[79]

Dismantling the missions would take place in various ways, including the internment and deportation of the Germans who worked for them and the transfer of their activity to other missionary groups. The Government of India also had its eyes on the commercial activities of the Basel Mission in particular. Following the legislation against enemy businesses, the Basel Trading Company required its directors of German origin to resign and then face internment. Despite this, the Government of India would only allow the Company to continue working under the supervision of the Controller of Enemy Property with a view to sequestration. The organisation transferred its commercial headquarters to London under the supervision of J. P. Werner & Co, who acted as agents for the British Government. The industrial activities in India therefore continued during the War despite the removal of the German missionaries. However, at the conclusion of peace, the British Government sequestered the property of the Basel Trading Company in both the Gold Coast and India, leading to the passage of the Basel Mission Trading Act in 1920.[80] This action represented one aspect of a wider determination by the British Government at the end of the war to gain control of any company 'under German influence' on a global scale.[81]

As the war progressed and Germanophobic feeling increased, the Government of India, mimicking actions taken in both London and other parts of the British Empire, took an increasingly hard line on the German missions and their property, even though German missionaries had largely disappeared as a result of deportation by the middle of 1916. By this time, the Government of India had decided, after consultation with the Foreign Office in London, to exclude German and Austrian missionaries at the end of the war. In fact, from this time, it rejected virtually all applications for foreign missionaries to travel to India, no matter what their nationality.[82] Furthermore, as the war progressed and any German activity became marginalised, the Government of India increasingly came to see all the possessions of the missions as enemy property, so that on 1 June 1918 they became subject to the Trading with the Enemy Act,[83] meaning their sale, but only if this could happen 'without impairing seriously the educational or other charitable work' of a mission which would include 'churches, schools and missionaries' houses'. It therefore seems that the Government of India had its eyes on fairly limited resources because these proposals did not cover the property of the 'Basel Mission Industrial Company', regarded as 'a separate and distinct question'.[84]

The solution to the issue of missionary property came at the end of the war, formalising procedures already in operation in which both the National Christian Council and other churches played a role in administering the property and activities of the German missions following internment and deportation between 1914 and 1916. The Enemy Missions Act of 1921, however, transferred the property of the missions to two trusts in the form of the Missions Trust of Southern India and the Missions Trust of Northern India.[85]

But during the course of the War, the German missions had come to agreements with other bodies and churches to ensure the continuance of their work. Thus, the Church of the Sweden Mission took over the work of Leipzig, with which it had close connections, on condition that it did not sell any of its property. Leipzig schools, together with those of Hermannsburg and Breklum, came under the control of a committee appointed by the Madras Representative Council of Missions and recognised by the Madras Government. The American Lutheran Mission took responsibility for the Hermannsburg and Breklum Missions. The Anglican Bishop of Chotar Nagpur, meanwhile, looked after the Gossner Mission and proposed a merger between the Anglican and Gossner churches at the end of the War – but this led to hostility from both sides, leading to the solution of an autonomous Lutheran Church, supervised by an independent Advisory Committee. An American-based Emergency Fund to Preserve our Lutheran Missions in India had made an appeal in 1916 to assist Breklum, Gossner, Hermmansburg and Leipzig in view of the hardship they faced.[86]

The activities of the Basel Mission in India proved more difficult to control because it 'carried on far more extensive and complicated work than other missions',[87] which meant a series of groups took over its functions. In fact, after the internment of all the German missionaries had taken place by the middle of 1915, the work continued as a result of the efforts of three Britons and 29 Swiss – or about a fifth of the previous number of personnel. This meant that 17 main stations remained unoccupied while seven did not even have an Indian priest.[88] From an administrative point of view, a Swiss Mission Committee took over the running of Basel activities in January 1916, although this proved a short-term solution.[89] A more permanent answer arrived at the end of the War under the auspices of the National Missionary Council of India, which transferred the work of Basel to a series of other bodies[90] in the following way: the churches in Malabar joined the South India United Church; the Calicut College would work with the Madras Christian College; activity in North Canara came under the control of the National Missionary Society, which already worked there, together with the Syrian Church; the Wesleyan Mission took over the churches on the Nilgiris; Swiss Missionaries would man the South Maratha and South Canara districts under the control of the National Missionary Council.[91]

As a result of the efforts of other churches and missionary societies, the activities of the German groupings would continue during the War and beyond, despite the loss of their leaders as a result of internment and deportation. Another factor which allowed continuity lay in the role of Indians in these churches by the outbreak of the First World War, which would continue during the conflict. One account of the activities of the Gossner Mission, which tackled the stance of Indians towards the war, claimed that the educated 'understood fully the difference between the political and religious' and could therefore conceive that Britain and Germany could go to war whereas 'the great mass of our Christians and the heathen ... could not possibly imagine that the sahibs, the white masters, could have a war between themselves'.[92] Despite this, the Indian employees of the missions inevitably played a larger role in the activities of the European-led groupings.[93] In Jeypur, where Breklum Germans operated, the 'Christians and especially the native assistants showed themselves extraordinarily industrious and took it upon themselves to continue the work in hand'. Consequently, normal religious activity continued, and 1,500 baptisms took place in 1915 and 1916.[94] Nevertheless, some decline inevitably occurred as revealed in the statistics which, for example, Leipzig continued to keep. Thus, while the 'soul count' stood at 21,474 at the end of 1915, it had fallen to 20,782 in 1916. The number of pupils had declined from 12,369 to 12,312 in the same period although the number of schools appears to have increased from 254 to 260.[95]

Trading with the enemy in the view of British authorities therefore incorporated not simply commodities and money but also souls. The London-led persecution of German minorities could not ignore the presence of German organisations in the British Empire as a whole,[96] and therefore made efforts to close down the economic activities of the missions by extending enemy trading legislation, while also controlling their religious work. In both cases, however, decades or centuries of labour did not go to waste because British and other international organisations took over the work established by the Germans, while the converted Indians also played a major role on the ground. Despite the violent nationalism created by the First World War, Christian brotherhood ultimately survived in India.

The implementation of internment

While the British authorities did not eradicate Lutheranism from India, they removed those responsible for leading and perpetuating it. Before their elimination took place, the Government of India, imitating actions in the UK and other parts of the Empire, introduced internment, impacting upon all Germans in the country.

Although incarceration in India fitted into an imperial internment process, which moved Germans and other enemies of the British Empire from one part of the world to another, the Government of India had its own traditions of internment which began in the second half of the nineteenth century[97] and would continue during the South African War of 1899–1902, when as many as 9,000 prisoners would face transportation to and internment in India. The most important camp during the conflict consisted of Ahmednagar, which appears to have housed as many as 1,000 prisoners, while others emerged in Bellary and Trichinopoly.[98] The first two would come back to life during the First World War.

L. Tesch experienced internment early in the Great War, having attempted to travel to Calcutta as a reservist with the intention of sailing either to the German colony in Kiautschou or the Persian Gulf. He claimed that he became a 'prisoner of war' on 6 August in Sakchi, 285 kilometres west of Calcutta, although this meant that he could not leave this city where he remained under observation.

> At 9.30 on the evening of 21 October soldiers suddenly appeared, surrounded the houses and ordered us to pack and travel to Calcutta in half an hour. People were hauled away from their beds and from their work. In a coolie wagon with blacks to the left and right we were taken to Calcutta during the night, marched to Fort William with half a company of soldiers and were accommodated there. On the 23rd we travelled through India to Ahmednagar, this time in 1st and 2nd class wagons.

Tesch pointed out that some Ahmednagar internees had initially spent time in prisons, 'for example in the house of correction in Byculla near

Bombay'.[99] Other prisoners had already arrived at Ahmednagar even before Tesch.[100]

The internment of missionaries took place in a rather haphazard manner. Despite the regulations introduced against all Germans at the beginning of the War, most missionaries 'were at the first allowed a considerable amount of liberty, and were permitted to continue their work'.[101] However, some faced arrest and incarceration early on. In October 1914, the Leipzig employees Otto Handmann and Johannes Ruckdäschel had to travel to Fort St George in Madras for internment in Ahmednagar, where their wives also wanted to join them.[102] Meanwhile, a handful of Gossner missionaries faced arrest and internment in Ahmednagar from the following month.[103] Some intensification of internment appears to have taken place at the end of January 1915,[104] when those affected included Georg Hammitzsch of the Leipzig Mission. 'On 27 January I completely unexpectedly became a prisoner of war. At midnight I was taken from my house. The separation from my dear wife and both of my children was very hard. A slice of luck, indeed an act of providence, was the fact that Mrs Handmann, who we had taken into our house after the internment of her husband, comforted my wife.' Hammitzsch initially faced transportation to Fort St George, where he remained alone for two and a half days, but then travelled 700 miles north to Ahmednagar.[105]

Albrecht Oepke pointed to the fact that the early war experiences of missionaries depended upon the organisation for which they worked. During the first year of the conflict, only the three aforementioned Leipzig missionaries (from a total of 21) faced confinement. The Hermannsburg Mission lost 12 men at the end of November. In early December, the Breklum missionaries and their wives and children travelled about 250 kilometres south of their Jeypur station to a former convalescent home in Waltair, where a small number would remain until the end of the following year (Figure 6.1). The 16 males of military age faced transportation to Fort St George and then Ahmednagar.[106]

The Basel employees counted the largest number of internees by the beginning of 1915, following arrests during November and December. A total of 107 faced expulsion from their stations, with 58 men, 20 women, two sisters and 22 children experiencing confinement. The men went to Ahmednagar while the women and children went to Bellary. Johann Jakob Jaus remembered: 'It was on 28 December 1914 that we had to leave our beloved Calicut. Once again the people gathered around us to give us a last firm handshake. The dear old home, the church – to which I was entrusted 33 years previously and had preached so often – and the mission station, disappeared from our view.'[107] The

Figure 6.1 Waltair sanatorium and internment camp

breaking up of families, caused by the separation of fathers from wives and children, led to inevitable distress.[108]

Although hundreds of Germans, both missionaries and others, faced incarceration by the spring of 1915, the Government of India hoped that further arrests would not take place. However, as in Britain, the sinking of the *Lusitania* led to an intensification of anti-German feeling among Anglo-Indian opinion with demands for increasing measures against Germans, including missionaries, which would also include internment.[109] On 23 May, the Government of India further restricted the movement of 'all foreigners' in the country, which Oepke interpreted as not only leading to wholesale internment but also preventing individuals from leaving their homes.[110] On 13 August, in a press communique, the authorities confirmed the internment of all men of military age (17–45) in Ahmednagar, as well as the deportation of women and children and those beyond military age.[111]

Incarceration therefore continued during the summer of 1915, as the experience of the Gossner missionaries in Ranchi reveals. On the morning of 30 June, 'police and native soldiers' surrounded the mission building and informed those who had military obligations as reservists that 'they must start for Ahmednagar by railway at 4 o'clock in the afternoon'. On 17 July, the remaining missionaries and their families received information that they should vacate the station[112] and by the beginning of August all had faced internment. While those of military age went to Ahmednagar, those of other age groups, together with women and children, lived in a barracks in Dinapur.[113]

Actually establishing the total number of Germans interned in India during the course of the War proves problematic because most of the counting took place at a regional or even at a camp level. Some snippets of official information provide snapshots at particular moments. The press communique of 13 August 1915 suggested a total of 1,143 in Ahmednagar. In addition, an accompanying table counted 1,232 others which it broke down in the following way. Those 'concentrated at various centres away from their homes' totalled 324 missionaries and 230 'others'. 'Numbers resident at their normal place of residence' totalled 265 missionaries and 286 others. At the same time 127 remained 'unspecified'. It proves difficult to penetrate and interpret these figures but it seems that the Government of India only counted those males of military age as internees and only regarded Ahmednagar as a 'prisoners of war camp'. Those 'concentrated at various centres away from their homes' experienced some sort of restriction upon their movement.[114] Three years later, a telegram from the Viceroy stated that since August 1914, 1,682 Germans and Austro-Hungarians 'are confined as prisoners of war and 523 are subject to detention and other restrictions in selected areas. Numbers exempted from detention is approximately 80 men, 220 women and 36 children who were settled all over India. Of the 220 women 184 are wives. A large majority of men are well over military service.' The telegram also pointed to 898 people who had faced repatriation.[115] Meanwhile, in October 1919, the India Secretary, Edwin Montagu, suggested that 'the total number now subjected to any restriction ... is 1,257, of whom ninety-one are actually interned'.[116] It proves difficult to come to any conclusions about the numbers of people who experienced internment because of the confusing language used by the government. This contrasted with the views of those incarcerated. An account of the Breklum mission described Waltair as a 'concentration camp'.[117] It seems likely that over 2,000 faced internment in India, mostly in Ahmednagar.

The internment camps

More accurate figures emerge when examining the individual camps themselves, especially through the efforts of the US and, subsequently, Swiss consulates which held responsibility for German interests in Britain and its Empire during the Great War.[118] Clearly, the key internment camp recognised by both the Government of India and the US and Swiss consulates – and remembered by many of those who spent

THE IMPACT OF THE GREAT WAR

time there – was Ahmednagar, the symbol of internment in British India during the Great War which also proved the longest lasting. A series of other places of incarceration also emerged, most notably: Belgaum, which housed men, women and children; Kataphar in the hill station of Darjeeling; Yercaud, another hill station; Bellary; Ramandroog; and Sholapur, established in 1918 to house internees on behalf of the Siamese Government (Figure 6.2). Nevertheless, as the

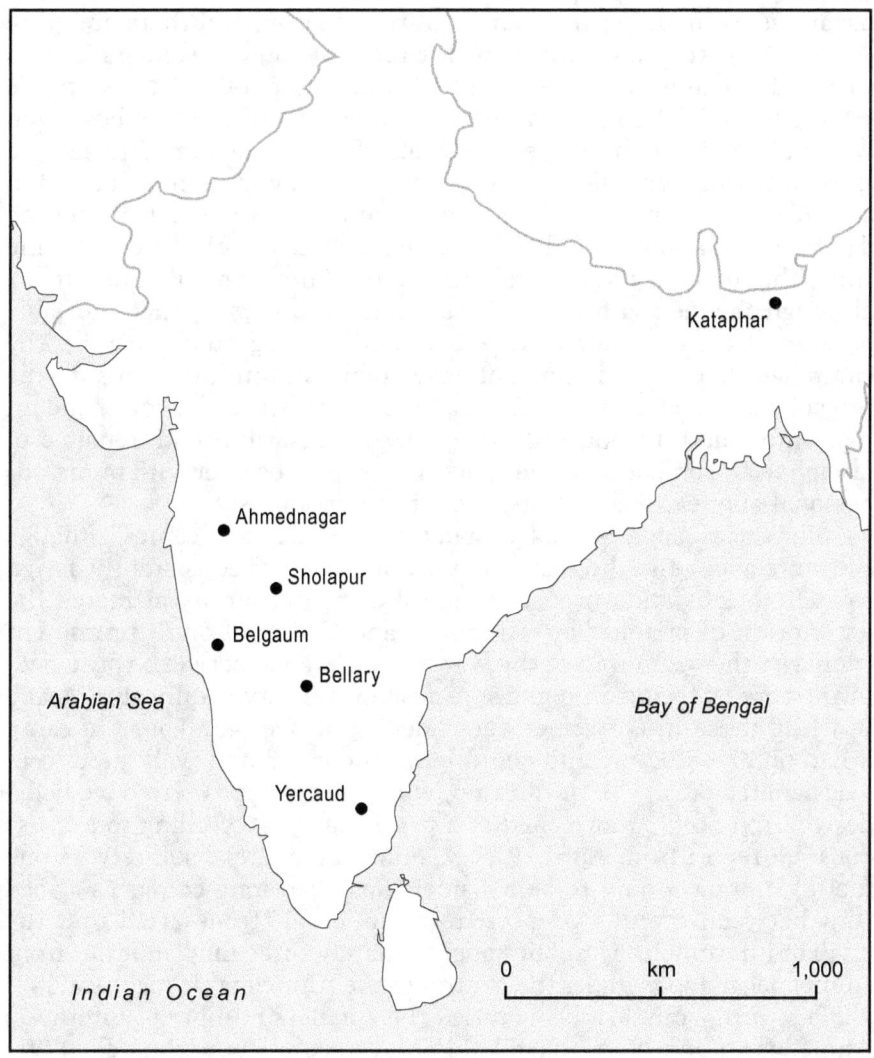

Figure 6.2 Location of major internment camps in India, 1914–20

narrative above has indicated, other short-lived camps also emerged during late 1914 and 1915 to house missionaries before deportation, including Waltair for Breklum and Dinapur for Gossner.

Ahmednagar therefore became the most enduring and emblematic camp in India during the Great War, and also held the largest number of prisoners. The first internees appear to have arrived here in the autumn of 1914, perhaps as early as August of that year following the publication of the Foreigners Ordinance on the 22nd of that month.[119] The first US Embassy report appeared in December of 1914.[120] 'Ahmednagar has for many years been a military station, and there are quite a number of stone built barracks in which the English soldiers used to live.'[121] The camp 'is situated about 100 miles east of Bombay in latitude 19°5 longitude 74.55 at an altitude of about 2000' feet.[122] Those who wrote about it, including both US and Swiss consular officials and those internees who did not complain about it, viewed it as located in a basically healthy spot. Although 'in summer rather hot during the day time ... the nights and the morning are fairly cool'.[123] At the same time 'the air is dry and suitable for most Europeans, it rains little', although the 'period from December until February is uncomfortable because of the constant wind which carries along much dust'.[124] The camp had its own commandant answerable, in military terms, to the Brigadier General of the 6th Poona Divisional Area. The commandant had 'immediate responsibility for the organisation, maintenance of discipline and proper observance of camp orders, together with numerous personal applications or complaints from prisoners'.[125]

Ahmednagar appears to have contained three different camps, although accounts about the three different sections do not consistently assign their functions and purpose. A and B camps generally attracted the description of prisoner of war camps and C that of civil internment camp. At the beginning of the war, the difference between those held in the three depended upon age. Those of military age lived in A and B, while those in C were either under 17 or over 45. Those in camp B had obtained parole and could leave the camp and walk around in a designated area. The third camp, which never appears to have had a designation of 'C', functioned as a parole camp. According to a Swiss consular report from April 1917, A and B camp 'are absolutely on one footing and have only to be considered as 2 separate camps as a road runs between them'. A report from January 1916 asserted that the civilian internment camp 'lies approximately three English miles from Ahmednagar and is under the control of the Ahmednagar magistrate'.[126]

This third camp always counted the smallest number of internees. Ahmednagar appears to have held an average of approximately 1,200 prisoners at any one time. Although the Swiss Embassy report of April

1917 mentioned 'about 2,000', this seems rather high compared to accounts giving more precise figures.[127] In the early autumn of 1915, '1,151 prisoners were interned in Camps "A" and "B"' made up of 966 Germans and 185 Austrians and divided between 791 in A and 360 in B, although the US consular official who wrote the report from which these figures emerge thought that 'the recent internment of others from various parts of India' may have brought the total closer to 1,200. This report also identified '127 detenus, of which 96 were German and 31 Austro-Hungarian' in the 'civil concentration camp' which 'is located about three miles from the military camp in the midst of open country'.[128] In the following summer, another US consular official counted 736 in camp A, 282 in camp B and 177 in the 'parole camp', making a total of 1,195. 'In addition to these, 89 men have been temporarily transferred to a military camp in Dagshai, a hill station in the Punjab ... upon the recommendation of the general medical officer of the camp' as they required 'a change of climate to enable them to convalesce more quickly'. In terms of nationality, the 1,264 prisoners, including those in Dagshai, broke down into 1,075 Germans, 207 Austrians and two Bulgarians.[129] A Red Cross report from the spring of 1917 stated that Ahmednagar held '1,621 persons, of whom 452 were military (apparently captured crews of German ships), the rest civilians'.[130] The only other figures about the numbers of internees in Ahmednagar come from as late as October 1919, just before the completion of deportation from India, when a letter from the Swiss Consul in Bombay pointed to between 2,000 and 2,500 people still interned in the five camps of Ahmednagar, Belgaum, Sholapore, Ramandroog and Yercaud, with the majority 'c.1700' in Ahmednagar.[131] In fact, Ahmednagar continued to function into 1920 and even early 1921 when it held German and Cossack refugees from the Russian Revolutionary Wars, although they seem to have left by April 1921.[132]

As the Red Cross reports pointed out, the camps contained a range of internees. In the autumn of 1915, the US Consul asserted that the majority 'are civilians, who were previous to the war residing in India and engaged in various occupations, such as merchants, bankers, professional men, priests, missionaries, medical men, and also officers and crews of captured merchant steamers'.[133] As this extract indicates, Ahmednagar remained a male camp. Much information has survived on missionaries. In August 1915, a total of 106 German missionaries lived in Camp A, originating from the following organisations: Basel, 68; Gossner, 19; Hermannsburg, three; Leipzig, seven; Kurku, one; Moravian, one; American Missouri, one; Salvation Army, one; YMCA, one; 'Neukirchen', three; 'Seven Days Adventists', one.[134] Although most missionaries would face deportation during 1915 and 1916, some still remained well into 1916. Others lived in Camp B.[135] The August 1915 list ignored those employed by the Roman Catholic Church in India, whose numbers appear to have totalled 60, although they seem to have spent no more than a few months in Ahmednagar.[136] The Basel missionaries interned here included Jakob Maue, who had first arrived in India in 1899 and spent 18 months in Ahmednagar,[137] and Georg Probst, who remained for 19 months.[138]

Doctor of Philosophy Hebert Müller, meanwhile, who presumably worked in India as an academic at the outbreak of war, recorded the time he spent in Ahmednagar in a detailed typescript which he wrote when he returned to Berlin: 'I was interned in Ahmednagar from 18 November 1914 until 30 March 1916.'[139] Other academics in Ahmednagar included Otto Strauß, who held a chair in Comparative Philology in Calcutta at the outbreak of war and faced incarceration there between 1915 and 1920 – during which time he learnt Russian and used the knowledge he gained to translate a Russian commentary on Buddhism into German, published in Munich after his return to Germany.[140] Meanwhile, Otto Schrader, Director of the Adyar Library in Madras from November 1905, experienced internment in Ahmednagar from December 1914. There he tried to continue with his research by learning Tibetan and Siamese and also worked with his friend and assistant Johan van Manen. He returned to Germany after release in 1920 and took up the post of Professor of Indology and Comparative Linguistic Studies at the University of Kiel in the following year.[141]

Those people who came from other parts of the world to face internment in Ahmednagar have also left a record. Women and children incarcerated in India on behalf of the Siamese Government[142] spent most of their time in Sholapur, while males lived in Ahmednagar.[143] The other major foreign origin of German internees in Ahmednagar was that of East Africa – those transported at the start of the War.[144] While men of military age experienced incarceration here, totalling 158 in September 1917, a further 56 'non-combatant prisoners of war including women and children' from East Africa endured internment in Belgaum at this time.[145] Other Ahmednagar internees from beyond India included Major Richard Dinkelmann and Lieutenant Bernard Waurick who strayed into Indian territory at the end of 1916 while travelling home from Tsingtau to Germany with Norwegian passports.[146]

Although the missionaries in particular spent a relatively short spell of time in Ahmednagar, the experiences of some of the scholars points to the fact that other Germans remained for up to five years there. A whole series of both official and personal sources allows a reconstruction of the realities of everyday life in Ahmednagar. The US and Swiss Embassy faced a barrage of complaints throughout the War, partly explained by the fact that the internees had too much time on their hands as civilian prisoners could not work under the Hague Convention.[147]

Most complaints focused upon serious issues. For example, physical mistreatment and even murder, even though this remained rare. In July 1916, four prisoners wrote to the US Consul about their experience following their capture after escaping from Ahmednagar. They remained at liberty between 5 and 22 December 1915 but, upon apprehension near Ratnagiri 400 kilometres away, faced incarceration in the local prison until 28 December.

> On our arrival at the jail we were forced to divest ourselves of our clothes and native Wardens and Policemen who gave this order made a minute bodily examination. We objected to such degrading treatment and asked for the presence of some competent authority. The jail-superintendent, a Parsee, who appeared abruptly, rejected our moral objection to such shameful and degrading treatment, nay, the proceeding was even intensified and such parts of the human rectum had to submit to visitation.

The letter continued with details about the food and the 'escort to Bombay consisting of Europeans and Natives ... heavily armed with revolvers besides fixed bayonets but in spite of this we were handcuffed.' Within the police jail in Bombay 'a call of nature had to take place on the floor within the space of confinement with signs of our predecessors still apparent. From the Bombay jail we were transported to the station again handcuffed followed by a crowd of native spectators.' As this extract suggests and, as is made clear later in the letter, they especially objected to 'such detestable, uncivilised and degrading (to us Europeans) handling at the hands of the Natives'.[148] Despite the racist indignation revealed in the above extracts, a worse fate befell those prisoners at Ahmednagar shot by sentries in October 1914 and May 1918. These ultimately remained isolated incidents. A court of enquiry following the 1918 shooting explained it by the fact that the prisoners went too close to the boundary fence.[149]

Ahmednagar internees spent much time complaining about their housing conditions, usually investigated by the US and Swiss consuls and the British authorities. Particular areas of concern included overcrowding, leaky roofs and the absence of proper floors.[150] The British authorities answered complaints partly by comparing the situation of internees at Ahmednagar with that of British troops housed there before the outbreak of war,[151] as well as by refuting complaints in a detailed and systematic manner.[152] At the same time, one senior British soldier pointed to the fact that 'there are a large number of well-to-do prisoners who cannot but feel considerable difference between their present mode of life and that to which they have been previously accustomed'.[153] The reports carried out by the Red Cross and the US and Swiss consular officials painted a fairly objective and positive picture of Ahmednagar.[154] One Swiss consular official declared: 'I think the space allotted to each prisoner is sufficient, and where there are complaints in this respect, it is probably due to the prisoners according to the custom amongst Europeans in the tropics having an enormous amount of luggage with them which of course takes up a good deal of space.'[155]

Prisoners also regularly complained about illness and disease. The most detailed allegations came from the returning Dr Finck in June 1917 who made claims about inadequate arrangements for operations and a lack of precautions against malaria and dysentery, which the British authorities dismissed.[156] They also provided statistics to demonstrate the relative health of the internees compared to British troops.[157] By June 1915, a total of 71 Ahmednagar internees had spent time in the camp hospital. The most common conditions comprised 11 cases of venereal disease, all contracted prior to arrival, and nine of malaria, six of them previously infected. The medical officer in charge of prisoners of war proudly declared: 'There has only been one death ... an old standing case of diabetes.'[158] The most serious outbreak of disease occurred in the second half of 1916 in the form of bubonic plague, originating from the district of Ahmednagar, where it began in July of that year. The infection affected camp B in November when Richard Krueder fell victim and died. In fact, because of the outbreak in the adjoining areas, the camp authorities had already taken measures to prevent its spread. The prisoners left camp B and moved to tents while cleaning and disinfection took place. Inoculation also occurred. Camp B and the parole camp remained free of the disease.[159]

The male-only prisoners in Ahmednagar devoted a lot of mental energy to their absent wives with whom they wished to reunite. In the early stages of confinement, not only could their wives not visit them, but they could only write one letter per month.[160] In February 1915, the German prisoners requested internment in the same camp as their wives and families who 'in several instances have been subjected to affronts and covert insults by various people, both Europeans and Natives, in spite of the protection Government afford them'.[161] While family reunification did not take place for Ahmednagar internees, the authorities relaxed the restrictions on writing and visits. By December, prisoners could write one letter per week.[162] By early January, wives could also visit their husbands for up to four days as long as they registered their names with the nearest American consulate. They would either stay at the American Mission or, in the case of those visiting parole prisoners, could use one of two bungalows in Mackenzie Road in Ahmednagar as long as they paid 'Rs. 5 per head per diem, which includes hire of bungalows, servants and food (breakfast, lunch, tea and dinner if required)'.[163] Despite the separation which took place, it appears that the Government of India had initially considered interning families in Ahmednagar but, as a Home Department Civil Servant made clear: 'We had Concentration Camps in South Africa for Boer women and children. Were we to send these people to Ahmednagar we can be certain that atrocity mongers would, sooner or later, make out that we had made them prisoners of war and sent them to a Concentration Camp.' Although this reservation did not prevent the establishment of other mixed camps, it formed part of discussions leading to a decision to provide separation allowances for wives and children which should not 'exceed the amount that the average family of a British soldier, proceeded on service has to live on'.[164]

Despite the complaints of the Ahmednagar internees, they managed to establish a 'prison camp society' characteristic of other places of internment during the Great War. This involved the development of social activity and led to the evolution of community. The fact that civilian internees could not work under the Hague Convention meant they had to find alternative ways of giving their days meaning in order to prevent the spread of barbed wire disease – a type of psychosis caused by internment.[165] In the first place, the prisoners established committees which both helped in the more efficient running of the camp and also facilitated social and other activity,[166] including religion and sport.[167] Theatre took off, as it did in camps throughout the world during the Great War.[168] Educational activity also developed, with much interest taken in the study of Oriental languages,[169] presumably because of the presence of German scholars – which also helped the development of 'a little university' with lectures on 'the history of dogma, church history, geography, Indian botany, Sanskrit ... and Tibetan'. The first two subjects also point to the presence of missionaries.[170] The internees also developed a sense of national consciousness which did not exist in the pre-War years. Partly imposed upon them through the measures taken by the British Government, they celebrated events such as the Kaiser's birthday.[171]

Although Ahmednagar became the largest, longest lasting and most emblematic camp in India, at least nine other places of internment also developed. Another long-lasting camp – established during 1915 and located about 250 miles south-east of Bombay on the site of a former military station approximately 1,700 above sea level – Belgaum seems to have initially housed the wives and children of those Germans deported from East Africa, who protested at the idea of repatriation because of the amount of movement they had already experienced during the War. Considerably smaller than Ahmednagar, it seems to have reached a maximum capacity of 214 people. Although women and children initially dominated, the proportion of men gradually increased as the war progressed, as did the percentage of those who resided in India before 1914. Belgaum therefore attracted the description of a 'family camp', emphasised by the birth of children here, although at least two internees died. The accommodation consisted of two large buildings divided into sections by partitions which appear to have housed individual families with up to five rooms and even two bathrooms. Servants lived in separate quarters nearby. Most of the reports on this camp remained positive. Although the children who spent part of their childhood there could receive education in a nearby Catholic convent, parents worried about the quality of this teaching compared with that they would have received in Germany. Belgaum, like Ahmednagar, survived until the end of 1919.[172]

It seems unclear how many Basel missionaries endured incarceration in the former barracks in Bellary, about 500 kilometres to the north-west of Madras, which appears to have started taking in its new residents in January 1915, but the total number of internees never exceeded a few dozen people, made up mostly of women and children, together with some males beyond military age. Jakob Jaus, who wrote two different accounts of internment there, painted a basically positive picture of the accommodation and treatment, although his portrait of the experiences of children pointed to their negative reaction to unfamiliar surroundings, relieved by events such as the celebration of birthdays. The women and children sailed to Germany in November 1915, leaving just 11 internees – a mixture of Germans and Austro-Hungarians – by February 1916. According to a US consular report, the 11 consisted of six missionaries 'two industrials, and the other three were engaged in railway construction in East Africa'. These disappeared because by March of the following year Bellary was acting as home to 137 Turkish prisoners of war.[173] The other camps which held Breklum and Gossner missionaries, in the form of Waltair and Dinapur respectively,[174] also seem to have lost their religious inhabitants by early 1916 as no records exist after this time.

The only other significant camp for Germans in India during the Great War consisted of Sholapur, which took Germans and Austrians deported by the Siamese Government from March 1918. It does not appear to have housed more than 150 internees at any stage.[175] About 20 of the Siamese prisoners spent time in Yercawd (or Yercaud) in the summer of 1918, which also appears to have held a variety of other internees, including some from Ahmednagar, individuals taken from ships and others from East Africa. This seemed an almost idyllic camp near a Roman Catholic mission. At an altitude of 4,500 feet, Yercaud also served as a health resort in the Madras Presidency used by retired Europeans previously employed in coffee and rubber plantations in surrounding areas. The first internees arrived here in the autumn of 1917. They lived in bungalows rented from the owners by the government, although as parole prisoners they had considerable freedom – meaning they could take walks in the surrounding hills. The number of prisoners held here totalled between 100 and 200 during its two years of existence. One Swiss Embassy report commented upon the appreciation displayed by the prisoners.[176]

These type of hill camps also existed in Kataphar, Ramandroog and Dagshai.[177] Kataphar and Ramandroog acted as recuperation stations for prisoners held in Ahmednagar. Kataphar, located near Darjeeling at an altitude of 8,000 feet, served as the summer hill station of the Government of Bombay. The prisoners here lived in army barracks of stone with timber roofs. In February 1916, Kataphar held 44 people consisting of: 35 Germans, eight Austrians and one Montenegrin – nine men, 17 women and 18 children. Like those in Yercaud, the internees could walk in the surrounding countryside as far as they wished.[178] Ramandroog acted as a camp for convalescing prisoners in Ahmednagar, situated about 3,000 feet above sea level over 500 kilometres to the south of Ahmednagar. In July 1918, it held 84 prisoners, although the total appears to have reached 232 at the beginning of 1920, presumably awaiting repatriation.[179]

The end of the Germans in India

Most male members of the German community in India in 1914 therefore experienced internment, although its nature remained humane. While complaints certainly surfaced, especially in Ahmednagar, deliberate mistreatment remained rare. But despite the tolerable nature of internment in India, the whole decision to deprive Germans of their liberty requires questioning, driven as it was by a hostile Anglo-Indian public opinion and by the globalisation of policy against enemies throughout the British Empire during the First World War.

Together with internment and legislation against Germans and their property in India and elsewhere in the British Empire, the final element in the battle against German civilians consisted of the euphemistically labelled repatriation, which, to quote the policies of the anti-German British Empire Union, formed part of a policy that aimed at 'the Extirpation – Root and Branch and Seed – of German Control and Influence from the British Empire'[180] – meaning deportation from British territories throughout the world.[181] In the case of India, repatriation took place in two phases in late 1915 and early 1916 and in 1919 and 1920.

The decision to undertake repatriation appears to have evolved during the summer of 1915, at the same time as the introduction of wholesale internment. A letter from the Viceroy of 13 July stated that Germans 'exhibit more embittered feelings towards us'. After alleging the presence of 3,108 hostile aliens in India (including internees), the letter also stated that the 'effect of supervising so large a number constitutes a severe tax on our officers who are fully employed otherwise and certain expenditure is necessitated'. The letter pointed to 'home policy' of repatriating 'all hostile foreign women and males who are not of military age ... It is proposed to adopt a similar policy here.' This initial decision followed an exchange of correspondence involving the Government of India, the Colonial and Foreign Offices and the Admiralty.[182] The Government of India made the new policy public in the communiqué of 13 August 1915 declaring the adoption of 'a general policy of repatriating all German and Austrian women and children and men of non-military age who are not interned as prisoners of war at Ahmednagar, and this will be affected as soon as the necessary arrangements can be completed'.[183] On the same day, the Home Department of the Government of India wrote to Chamberlain about the German missions asserting that 'we have no hesitation in recommending that we should aim at their immediate removal',[184] confirmed by an Inter-Departmental Conference regarding German and Austrian Missions on 2 November, involving representatives from the India Office, Colonial Office and Foreign Office, which recommended 'the final removal of missions that were German or Austrian, pure and simple'.[185] These developments actually meant the repatriation of both those still at liberty and most interned missionaries.

By this time, deportation had already begun. In the second half of August 1915, the headquarters of the individual German missions received letters informing them of the decision reached on the 13th.[186] Between 30 October and 23 November, Carl Paul, the Basel mission inspector stationed in Triwallur, claimed that he received 'not less than ten official communications from the government authorities concerning every possible detail in preparation for the journey'.[187] By late September, the Viceroy had come to an agreement with the Admiralty about using the SS *Golconda* for the deportations.[188] The name of this ship, together with that of Ahmednagar, became etched on the memory of the repatriated German missionaries as symbols of the end of their Indian lives.[189] As Karl Foertsch, the Chief Inspector of the Gossner Mission, wrote: 'Golconda, thy name will never disappear from our memory as long as we live.' (Figure 6.3).[190]

THE IMPACT OF THE GREAT WAR

Figure 6.3 The *Golconda*

The ship actually made two sailings. The first departed in late November 1915, picking up passengers in Calcutta, Madras and Bombay and then sailing on to Cape Town and Tilbury, following a decision in August 1915 that 'no alien enemies should pass through the Suez Canal'.[191] Those picked up in Calcutta included 'acting-consul Brill of Madras' who claimed that he 'travelled from Ahmednagar to Calcutta under a military escort on 13 November'.[192] The ship appears to have departed from here on 15 November with '470 deportees' according to a telegram from the Viceroy.[193] It appears to have arrived in Madras on 23 November. Those who embarked there included the Basel missionaries held in Bellary, released on 22 November. The 'march outside' was not 'a victory parade'. Instead, there was 'an indescribably serious atmosphere. Sadness and joy, fear and hope were fighting within us.'[194] On the other hand the children interned there 'cheered with joy' at the fact that they would travel by train and then by ship to Europe.[195] The *Golconda* sailed on to Bombay, where those it picked up included the Basel missionary Jakob Maue, who arrived there by railway. 'On the way we met various missionaries together with their wives and children.'[196]

According to Karl Foertsch, 823 individuals travelled upon the ship. Missionaries – including 'sisters', wives and children from all of the major missionary groups – totalled 336. Foertsch also included 176 'German and Austrian families, businessmen, officials etc.', while the remainder consisted of the crew.[197] A range of travellers also left descriptions of the sea passage, which resembled, in many ways, the experience of internment in the sense of remaining helpless and waiting for something to happen. Christmas proved one of the highlights of the journey.[198] Negative accounts emerged, including the one from Brill.[199] The US Ambassador carried out investigations into complaints about the advisability of the journey in view of the threat of sinking by submarine.[200] The first journey of the *Golconda* ended in Tilbury docks on 12 January after 52 days at sea.[201] The second began on 19 April 2016 and involved mostly missionaries, although Herbert Müller also travelled on this occasion. The ship left Bombay and made just one stop in Cape Town, where it picked up 50 men from the internment camp in Petermaritzburg. By the time it reached Tilbury on 17 May it carried about 500 people.[202]

Upon landing in Tilbury, whether on the first or second journey of the *Golconda*, not all the expellees went directly to Germany, as males spent a short spell in the Alexandra Palace internment camp in north London (Figure 6.4).[203] One account of the arrival in Tilbury on 12 January put this news in stark terms. 'An announcement then struck us like a clap of thunder: "All men without exception shall be held back in London; only women and children can proceed further".'[204] The same happened to those who arrived in May. Those women and children who landed on 12 January faced transfer to the *Mecklenburg* on the following day bound for Vlissingen.[205] Similarly, those women and children arriving in May went immediately to the *Kilkenny*.[206] The males from both journeys actually only spent a few weeks in Alexandra Palace before returning to Germany.[207]

While the national identity of the missionaries may have played second fiddle to religious belief before 1914, their Germanisation by the British authorities in India and the wartime German nationalism which greeted them when setting foot on German soil[208] confirmed their new attachment to the country of their birth. Foertsch described

THE IMPACT OF THE GREAT WAR

Figure 6.4 George Kenner, 'Returned German Missionaries in Alexandra Palace'

the feeling when reaching Germany as follows: 'Goch, German soil. Who can describe the exhilaration of the travellers!'[209] Otty Jessen, who worked for Breklum, used even more nationalistic language. Upon arrival in Schleswig-Holstein in May 1916, she wrote of her 'journey through the blooming German country! We reminisced about the hot, barren, dead stretches, that we had survived in India.' In contrast, 'the German Fatherland' contained 'green, lush, meadows. Oh Germany, how has the Lord so richly blessed you before all other lands.'[210] While this last sentence combines religion and nationalism, no German missionary would have used such language at any time in the nineteenth century. The reception which the missionaries received from the organisations which employed them placed less emphasis on praising the Fatherland and more on looking back on the wartime experiences of those who worked for them and on expressing gratitude towards their God. Apart from the holding of services to greet the return of the missionaries,[211] the missions also provided them with financial assistance, in the case of Leipzig using donations.[212]

While the majority of German missionaries and their families had returned home in early 1916, the two journeys of the *Golconda* formed the first part of the process of repatriation that was finally completed in 1920. In the middle of August 1918, '898 German and Austro-Hungarians have been repatriated, 1,682 are confined as prisoners of war and 523 are subject to detention.' In addition, 80 men, 220 women and 26 children were 'exempted from detention'.[213]

Final repatriation from India did not take place until 1920, with many of those forced to leave having no desire to return to a Germany they might not have seen for decades. In October 1919, the Swiss Consul in Bombay counted 2,500 internees held at Ahmednagar, Belgaum, Sholapur, Ramandroog and Yercaud.[214] By this time, some men had endured confinement for over five years – including four who worked for the Indian sales organisation of the Badische Aniline and Soda Factory in Ludwigshafen.[215]

Some Germans actually remained until the end of 1920 because of the unavailability of shipping. All British transportation initially returned home British troops stationed abroad, which meant that German shipping would have to become available for the long sea journey from the Indian Ocean – which did not happen until late 1919. Although repatriation of internees from the British mainland took place during the course of 1919,[216] return to Germany for those still in India appears to have taken place in two main batches using the SS *Main* in December 1919, and a much smaller number on the SS *Patricia* in the following October.

The *Main* left Bombay on 30 December. The journey home proved more complicated than expected due to an outbreak of Spanish Influenza, which had become a pandemic at the end of the War. Consequently, the ship landed in Port Said and left 689 prisoners in a camp there, including 300 Germans from East Africa and approximately 250 seamen captured in the Indian Ocean and held in India since the beginning of the War. The internees themselves returned home in two groups. The *Main* reached Rotterdam on 6 February with 65 officers, 171 crew and 976 civilians, made up of 854 men, 60 women and 62 children. Those left in Port Said would have to remain there until 26 March 1920 when they departed on the *Christian Rede*, reaching Hamburg several weeks later.[217] The *Main* appears to have deported the overwhelming majority of the Germans remaining in India, as only 42 travelled on the *Patricia*, which arrived in Liverpool on 18 October 1920. They continued by rail to Grimsby and departed for Hamburg.[218]

Some of the Germans in India at the end of the War had no desire to return to Europe, including some from Siam and their wives and children who wanted the *Main* to take them home.[219] While the males may not have visited Europe for decades, their wives and children would never have seen it. Despite this, '117 men to whom are to be added 27 women and children' from this group actually travelled to Europe. A handful of Germans appear to have returned to Siam on condition that they renounced their German nationality, although the Government of India could not account for several dozen other people from this group.[220] The Siamese Government also agreed to accept women and children if they chose not to accompany their enemy alien husbands back to Europe.[221] Six other Germans and one Austrian, meanwhile, received permission to travel to the Dutch East Indies.[222]

The internees displayed much concern at the fate of their possessions. Indian regional governments made the decision about the amount of luggage which they could take with them, in some cases as much as possible 'and that which is left behind will be vested in the Custodian and sold'.[223] However, the Government of India appears to have changed this decision in the following year so that 'in cases where the personal effects of such persons have been sold, the sale proceeds, whether vested or not, may be restored to them if they apply for the money after deduction of freight, storage and commission, if any'.[224]

By the end of 1920, the story of the Germans in India had therefore come to an end. The Government of India tried to make this permanent by attempting to prohibit the entry of further Germans to the country for a period of up to five years after the conclusion of peace,[225] a policy which reflected the desire to completely cleanse the Empire of all enemy aliens.[226] The First World War therefore utterly transformed the position of the Germans in India. Earnestly working away, whether as missionaries, scholars or businessmen, and remaining largely anonymous for the preceding century, the Great War completely changed their position. While they had a complexity of identities before 1914, whether religions, racial or even national, the conflict turned them into Germans whether they liked it or not. Even if they had become fully integrated into European society through marriage, the Great War meant that all other identities became irrelevant. Like Germans all over the world, they faced the full wrath of the British Empire and, in this case, the Government of India.

Notes

1 Panikos Panayi, 'Minorities', in Jay Winter, ed., *The Cambridge History of the First World War*, Vol. III, *Civil Society* (Cambridge, 2014), pp. 221–9.
2 See Chapter 1.
3 See, for example, the special issue of the *Journal of Genocide Research*, vol. 10. no. 1 (2008).
4 Panikos Panayi, ed., *Germans as Minorities during the First World War: A Global Comparative Perspective* (Farnham, 2014); Frederick C. Luebke, *Germans in Brazil: A Comparative History of Cultural Conflict during World War I* (Baton Rouge, LO, 1987), pp. 119–201; Jörg Nagler, *Nationale Minoritäten im Krieg: 'Feindliche Ausländer' und die amerikanische Heimatfront während des Ersten Weltkriegs* (Hamburg, 2000).
5 Panikos Panayi, *The Enemy in Our Midst: Germans in Britain During the First World War* (Oxford, 1991); idem., *Prisoners of Britain: German Civilian and Combatant Internees during the First World War* (Manchester, 2012); Stefan Manz,

Migranten und Internierte: Deutsche in Glasgow, 1864–1918 (Stuttgart, 2003), pp. 231–95.
6   Gerhard Fischer, *Enemy Aliens: Internment and the Homefront Experience in Australia, 1914–1920* (St Lucia, 1989).
7   Bohdan S. Kordan, *Enemy Aliens, Prisoners of War: Internment in Canada during the Great War* (Montreal, 2002).
8   Andrew Francis, 'To Be Truly British We Must Be Anti-German': New Zealand, *Enemy Aliens and the Great War Experience, 1914–1919* (Oxford, 2012).
9   Tilman Dedering, '"Avenge the Lusitania": The Anti-German Riots in South Africa in 1915', in Panayi, *Germans as Minorities*, pp. 235–62.
10 Fischer, *Enemy Aliens*, pp. 138–54; Panayi, *Prisoners of Britain*, pp. 54–60; Francis,'To Be Truly British We must Be Anti-German', pp. 113–52.
11 See, for example: Sir Charles Prestwood Lucas, ed., *The Empire at War*, five volumes (London, 1921–6); idem., *The War and the Empire: Some Facts and Deductions* (London, 1919); Charles E. Carrington, 'The Empire at War, 1914–1918', in E. A. Benians, Sir James Butler and Charles E. Carrington, eds, *The Cambridge History of the British Empire*, Vol. 3 (Cambridge, 1959), pp. 605–44; Robert Holland, 'The British Empire and the Great War, 1914–1918', in Judith M. Brown and W. R. Louis, eds, *The Oxford History of the British Empire*, Vol. 4, *The Twentieth Century* (Oxford, 1999), pp. 114–38; Ashley Jackson, ed., *The British Empire and the First World War* (Abingdon, 2015).
12 See, for example, Kaushik Roy, ed., *War and Society in Colonial India* (Oxford, 2006), which contains no essay on the First World War.
13 See, for example: David Omissi, ed., *Indian Voices of the Great War: Soldiers' Letters, 1914–18* (London, 2014); George Morton-Jack, *The Indian Army on the Western Front: India's Expeditionary Force to France and Belgium in the First World War* (Cambridge, 2014); Santanu Das, 'Indians at Home, Mesopotamia and France, 1914–1918: Towards an Intimate History', in Santanu Das, ed., *Race, Empire and First World War Writing* (Cambridge, 2011), pp. 70–89.
14 Government of India, *India's Contribution to the Great War* (Calcutta, 1923), pp. 96–7.
15 Dewitt Ellinwood and S. D. Prahan, 'Introduction', in Dewitt Ellinwood and S. D. Prahan, eds, *India and World War 1* (Columbia, MO, 1978), p. 5.
16 Judith Brown, 'War and the Colonial Relationship: Britain, India, and the War of 1914–1918', in M. R. D. Foot, ed., *War and Society* (London, 1973), p. 106.
17 Ibid., pp. 93–4.
18 Ibid., pp. 91–2.
19 See the following contributions to Panayi, *Germans as Minorities*: Panayi, 'Germans as Minorities', pp. 10–14; Tammy M. Proctor, '"Patriotic Enemies": Germans in the Americas, 1914–1920', pp. 213–33; Dedering, '"Avenge the Lusitania"'. See also: Panikos Panayi, *Enemy*, pp. 153–258; Luebke, *Germans in Brazil*, pp. 119–201; Eric Lohr, *Nationalizing the Russian Empire: The Campaign against Enemy Aliens during World War I* (Cambridge, MA, 2003), pp. 31–54; Gerhard Fischer, 'Fighting the War at Home: The Campaign against Enemy Aliens in Australia during the First World War', in Panikos Panayi, ed., *Minorities in Wartime: National and Racial Groupings in Europe, North America and Australia during the Two World Wars* (Oxford, 1993), pp. 263–86.
20 Simon J. Potter, *News and the British World: The Emergence of an Imperial Press System 1876–1922* (Oxford, 2003), especially Chapter 8 on 'The Imperial Press System in the First World War'.
21 Panayi, *Enemy*, pp. 153–222.
22 *Madras Mail*, 17 July 1915.
23 This is reported in *Evangelisches Missions Magazin*, December 1915, pp. 543–4.
24 European Association, *Thirty-First Annual Report* (Calcutta, 1915), p. 7.
25 Ibid., pp. 2–3, 8.
26 Ibid., p. 12.
27 European Association, *Thirty-Second Annual Report* (Calcutta, 1916), pp. 35–47.

28 *European Association Gazette*, August 1915.
29 See, for example: Francis, 'To Be Truly British We Must Be Anti-German', pp. 153–80; Anthony Lentin, *Banker, Traitor, Scapegoat, Spy? The Troublesome Case of Sir Edgar Speyer* (London, 2013); Christopher T. Husbands, 'German academics in British universities during the First World War: the case of Karl Wichmann', *German Life and Letters*, vol. 60 (2007), pp. 493–517; Proctor 'Patriotic Enemies', p. 219.
30 BL/IOR/L/MIL/7/12399, the Secretary, The European Association to the Secretary of State for India, 20 March 1916.
31 *Hansard*, Commons, fifth series, LXXXII, 449, 9 May 1916.
32 *Hansard*, Commons, fifth series, LXXIII, 9–10, 5 July 1915.
33 BL/IOR/ Mss Eur B235/3, Memoirs of Colonel Harry Ross, Indian Army, 1914–19.
34 J. Maue, *In Feindes Land: Achtzehn Monate in englischer Kriegsgefangenschaft in Indien und England* (Stuttgart, 1918), pp. 6–8.
35 *Madras Mail*, 17 July 1915.
36 K. Baago, *A History of the National Christian Council of India, 1914–1964* (Nagpur, 1965), p. 24.
37 BMA/C/5/5/3a, To the German Missionaries of South India, 31 August 1914.
38 BMA/C/5/5/3a, Conference of Missionary Societies in Great Britain and Ireland, letter of 27 August 1914.
39 AFST/LMW/II.31.8.62, Madras Representative Council of Missions to the German Missionaries in India, 25 December 1914. See *Harvest Field*, 1915, p. 28, for details of the funds raised.
40 AFST/LMW/II.31.8.62, Madras Representative Council of Missions to the German Missionaries in India, 25 December 1914.
41 BMA/C/3/14, Madras Representative Council of Missions to the German Missionaries in South India, 8 September 1915.
42 See especially an editorial entitled 'The Treatment of Our Enemies', *Harvest Field*, May 1915, pp. 169–70.
43 *Harvest Field*, January 1915, p. 6.
44 Bernard Lucas, 'The Position of the German Missionaries', *Harvest Field*, August 1915, pp. 293–8.
45 Panayi, *Enemy*, pp. 45–69; Fischer, *Enemy Aliens*, pp. 65–76; Francis, 'To Be Truly British We Must Be Anti-German', pp. 80–9.
46 Panayi, ibid, pp. 46–61; NA/CO323/681, Memorandum on Foreigners in India, 30 September 1914.
47 NA/CO323/681, Memorandum on Foreigners in India, 30 September 1914.
48 IOR/L/PJ/6/1399/3517, Communiqué, 13 August 1915.
49 NAI/Foreign and Political/Secret War/September1914/16–25-W, Cancellation of all licenses held by Germans and Austrians under the Arms Act Rules.
50 NA/FO383/36, Legislative Department, Notification, Simla, 20 August 1914, An Ordinance to provide for the exercise of more effective control over foreigners in British India, Ordnance No. III of 1914.
51 IOR/L/PJ/6/1399/3517, Communiqué, 13 August 1915.
52 NA/FO383/36, Legislative Department, Notification, Simla, 20 August 1914, An Ordinance to provide for the exercise of more effective control over foreigners in British India, Ordnance No. III of 1914.
53 BMA/C/5/5/3a, Notice No. 6583 of 1914, 28 August 1914.
54 NA/FO383/36, Government of India, Legislative Department. Notification. Simla, 5 September 1914, An ordinance to provide for the control of persons entering British India, whether by sea or land, in order to protect the State from danger of anything prejudicial to its safety, interests or tranquillity, Ordinance No. V. of 1914.
55 NAI/LegislativeB/Legislative/September1914/305, Copy of a Telegram from the Secretary to the Government of India, Marine Department to the Chief Secretary to the Government of Madras, 24 September 1914.
56 NA/FO383/105, Memorandum, No. 2 on Foreigners in India, 26 August 1915.

57 NAI/Home/PoliticalA/September1915/440–445, Enquiry from the Government of Bombay whether a British born woman married to an alien enemy is a foreigner for the purposes of the Foreigners Act 1864 and the Foreigners Ordinance 1914 in the case of Mrs Geeta M. Drill, Letter from S. R. Hignell, 15 September 1915. For the position of women in Britain, see Zoë Denness, 'Gender and Germanophobia: The Forgotten Experiences of German Women in Britain, 1914–1919', in Panayi, *Germans as Minorities*, pp. 71–97.
58 NA/FO383/30, Secretary of State to Viceroy, Home Department, 21 May 1915.
59 http://gaebler.info/ahnen/gaebler/else.htm#0, Else Gaebler, 'Unsere Kriegserlebnisse', *Braunschweiger Volkskalender*, 1918, accessed 4 December 2015.
60 Karl Foertsch, *Unter Kriegs-Wettern: Kriegserlebnisse der Gossnerschen Missionare in Indien* (Berlin, 1916), pp. 2–9; AA/R140765, Hans to Ewald [no surnames given], 16 October 1914.
61 NAI/Home/PoliticalA/September1914/244–57, Treatment of Germans and Austrians of combatant ages.
62 AFST/LMW/II.31.7.21, Ernst Brutzer, 'Persönliche Erlebnisse in Indien 1914–1919', p. 8; NAI/Home/PoliticalA/September1914/244–57, Treatment of Germans and Austrians of combatant ages.
63 Otto Waack, et al., *Indische Kirche und Indien-Mission*, Vol. 2, *Die Geschichte der Jeypore-Kirche und der Breklumer Mission (1914–1939)* (Erlangen, 1996), p. 22.
64 Panayi, *Enemy*, pp. 132–49; Francis, *To Be Truly British We Must Be Anti-German*, pp. 181–213; Daniela L. Caglioti, 'Germanophobia and Economic Nationalism: Government Policies against Enemy Aliens in Italy during the First World War', in Panayi, *Germans as Minorities*, pp. 147–70.
65 BA/R901/85518, Government of India, Department of Commerce and Industry to All Local Governments and Administrations, 30 August 1915.
66 NA/CO323/717, B. C. Allen, Chief Secretary to the Chief Commissioner of Assam to Secretary to the Government of India, Department of Commerce and Industry, 18 October 1915.
67 NAI/Foreign and Political/WarB/May1915/152, Question of a stricter surveillance regime being exercised over Germans and Austrians in India and the extension of the age-limit of persons of those nationalities to be treated as prisoners of war, pp. 13–16.
68 See, for example, NA/CO323/717, A. W. Pim, Secretary to the Government, United Provinces, Industries Department, to Secretary to the Government of India, Department of Commerce and Industry, 28 October 1915.
69 NAI/Commerce and Industry/Commerce and TradeA/December1914/43–49, Hostile Foreigners Trading in India; NAI/Commerce and Industry/Commerce and TradeA/August1916/67–69, The Enemy Trading (winding up) Order; BA/R901/85513, Memorandum on the Treatment accorded to Enemy Interests in British India, October 1915; NA/CO323/717, Memorandum No. 3, on Foreigners in India, December 1916; H. Campbell, *The Law of Trading with the Enemy in British India* (Calcutta, 1916), pp. 401–22.
70 NAI/Home/WarB/April1920/21–22, Authorisation of the Custodian of Enemy Property to exempt from sale personal effects of repatriated Germans and Austrians up to the value of Rs100 in each case.
71 BA/R901/85511, Letter from R. E. Enthoven, 15 January 1915.
72 BA/R901/85511, *Capital*, January 1915.
73 NAI/Foreign/WarB/March1916/7, Copy of a letter, dated Ahmednagar 27 October 1915, from G. v. Berckfeldt, Camp A, Section II, to the American Consul, Bombay.
74 NA/FO383/108, Letter from American Consulate General, 29 January 1915.
75 NAI/Home/PoliticalA/June1915/406–422, Letter of H. Sharp, 1 December 1914, pp. 9–10.
76 NAI/Home/PoliticalA/June1915/406–422, pp. 39–53.
77 NAI/Home/PoliticalA/June1915/406–422, Letter from Secretary to the Government of India, Home Department, 15 June 1915, pp. 65–6.

78 NA/CO/323/717, Memorandum on Foreign Missionaries in India, 8 December 1916.
79 NA/CO323/681, Government of India, Home Department to Austen Chamberlain, 13 August 1915.
80 BL/IOR/L/AG/50/15, Statement of the Claim of the Basel Trading Company Against the United Kingdom Government, 1950; NA/CO/323/717, Extract from a letter from Mr. Adolf ... Manager of the Brick Work Factory at Cadacel, 5 April 1916; Gustave Adolf Wanner, *Die Basler Handels Gesellschaft A. G., 1859–1959* (Basel, 1959), pp. 377–9.
81 R. F. Roxburgh, 'German property in the war and the peace', *Law Quarterly Review*, vol. 37 (1921), p. 56.
82 NA/CO/323/717, Memorandum on Foreign Missionaries in India, 8 December 1916.
83 NA/CO323/778/71, From Viceroy, Home Department, 30 July 1918.
84 NA/CO323/778/71, J. H. Oldham to Under Secretary of State, India Office, 30 August 1918.
85 NA/CO323/868, Enemy Missions Act, 1921; *Harvest Field*, 1919, p. 259.
86 NA/CO323/717, p. 495, 'Remember Our Distressed Brethren in the Faith Whose Noble Work is Now Paralysed by the War', n.d.; *Harvest Field*, 1919, pp. 10–12, 260–1; Baago, *History of the National Christian Council*, pp. 25–6; AFST/LMW/II.31.11.10.I, In dem Herrn geliebte Freunde, 28 December 1915; AFST/LMW/II.31.11.23, Protokoll No. 11 des Kirchenrats (Madras, 9. März 1916); AFST/LMW/II.31.11.23, Uebersetzung eines über Upsala am 8. März 1916 in Leipzig eingetrofennen Protokolls; Waack, *Indische Kirche*, pp. 36–51; *Evangelisches Missions-Magazin*, 1917, pp. 41–3.
87 *Harvest Field*, 1919, p. 261.
88 Wilhelm Schlatter and Hermann Witschi, *Geschichte der Basler Mission*, Vol. 4, *1914–1919* (Basel, 1965), p. 225.
89 Ibid., pp. 232–7; *Allgemeine Missions Zeitschrift*, 1918, pp. 228–9.
90 BMA/C/5/5/3b, Resolutions of the National Missionary Council of India, taken at its Annual Meeting, 18 November 1918.
91 BMA/C/5/5/3b, H. Guildford to the Madras Representative Council of Missions, 5 September 1918; *Harvest Field*, 1919, pp. 261–2.
92 Foertsch, *Unter Kriegs-Wettern*, p. 13.
93 *Evangelisches Missions-Magazin*, 1918, pp. 366–8; *Die Biene auf dem Missionsfelde*, January/February 1920, pp. 8–12.
94 *Evangelisches Missions-Magazin*, 1917, p. 271.
95 *Achtundneunzigster Jahresbericht der Evangelisch-lutherischen Mission zu Leipzig, verfassend den Zeitraum vom 1. Januar bis 31. Dezember 1916* (Leipzig, 1917), p 11.
96 See Schlatter and Witschi, *Geschichte der Basler Mission*; Julius Richter, *Der deutsche Krieg und die deutsche evangelische Mission* (Gütersloh, 1915); Wilhelm Oehler, *Geschichte der deutschen evangelischen Mission*, Vol. 2, *Reife und Bewährung der deutschen evangelischen Mission, 1885–1950* (Baden-Baden, 1951), pp. 278–95.
97 Aidan Forth, 'Britain's archipeligo of camps: labour and detention in a Liberal Empire', *Kritika*, vol. 16 (2015), pp. 651–80, places these traditions into a wider imperial perspective.
98 NAI/Public Works/Civil WorksA/April1902/29–31, Letter from the Government of India, Military Department, 18 March 1901 to the Adjutant General in India; NAI/Revenue and Agriculture/Archaeology and EpigraphyA/February 1903/23/27/1903, Allegations made by Dr Vogel, Archaeological Survey Punjab Circle, regarding the treatment of Boer prisoners of War in India; Isabel Hofmeyr, 'South Africa's Indian Ocean: Boer prisoners of war in India', *Social Dynamics*, vol. 38 (2012), pp. 363–80; Floris Van der Meuwe, *Sport in die Boere-krygsgevangekampe tydens die Anglo-Boereoorlog, 1899–1902* (Stellenbosch, 2013), pp. 121–46.
99 BA/R901/83007, letter from L. Tesch, 1 February 1915.
100 AA/R48283, Verhandelt zu Ahmednagar (Indien) 21. Oktober 1914.

101 *Harvest Field*, 1915, p. 346.
102 AFST/LMW/II.31.11.23, 'Das indische Missionsgebiet (Fortzetzung vom 8.12.14)'.
103 Foertsch, *Unter Kriegs-Wettern*, pp. 10–11.
104 Albrecht Oepke, *Ahmednagar und Golconda: Ein Beitrag zur Erörterung der Missionsprobleme des Weltkrieges* (Leipzig, 1918), p. 12.
105 AFST/LMW/II.31.11.10.I, letter from Georg Hammitzsch, 12 April 1915.
106 Waack, *Indische Kirche*, p. 23; Oepke, *Ahmednagar und Golconda*, pp. 13–14; E. Pohl, *Schiff in Not: Die Breklumer Mission in Indien in und nach dem Kriege* (Breklum, 1929), p. 11; Otty Jessen, *Vertrieben* (Breklum, 1917), pp. 17–35.
107 Oepke, ibid., pp. 14–15; BMA/C3/13, letter to His Excellency the Governor of Madras Presidency, 3 March 1915; Johann Jakob Jaus, *Als Kriegsgefangener: Von Indien nach Deutschland* (Stuttgart, 1916), p. 15.
108 Johann Jakob Jaus, *Kriegsgefangene Missionskinder* (Stuttgart, 1916), pp. 4–8.
109 AFST/LMW/II.31.7.21, Ernst Brutzer, 'Persönliche Erlebnisse in Indien 1914–1919'; NA/FO383/241, Supplement to the *Allgemeine Missions-Zeitschrift*, April 1916, pp. 6–8. For the impact of the *Lusitania* sinking on British internment policy, see Panayi, *Prisoners of Britain*, pp. 50–4.
110 Oepke, *Ahmednagar und Golconda*, pp. 32–3.
111 IOR/L/PJ/6/1399/3517, Communiqué, 13 August 1915.
112 NA/FO383/241, Supplement to the *Allgemeine Missions-Zeitschrift*, April 1916, pp. 8–10.
113 Ibid.; BA/R67/1627, German Red Cross report on Dinapur, 29 January 1916; Foertsch, *Unter Kriegs-Wettern*, pp. 38–44.
114 IOR/L/PJ/6/1399/3517, Communiqué, 13 August 1915.
115 BL/IOR/L/PJ/6/1539, File 2960, Telegram from Viceroy, 15 August 1918.
116 *Hansard*, Commons, fifth series, CCXX, 52–3, 22 October 1919.
117 Pohl, *Schiff in Not*, p. 11.
118 See Richard B. Speed III, *Prisoners, Diplomats and the Great War: A Study in the Diplomacy of Captivity* (London, 1990); Panayi, *Prisoners of Britain*, p. 26.
119 NA/FO383/103, Letter from Adjutant General in India, 2 February 1915.
120 BA/R67/251, Amerikanisches Konsulat Bombay to Staatssekretar, Washington DC, 19 December 1914.
121 BA/R901/83083, Swiss Consular report, 23 April 1917.
122 NA/FO383/34, Letter from India Office, 18 August 1915.
123 BA/R901/83083, Swiss Consular report, 23 April 1917.
124 *Die Biene auf dem Missionsfelde*, February 1916.
125 NA/FO383/237, Report on Military and Civil Camps at Ahmednagar, India, by James Smith, American Consul-General at Calcutta, 2 October 1915.
126 NA/FO383/237, Report on Military and Civil Camps at Ahmednagar, India, by James Smith, American Consul-General at Calcutta, 2 October 1915; BA/R901/83083, Swiss Consular report, 23 April 1917; BA/R67/251, Interner Bericht 57, 15.1.1916.
127 BA/R901/83083, Swiss Consular report, 23 April 1917.
128 NA/FO383/237, Report on Military and Civil Camps at Ahmednagar, India, by James Smith, American Consul-General at Calcutta, 2 October 1915.
129 NA/FO383/240, Report on Military and Civil Camps at Ahmednagar, India, by James Smith, American Consul-General at Calcutta, date of visit July 5 to 10 1916.
130 Emanuel Schoch, F. Thormeyer, and F. Blanchod, eds, *Reports on British Prison Camps in India and Burma Visited by the International Red Cross Committee in February, March and April 1917* (London, 1917), p. 25.
131 BMA/C3/13, Consulate General for Switzerland, Bombay to General-Direktion, Norddeustche Versicherungsgesellschaft, 2 October 1919.
132 AA/R48342, Verbalnote, 18 January 1921; NAI/Foreign and Political/External B/July1921/112–23, Evacuation of the Ahmednagar Civil Refugees Camp and retention by the Govt. of Bombay of the use of the Belgaum and Deolali camps for refugees
133 NA/FO383/237, Report on Military and Civil Camps at Ahmednagar, India, by James Smith, American Consul-General at Calcutta, 2 October 1915.

134 BMA/C3/13, List of Protestant Missionaries in Prisoners of War Camp A, Ahmednagar, August 1915.
135 *Evangelische Lutherische Freikirche*, 10 September, 22 October, 3 December 1916.
136 Ernest R. Hull, *The German Jesuit Fathers of Bombay: By an Englishman Who Knows Them* (Bombay, 1915), p. 99; Alfons Väth, *Die deutschen Jesuiten in Indien: Geschichte der Mission von Bombay-Puna* (Regensburg, 1920), pp. 231–4; *Die katholischen Missionen*, no. 4 (1915–1916), p. 83.
137 Maue, *In Feindes Land*, pp. 15–23.
138 Hans Georg Probst, *Unter indischer Sonne: 19 Monate englischer Kriegsgefangenschaft in Ahmednagar* (Herborn, 1917).
139 BA/R901/83964, Herr Dr Herbert Müller, 'Im Gefangenen-Lager Ahmednagar'.
140 Elpidius Pax, 'Otto Strauß', *Zeitschrift der Deutschen Morgenländischen Gesellschaft*, vol. 100 (1950), p. 43.
141 Joachim Friedrich Sprockhoff, 'Friedrich Otto Schrader zum Gedächtnis', *Zeitschrift der Deutschen Morgenländischen Gesellschaft*, vol. 113 (1963), p. 3.
142 See Chapter 2.
143 NA/FO383/536, Major A. H. Bingley to Secretary, Military Department, India Office, London, 7 March 1919; AA/R48338, Norddeutscher Lloyd to Auswärtiges Amt, 10 September 1919.
144 See Chapter 2.
145 NA/FO383/436, J. E. C. Dukes to Consul for Switzerland at Bombay, 22 October 1917.
146 Details of the arrests can be found in: BL/IOR/L/PS/10/644.
147 J. C. Bird, *Control of Enemy Alien Civilians in Great Britain, 1914–1918* (London, 1986), p. 280.
148 NAI/Army/Secretary of State/1179–83/July 1916, letter from Carl Marnitz, Hans Moller, Adolf Ringetholtz and Ludwig Politzer to US Consul, 5 July 1916.
149 The 1914 shooting of Walter Luley can be traced in AA/R48283. For the killing of Johann Anderka and the wounding of Karl Rötticher in 1918, see NA/FO383/515, List of enclosures to despatch No. 73 (Army), dated 4 October 1918, from the Government of India in the Army Department, to his Majesty's Secretary of State.
150 See, for example: NA/FO383/164, Draft letter from Foreign Office to United States Charge d'Affaires, 16 October 1916; BA/R901/83083, Statement by D. A. Finck, Gardelegen, 26 June 1917.
151 NA/FO383/163, G. C. Walker, Statement showing the authorised accommodation and actual number of prisoners in the building, 19 May 1916.
152 See, for example, BA/R901/83083, General Officer Commanding, 6th (Poona) Divisional Area to the Adjutant General in India, 17 January 1917.
153 NA/FO383/163, General Officer Commanding, 6th (Poona) Divisional Area to the Adjutant General in India, 3 May 1916.
154 See, for example, Schoch, Thormeyer and Blanchod, *Reports*, pp. 25–7; NA/FO383/237, Report on Military and Civil Camps at Ahmednagar, India, by James Smith, American Consul-General at Calcutta, 2 October 1915; NA/FO383/240, Report on Military and Civil Camps at Ahmednagar, India, by James Smith, American Consul-General at Calcutta, date of visit July 5 to 10 1916.
155 BA/R901/83083, Swiss Consular report, 23 April 1917.
156 BA/R901/83083: Statement by D. A. Finck, Gardelegen, 26 June 1917; General Officer Commanding, 6th (Poona) Divisional Area to the Adjutant General in India, 17 January 1917.
157 See the tables attached to NA/FO383/163, General Officer Commanding, 6th (Poona) Divisional Area to the Adjutant General in India, 3 May 1916.
158 NA/FO383/237, Major W. W. Browne, R.A.M.C., Medical Officer in Charge of Prisoners of War to Commandant, Prisoners of War, Ahmednagar, 28 July 1915.
159 NA/FO383/347: Officer Commanding Station Hospital, Ahmednagar to Assistant Director, Medical Services, 6th (Poona) Divisional Area, 13 November 1916; Senior Medical Officer Ahmednagar Brigade, A Report in Continuation of my No. 4646, 27 January 1917.

160 BA/R901/83828, American Consulate, Bombay to Secretary of State, Washington DC, 19 December 1914.
161 BA/R901/83006, Letter from Ahmednagar internees through the Ahmednagar Commandant to the Viceroy, 10 February 1915.
162 BA/R901/83828, American Consulate, Bombay to Secretary of State, Washington DC, 19 December 1914.
163 See two letters in BA/R901/83009, from the American Consulate, Bombay, dated 14 and 30 December 1914 entitled 'To the Wives of Prisoners of War at Ahmednagar'.
164 NAI/Home/PoliticalA/September1914/394–397, Grant of allowance to the wives and children of prisoners of war interned at Ahmednagar.
165 See: John Davidson Ketchum, *Ruhleben: A Prison Camp Society* (Toronto, 1965); Matthew Stibbe, *British Civilian Internees in Germany: The Ruhleben Camp, 1914–18* (Manchester, 2008); Panikos Panayi, '"Barbed Wire Disease" or a "Prison Camp Society": The Everyday Lives of German Internees on the Isle of Man, 1914–1919', in Panayi, *Germans as Minorities*, pp. 99–121.
166 BA/R67/251, Interner Bericht 57, 15.1.1916; NA/FO383/237, Report on Military and Civil Camps at Ahmednagar, India, by James Smith, American Consul-General at Calcutta, 2 October 1915.
167 BA/R901/83964, Herr Dr Herbert Müller, 'Im Gefangenen-Lager Ahmednagar'.
168 See the theatre programmes from Camp A in BA/MA/MSG200/1847 and BA/MA/MSG200/1977. The classic study of theatre in First World War camps is Hermann Pörzgen, *Theater ohne Frau: Das Bühnenleben der Kriegsgefangenen Deutschen 1914–1920* (Königsberg, 1933).
169 NAI/Foreign and Political/War B/November 1917/16–17, Question of allowing prisoners of war to study Eastern languages.
170 BA/R901/83964, Herr Dr Herbert Müller, 'Im Gefangenen-Lager Ahmednagar'.
171 Probst, *Unter indischer Sonne*, pp. 67–74.
172 Schoch, Thormeyer and Blanchod, *Reports*, pp. 35–9; BL/IOR/L/PJ/6/1398/3470, Telegram from Viceroy, 2 October 1915; NA/FO383/163, letter to His Excellency the Viceroy, 19 August 1915; NA/FO383/203, Foreign Office to US Ambassador, 18 October 1916; NA/FO383/237, US Consular Report on the Civil Concentration Camp at Belgaum, 6 October 1915; BA/R67/822, US Consular Report on the Civil Concentration Camp at Belgaum, 11 July 1916; NAI/Home/PoliticalB/December1916/53, Revised list of hostile aliens interned in the Civil camp at Belgaum; NAI/Home/WarB/January1920/65–66, Report of the death of the prisoner of war Reuss in Belgaum; NAI/Home/War/B/February 1920/File 414, Report of the birth on the 27th January 1920 of a girl to Mrs Luders in the Belgaum civil camp; NAI/Home/War/B/March1920/File 81, Report of the birth of daughters to Mrs Mensching and Mrs Linde in Belgaum; NAI/Home/WarB/June1920/2, Swiss Consular report on Belgaum, 26 and 27 July 1918; BMA/C3/13, Consulate General for Switzerland, Bombay to General-Direktion, Norddeustche Versicherungsgesellschaft, 2 October 1919.
173 Jaus, *Als Kriegsgefangener*, pp. 18–18; Jaus, *Kriegsgefangene Missionskinder*, pp. 7–17; BA/R901/83082, American Consular report on Bellary, 5 February 1916; Schoch, Thormeyer and Blanchod, *Reports*, pp. 40–3.
174 See pp. 202, 203, 204, 206.
175 NAI/Home/PoliceB/April918/31, List of prisoners of war from Siam interned in the civil camp at Sholapur; BMA/C3/13, Consulate General for Switzerland, Bombay to General-Direktion, Norddeustche Versicherungsgesellschaft, 2 October 1919.
176 NAI/Home/PolitcalA/December1917/370–83, Transfer of German Civilians to civil camp at Yercawd; NAI/Home/WarB/June1920/2, Swiss Consul Report on Yercaud, 31 July to 1 August 1918; BMA/C3/13, Swiss Consul Report on Yercaud, 3 October 1919.
177 Little information survives on Dagshai, but it is mentioned in NA/FO383/432, Senior Medical Officer, Ahmednagar to Commandant, Prisoners of War Camp Ahmednagar, 14 July 1917. Dagshai appears to lie about 65 kilometres south-west of Simla. See also NAI/Home/Police/January1919/142–57, Chief Secretary to the

THE IMPACT OF THE GREAT WAR

Government of Bengal to Secretary to the Government of India, Home Department, 5 September 1918, which mentions camps at Tadkah, Bankura and Berhampore, although these do not appear to have held Germans.

178 NA/FO383/432, Senior Medical Officer, Ahmednagar to Commandant, Prisoners of War Camp Ahmednagar, 14 July 1917; BA/R901/83082, American Consul Report on Kataphar, 8 March 1916; Schoch, Thormeyer and Blanchod, *Reports*, pp. 45–6.
179 NAI/Home/WarB/June1920/2, Swiss Consul Report on Ramandroog, 23–25 July 1918; BA/R67/1118, Deutsche Kriegsgefangene Ramandroog; Albert Achilles, *Erinnerungen aus meiner Kriegsgefangenschaft im Mixed-Transit-Camp Ahmednagar und Erholungslager Ramandrog in Indien während des ersten Weltkrieges 1914–1920* (Berlin, 1977), pp. 51–95.
180 Panikos Panayi, 'The British Empire Union in World War I', *Immigrants and Minorities*, vol. 8 (1989), pp. 113–28.
181 Panayi, *Prisoners of Britain*, pp. 279–98; Fischer, *Enemy Aliens*, pp. 280–314.
182 NA/CO323/681, Repatriation from India of certain alien enemies and question of use by alien enemies of the Suez Canal route, 5 August 1915.
183 BL/IOR/L/PJ/6/1399/3517, Communiqué, 13 August 1915.
184 NA/FO383/36, Government of India, Home Department to Austen Chamberlain, 13 August 1915.
185 NA/CO323/681, Inter-Departmental Conference regarding German and Austrian Missions on 2 November 1915.
186 AFST/LMW/II.31.11.10, An die lieben Angehörigen unserer Missionsgeschwister, sowie an die Herren Mitglieder unserer beiden Vorstände, 17 September 1915.
187 Carl Paul, *Vom Missionsfeld Vertrieben: Ein Kriegserlebnis der Leipziger Mission* (Leipzig, 1916), pp. 9–10.
188 NA/FO383/237, Viceroy to Secretary of State, Home Department, 28 September 1915.
189 See, especially: Oepke, *Ahmednagar und Golconda*; and Therese Zehme, *Heimkehr mit der Golconda: Wie es den Kindern unserer vertriebenen indischen Missionare erging* (Leipzig, 1916).
190 Foertsch, *Unter Kriegs-Wettern*, p. 64.
191 NA/FO383/237, Secretary of State to Viceroy, 10 August 1915.
192 NA/FO383/237, Extract from report of Acting-Consul Brill of Madras on his internment in India, journey on the 'Golconda', and re-internment in England.
193 NA/FO383/105, Telegram from the Viceroy, 9 November 1915.
194 Jaus, *Als Kriegsgefangener*, p. 28.
195 Jaus, *Kriegsgefangene Missionskinder*, p. 17.
196 Maue, *In Feindes Land*, p. 23.
197 Foertsch, *Unter Kriegs-Wettern*, p. 65.
198 Ibid., pp. 67–73; Jaus, *Als Kriegsgefangener*, pp. 34–9.
199 NA/FO383/237, Extract from report of Acting-Consul Brill of Madras on his internment in India, journey on the 'Golconda', and re-internment in England.
200 *Correspondence with the United States Ambassador Respecting the Safety of Alien Enemies Repatriated from India on the S.S. 'Golconda'* (London, 1916); *Further Correspondence with the United States Ambassador Respecting the Safety of Alien Enemies Repatriated from India on the S.S. 'Golconda'* (London, 1916).
201 Foertsch, *Unter Kriegs-Wettern*, p. 73; Schlatter and Witschi, *Geschichte der Basler Mission*, p. 221.
202 'Die Letzte Fahrt der Golconda', *Evangelische Lutherische Freikirche*, 2 July 1916; BA/R901/83964, Herr Dr Herbert Müller, 'Im Gefangenen-Lager Ahmednagar'.
203 See Panayi, *Prisoners*, pp. 90–1.
204 'Kriegsgefangen in Indien', *Evangelische Lutherische Freikirche*, 25 March 1917.
205 Jaus, *Als Kriegsgefangener*, pp. 42–3.
206 Jessen, *Vertrieben*, pp. 110–15.
207 Herr Dr Herbert Müller, 'Im Gefangenen-Lager Ahmednagar'; Pohl, *Schiff in Not*, pp. 26–9; Probst, *Unter indischer Sonne*, pp. 124–31; Maue, *In Feindes Land*, pp. 26–31.

208 Matthew Stibbe, *German Anglophobia and the Great War, 1914–1918* (Cambridge, 2001).
209 Foertsch, *Unter Kriegs-Wettern*, p. 74.
210 Jessen, *Vertrieben*, p. 118.
211 Paul, *Vom Missionsfeld vertrieben*, pp. 28–46; Christian Roemer, *Heimkehr aus Feindesland: Begrüßungsfeier f. die aus engl. Gefangenschaft freigewordenen Basler Missionsgeschwister in d. Stiftskirche zu Stuttgart 12. Juni 1916* (Stuttgart, 1916).
212 AFST/LMW/II.31.11.10.I, Eingegangene Gaben für die aus Indien heimgekehrten Missionsgeschwister. n.d.
213 BL/IOR/L/PJ/6/1539/2960, Telegram from the Viceroy, 15 August 1918.
214 AA/R48339, Swiss Consulate Bombay to Swiss Political Department, Bern, 18 October 1919.
215 AA/48338, Badische Anilin & Soda Fabrik, Ludwigshafen, to Friedens-Kommission, Berlin, 18 September 1919.
216 Panayi, *Prisoners*, p. 278; AA/R48338, Wako Goette to Leg. Rat Martius, 10 October 1919.
217 Two sources trace the fate of those who originally boarded the *Main*: AA/R48340; and N. O. Tera, *Meine 800: Heimkehr aus Ahmednagar: 'Der Käpt'n erzählt'* (Hanover, 1934). *Die Katholische Mission*, 1919/1920, p. 133, claims 2,400 people originally sailed on the *Main* including 50 Catholic missionaries. For the influenza epidemic at the end of the First World War, see Howard Phillips and David Killingray, eds, *The Spanish Influenza Pandemic of 1918–19: New Perspectives* (London, 2003).
218 NAI/Home/PoliceB/February1921/106–107, List of Germans repatriated in the SS *Patricia*; AA/R48341, Society of Friends of Foreigners in Distress to E Schroetter, 2 October 1920.
219 AA/R48339, letter from Foreign Office, 1 December 1919.
220 See the correspondence in NAI/ForeignandPoliticalB/External/September 1921, 353–424, Matters connected with the disposal of German and Austrian prisoners of war interned on behalf of the Siam government.
221 NAI/Home/WarA/June1919/11–22, Repatriation of Germans and Austrians in India on behalf of the Siamese Government and the disposal of women of Siamese origin married to Germans and Austrians at the time of the repatriation of their husbands.
222 NAI/Home/War/February1920/123–36, Grant of permission to Mr Hoeppner, a German interned at Yercaud, to go to Sumatra; NAI/Foreign and Political/ ExternalA/9/1920/897–914, Grant of permission to Germans and Austrian prisoners of war in civil and military camps in India to proceed to the Dutch East Indies at their own expense.
223 NAI/Home/WarB/December1919/238–249, Details of the arrangements in connection with the repatriation of German and Austrian prisoners of war and civilians interned in India, minute of 23 September 1919.
224 NAI/ Foreign and Political/ExternalB/September1921/347, Government of India, Depart. of Commerce, to all local governments and administrations, 12/11/1920.
225 NA/CO323/844, India Office, Admission into India of Aliens desiring to undertake Missionary, Educational, or other Philanthropic Work in India after the War, January 1920; BL/IOR/L/PJ/6/1569/1126, Government of India Press Communiqués, 'Exclusion of former Enemy Nationality from India for a Period of Five Years from the Conclusion of the War', 1919–20.
226 Panayi, 'Germans as Minorities', pp. 16–17.

CHAPTER SEVEN

Endings, new beginnings and meanings

Endings

The events of the First World War brought to an end a continuous presence of Germans in India dating back at least as far as Ziegenbalg. The ethnic cleansing which took place appears almost total. According to one official document from March 1920, only 62 Germans avoided repatriation, made up of 40 men, 17 women and six children, although even these would have sailed home on the *Patricia*. Over 3,200 Germans and Austrians had 'recently been repatriated'.[1]

Those who wished to return in the immediate aftermath of the War received no sympathy from the Government of India, no matter how long they may have resided in the country. They included Franz von Berckefeldt, born in Germany in 1877 and taking up residence in India in 1891 where he would remain until 1914 – with the exception of spells in the USA and Western Australia. He had established a business in Agra but faced internment, had his concern liquidated and experienced repatriation to Europe on board the *Patricia*. Absent from India when the War broke out, he decided to return on the advice of an Indian lawyer in an attempt to gain a certificate of British nationality in October 1914. Facing incarceration by the end of the year, he wrote to the Secretary of State for India from Emmerich in March 1921 asking for permission either to return to the country or to reside in Great Britain, partly because of the fact that he had a British-born wife and two sons with British nationality. The police official at the Government of India dismissed this plea after digging up a series of allegations against Berckefeldt, focusing upon a pre-War misdemeanour while working 'in the bone trade' when he had committed 'a public nuisance in keeping a stock of bones which had become offensive and was fined Rs.200'. During the War 'the Government of the United provinces ... had little confidence in the friendliness of his sentiments and considered his internment eminently desirable'. While in Ahmednagar 'he evaded censorship by smuggling two letters containing complaints against bad treatment'. Although the Government of India re-examined his case following his appeal against repatriation 'the Government of the United Provinces ... considers Mr von Berckefeldt's return to India to be undesirable in view of his objectionable character and reputation'. He essentially stood no chance in view of 'the general policy of exclusion of Germans for a period of five years'.[2]

The lack of leniency on the part of British officialdom became further apparent with the deportation of missionaries, some of whom had resided in India for decades. Basel employees with the longest service included Gotthilf Benner, born in Gehringen in Württemburg in 1850 and moving to India in 1887 where he worked in a variety of stations. Although he had returned home in between, he had spent most of his life in India, facing deportation on the *Golconda* in January 1916 after experiencing internment.[3] A similar story emerges in the case of Leipzig workers. Those arriving just before the War broke out included Berta Hübener, born in Belitz in Mecklenburg in 1887, sailing to Colombo in 1912 and working in Coimbatore. She actually had her appendix removed in the summer of 1914 and returned with the *Golconda* in November 1915.[4] Meanwhile, Theodor Meyner, born in Zöllnitz in Sachsen-Altenburg in 1864, had settled in India in 1887 and spent most of the next 28 years there, returning on the same journey as Hübener.[5]

New beginnings

Return on the *Golconda* in November 1915 did not quite signal the end of the Indian lives of either Hübener or Meyner. Despite the strict policy of excluding Germans during the early 1920s, by the second half of that decade the situation had changed, meaning that by the 1930s a German community of the type imagined by the German nationalists of the late nineteenth century had emerged, although it remained small. By the second half of the 1930s, in common with German groupings in other parts of the world, it had become at least partly Nazified,[6] as revealed in a publication launched in 1936 entitled *Die Deutschen in Indien*.

Even before the spread of Nazi influence, a German Society had emerged in Bombay in 1932, perhaps reviving the similar organisation which had existed on the eve of the Great War, and – on this occasion – including both Britons and Germans in its leadership. Its aims included: the spread of the study of the German language; the opening of a German library in Bombay; and the establishment of a newspaper. Education stood at the centre of its activity.[7] Four years later a German

Club had emerged in Bombay, although it seems unclear if this evolved from the German society. This appeared to pursue more down-to-earth activities, including dancing. A sport club had also emerged. The Nazification of the Germans in Bombay had resulted in the emergence of a Strength Through Joy branch by this time, which organised a series of excursions including a visit to Candy.[8] This Nazification would continue into the late 1930s such that in 1939 the National Socialist Sporting Organization of Calcutta celebrated its fifth anniversary.[9]

The Nazis established the type of nationalist organisation for which their predecessors in the late nineteenth century had strived. The German activity which had characterised the pre-War years also re-emerged. In fact, despite the disappearance of the German missionaries, the religious work which they had established would continue even in their initial absence during the early 1920s, when other groupings took over the work of the larger German missionary organisations.[10] The German missionaries did not actually receive permission to return until 1926, although some Basel employees had arrived a couple of years earlier. The first Leipzig missionaries began settling in 1925, followed by Breklum and Gossner employees. The type of activity which characterised the nineteenth century re-emerged, although not on quite the same scale.[11] As indicated above, some of those deported during the War would return in the 1920s. Thus Berta Hübener, upon settling in Leipzig in 1916, found employment as a teacher and then in the publicity organisation of the Leipzig Mission but would move back to India in October 1926 when she would work in Porayar and Mayavaram, subsequently taking up a post as a school inspector in 1936.[12] Theodor Meyner moved back to India from 1927 but returned to Germany for good in 1931.[13]

Academics and travellers also resurfaced in India during the interwar years. Manjapra's *Age of Entanglement* covers both the nineteenth and twentieth centuries, although his focus upon the years after the First World War devotes little attention to the actual presence of Germans in India.[14] Andreas Nehring's study of the anthropological research carried out by Leipzig missionaries, meanwhile, stretches until 1940.[15] Walter Leifer's pioneering volumes on the relationship between Germans and India does not regard the end of the First World War as a caesura.[16] In fact, the rebirth of the German communities during the 1920s and 1930s remained short lived because of the reintroduction of internment in 1940, again mirroring developments in Britain.[17]

Meanings

The history of the Germans in India from the early nineteenth until the early twentieth century, which the missionaries and the organisations for which they worked in particular helped to preserve, has allowed the construction of a narrative tracing their journeys, everyday experiences, identities and relations with Britons and Indians. However rich the stories they left behind, they remain a small group within the history of either nineteenth-century diasporas or the history of the German diasporas more generally during this period: a micro-minority giving rise to this micro-history. But the salient characteristics of their story help to provide an understanding of the following areas: the global history of the nineteenth and early twentieth centuries; German history; the history of the British Empire in India; and Indian history.

Before placing them into these contexts, a recap of their specific characteristics will assist in this contextualisation. This volume has argued that the Germans in India constituted an elite minority, as indicated by their education and their occupations. They differed from the 'low and licentious Europeans' identified by Harald Fischer-Tiné who, in any case, uses the term Europeans in a loose way, like most scholars and contemporaries. As the census statistics of the early twentieth century illuminate, the overwhelming majority of so-called Europeans essentially consisted of Britons. This study has made clear that the Germans in India constituted a distinct grouping. The missionaries created their own compounds which, while of necessity became multilingual, remained outposts of German Lutheranism. By the outbreak of the First World War, the type of German community which had evolved in other parts of the world had done so in a micro-form in Bombay. Whether religious or not, those of German birth living in India of necessity interacted with elite British society to the extent of intermarrying, but this did not change the distinctiveness of many of them. This became clear during the First World War when European society broke down into its constituent parts, mirroring the situation elsewhere in the British and German empires. While racial hierarchies may have survived, they became fractured, again mirroring other parts of the British and German empires, as well as anywhere else in the world where German minorities lived. Some poorer Germans may have lived in India, such as sailors, but they remained temporary visitors. The longer term residents generally constituted an educated group which had evolved in the country through global networks established during the course of the nineteenth century, especially scholars and those employed by the missionary organisations.

The small group of Germans in India reflect wider developments in global, German, British imperial and Indian history. Beginning with global history, the movement of a few thousand Germans to India mirrors the migration history of the nineteenth century. While population movement may have taken place on a significant scale before the age of steam, the development of ocean-going liners during this period made movement much easier. We can only consider these as underlying factors which, while they remain central to the movement of the few thousand Germans who moved to India during the nineteenth century, did not ultimately cause them to progress to the country. The epic journeys recounted by some of the missionaries who sailed to India ultimately point to the power of Pietism: those who risked their lives to travel to an unknown land adhered to a messianic faith.

But this belief had a grounding in knowledge of the land to which they sailed. Missionaries in particular depended upon networks which eased their journey from Württemberg or Saxony, meaning that their co-religionists greeted them when they arrived in an otherwise unfamiliar environment and took them to their new place of work. As both historians and social scientists have demonstrated, migration cannot function without networks. The German elite migrants in India symbolise a nineteenth-century world of migration based upon connections revolving around place of origin, family and occupation. The German missionaries who moved to India formed part of broader missionary networks which incorporated other parts of the world. The mission brides identified by Dagmar Konrad who were prepared for marriage in Basel did not just travel to India but also went to the Gold Coast, Cameroon and China.[18] The arguments put forward by Jon Miller in his study of Basel missionaries, especially regarding religious activity as an opportunity for social mobility, may focus upon West Africa, but they apply equally to those who made their way to India.[19] The Basel Mission and its historians thought on a global scale, epitomised by the standard history written by Schlatter and Witschi.[20] They wrote and thought globally because their subject matter consisted of a truly international organisation. Although the collection of essays on colonial Switzerland edited by Patricia Purtschert and Harald Fischer-Tiné does not contain an essay on the Basel Mission (perhaps because of the approach taken), this organisation appears fundamental in any notion of Swiss imperialism.[21] Those Germans employed by the Basel Mission in India therefore do not only live in the British Empire but also form part of Swiss imperialism.

Perhaps more than any other group, missionaries symbolise the global nineteenth century constructed by Osterhammel. Whether they worked for Basel, the German-based organisations, or the British groupings, those international proselytisers born on German soil simply reflect British, American and other organisations. The CMS's classic multi-volume history of its activities, by Eugene Stock – predating the equivalent work of Schlatter and Witschi on Basel – provides an international overview of its activities throughout the world.[22] If empire played the determining role in nineteenth-century internationalisation and the increasing connectedness of the world, mission organisations form part of a parallel imperialism. In one sense they remain a key tenet of the growth of empire, generally following the flag although – as the Germans in India have demonstrated – a subtler relationship existed between political control and the spread of Christianity.

The global Christian network finds reflection in the activities of some of the other elite German groups. While the work of Ulrike Kirchberger has demonstrated this process in the case of German scholarly networks in the British Empire, Tamson Pietsch has looked at the development of academic networks among white British scholars in particular within the Dominions and the United Kingdom, [23] and Elleke Boehmer has examined the role of academic networks in bringing educated Indians to Britain.[24] The German Indologists identified by Valentina Stache-Rosen did not simply travel to India, but also to other parts of 'the East'. Ernst Trumpp, for example, born in Besigheim in Württemberg in 1828, worked in Bombay, Karachi, Lahore and Peshawar, as well as spending time in Jerusalem.[25]

The development of international business provided perhaps the best indication of globalisation during the nineteenth century. Cornelius Torp has demonstrated the ways in which the growing German economy inevitably became international from the 1860s, as the country industrialised and came close to Britain in its share of world export markets.[26] Those German businessmen living in India symbolise the growth of the German economy during the nineteenth century, often working as agents for German firms. As with the missionaries and scholars, this group of elite migrants lived not simply in India, but in locations throughout the world, as demonstrated in the collection edited by Markus Denzel which contains essays on North America, Latin America, sub-Saharan Africa, the near and far East and Oceania. This collection does not, however, focus simply upon the nineteenth century but begins in the fifteenth century and ends in the twentieth,[27] pointing to the fact that globalisation, and the elite and other migrants which followed this process, did not begin or end between 1800 and 1914. The middle-class bankers and industrialists who lived in Britain in the Victorian and Edwardian years[28] had predecessors from the middle of the seventeenth century, as Margrit Schulte Beerbühl has demonstrated.[29]

The Germans in India therefore serve as a symbol of nineteenth- and even pre-nineteenth-century globalisation. An elite group, they mirror other educated migrants of our period. What do they tell us about German history? Most importantly, they point to the importance of migration in the evolution of this country both before and after 1871. Although contemporary writers recognised the importance of emigration for the evolution of the modern German nation state, Klaus J. Bade became the historian who firmly placed population movement at the centre of German history. His pioneering *Vom Auswanderungsland zum Einwanderungsland* pointed to the fact that, while Germany served as an exporter of population for most of the nineteenth century, by its conclusion – as the country evolved into the largest continental European economy – it developed a need for labour which turned it into a net importer of people.[30] Emigration and immigration went together with internal migration as part of the industrialisation and urbanisation process of the nineteenth century. By 1871, nearly 38 per cent of Germans did not reside in the locality in which they were born, while by 1907 almost half of all Germans had moved from their place of birth.[31]

Our concern lies with those who emigrated. Bade's work proves particularly important here, especially his edited collection entitled *Deutsche im Ausland Fremde in Deutschland*, driven, as its subtitle (*Migration in Geschichte und Gegenwart*) suggests, by a desire to educate German public opinion about the link between immigration and emigration in German history. Its importance from our point of view lies in the fact that the contributions recognised the existence of both larger and smaller German groups throughout the world.[32] Two decades after Bade, H. Glenn Penny and Stefan Rinke suggested that: 'Historians need not fear thinking about Germans abroad as an integral part of German history' in a special issue of *Geschichte und Gesellschaft* which they edited.[33] One of the contributors, David Blackbourn, stresses the global nature of these *Auslandsdeutsche* as well as demonstrating their pre-modern existence, which also include elites.[34] This contrasts with many of the individual studies of German migrant groups which generally focus upon large-scale communities during the nineteenth century. Great Britain has attracted particular attention. Much of this has focused upon refugees from Nazism, summed up in the 1991 volume under the overall editorship of Werner Mosse, which, in this case, essentially deals with elite migrants from the eighteenth to the twentieth century,[35] linking them to Germans in India. However, much of the research on the German community in Britain has focused upon the nineteenth and early twentieth centuries, including the First World War, essentially pioneered by my own work on a national scale and taken forward especially by Stefan Manz's micro-study of Glasgow. Both of us recognise the social and occupational diversity of the Germans in Britain, which includes the presence of elite groups such as teachers, academics and businessmen, often tied into transnational and international networks.[36] Most research on the German diaspora has tended to focus upon two locations in particular in the form of Russia and the Americas, especially the USA. The former group, which became especially identifiable in the era of Catherine the Great, has resulted in the evolution of a vast historiography in view of its size by the outbreak of the First World War. Key books here include: the collection edited by Dittmar Dahlmann and Ralph Tuchtenhagen on the Volga Germans in the half century leading up to the Russian Revolution, which includes contributions on economics and employment, politics and rights, society and culture, church and schooling and language and literature;[37] Gerd Stricker's large edited collection on the Germans in Russia, stretching to the Second World War and covering a variety of groups living in large cities (especially St Petersburg) the Volga region and the Black Sea;[38] and Victor Dönninghaus's study of the Moscow Germans, a detailed history of this group which focuses especially upon the development of community organisations and the catastrophic consequences of the First World War, which virtually wiped out this group, especially as a result of pogroms.[39] As Dahlmann has pointed out elsewhere, two important characteristics of the Germans in Russia consist of their heterogeneity and their relatively privileged position by the outbreak of the First World War.[40] A similarly huge historiography has also emerged on the Germans in America dating back to the nineteenth century. One of the key scholars here consists of Frederick C. Luebke, whose pioneering volume on the Germans during the First World War[41] formed the basis of subsequent work which placed the settlement of Germans in the USA into a broader transatlantic migration of Germans.[42] His research has given rise to a series of studies of the Germans in South America, a field in which Luebke, once again, provided the spark through his study on Brazil.[43] These new studies include Silke Nagel's volume on Mexico, which compares the US and German communities in the country with a focus on business activity, ethnic community and the consequences of the two World Wars.[44] Katharina Tietze de Soto's short account of German settlement in the Chilean province of Concepción covers the history of an elite group. In this particular instance, Germans played a significant role in the development of industry, banking and trade.[45]

These examples simply illustrate the globalisation of Germany during the nineteenth century as a result of migration. By 1914, Germans had become a truly worldwide minority. The Germans in India form a small cog in the large clock of international *Deutschtum*, with its main wheel spinning in Berlin and other significant ones whirring in Russia and the USA, as well as all over the world. While Germans may have migrated in significant numbers from the eighteenth century and witnessed a large increase during the nineteenth, the formation of the Kaiserreich led a series of organisations based in the Fatherland to start claiming the areas in which Germans had settled throughout the globe as German space – as Stefan Manz has illustrated in his study of the construction of the German diaspora from 1871 to 1914 focusing especially upon Russia and the USA and examining the role of the German Navy League, the Protestant Church and the *Allgemeiner Schulverein für das Deutschtum im Ausland*, concerned with the survival of language through the spread of German schooling abroad. While these organisations may have devoted most of their attention towards the largest settlements of Germans, they did not ignore the smallest as the example of India has demonstrated. For such groups, it formed part of German space.[46] The work of Manz builds upon the broader German globalisation perspective taken by Sebastian Conrad.[47] Moving away from the work of Bade, who essentially took a social history perspective emerging from a concern with the causes of migration into and out of Germany, Conrad's work offers a new approach which views the German diaspora as part of the globalisation of Germany by the early twentieth century which includes colonialism, a concrete example of German international power, but also significantly examines migration into Germany, especially of Poles, linking his work to Bade's research.

German imperial power and the movement of people into and out of Germany provide two of the clearest indications of German globalisation by the end of the nineteenth century, therefore placing Germany firmly into the internationally connected world which had emerged by this time. The events of the First World War would mean that German globalisation came crashing down, especially with the successes of the British Empire, a process which involved the elimination German diasporas.

Before examining this issue, we should return more specifically to the position of the Germans in India in the globalisation of Germany during the nineteenth century. While they point to the expansion of German trade by 1914, the groups which have left the most significant records, the missionaries and the academics, point to the international success of Lutheranism and German scholarship. We need to stress once again that India became just one area in which groups such as the Basel and Leipzig missions operated, reflecting the activities of both other German bodies and groups from other parts of the Protestant world, as well as Rome, which had become globalised centuries before Protestantism. Karl Graul, Hermann Gundert and Johannes Gossner thought globally decades before Bismarck, Caprivi and Kaiser Wilhelm II. Similarly, German Orientalists began studying and travelling to the 'the East', stretching from Asia Minor, decades – if not centuries – before the formation imperial Germany.

The Germans in India therefore point to the globalisation of Germany before the period studied by Manz and Conrad. But what does their history tell us about the British Empire in India? It helps to elucidate two questions in particular. First, European means European. While the overwhelming majority of those who attracted this description hailed from the British Isles by 1900, this study has demonstrated that continental Europeans lived unique lives separate from the British in India. This became clear as a consequence of the First World War, when British imperial power, reaching its zenith, crushed German minorities throughout the world. The Germans in India formed one small pawn in the exercise of British global power during the Great War.

The 1901 and 1911 census statistics not only demonstrate that Europeans formed a tiny percentage of the population of India in this period, but that the overwhelming majority of this group originated in the British Isles.[48] Yet both contemporary writers and historians have routinely used the concept of Europeans interchangeably with British. One of the most obvious contemporary examples of this conflation was the European Association, formed in the 1880s, but whose main aim in the early stages of the First World War consisted precisely of breaking up any concept of European society in India by purging the country of Germans. Similarly, both Harald Fischer-Tiné and Sarmistha De essentially write about Europeans in India while referring almost exclusively to the British. Not all historians have demonstrated this level of carelessness in their use of terminology. The now rather dated *Bound to Exile* by Michael Edwardes focused purely on the British elites,[49] as did the later *Ruling Caste* by David Gilmour.[50] Both of these authors leave no doubts as to the subject of their study: the British elites in India. Similarly, Elizabeth Buettner's study of British families in India consciously uses the phrase Britons in her subtitle and, like Edwardes and Gilmour, focuses purely upon this group.[51] Buettner also tackled the issue of Europeans in India in an article in which she leads us to the other synonym which often comes into use when the concept of Europeans arises: whiteness.[52]

The study has made clear several points about whiteness, Europeans and Britons in India. First, the Germans constitute genuine continental Europeans living in India. For much of the period under consideration they certainly had close connections with the British ruling elites, especially in the case of missionaries. The German Christians worked closely with their British brethren, as did academics and businessmen. The last two categories would appear to have become fully integrated into British society, as a reading of Flex would suggest. Many of the academics who secured jobs in India would have worked in environments in which they interacted with both Britons and Indians. The missionaries also worked with Britons, especially in the earlier nineteenth century when they tried to establish their operations, yet – as the Victorian and Edwardian eras progressed and their mission stations became firmly established – these became islands of a type of Germanness or Europeaness in which Britons remained absent. These multilingual groups who used their own German dialects, high German, English and Indian languages, remained distinct from the British in India – whether elites or the populations considered by De and Fisher-Tiné. In linguistic terms, these constituted unique worlds, although they mirrored German mission stations which had emerged throughout the world. This study therefore tells us that, while the overwhelming majority of Europeans in India originated in the British Isles, at least one significant group came from continental Europe and therefore needs distinguishing from the British elites and non-elites.

This becomes clear during the First World War. Whatever relationships Germans may have developed with Britons before 1914, which made them part of the 'white race', these came crashing down as a result of the conflict. People who may have given little thought to their German identity and nationality and the fact that they differed from the British, now found themselves stigmatised as Germans leading to their marginalisation through legislation and internment and to the loss of property and ultimate deportation.

This points to the second issue which the history of the Germans in India illustrates about the British Empire. The First World War experience demonstrates both the power and the unity of this entity. The global nature of this conflict necessitated global solutions. India contributed hundreds of thousands of troops to the war effort, pointing to the type of mobilisation which characterised other parts of the Empire. This mobilisation included dealing with the enemy (or perceived enemy) within. India followed the lead of London. The actions carried out against the German population in Great Britain found reflection not simply in India but throughout the Empire. Enemy aliens faced incarceration whether they lived in Sydney, Bombay or the Canadian prairies. They faced arrest and transportation to the nearest internment camp in whichever sea they might find themselves sailing in the late summer or autumn of 1914. While the Government of India may have acted on its own initiative in the use of Ahmednagar as the main site of internment, similar places of incarceration emerged throughout the Empire. The obvious innocence of the Germans in India, reflecting their position throughout British imperial possessions, could not prevent the global behemoth from crushing all of those which it viewed as posing any threat to imperial victory including those who may have lived in a mission station for decades with no properly developed sense of German national consciousness. As the classic studies of the Empire at War, published in its immediate aftermath, emphasised: 'It was not the United Kingdom, with an overseas tail attached to it, that went to war; it was the whole great world-wide unit, the British Empire, acting as one, with very rare exceptions feeling and thinking as one.'[53]

The Great War therefore confirmed the reality of German lives in India from the early nineteenth century. While they may have fitted comfortably into the elites at the top of the racial hierarchy, and while they may have constituted part of European society in the true sense of this phrase, they had always remained a distinct if miniscule group in British India, even though they made little effort to emphasise their difference in any overt manner. The history of the German elites in India demonstrates that European society did not simply consist of Britons, and also points to imperial unity through their persecution during the Great War.

What does the presence of the Germans in India tell us about Indian history? On the surface very little. Within the population of the country as a whole in the century before the First World War they constituted a micro-minority: 1,860 from 315,156,396 in 1911.[54] The overwhelming majority of Indians would have had no contact with them. Even in the areas where the missionaries preached, they used Indian intermediaries. While some intermarriage may have taken place, it remained rare. The children of such unions have left little trace, other than the Kaundinyas, taken under the wing of Hemann Mögling and therefore allowed entry into Basel society. Hermann Kaundinya and his wife Marie Reinhardt had 11 children, five of whom died young, while two others worked for the mission and another found employment in Ghana as a trader for the Basel Mission, according to one source.[55] In fact, R. Kaundinya actually worked as a trader in German East Africa, as revealed in a memoir of his experiences published in 1918. The picture at the front of this publication shows him with his German wife and his multi-ethnic daughters Rani and Hilde. He writes in the tone of a German nationalist revealing little consciousness of his Indian heritage, although he also tells us that he had worked for 23 years as a planter in India upon arrival in Kilossa to the west of Daressalam in 1907. While his narrative ends with an indignant account of the consequences of the First World War in East Africa, he does not reveal his own fate. [56]

The grandiose claims made by those who wrote the histories of the activity of their organisation during the nineteenth century, together with the annual reports of Basel and Leipzig, suggested that German spiritual power had conquered vast swathes of the country. Except that a deconstruction of the figures again points to the fact that the converts remained small Christian islands in an ocean of Hinduism. Even one conversion often required an extraordinary amount of effort. The history of the Germans in India therefore suggests a demographic and a religious truth. Demographically, India has remained a state in which immigrants remained largely absent. Returning to the 1911 census, a total of only 650,768 foreigners lived in the country meaning a percentage of just 0.2 per cent, remarkably low by Western standards. The explanation would lie in the lack of industrialisation and the huge 'surplus' population which lived in the country. Despite the vast literature on the Indian diaspora, relatively few Indians have emigrated, originating from few areas – above all Gujurat and the Punjab.

But we need to move away from raw statistics. As the Germans demonstrated, Europeans who moved to India settled mostly as elites. While they did not control the country in the same way as the British did, they played an important role in the development of Indology, or the academic study of India. Only a minority of German scholars working on India may have actually travelled to the country but, if they include missionaries, they gave a literary form to some languages as well as studying the country in depth for the first time. At the same time, although the German missionaries may ultimately have converted relatively few Indians, they nevertheless had a larger impact through the schools which they established, without which tens of thousands, hundreds of thousands or even millions of Indians (if we take a long-term perspective which looks at the survival of the schools established during the nineteenth century after their transfer to other organisations during the First World War) would never have had the chance of an education – pointing to the importance of missionaries in the spread of education globally during the nineteenth century, despite its religious, racial and gendered message,[57] and again emphasising the global nature of missionary activity. The intermediaries played a central role in the spread of Lutheran Christianity and, increasingly, as the nineteenth century progressed, they moved to the centre of this religion when they became pastors. This process became more noticeable as a result of the ethnic cleansing of the First World War when this religion became increasingly Indian, not just in terms of worshippers but also employees.

Despite the relatively few Indians in terms of the overall population upon which the German missionaries may have impacted, they form part of the mosaic of Christian activity in India which predates the nineteenth century. While Bartholomäus Ziegenbalg and Heinrich Plütschau may have first brought Protestantism into India at the start of the eighteenth century, 200 years later the organisation which they had created had morphed into the Leipzig Mission. Leipzig constituted one piece of the mosaic which, as well as counting a variety of Protestant groups from continental Europe, Great Britain and North America, also included Roman Catholic activity which predated the Tranquebar Church. Understood as part of the tapestry of Christianity, the Germans formed part of a network of welfare activity impacting upon millions of Indians, as emphasised in numerous missionary publications.

We can therefore read the story of the Germans in India in relative isolation. The richness of the material which they have left allows a reconstruction of the history of a micro-minority evolving in the age of empire and war. An apparently integrated group within the British elites, the Great War destroyed lives and communities. Yet their story reflects that of German communities throughout the world in the same period, if on a much smaller scale. At the same time, it illustrates nineteenth-century globalisation, again reflecting the centrality of migration in this process. Most importantly, this history questions the whole concept of 'European' in India.

Notes

1. BL/IOR/L/PJ/6/1660/1746, Memorandum on 'Repatriation of Germans Interned in India', March 1920.
2. This narrative emerges from two letters, giving contradictory information about Berckefeldt's personal history in India, in BL/IOR/L/PJ/6/1329/4262: Government of India, Home Department (Police) to Sir William Duke, 9 December 1920; Franz von Berckefeldt to Secretary of State for India, 7 March 1921.
3. BMA/Q-30.3,5, Gebietslisten, Indien, Männer 1, Brüder no. 997.
4. www.lmw-mission.de/de/missionar-205.html, Leipziger Missionswerk, Berta Hübener, accessed 24 February 2016.
5. www.lmw-mission.de/de/missionar-112.html, Leipziger Missionswerk, Theodor Meyner, accessed 3 November 2015.
6. See, for example, Ronald C. Newton, *The 'Nazi Menace' in Argentina, 1931–1947* (Stanford, CA, 1992).
7. BA/R57Neu/1224/2, Deutsche Gesellschaft, Bombay, 15 January 1932.
8. *Die Deutschen in Indien*, September 1936.
9. Ibid., April 1939.
10. See Chapter 6 for details of the organisations which took over responsibility for individual German missionary work. For the early 1920s, see: Hermann Witschi, *Geschichte der Basler Mission*, Vol. 5, *1920–1940* (Basel, 1970), pp. 223–7; K. Hartenstein, *Das werden einer jungen Kirche im Osten: 100 Jahre Basler Missionsarbeit in Indien* (Stuttgart, 1935), pp. 118–21.
11. Witschi, ibid., pp. 232–300; Wilhelm Oehler, *Geschichte der deutschen evangelischen Mission*, Vol. 2, *Reife und Bewährung der deutschen evangelischen Mission, 1885–1950* (Baden-Baden, 1951), pp. 346–61.
12. www.lmw-mission.de/de/missionar-205.html, Leipziger Missionswerk, Berta Hübener, accessed 3 November 2015.
13. www.lmw-mission.de/de/missionar-112.html, Leipziger Missionswerk, Theodor Meyner, accessed 3 November 2015.
14. Kris Manjapra, *Age of Entanglement: German and Indian Intellectuals across Empire* (London, 2014).
15. Andreas Nehring, *Orientalismus und Mission: Die Repräsentation der tamulischen Gesellschaft und Religion durch Leipziger Missionare 1840–1940* (Wiesbaden, 2003).
16. Walter Leifer: *India and the Germans: 500 years of Indo-German Contacts* (Bombay, 1977); *Bombay and the Germans* (Bombay, 1975).
17. Paul von Tucher, *German Missions in British India: Case and Crisis in Missions* (Self Publication, 1980). For internment in Britain during the Second World War, see the relevant contributions to: David Cesarani and Tony Kushner, eds, *The*

Internment of Aliens in Twentieth Century Britain (London, 1993); and Richard Dove, ed., *'Totally un-English?' Britain's Internment of 'Enemy Aliens' in Two World Wars* (Amsterdam, 2005).
18 Dagmar Konrad, *Missionsbräute: Pietistinnen des 19. Jahrhunderts in der Basler Mission* (Münster, 2001).
19 Jon Miller, *The Social Control of Religious Zeal: A Study of Organizational Contradictions* (New Brunswick, NJ, 1994).
20 Wilhelm Schlatter and Hermann Witschi, *Geschichte der Basler Mission*, five volumes (Basel, 1916–70).
21 Patricia Purtschert and Harald Fischer-Tiné, eds, *Colonial Switzerland: Rethinking Colonialism from the Margins* (Basingstoke, 2015).
22 Eugene Stock, *The History of the Church Missionary Society: Its Environment, its Men and its Work*, four volumes (London, 1899–1916).
23 Tamson Pietsch, *Empire of Scholars: Universities, Networks and the British Academic World, 1850–1939* (Manchester, 2013).
24 Elleke Boehmer, *Indian Arrivals, 1870–1915: Networks of British Empire* (Oxford, 2015).
25 Valentina Stache-Rosen, *German Indologists: Biographies of Scholars in Indian Studies Writing in German* (New Delhi, 1981), pp. 35–6.
26 Cornelius Torp, *The Challenges of Globalization: Economy and Politics in Germany, 1860–1914* (Oxford, 1914).
27 Markus A. Denzel, ed., *Deutsche Eliten in Übersee (16. bis frühes 20. Jahrhundert)* (St Katharinen, 2006).
28 Panikos Panayi, *German Immigrants in Britain during the Nineteenth Century, 1815–1914* (Oxford, 1995), pp 133–43; Stefan Manz, *Migranten und Internierte: Deutsche in Glasgow, 1864–1918* (Stuttgart, 2003), pp. 48–110.
29 Margrit Schulte Beerbühl, *The Forgotten Majority: German Merchants in London, Naturalization and Global Trade, 1660–1815* (Oxford, 2015).
30 Klaus J. Bade, *Vom Auswanderungsland zum Einwanderungsland? Deutschland, 1880–1980* (Berlin, 1983).
31 John E. Knodel, *The Decline of Fertility in Germany, 1871–1939* (Princeton, 1974), p. 192.
32 Klaus J. Bade, ed., *Deutsche im Ausland Fremde in Deutschland: Migration in Geschichte und Gegenwart* (Munich, 1992).
33 H. Glenn Penny and Stefan Rinke, 'Germans abroad: respatializing historical narrative', *Geschichte und Gesellschaft*, vol. 41 (2015), p. 173.
34 David Blackbourn, 'Germans abroad and Auslandsdeutsche: places, networks and experiences from the sixteenth to the twentieth century', *Geschichte und Gesellschaft*, vol. 41 (2015), pp. 321–46.
35 Werner E. Mosse, et al., eds, *Second Chance: Two Centuries of German–speaking Jews in the United Kingdom* (Tübingen, 1991).
36 Panayi, *German Immigrants*, pp 133–43; Manz, *Migranten und Internierte*.
37 Dittmar Dahlmann and Ralph Tuchtenhagen, eds, *Zwischen Reform und Revolution: Die Deutschen an der Wolga 1860–1917* (Essen,1994).
38 Gerd Stricker, ed., *Deutsche Geschichte im Osten Europas: Rußland* (Berlin, 1997).
39 Victor Dönninghaus, *Die Deutschen in der Moskauer Gesellschaft: Symbiose und Konflikte (1494–1941)* (Munich, 2002).
40 Dittmar Dahlmann, 'The Russian Germans: A Heterogeneous Minority during the First World War', in Panikos Panayi, ed., *Germans as Minorities During the First World War: A Global Comparative Perspective* (Farnham, 2014), pp. 171–5.
41 Frederick C. Luebke, *Bonds of Loyalty: German Americans and World War I* (De Kalb, IL, 1974).
42 Frederick C. Luebke, *Germans in the New World: Essays in the History of Immigration* (Chicago, IL, 1990).
43 Frederick C. Luebke, *Germans in Brazil: A Comparative History of Cultural Conflict during World War I* (Baton Rouge, 1987).

44 Silke Nagel, *Ausländer in Mexiko: Die 'Kolonien' der deutschen und US-amerikanischen Einwanderer in der mexikanischen Hauptstadt 1890–1942* (Frankfurt, 2005).
45 Katharina Tietze de Soto, *Deutsche Einwanderung in die chilenische Provinz Concepción 1870–1930* (Frankfurt, 1999).
46 Stefan Manz, *Constructing a German Diaspora: The 'Greater German Empire', 1871–1914* (London, 2014).
47 Sebastian Conrad, *Globalization and the Nation in Imperial Germany* (Cambridge, 2011).
48 See the statistical breakdown in Chapter 1.
49 Michael Edwardes, *Bound to Exile: The Victorians in India* (London, 1969).
50 David Gilmour, *The Ruling Caste: Imperial Lives in the Victorian Raj* (London, 2005).
51 Elizabeth Buettner, *Empire Families: Britons and Late Imperial India* (Oxford, 2004).
52 Elizabeth Buettner, 'Problematic spaces, problematic races: defining Europeans in Late Colonial India', *Women's History Review*, vol. 9 (2000), pp. 277–98.
53 Sir Charles Lucas, ed., *The Empire at War*, Vol. 1 (Oxford, 1921), p. 298.
54 *Census of India, 1911*, Vol. 1, Part II – *Tables* (Calcutta, 1913), p. 125.
55 Waltraud Haas, 'Kaundinya, Hermann Anandrayo', in Gerald H. Anderson, ed., *Biographical Dictionary of Christian Missions* (Grand Rapids, MI, 1999), p. 355.
56 R. Kaundinya, *Erinnerungen aus meinen Pflanzerjahren in Deutsch-Ost-Afrika* (Leipzig, 1918).
57 Felicity Jensz, 'Missionaries and indigenous education in the 19th-century British Empire', *History Compass*, vol. 10 (2012), pp. 294–317.

BIBLIOGRAPHY

Primary sources

Archival material
Archiv der Frankeschen Stiftung, Halle
LMW, Leipziger Missionswerk

Archiv der Basel Mission, Basel
C, India

Auswärtiges Amt, Politisches Archiv, Berlin
R48283, Ermordung Walter Luley in Ahmednagar, 1914
R48338, Heimschaffung der Kriegsgefangenen aus Indien, Aug–Nov 1919
R48339, Heimschaffung der Kriegsgefangenen aus Indien, Nov–Dec 1919
R48340, Heimschaffung der Kriegsgefangenen aus Indien, Jan–April 1920
R48341, Heimschaffung der Kriegsgefangenen aus Indien, April–Nov 1920
R48342, Heimschaffung der Kriegsgefangenen aus Indien, 12/1920–1923
R62397, German Schools in India, 1904–9
R140765, Letter from Germans describing conditions since outbreak of war
R140857, Cochin Consulate, 1910–14
R140877, Calcutta Consulate, 1905–7
R140878, Calcutta Consulate, 1907–10
R140879, Calcutta Consulate, 1910–13
R140884, Bombay Consulate, 1909–14
R251730, Cochin Consulate, 1873–97

British Library, London
IOR, India Office Records

Bundesarchiv Berlin, Lichterfeld
R57 NEU, Deutsches Auslands Institut
R67, Archiv des Ausschusses für deutsche Kriegsgefangene des Frankfurt Vereins vom Roten Kreuz/Archiv für Kriegsgefangenenforschung, Frankfurt am Main
R901, Auswärtiges Amt

Bundesarchiv, Militärarchiv, Freiburg
MSG200, Elsa-Brändström-Gedächtnisarchiv: Kriegsgefangenenwesen 1867 bis Gegenwart
RM3, Reichsmarineamt

Evangelisches Zentralarchiv
5/3132, Reports on Calcutta, 1909–11

THE GERMANS IN INDIA

Geheimes Staatsarchiv, Preußischer Kulturbesitz
III. HA MdA. Ministerium des auswärtigen Angelegenheiten, III Nr. 13903

National Archives, London
Colonial Office Papers, CO323
Foreign Office Papers, FO383

National Archives of India, Delhi
Army/Secretary of State
Commerce and Industry/Commerce and TradeA
Foreign and Political/ExternalA
Foreign and Political/ExternalB
Foreign and Political/Secret War
Foreign and Political/WarB
Foreign/WarB
Home/PoliceB
Home/PoliticalA
Home/PoliticalB
Home/WarA
Home/WarB
LegislativeB/Legislative
Public Works/Civil WorksA
Revenue and Agriculture/Archaeology and EpigraphyA

University of Birmingham, Cadbury Research Library, Birmingham
Church Missionary Society Records, CMS

Printed works

Official publications

Census of India 1891: *General Tables for British Provinces and Feudatory States.* Vol. 1, *Statistics of Area; Population; Towns and Villages; Religion; Age; Civil Condition; Literacy; Parent-tongue; Birth-place; Infirmities, and Occupation* (London, 1892).

Census of India, 1911, Vol. 1, Part II – *Tables* (Calcutta, 1913).

Correspondence with the United States Ambassador Respecting the Safety of Alien Enemies Repatriated from India on the S.S. 'Golconda' (London, 1916).

Deutsches Kolonial-Handbuch, 13th Edition (Berlin, 1913).

Further Correspondence with the United States Ambassador Respecting the Safety of Alien Enemies Repatriated from India on the S.S. 'Golconda' (London, 1916).

Gaffky, Georg, Pfeiffer, Richard, Sticker, Georg and Dieudonné, Adolf, *Bericht über die Thätigkeit der zur Erforschung der Pest i. J. 1897 nach Indien entsandten Kommission* (Berlin, 1899).

Government of India, *India's Contribution to the Great War* (Calcutta, 1923).

Hansard, Commons, Lords, fifth series, 1914–19.

Schoch, Emanuel, Thormeyer, F. and Blanchod, F., eds, *Reports on British Prison Camps in India and Burma Visited by the International Red Cross Committee in February, March and April 1917* (London, 1917).

BIBLIOGRAPHY

Newspapers and periodicals
Allgemeine Missions Zeitschrift
Allgemeine Missions Zeitung
Beiblatt zur Allgemeinen Missions=Zeitschrift
Der evangelische Heidenbote
Deutsche Erde
Die Biene auf dem Missionsfelde
Die Deutschen in Indien
Die katholischen Missionen
Dresdener Missions-Nachrichten
Echo aus Indien
European Association Gazette
Evangelische Heidenbote
Evangelische Lutherische Freikirche
Evangelisch-lutherisches Missionsblatt
Evangelisches Missions-Magazin
Harvest Field
Indian Forester
Madras Mail
Magazin für die neueste Geschichte der evangelischen Missions- und Bibelgesellschaften

Publications of organisations
Achtundneunzigster Jahresbericht der Evangelisch-lutherischen Mission zu Leipzig, verfassend den Zeitraum vom 1. Januar bis 31. Dezember 1916 (Leipzig, 1917).
Achtzigster Jahresbericht der Evangelischen Missionsgesellschaft zu Basel auf 1. Juli 1895 (Basel, 1895).
Allgemeiner Deutscher Schulverein zur Erhaltung des Deutschtums im Auslande, ed., Handbuch des Deutschtums im Auslande, nebst einem Adressbuch der deutschen Auslandschulen, zwei Kartenbeilagen und fünf Kartenskizzen (Berlin, 1906).
Basel German Evangelical Missionary Society, *Report of the Basel German Evangelical Missionary Society. Forty-Fourth Year. 1859. Twentieth Report of the German Evangelical Mission in South-Western India* (Mangalore, 1860).
Basel German Evangelical Missionary Society, *Report of the Basel German Evangelical Missionary Society. Forty-Ninth Year. 1864. Twenty Fifth Report of the German Evangelical Mission in South-Western India* (Mangalore, 1865).
Basel German Evangelical Missionary Society, *Report of the Basel German Evangelical Mission in South-Western India for 1870* (Mangalore, 1871).
Bericht über die Arbeit der Schleswig-Holsteinischen Evangelisch Lutherischen Missionsgesellschaft für die Zeit vom 1. April 1900 bis dahin 1901 (Breklum, 1901).
Church Missionary Society, *Register of Missionaries, Clerical, Lay, & Female, and Native Clergy, from 1804 to 1904* (London, 1904).
European Association, *Thirty-First Annual Report* (Calcutta, 1915).
European Association, *Thirty-Second Annual Report* (Calcutta, 1916).

Evangelische Missions-Gesellschaft, *Album der Basler Mission: Bilder aus Indien* (Basel, 1860).
Evangelische Missionsgesellschaft (Basel), *Verzeichnis der Basler Missions-Stationen in Indien: Mit Bezeichnung der Eigentumsverhältnisse* (Basel, 1888–91).
German Evangelical Mission, *The Fifteenth Report of the German Evangelical Mission on the Western Coast of India* (Mangalore, 1855).
German Lutheran Mission (Tirhut, India), *The Twenty Sixth Annual Report of the German Mission in Tirhoot* (Muzaffarpur, 1866).
Jahresbericht des Stettiner Hilfsvereins für die Goßnersche Mission für das Jahr 1910 (Stettin, 1911).
Missions-Ordnung: Zusammenstellung wichtiger Bestimmungen für die Missionare der Evangelisch-Lutherischen Mission in Indien (Leipzig, 1908).
Neunundneunzigster Jahresbericht der Evangelischen Missions-Gesellschaft zu Basel auf 1. Juli 1914 (Basel, 1914).
Neunzigster Jahresbericht der evangelischen Missions-Gesellschaft zu Basel auf 1. Juli 1905 (Basel, 1905).
Sechzigster Jahresbericht der evangelischen Missionsgesellschaft zu Basel auf 1. Juli 1875 (Basel, 1875).
Siebenzigster Jahresbericht der Evangelischen Missionsgesellschaft zu Basel auf 1. Juli 1885 (Basel, 1885).
Vierundvierzigster Jahresbericht der evangelischen Missionsgesellschaft zu Basel auf 1. Juli 1859 (Basel, 1859).
Zweiundneunzigster Jahresbericht der Evangelisch-lutherischen Mission zu Leipzig (Leipzig, 1911).

Contemporary books, articles and memoirs
Achilles, Albert, *Erinnerungen aus meiner Kriegsgefangenschaft im Mixed-Transit-Camp Ahmednagar und Erholungslager Ramandrog in Indien während des ersten Weltkrieges 1914–1920* (Berlin, 1977).
Anton, A., *Von Darmstadt nach Ostindien: Erlebnisse und Abenteuer eines Musikers auf der Reise durch Arabien nach Lahore: Die denkwürdigen Ereignisse der letzten Jahre* (Darmstadt, 1860).
Baierlein, E. R., *Die evangelische lutherische Mission in Ostindien* (Leipzig, 1874).
Baierlein, E. R., *The Land of the Tamulians and its Missions* (Madras, 1875).
Baierlein, E. R., *Unter den Palmen: Im Lande der Sonne* (Leipzig, 1890).
Bongard, Oscar, *Die Reise des Deutschen Kronprinzen durch Ceylon und Indien* (Berlin, 1911).
Bonsels, Waldemar, *Mein Austritt aus der Baseler Missions-Industrie und seine Gründe: Ein offener Brief an die Baseler Missions-Gemeinde in Württemberg und der Schweiz* (Munich-Schwabing, 1904).
Bonsels, Waldemar, *Indienfahrt* (originally 1912; Gloucester, 2008).
Bracker, Detlef, *Burgen der Finsternis in Indien* (Breklum, 1916).
Brandis, Dietrich, *Indian Trees: An Account of Trees, Shrubs, Woody Climbers, Bamboos and Palms Indigenous or Commonly Cultivated in the British Indian Empire* (London, 1906).

BIBLIOGRAPHY

Burkhardt, Gustav Emil, *Dr. G. E. Burkhardt's kleine Missions-Bibliothek*, three volumes (Leipzig, 1879–1880).
Cassel, Paulus, *Vom Nil zum Ganges: Wanderungen in die orientalische Welt* (Berlin, 1880).
Chatterton, Eyre, *The Story of Fifty Years' Mission Work in Chhota Nagpur* (London, 1901).
Dahlmann, Joseph, *Indische Fahrten*, two volumes (Freiburg im Breisgau, 1908).
Dalton, Hermann, *Johannes Goßner: Ein Lebensbild aus der Kirche des neunzehnten Jahrhunderts* (Berlin, 1878).
Dalton, Hermann, *Indische Reisebriefe* (Gütersloh, 1899).
Deussen, Paul, *Erinnerungen an Indien* (Leipzig, 1904).
Eggers, August, *Die Deutsch-Asiatische Bank und ihre Aufgaben* (Berlin, 1890).
Ehlers, Otto E., *An Indischen Fürstenhöfen* (Berlin, 1894).
Eppler, Christoph Friedrich, *Karl Gottlieb Pfander: Ein Zeuge der Wahrheit unter den Bekennern des Islam* (Basel, 1888).
Eppler, Paul, *Geschichte der Basler Mission 1815–1899: Mit vier Kartenskizzen* (Basel, 1900).
Fischer, Hermann, *Geographie der schwäbischen Mundart mit einem Atlas von achtundzwanzig Karten* (Tübingen,1895).
Flex, Oscar, *Pflanzerleben in Indien: Kulturgeschichtliche Bilder aus Assam* (Berlin, 1873).
Foertsch, Karl, *Unter Kriegs-Wettern: Kriegserlebnisse der Gossnerschen Missionare in Indien* (Berlin-Friedenau, 1916).
Garbe, Richard, *Indische Reiseskizzen* (Berlin, 1889).
Gehring, Alwin, *Erinnerungen aus dem Leben eines Tamulenmissionars* (Leipzig, 1906).
Gehring, Alwin, *Das Tamulenland, seine Bewohner und die Mission* (Leipzig, 1927).
Geiser, Alfred, *Deutsches Reich und Volk*, 2nd Edition (Munich, 1910).
Gengnagel, Ludwig, *Sieg des Evangeliums in einem Brahmanen-Herzen* (Basel, 1883).
Gloyer, Ernst, *Jeypur, das Haupt-Arbeitsfeld der Schleswig-Holsteinischen evangelisch-lutherischen Missionsgesellschaft zu Breklum auf der Ostküste Vorderindiens* (Breklum, 1901).
Graul, Karl, *Explanations Concerning the Principles of the Leipzig Missionary Society, with Regard to the Caste Question* (Madras, 1851).
Graul, Karl, *Reise nach Ostindien über Palästina und Egypten von Juli 1849 bis April 1853*, five volumes (Leipzig, 1854–6).
Grundemann, Reinhold, *Allgemeiner Missions-Atlas nach Originalquellen* (Gotha, 1869).
Grundemann, Reinhold, *Missions-Studien und Kritiken in Verbindung mit einer Reise nach Indien* (Gütersloh, 1894).
Grundemann, Reinhold, *Kleine Missions-Geographie und -Statistik zur Darstellung des Standes der evangelischen Mission am Schluss des 19. Jahrhunderts* (Stuttgart, 1901).
Gründler, O., *Frauenelend und Frauenmission in Indien* (Berlin, 1895).

Gundert, Hermann, *Aus dem Briefnachlass von Hermann Gundert* (Stuttgart, 1907).
Gundert, Hermann, *Herrmann Mögling: Ein Missionsleben in der Mitte des 19. Jahrhunderts* (Stuttgart, 1882).
Gundert, Hermann and Mögling, H., *The Life of Samuel Hebich: By Two of His Fellow-Labourers* (originally London, 1876; Memphis, TN, 2012).
Haccius, Georg, *Die letzten Erlebnisse unserer indischen Schwestern* (Hermannsburg, 1916).
Haeckel, Ernst, *Indische Reisebriefe* (Berlin, 1883).
Handmann, Richard, *Umschau auf dem Gebiete der evangelisch-lutherischen Mission in Ostindien* (Leipzig, 1888).
Handmann, Richard, *Die Evangelisch-lutherische Tamulen-Mission in der Zeit ihrer Neubegründung* (Leipzig, 1903).
Hebich, Samuel, *Züge aus dem Leben und Wirken des Missionars Samuel Hebich* (Elberfield, 1864).
Heilmann, Karl, *Missionskarte der Erde nebst Begleitwort: Mit besonderer Berücksichtigung der deutschen Kolonien* (Gütersloh, 1897).
Hermann, G., *Karl Graul und seine Bedeutung für die lutherische Mission* (Halle, 1867).
Hesse, Hermann, *Aus Indien* (Berlin, 1913).
Hesse, Hermann and Adele, *Zum Gedächtnis useres Vaters* (Tübingen, 1930).
Hesse, Johannes, *Die Heiden und Wir: 220 Geschichten und Beispiele aus der Heidenmission* (Calw, 1906).
Hoffmann, Frau Adolf, *Sie reden noch: Sieben Lebensbilder aus der Missionsarbeit der Frau* (Basel, 1926).
Hoffmann, Wilhelm, *Die Erziehung des weiblichen Geschlechts in Indien: Ein Aufruf an die christlichen Frauen Deutschlands* (Stuttgart, 1841).
Huber, F. G., 'Auswanderung and Auswanderungspolitik im Königreich Württemberg', in Eugen von Philippovich, ed., *Auswanderung und Auswanderungspolitik in Deutschland* (Leipzig, 1892).
Hull, Ernest, *The German Jesuit Fathers of Bombay: By an Englishman who Knows them* (Bombay, 1915).
Irion, Christan, *Malabar und die Missionsstation Talatscheri* (Basel, 1864).
Johann Jakob, *Als Kriegsgefangener: Von Indien nach Deutschland* (Stuttgart, 1916).
Jaus, Johann Jakob, *Kriegsgefangene Missionskinder* (Stuttgart, 1916).
Jaus, Johann Jakob, *Samuel Hebich: Ein Zeuge Jesu Christi aus der Heidenwelt* (Stuttgart, 1922).
Jessen, Otty, *Vertrieben* (Breklum, 1917).
Jolly, Julius, *Georg Bühler, 1837–1898* (Strasbourg, 1899).
Joseephy, Fritz, *Die deustche überseeische Auswanderung seit 1871* (Berlin, 1912).
Kauffmann, Oscar, *Aus Indiens Dschungeln: Erlebnisse und Forschungen*, two volumes (Leipzig, 1911).
Kaundinya, R., *Erinnerungen aus meinen Pflanzerjahren in Deutsch-Ost-Afrika* (Leipzig, 1918).

BIBLIOGRAPHY

Kausch, Hans, *Festschrift zum 75. jährigen Bestehen der Gossnerschen Mission* (Friedenau-Berlin, 1911).

Kausch, Hans and Hahn, F., *50 Bilder aus der Goßnerschen Kols-Mission mit erläuterndem Text und Karte* (Berlin, 1894).

Kleinschmidt, P. Beda, *Auslanddeutschtum und Kirche*, Vol. 2, *Die Auslanddeustchen im Übersee* (Münster, 1930).

Koch, Robert, *Reiseberichte über Rinderpest, Bubonenpest in Indien und Afrika, Tsetse- oder Surrakrankheit, Texasfieber, tropische Malaria, Schwarzwasserfieber* (Berlin, 1898).

Koenigsmarck, Hans von, *Die Engländer in Indien: Reiseeindrücke* (Berlin, 1909).

Kröpke, Wilhelm, *Mein Flucht aus englischer Kriegsgefangenschaft 1916: Von Afrika über England nach Deutschland zur Flandern-Front* (Flensburg, 1937).

Kühnle, K., *Die Arbeitsstätten der Basler Mission in Indien, China, Goldküste und Kamerun: Mit Übersichtskarte und Stationsbildern* (Basel, 1896).

Langholf, E., *Die Gefangenschaft und Heimkehr unserer Indischen Missionare* (Hermannsburg, 1916).

Leupolt, Charles Benjamin, *Further Recollections of an Indian Missionary* (London, 1884).

Limbach, S., *Bilder aus dem Südindischen Volksleben* (Basel, 1893).

Lorbeer, Helene, *Frauenleben und Frauenelend am heiligen Ganges* (Berlin, 1911).

Lucas, Anna, *Die Deutschen in Indien* (Bordelsholm, 1925).

Lucas, Sir Charles Prestwood, *The War and the Empire: Some Facts and Deductions* (London, 1919).

Lucas, Sir Charles Prestwood, ed., *The Empire at War*, five volumes (London, 1921–6).

Maue, J., *In Feindes Land: Achtzehn Monate in englischer Kriegsgefangenschaft in Indien und England* (Stuttgart, 1918).

Mögling, H. and Weitbrecht, C., *Das Kurgland und die evangelische Mission in Kurg* (Basel, 1866).

Mohr, Friedrich Wilhelm and Hauff, Walter von, *Deutsche im Ausland* (Breslau, 1923).

Mönckmeier, Wilhelm, *Die deutsche Überseeische Auswanderung* (Jena, 1912).

Norden, Heinrich, *In englischer Gefangenschaft* (Kassel, 1915).

Nostitz, Grafin Pauline, *Travels of Doctor and Madame Helfer in Syria, Mesopotamia, Burmah and other Lands*, two volumes (London, 1878).

Noti, Severin, *Reisebriefe eines Missionars* (New York, NY, 1908).

Nottrott, L., *Die Gossner'sche Mission unter den Kolhs: Bilder aus dem Missionsleben* (Halle, 1874).

Oepke, Albrecht, *Ahmednagar und Golconda: Ein Beitrag zur Erörterung der Missionsprobleme des Weltkrieges* (Leipzig, 1918).

Paul, Carl, *Vom Missionsfeld vertrieben: Ein Kriegserlebnis der Leipziger Mission* (Leipzig, 1916).

Paul, D., ed., *Die Leipziger Mission Daheim und Draussen* (Leipzig, 1914).

Philippovich, Eugen von, ed., *Auswanderung und Auswanderungspolitik in Deutschland* (Leipzig, 1892).

Plath, Karl Heinrich Christian, *Eine Reise nach Indien: Für kleine und große Leute beschrieben* (Berlin, 1880).
Pohl, E., *Schiff in Not: Die Breklumer Mission in Indien in und nach dem Kriege* (Breklum, 1929).
Pörzgen, Hermann, *Theater ohne Frau: Das Bühnenleben der Kriegsgefangenen Deutschen 1914–1920* (Königsberg, 1933).
Probst, Hans Georg, *Unter indischer Sonne: 19 Monate englischer Kriegsgefangenschaft in Ahmednagar* (Herborn, 1917).
Prochnow, Johann Dettloff, *Johannes Gossner: Biographie aus Tagebüchern und Briefen* (Berlin, 1874).
Ramawarma, Jakob, *Der indische Fürstensohn Jakob Ramawarma: Erstling der Malabar-Prediger* (Basel, 1880).
Reuleaux, Franz, *Eine Reise quer durch Indien im Jahre 1881: Erinnerungsblätter* (Berlin, 1884).
Rhenius, J., *Memoir of C. T. E. Rhenius, Comprising Extracts from His Journals and Correspondence, with Details of Missionary Proceedings in South India* (London, 1841).
Ribbentrop, Berthold, *Forestry in British India* (Calcutta, 1900).
Richter, Julius, *Die deutsche Mission in Südindien: Erzählungen und Schilderungen von einer Missions-Studienreise durch Ostindien* (Gütersloh, 1902).
Richter, Julius, *Nordindische Missionsfahrten: Erzählungen und Schilderungen von einer Missions-Studienreise durch Ostindien* (Gütersloh, 1903).
Richter, Julius, *A History of Missions in India* (Edinburgh, 1908).
Roemer, Christian, *Heimkehr aus Feindesland: Begrüßungsfeier f. die aus engl. Gefangenschaft freigewordenen Basler Missionsgeschwister in d. Stiftskirche zu Stuttgart 12. Juni 1916* (Stuttgart, 1916).
Rosenberger, Erwin, *In indischen Liebesgassen: Aus dem Tagebuch eines Schiffsarztes* (Vienna, 1924).
Roxburgh, R. F., 'German property in the war and the peace', Law Quarterly Review, vol. 37 (1921).
Saint-Hilaire, J. Barthélemy, *Egypt and the Suez Canal: A Narrative of Travels* (London, 1857).
Schaeuffelen, Eugenie, *Meine indische Reise* (Munich, 1904).
Schäfer, Marie Elisabeth, *Was vier kleine Kriegsgefangene erlebten: Erzählung aus dem Weltkrieg* (Leipzig, 1917).
Schlagintweit, Adolphe, Hermann and Robert, *Report on the Proceedings of the Officers Engaged in the Magnetic Survey of India* (Madras, 1855).
Schlagintweit, Adolphe, Hermann and Robert, *Report upon the Progress of the Magnetic Survey of India, and of the Researches Connected with it in the Himalaya Mountains, from April to October 1855* (Agra, 1856).
Schlagintweit, Emil, 'Ostindische Kaste in der Gegenwart', Zeitschrift der Deutschen Morgenländische Gesellschaft, vol. 33 (1879).
Schlagintweit, Emil, *Indien in Wort und Bild*, two volumes (Leipzig, 1880–1).
Schlagintweit-Sakülünski, Hermann von, *Reisen in Indien und Hochasien: Eine Darstellung der Landschaft, der Cultur und Sitten der Bewohner, in*

BIBLIOGRAPHY

Verbindung mit klimatischen und geologischen Verhältnissen Basirt auf die Resultate der wissenschaftlichen Mission von Hermann, Adolph und Robert von Schlagintweit ausgefuhrt in den Jahren 1854–1858, three volumes (Leipzig, 1869–80).

Schimming, Otto, *13 Monate hinter dem Stacheldraht: Alexandra Palace, Knocakaloe, Isle of Man, Stratford* (Stuttgart, 1919).

Schölly, Traugott, *Samuel Hebich: Der erste Sendbote der Basler Mission in Indien* (Basel, 1911).

Schomerus, L., 'Mittel und Wege zur Erlösung im indischen Heidentum nach Theorie und Praxis', in D. Paul, ed., *Die Leipziger Mission daheim und draussen* (Leipzig, 1914).

Stock, Eugene, *The History of the Church Missionary Society: Its Environment, Its men and Its Work*, four volumes (London, 1899–1916).

Stosch, Georg, *Im fernen Indien: Eindrücke und Erfahrungen im Dienst der luth. Mission unter den Tamulen* (Berlin, 1896).

Stolz, C., *Die Basler Mission in Indien: Zugleich als Festschrift zum 50 jährigen Jubiläum der Kanara-Mission* (Basel, 1884).

Tera, N. O., *Meine 800: Heimkehr aus Ahmednagar: 'Der Käpt'n erzählt'* (Hanover, 1934).

Thomssen, G. N., *Samuel Hebich of India: A Master Fisher of Men*, 2nd Edition (Mangalore, 1915).

Väth, Alfons, *Die deutschen Jesuiten in Indien: Geschichte der Mission von Bombay-Puna* (Regensburg, 1920).

Voelcker, John Augustus, *Report on the Improvement of Indian Agriculture* (London, 1893).

Vöhringer, Gotthilf, *Meine Erlebnisse während des Krieges in Kamerun und in englischer Kriegsgefangenschaft* (Hamburg, 1915).

Wegener, Georg, *Das heutige Indien: Grundlagen und Probleme der britisch-indischen Herrschaft* (Berlin, 1912).

Weigle, Christian Gotthilf, *Basler Missionar in Südmaharatta* (Basel, 1879).

Weitbrecht, Mary, *Memoir of the Rev. J. J. Weitbrecht: Compiled from his Journals and Letters by his Widow* (London, 1854).

Winternitz, M., *Georg Bühler und die Indologie* (Munich, 1898).

Wirth, Alfred, 'Das Deutschtum in Asien', *Deutsche Erde*, vol. 1 (1902).

Wörrlein, Johann, *Christian Kohlmeier: Von 1888–1892 Missionar in Indien* (Hermannsburg, 1901).

Wörrlein, Johann, *Hermann Ernst Jügenmeier: Von 1888–1892 Missionar in Indien* (Hermannsburg, 1901).

Wörrlein, Johann, *Paul Otto Petersen: Von 1875 bis 1888 Missionar in Indien* (Hermannsburg, 1901).

Wörrlein, Johann, *Peter Wilhelm Heinrich Lüchow: Von 1880–1893 Missionar in Indien* (Hermannsburg, 1901).

Wörrlein, Johann, *Ist in Indien eine besondere Frauenmission nötig?* (Hermannsburg, 1902).

Wörrlein, Johann, *Vierzig Jahre in Indien: Erinnerungen eines alten Missionars* (Hermannsburg, 1913).

Zehme, Therese, *Heimkehr mit der Golconda: Wie es den Kindern unserer vertriebenen indischen Missionare erging* (Leipzig, 1916).
Zimmer, Max, *Unsere Reise durch Indien, Java u. Ceylon im Jahre 1910* (Baden-Baden, 1911).

Secondary sources

Published work

Adluri, Vishwa and Bagchee, Joydeep, *The Nay Science: A History of German Indology* (Oxford, 2014).
Alagodi, S. D. L., 'The Basel Mission in Mangalore: Historical and Social Context', in Reinhardt Wendt, ed., *An Indian to the Indians? On the Initial Failure and the Posthumous Success of the Missionary Ferdinand Kittel (1832–1903)* (Wiesbaden, 2006).
Alcock, Helga, *The Schlagintweit Brothers: Achievements in High Asia* (Totnes, 1981).
Anagol, Padma, 'Indian Christian Women and Indian Feminism', in Clare Midgely, ed., *Gender and Imperialism* (Manchester, 1998).
Anwar, Muhamad, *The Myth of Return: Pakistanis in Britain* (London, 1979).
Arielli, Nir and Collins, Bruce, eds, *Transnational Soldiers: Foreign Military Enlistment in the Modern Era* (Basingstoke, 2013).
Arnold, David, 'Introduction: Disease, Medicine and Empire', in David Arnold, ed., *Imperial Medicine and Indigenous Societies* (Manchester, 1988).
Arnold, David, *Colonizing the Body: State Medicine and Epidemic Disease in Nineteenth-century India* (London, 1993).
Arnold, David, *Technology and Medicine in Colonial India* (Cambridge, 2000).
Arnold, David, 'The white town of Calcutta under the rule of East India Company', Modern Asian Studies, vol. 34 (2000).
Ashton, Rosemary, *Little Germany: Exile and Asylum in Victorian England* (Oxford, 1986).
Baago, K., *A History of the National Christian Council of India, 1914–1964* (Nagpur, 1965).
Bade, Klaus J., *Vom Auswanderungsland zum Einwanderungsland? Deutschland, 1880–1980* (Berlin, 1983).
Bade, Klaus J., ed., *Population, Labour and Migration in 19th and 20th Century Germany* (Leamington Spa, 1987).
Bade, Klaus J., ed., *Deutsche im Ausland – Fremde in Deutschland: Migration in Geschichte und Gegenwart* (Munich, 1992).
Bade, Klaus J., *Migration in European History* (Oxford, 2003).
Bagchi, Kaushik, 'An Orientalist in the Orient: Richard Garbe's Indian journey, 1885–1886', Journal of World History, vol. 14 (2003).
Baines, Dudley, *Emigration from Europe 1815–1930* (London, 1991).
Ballhalchet, Kenneth, *Race, Sex and Class under the Raj: Imperial Attitudes and Policies and their Critics, 1793–1905* (London, 1980).

BIBLIOGRAPHY

Bara, Joseph, 'Unlocking Tribal Knowledge to the World: German Missionaries in Chotangapur, East India (c.1850–1930)', in Ulrich van der Heyden und Andreas Feldtkeller, eds, *Missionsgeschichte als Geschichte der Globalisierung von Wissen: Transkulturelle Wissensaneignung und -vermittlung durch christliche Missionare in Afrika und Asien im 17., 18. und 19. Jahrhundert* (Stuttgart, 2012).

Basel Mission Work in India: A Chronology', in Godwin Shiri, ed., *Wholeness in Christ: The Legacy of the Basel Mission in India* (Mangalore, 1985).

Bassler, Gerhard P., edited and translated by Heinz Lehmann, *The German Canadians, 1750–1937* (St John's, Newfoundland, 1986).

Bayly, Christopher, *Indian Society and the Making of the British Empire* (Cambridge, 1988).

Bayly, Christopher, *The Birth of the Modern World, 1780–1914* (Oxford, 2004).

Becker, Judith, '"Gehet hin in alle Welt": Sendungsbewustsein in der evangelischen Missionsbewegung der ersten Hälfte des 19.Jahrhunderts', Evangelische Theologie, vol. 72 (2012).

Becker, Judith, *Conversio Im Wandel: Basler Missionare Zwischen Europa und Sudindien und die Ausbildung Einer Kontaktreligiosität, 1834–1860* (Göttingen, 2015).

Becker, Judith, ed., *European Missions in Contact Zones: Transformation through Interaction in a (Post-) Colonial World* (Göttingen, 2015).

Beerbühl, Margrit Schulte, *The Forgotten Majority: German Merchants in London, Naturalization and Global Trade, 1660–1815* (Oxford, 2015).

Beerbühl, Margrit Schulte and Weber, Klaus, 'From Westphalia to the Caribbean: Networks of German Textile Merchants in the Eighteenth Century', in Andreas Gestrich and Margrit Schulte Beerbühl, eds, *Cosmopolitan Networks in Commerce and Society 1660–1914* (London, 2011).

Benians, E. A., Butler, Sir James and Carrington, Charles E., eds, *The Cambridge History of the British Empire*, Vol. 3 (Cambridge, 1959).

Bergunder, Michael, 'Proselytismus in der Geschitche des Indischen Christentums: Eine Ökumenische Bestandsaufnahme', in Ulrich van der Heyden and Jürgen Becker, eds, *Mission und Gewalt: Der Umgang christlicher Missionen mit Gewalt und die Ausbreitung des Christentums in Afrika und Asien in der Zeit von 1792 bis 1918/19* (Stuttgart, 2000).

Bhabha, Jacqueline and Shutter, Sue, *Women's Movement: Women under Immigration, Nationality and Refugee Law* (Stoke-on-Trent, 1994).

Bidermann, Willi, *Missionar in den Blauen Bergen: Andreas Köhlers Weg nach Indien* (Bietigheim-Bissingen, 1997).

Bird, J. C., *Control of Enemy Alien Civilians in Great Britain, 1914–1918* (London, 1986).

Bitchnell, Thomas and Caletrio, Javier, eds, *Elite Mobilities* (London, 2012).

Blackbourn, David, 'Germans abroad and Auslandsdeutsche: Places, networks and experiences from the sixteenth to the twentieth century', Geschichte und Gesellschaft, vol. 41 (2015).

Blanton, Casey, *Travel Writing: The Self and the World* (London, 2002).
Boehmer, Elleke, *Indian Arrivals, 1870–1915: Networks of British Empire* (Oxford, 2015).
Bolt, Christine, *Victorian Attitudes to Race* (London, 1971).
Bonsels, Rose-Marie, ed., *Indien als Faszination: Stimmen zur 'Indienfahrt' von Waldemar Bonsels* (Wiesbaden, 1990).
Brecht, Martin, 'Der Württemburgische Pietismus', in Martin Brecht and Klaus Deppermann, eds, *Der Pietismus im achtzehnten Jahrhundert* (Göttingen, 1995).
Brettell, Caroline B. and Hollifield, James F., 'Introduction: Migration Theory – Talking Across Disciplines', in Caroline B. Brettell and James F. Hollifield, eds, *Migration Theory: Talking Across Disciplines* (London, 2000).
Brötel, Dieter, 'Die deutsche "Kolonie" in Paris: Imperiale Aktivitäten jüdisch-deutscher Bankiers, 1860–1880', in Markus A. Denzel, ed., *Deutsche Eliten in Übersee: (16. bis frühes 20. Jahrhundert)* (St Katharinen, 2006).
Brown, Judith M., 'War and the Colonial Relationship: Britain, India, and the War of 1914–1918', in M. R. D. Foot, ed., *War and Society* (London, 1973).
Brown, Judith M., *Global South Asians: Introducing the Modern Diaspora* (Cambridge, 2006).
Brown, Judith M. and Louis, W. R., eds, *The Oxford History of the British Empire*, Vol. 4, *The Twentieth Century* (Oxford, 1999).
Bueltmann, Tanja, Gleeson, David T. and MacRaild, Don, eds, *Locating the English Diaspora, 1500–2010* (Liverpool, 2012).
Buettner, Elizabeth, 'Problematic spaces, problematic races: defining Europeans in late colonial India', Women's History Review, vol. 9 (2000).
Buettner, Elizabeth, *Empire Families: Britons and Late Imperial India* (Oxford, 2004).
Bugge, Henriette, *Mission and Tamil Society: Social and Religious Change in South India (1840–1900)* (Richmond, 1994).
Burgdorfer, F., 'Migration Across the Frontiers of Germany', in Walter F. Wilcox, ed., *International Migrations* (London, 1961 reprint).
Butt, Maggie, *Ally Paly Prison Camp* (South Pool, 2011).
Caglioti, Daniela Luigia, *Vita parallele: Una minoranza protestante nell'Italia dell'Ottocento* (Bologna, 2006).
Caglioti, Daniela Luigia, 'Germanophobia and Economic Nationalism: Government Policies against Enemy Aliens in Italy during the First World War', in Panikos Panayi, ed., *Germans as Minorities during the First World War: A Global Comparative Perspective* (Farnham, 2014).
Carrington, Charles E., 'The Empire at War, 1914–1918', in E. A. Benians, Sir James Butler and Charles E. Carrington, eds, *The Cambridge History of the British Empire*, Vol. 3 (Cambridge, 1959).
Carton, Adrian, *Mixed-race and Modernity in Colonial India: Changing Concepts of Hybridity across Empires* (London, 2012).
Castles, Stephen, Haas, Hein de and Miller, Mark J., *The Age of Migration: International Population Movements in the Modern World*, 5th Edition (Palgrave, 2013).
Cesarani, David and Kushner, Tony, eds, *The Internment of Aliens in Twentieth Century Britain* (London, 1993).

BIBLIOGRAPHY

Chapman, Stanley D., *The Rise of Merchant Banking* (London, 1984).
Chaudhuri, Nupur, 'Memsahibs and their servants in nineteenth century India', Women's History Review, vol. 3 (1994).
Cho, Joanne Miyang, Kurlander, Eric and McGetchin, Douglas T., eds, *Transcultural Encounters between Germany and India: Kindred Spirits in the Nineteenth and Twentieth Centuries* (London, 2014).
Choné, Aurélie, 'Die Stadt des Lichts, eine für den Fremden unsichtbare Stadt? Probleme der Wahrnehmungsperspektive von Benares in deutschsprachigen Indienreiseschriften (1880–1930)', in Manfred Durzak, ed., *Bilder Indiens in der deutschen Literatur* (Frankfurt, 2011).
Cleall, Esme, *Missionary Discourse: Negotiating Otherness in the British Empire, 1840–1900* (Basingstoke, 2012).
Coleman, Terry, *Passage to America: A History of Emigrants from Great Britain and Ireland to America in the Mid-Nineteenth Century* (London, 1992).
Conrad, Sebastian, *Globalization and the Nation in Imperial Germany* (Cambridge, 2010).
Conzen, Kathleen Neils, *Immigrant Milwaukee, 1836–1860: Accommodation in a Frontier City* (London, 1976).
Cowan, Robert, *The Indo-German Identification: Reconciling South Asian Origins and European Destinies, 1765–1885* (Rochester, NY, 2010).
Cox, Jeffrey, *Imperial Fault Lines: Christianity and Colonial Power in India, 1818–1940* (Stanford, 2002).
Cox, Jeffrey, *The British Missionary Enterprise Since 1700* (London, 2008).
Curtin, Philip D., *Death by Migration: Europe's Encounter with the Tropical World in the Nineteenth Century* (Cambridge, 1989).
Dahlmann, Dittmar, 'The Russian Germans: A Heterogeneous Minority during the First World War', in Panikos Panayi, ed., *Germans as Minorities During the First World War: A Global Comparative Perspective* (Farnham, 2014).
Dahlmann, Dittmar and Tuchtenhagen, Ralph eds, *Zwischen Reform und Revolution: Die Deutschen an der Wolga 1860–1917* (Essen, 1994).
Dahya, Badr, 'Pakistanis in Britain: Transients or Settlers?', Race, vol. 14 (1973).
Dalrymple, William, *White Mughals: Love and Betrayal in 18th-Century India* (London, 2004).
Das, Santanu, 'Indians at Home, Mesopotamia and France, 1914–1918: Towards an Intimate History', in Santanu Das, ed., *Race, Empire and First World War Writing* (Cambridge, 2011).
Daunton, Martin and Halpern, Rich, eds, *Empire and Others: British Encounters with Indigenous Peoples* (London, 1999).
David, Saul, *The Indian Mutiny* (London, 2002).
De, Sarmistha, *Marginal Europeans in Colonial India, 1860–1920* (Kolkata, 2008).
Dedering, Tilman, '"Avenge the Lusitania": The Anti-German Riots in South Africa in 1915', in Panikos Panayi, ed., *Germans as Minorities during the First World War: A Global Comparative Perspective* (Farnham, 2014).
Denness, Zoë, 'Gender and Germanophobia: The Forgotten Experiences of German Women in Britain, 1914–1919', in Panikos Panayi, ed., *Germans*

as Minorities Dduring the First World War: A Global Comparative Perspective (Farnham, 2014).
Denzel, Markus A., ed., Deutsche Eliten in Übersee: (16. bis frühes 20. Jahrhundert) (St Katharinen, 2006).
Devanesan, A., 'The Lutheran Mission', in B. Sobhanan, ed., A History of the Christian Missions in South India (Thiruvananthapuram, 1996).
Doerries, Reinhard R. 'German Transatlantic Migration from the Early Nineteenth Century to the Outbreak of World War II', in Klaus J. Bade, ed., Population, Labour and Migration in 19th and 20th Century Germany (Leamington Spa, 1987).
Dönninghaus, Victor, Die Deutschen in der Moskauer Gesellschaft: Symbiose und Konflikte (1494–1941) (Munich, 2002).
Dove, Richard, ed., 'Totally un-English?' Britain's Internment of 'Enemy Aliens' in Two World Wars (Amsterdam, 2005).
Durzak, Manfred, ed., Bilder Indiens in der deutschen Literatur (Frankfurt, 2011).
Dussort, Fae, '"Strictly Legal Means": Assault, Abuse and the Limits of Acceptable Behaviour in the Servant/Employer Relationship in Metropole and Colony 1850–1890', in Victoria K. Haskins and Claire Lowrie, eds, Colonization and Domestic Service: Historical and Contemporary Perspectives (Abingdon, 2015).
Eberhardt, Martin, Zwischen Nationalsozialismus und Apartheid: Die deutsche Bevölkerungsgruppe Südwestafrikas 1915–1965 (Münster, 2007).
Edwardes, Michael, Bound to Exile: The Victorians in India (London, 1969).
Ellinwood, Dewitt and Prahan, S. D., 'Introduction', in Dewitt Ellinwood and S. D. Prahan, eds, India and World War 1 (Columbia, MO, 1978).
Engberts, Christiaan, 'The rise of associational activity: early twentieth century German sailors' homes and schools in Antwerp and Rotterdam', Immigrants and Minorities, vol. 32 (2014).
Engelsing, Rolf, Bremen als Auswandererhafen 1683–1880 (Bremen, 1961).
Erickson, Charlotte, Emigration from Europe, 1815–1914 (London, 1976).
Erickson, Charlotte, Leaving England: Essays on British Emigration in the Nineteenth Century (London, 1994).
Fenske, Hans, 'International migration in the eighteenth century', Central European History, vol. 13 (1980).
Fernando, Leonard and Gispert-Sauch, G., Christianity in India: Two Thousand Years of Faith (London, 2004).
Findeis, Hans-Juergen, 'Language – Religion – Mission: Some Reflections on the Contribution of Missionaries to Indian Languages in the Context of Mission History', in William Madtha, Heidrun Becker, A. Murigeppa and H. M. Mahehshwari, eds, A Dictionary with a Mission: Papers of the International Conference on the Occasion of the Centenary Celebrations of Kittel's Kannada-English Dictionary (Mangalore, 1998).
Fischer, Gerhard, Enemy Aliens: Internment and the Homefront Experience in Australia, 1914–1920 (St Lucia, 1989).
Fischer, Gerhard, 'Fighting the War at Home: The Campaign against Enemy Aliens in Australia during the First World War', in Panikos Panayi, ed.,

BIBLIOGRAPHY

Minorities in Wartime: National and Racial Groupings in Europe, North America and Australia during the Two World Wars (Oxford, 1993).

Fischer, Rudolf, *Die Basler Missionsindustrie in Indien 1850–1913: Rekrutierung und Disziplinierung der Arbeiterschaft* (Zürich, 1978).

Fischer, Rudolf, 'Mission and Modernisation: The Basel Mission Factories as Agencies of Social Change (1850–1914)', in Godwin Shiri, ed., *Wholeness in Christ: The Legacy of the Basel Mission in India* (Mangalore, 1985).

Fischer-Tiné, Harald, *Low and Licentious Europeans: Race, Class and 'White Subalternity' in Colonial India* (Hyderabad, 2009).

Fleisch, Paul, *Hundert Jahre Lutherischer Mission* (Leipzig, 1936).

Foot, M. R. D., ed., *War and Society* (London, 1973).

Forth, Aidan, 'Britain's archipeligo of camps: labour and detention in a liberal empire', Kritika, vol. 16 (2015).

Francis, Andrew, *'To Be Truly British We Must Be Anti-German': New Zealand, Enemy Aliens and the Great War Experience, 1914–1919* (Oxford, 2012).

Franz, Eckhart G., 'Freiheit jenseits des Meeres: Hessische Polit-Emigration nach Übersee im 19. Jahrhundert', in Markus A. Denzel, ed., *Deutsche Eliten in Übersee (16. bis frühes 20. Jahrhundert)* (St Katharinen, 2006).

Frenz, Albrecht, *Hermann Gundert: Schriften und Berichte aus Malabar* (Stuttgart, 1983).

Frenz, Albrecht, *Hermann Gundert: Tagebuch aus Malabar, 1837–1859* (Stuttgart, 1983).

Frenz, Albrecht, 'Dr. Hermann Gundert: A Biography', in Albrecht Frenz and Scaria Zacharia, eds, *Dr. Hermann Gundert and Malayalam Language* (Changanassery, 1993).

Frenz, Albrecht, *Hermann Gundert: Reise nach Malabar* (Ulm, 1998).

Frenz, Albrecht, 'Berichte über Aufstände der Mappilas in Hermann Gunderts Briefen und in seinem Tagebuch', in Ulrich van der Heyden and Jürgen Becker, eds, *Mission und Gewalt: Der Umgang christlicher Missionen mit Gewalt und die Ausbreitung des Christentums in Afrika und Asien in der Zeit von 1792 bis 1918/19* (Stuttgart, 2000).

Frenz, Albrecht, *Freiheit hat Gesicht. Anadapur – eine Begegnung zwischen Kodagu und Baden-Württemberg. Pauline Franziska Mögling, Herrmann Anandrao Kaundinya, Herrmann Friedrich Mögling – Stephanas Somaya Almanda, Otto Kaufmann. Briefe, Berichte und Bilder versehen mit Einleitung, biografischen Skizzen und Anhang* (Stuttgart, 2003).

Frenz, Albrecht, *Eine Reise in die Religionen: Herrmann Mögling (1811–1881), Missionar und Sprachforscher in Indien, zum 200. Geburtstag* (Heidelberg, 2011).

Frenz, Albrecht and Zacharia, Scaria, eds, *Dr. Hermann Gundert and Malayalam Language* (Changanassery, 1993).

Frykenberg, Robert Eric, *Christianity in India: From beginnings to the Present* (Oxford, 2008).

Frykenberg, Robert Eric and Low, Alaine M., eds, *Christians and Missionaries in India: Cross-Cultural Communication since 1500, with Special Reference to Caste, Conversion and Colonialism* (Grand Rapids, MI, 2003).

Fuechtner, Veronika and Rhiel, Mary, eds, *Imagining Germany Imagining Asia: Essays in Asian-German Studies* (Rochester, NY, 2013).

Fulbrook, Mary, *Piety and Politics: Religion and the Rise of Absolutism in England, Württemberg and Prussia* (Cambridge, 1983).
Fulbrook, Mary and Rublak, Ulinka, 'The "social self" and ego-documents', German History, vol. 28 (2010), pp. 263–72.
Ganeshan, Vidhagiri, *Das Indienbild deutscher Dichter um 1900: Dauthendey, Bonsels, Mauthner, Gjellerup, Hermann Keyserling und Stefan Zweig: Ein Kapitel deutsch-indischer Geistesbeziehungen im frühen 20. Jahrhundert* (Bonn, 1975).
Ganeshan, Vidhagiri, *Das Indienerlebins Hermann Hesses*, 2nd Edition (Bonn, 1980).
Genschorek, Wolfgang, *Robert Koch* (Leipzig, 1975).
Gense, James H., *The Church at the Gateway of India, 1720–1960* (Bombay, 1960).
Gestrich, Andreas and Schulte Beerbühl, Margrit, eds, *Cosmopolitan Networks in Commerce and Society 1660–1914* (London, 2011).
Ghose, Indira, *Memsahibs Abroad: Writings by Women Travellers in Nineteenth Century India* (Oxford, 1998).
Ghosh-Shantinikaten, Pranabendra Nath, 'Johann Gottfried Herder's Image of India', in Heinz Mode and Hans-Joachim Peuke, eds, *Indien in der deutschen Literarischen Tradition* (Halle, 1979).
Gilley, Sheridan and Stanley, Brian, eds, *The Cambridge History of Chritianity*, Vol. 8, *World Christianities c.1815–c.1914* (Cambridge, 2006).
Gilmour, David, *The Ruling Caste: Imperial Lives in the Victorian Raj* (London, 2005).
Glasenapp, Helmuth von, *Indien in der Dichtung und Forschung des deutschen Ostens* (Königsberg, 1930).
Glasenapp, Helmuth von, *Image of India* (New Delhi, 1973).
Gläsle, Rosemarie, *Pauline und ihre Töchter: 'Missionsbräute' als lebenslange Weggefährtinnen Basler Missionare in Indien und China* (Erlangen, 2012).
Grafe, Hugald, *Evangelische Kirche in Indien: Auskunft und Einblicke* (Erlangen, 1981).
Grimshaw, Allen D., 'The Anglo-Indian community: the integration of a marginal group', Journal of Asian Studies, vol. 18 (1959).
Grove, Richard, *Green Imperialism* (Cambridge, 1995).
Gründler, O., *Frauenelend und Frauenmission in Indien* (Berlin, 1895).
Guha, Ramachandra, 'Dietrich Brandis: A Vision Revisited and Reaffirmed', in Mark Poffenberger and Betsy McGean, eds, *Village Voices, Forest Choices: Joint Forest Management in India* (Oxford, 1996).
Haas, Waltraud, *Erlitten und Erstritten: Der Befreiungsweg von Frauen in der Basler Mission 1816–1966* (Basel, 1994).
Haas, Waltraud, 'Kaundinya, Hermann Anandrayo', in Gerald H. Anderson, ed., *Biographical Dictionary of Christian Missions* (Grand Rapids, MI, 1999).
Hardiman, David, *Missionaries and Their Medicine: A Christian Modernity for Tribal India* (Manchester, 2008).
Harper, Marjory and Constantine, Stephen, *Migration and Empire* (Oxford, 2014).
Harris, Janet, *Alexandra Palace: A Hidden History* (Stroud, 2005).

BIBLIOGRAPHY

Hartenstein, K., *Das Werden einer jungen Kirche im Osten: 100 Jahre Basler Missionsarbeit in Indien* (Stuttgart, 1935).

Haskins, Victoria K. and Lowrie, Claire, eds, *Colonization and Domestic Service: Historical and Contemporary Perspectives* (Abingdon, 2015).

Havanur, Srinivasa, 'Contribution of the Basel Mission to Kannada Literature', in Godwin Shiri, ed., *Wholeness in Christ: The Legacy of the Basel Mission in India* (Mangalore, 1985).

Hawes, Christopher J., *Poor Relations: The Making of a Eurasian Community in British India, 1773–1833* (Richmond, 1996).

Hesmer, Herbert, *Leben und Werk von Dietrich Brandis, 1824–1907: Begründer der tropischen Forstwirtschaft, Förderer der forstlichen Entwicklung in den USA, Botaniker und Ökologe* (Opladen, 1975).

Hesse, Marie Gundert, *Marie Hesse: Ein Lebensbild in Briefen und Tagebüchern* (Frankfurt am Main, 1977).

Heyden, Ulrich van der und Feldtkeller, Andreas, eds, *Missionsgeschichte als Geschichte der Globalisierung von Wissen: Transkulturelle Wissensaneignung und -vermittlung durch christliche Missionare in Afrika und Asien im 17., 18. und 19. Jahrhundert* (Stuttgart, 2012).

Hiery, Hermann Joseph, *Das Deutsche Reich in der Südsee: Eine Annäherung an die Erfahrungen verschiedener Kulturen* (Göttingen, 1995).

Hippel, Wolfgang von, *Auswanderung aus Südwestdeutschland: Studien zur württembergischen Auswanderung und Auswanderungspolitik im 18. und 19. Jarhundert* (Klett-Gotha, 1984).

Hobsbawm, Eric, *The Age of Empire, 1875–1914* (Harmondsworth, 1987).

Hoerder, Dirk, *Labor Migration in the Atlantic Economies: The European and North American Working Classes during the Period of Industrialization* (London, 1985).

Hoerder, Dirk, *Cultures in Contact: World Migrations in the Second Millenium* (London, 2002).

Hoerder, Dirk, 'Segmented Macrosystems and Networking Individuals: The Balancing Functions of Migration Processes', in Jan and Leo Lucassen, eds, *Migration, Migration History, History: Old Paradigms and New Perspectives* (Oxford, 2005).

Hoerder, Dirk, *Geschichte der deutschen Migration: Von Mittelalter bis heute* (Munich, 2010).

Hoerder, Dirk and Moch, Leslie Page, eds, *European Migration: Global and Local Perspectives* (Boston, 1996).

Hofmeyr, Isabel, 'South Africa's Indian Ocean: Boer prisoners of war in India', Social Dynamics, vol. 38 (2012).

Holland, Robert, 'The British Empire and the Great War, 1914–1918', in Judith M. Brown and W. R. Louis, eds, *The Oxford History of the British Empire*, Vol. 4, *The Twentieth Century* (Oxford, 1999).

Holsten, Walter, *Johannes Evangelista Goßner: Glaube und Gemeinde* (Göttingen, 1949).

Huber, Valeska, *Channelling Mobilities: Migration and Globalisation in the Suez Canal Region and Beyond, 1869–1914* (Cambridge, 2013).

Hümmerich, Franz, *Die erste deutsche Handelsfahrt nach Indien 1500/6* (Munich, 1922).

Husbands, Christopher T., 'German academics in British universities during the First World War: the case of Karl Wichmann', German Life and Letters, vol. 60 (2007).

Hutchinson, Mark and Wolffe, John, *A Short History of Global Evangelicalism* (Cambridge, 2012).

Huxley, Andrew, 'Dr Führer's Wanderjahre: the early career of a Victorian archaeologist', Journal of the Royal Asiatic Society of Great Britain and Ireland, Series 3, vol. 20 (2010).

Jackson, Ashley, ed., *The British Empire and the First World War* (Abingdon, 2015).

Jenkins, Jennifer M., 'Travelling to India in the 1850s: An Account by Fanny Würth-Leitner, One of Ferdinand Kittel's Travelling Companions', in William Madtha, Heidrun Becker, A. Murigeppa and H. M. Mahehshwari, eds, *A Dictionary with a Mission: Papers of the International Conference on the Occasion of the Centenary Celebrations of Kittel's Kannada-English Dictionary* (Mangalore, 1998).

Jenkins, Paul, 'The Church Missionary Society and the Basel Mission: An Early Experiment in Indo-European Cooperation', in Kevin Ward and Brian Stanley, eds, *The Church Mission Society and World Christianity, 1799–1999* (Richmond, 2000).

Jensz, Felicity, 'Missionaries and indigenous education in the 19th-century British Empire', History Compass, vol. 10 (2012).

Johnson, Donald Clay, 'German influences on the development of research libraries in nineteenth century Bombay', Journal of Library History, vol. 21 (1986).

Juneja, Monica, 'Mission und Begegnung: Gestaltung und Grenzen eines kommunikativen Raumes', in Monica Juneja and Margrit Pernau, eds, *Religion und Grenzen in Indien und Deutschland: Auf dem Weg zu einer transnationalen Historiographie* (Göttingen, 2008).

Jürgens, Hanco, 'German Indology avant la letter: The Experiences of the Halle Missionaries in Southern India', in Douglas T. McGetchin, Peter J. Park and Damodar Sardesai, eds, *Sanskrit and Orientalism: Indology and Comparative Linguistics in Germany, 1750–1958* (New Delhi, 2004).

Kade-Luthra, Veena, ed., *Sehnsucht Nach Indien: Ein Lesebuch von Goethe bis Grass* (Munich, 1991).

Kamphoefner, Walter D., *The Westfalians: From Germany to Missouri* (Princeton, NJ, 1987).

Karnick, Kamal, 'Warheit und Dichtung in Bonsels "Indienfart"', in Rose-Marie Bonsels, ed., *Indien als Faszination: Stimmen zur "Indienfahrt" von Waldemar Bonsels* (Wiesbaden, 1990).

Keil, Hartmut and Jentz, John B., *German Workers in Industrial Chicago, 1850–1910: A Comparative Perspective* (DeKalb, IL, 1983).

Kellenbenz, Hermann, 'The Herwarts of Augsburg and their Indian Trade during the First Half of the Sixteenth Century', in K. S. Mathew, ed., *Studies in Maritime History* (Pondicherry, 1990).

BIBLIOGRAPHY

Kenny, Judith T., 'Climate, race, and imperial authority: the symbolic landscape of the British hill station in India', Annals of the Association of American Geographers, vol. 85 (1995).
Kerr, Ian J., *Building the Railways of the Raj* (New Delhi, 1995).
Ketchum, John Davidson, *Ruhleben: A Prison Camp Society* (Toronto, 1965).
Kiernan, Victor, *The Lords of Human Kind: European Attitudes to Other Cultures in the Imperial Age* (Harmondsworth, 1972).
Kincaid, Dennis, *British Social life in India, 1608–1937* (London, 1973).
King, Richard, *Orientalism and Religion: Postcolonial Theory, India and the Mystic East* (Abingdon, 1999).
Kirchberger, Ulrike, *Aspekte deutsch-britischer Expansion: Die Überseeinteressen der deutschen Migranten in Großbritannien in der Mitte des 19. Jahrhunderts* (Stuttgart, 1999).
Kirchberger, Ulrike, 'Deutsche Naturwissenschaftler im britischen Empire: Die Erforschung der außereuropäischen Welt im Spannungsfeld zwischen deutschem und britischen Imperialismus', Historische Zeitschrift, vol. 271 (2000).
Kirchberger, Ulrike, 'German scientists in the Indian Forest Service: a German contribution to the Raj?', Journal of Imperial and Commonwealth History, vol. 29 (2001).
Kirchberger, Ulrike, '"Fellow-Labourers in the Same Vineyard": Germans in British Missionary Societies in the First Half of the Nineteenth Century', in Stefan Manz, Margrit Schulte Beerbühl and John R. Davis, eds, *Migration and Transfer from Germany to Britain* (Munich, 2007).
Knabe, Wolfgang, *Auf den Spuren der ersten deutschen Kaufleute in Indien: Forschungs Expedition mit der Mercator entlang der Westküste und zu den Aminen* (Anhausen, 1993).
Knodel, John E., *The Decline of Fertility in Germany, 1871–1939* (Princeton, 1974).
Konrad, Dagmar, *Missionsbräute: Pietistinnen des 19. Jahrhunderts in der Basler Mission* (Münster, 2001).
Kordan, Bohdan S., *Enemy Aliens, Prisoners of War: Internment in Canada during the Great War* (Montreal, 2002).
Korschorke, Klaus, eds., *Etappen der Globalisierung in christentumsgeschichtlicher Perspektive* (Wiesbaden, 2012).
Kuntsmann, Friedrich, *Die Fahrt der ersten Deutschen nach dem portugiesischen Indien* (Munich, 1861).
Kurup, Kuttamath K. N., 'Contribution of the Basel Mission in Malabur to Malayalam Languages and Literature', in Godwin Shiri, ed., *Wholeness in Christ: The Legacy of the Basel Mission in India* (Mangalore, 1985).
Lattek, Christine, *Revolutionary Refugees: German Socialism in Britain, 1840–1860* (London, 2006).
Lehmann, Arno, *Es begann in Tranquebar: Die Geschichte der ersten evangelischen Kirche in Indien* (Berlin, 1955).
Leifer, Walter, *Bombay and the Germans* (Bombay, 1975).
Leifer, Walter, *India and the Germans: 500 years of Indo-German Contacts* (Bombay, 1977).
Lentin, Anthony, *Banker, Traitor, Scapegoat, Spy? The Troublesome Case of Sir Edgar Speyer* (London, 2013).

Liebau, Heike, 'Deutsche Missionare als Indienforscher: Benjamin Schultze – Ausnahme oder Regel', Archiv für Kulturgeschichte, vol. 76 (1994).

Liebau, Heike, 'Country Priests, Catechists and Schoolmasters as Cultural, Religious and Social Middlemen in the Context of the Tranquebar Mission', in Robert Eric Frykenberg and Alaine M. Low, eds, *Christians and Missionaries in India: Cross-Cultural Communication since 1500, with Special Reference to Caste, Conversion and Colonialism* (Grand Rapids, MI, 2003).

Liebau, Heike, *Cultural Encounters in India: The Local Co-workers of the Tranquebar Mission, 18th to 19th Centuries* (New Delhi, 2013).

Liebau, Heike, Nehring, Andreas and Klosterberg, Brigitte, eds, *Mission und Forschung: Translokale Wissensproduktion zwischen Indien und Europa im 18. und 19. Jahrhundert* (Halle, 2010).

Lohr, Eric, *Nationalizing the Russian Empire: The Campaign against Enemy Aliens during World War I* (Cambridge, MA, 2003).

Lokies, Hans, *Die Gossner-Kirche in Indien: Durch Wachstumskrisen zur Mündigkeit* (Berlin, 1969).

Lucassen, Jan and Leo, eds, *Migration, Migration History, History: Old Paradigms and New Perspectives* (Oxford, 2005).

Lüdemann, Joachim, *August Mylius (1819–1887): Lutherische Missionarsexistenz in Tamilnadu und Andhra Pradesh* (London, 2003).

Luebke, Frederick C., *Bonds of Loyalty: German Americans and World War I* (De Kalb, IL, 1974),

Luebke, Frederick C., *Germans in Brazil: A Comparative History of Cultural Conflict during World War I* (Baton Rouge, LO, 1987).

Luebke, Frederick C., *Germans in the New World: Essays in the History of Immigration* (Chicago, IL, 1990).

Mack, Julia Ulrike, *Menschenbilder: Anthropologische Konzepte und stereotype Vorstellungen vom Menschen in der Publizistik der Basler Mission 1816–1914* (Zurich, 2014).

MacKenzie, John M., *The Empire of Nature: History, Conservation and British Imperialism* (Manchester, 1988).

Macraild, Donald and Delaney, Enda, eds, *Irish Migration, Networks and Ethnic Identities since 1750* (London, 2007).

Madtha, William, Becker, Heidrun, Murigeppa, A. and Mahehshwari, H. M., eds, *A Dictionary with a Mission: Papers of the International Conference on the Occasion of the Centenary Celebrations of Kittel's Kannada-English Dictionary* (Mangalore, 1998).

Magee, Gary B. and Thompson, Andrew S., *Empire and Globalisation: Networks of People, Goods and Capital in the British World, c.1850–1914* (Cambridge, 2010).

Major, Andrea, *Sovereignty and Social Reform in India: British Colonialism and the Campaign against Sati, 1830–1860* (London, 2011).

Mammen, E., Tomar, M. S., and Parameswaran, N., 'A salute to William Schlich', Indian Forester, vol. 91 (1965).

Manjapra, Kris, *Age of Entanglement: German and Indian Intellectuals across Empire* (London, 2014).

BIBLIOGRAPHY

Manktelow, Emily J., *Missionary Families: Race, Gender and Generation on the Spiritual Frontier* (Manchester, 2013).
Mann, Michael, 'Indien ist eine Karriere: Biographische Skizzen deutscher Söldner, Ratsherren und Mediziner in Südasien, 1500–1800', in Markus A. Denzel, ed., *Deutsche Eliten in Übersee (16. bis frühes 20. Jahrhundert)* (St Katharinen, 2006).
Manning, Patrick, *Migration in World History*, 2nd Edition (London, 2013).
Manz, Stefan, *Migranten und Internierte: Deutsche in Glasgow, 1864–1918* (Stuttgart, 2003).
Manz, Stefan, *Constructing a German Diaspora: The 'Greater German Empire', 1871–1914* (London, 2014).
Manz, Stefan, Schulte Beerbühl, Margrit and Davis, John R., eds, *Migration and Transfer from Germany to Britain* (Munich, 2007).
Marchand, Suzanne L., *German Orientalism in the Age of Empire: Religion, Race, and Scholarship* (Cambridge, 2009).
Marschalck, Peter, *Deustche Überseewanderung im 19. Jahrhundert* (Stuttgart, 1973).
Marshall, P. J., 'British society in India under the East India Company', Modern Asian Studies, vol. 31 (1997).
Mathew, K. S., ed., *Studies in Maritime History* (Pondicherry, 1990).
Mathieson, Alfred, *Hebich of India: A Passionate Soul-Winner* (Kilmarnock, 1936).
May, Andrew J., *Welsh Missionaries and British Imperialism: The Empire of Clouds in North-East India* (Manchester, 2012).
McGetchin, Douglas, *Indology, Indomania and Orientalism: Ancient India's Rebirth in Modern Germany* (Madison, NJ, 2009).
McGetchin, Douglas, Park, Peter J. and Sardesai, Damodar, eds, *Sanskrit and Orientalism: Indology and Comparative Linguistics in Germany, 1750–1958* (New Delhi, 2004).
Metcalf, Thomas R., *Ideologies of the Raj* (Cambridge, 1998).
Midgely, Clare, ed., *Gender and Imperialism* (Manchester, 1998).
Miller, Jon, *The Social Control of Religious Zeal: A Study of Organizational Contradictions* (New Brunswick, NJ, 1994).
Mizutani, Satoshi, *The Meaning of White: Race, Class, and the 'Domiciled Community' in British India 1858–1930* (Oxford, 2011).
Mode, Heinz and Peuke, Hans-Joachim, eds, *Indien in der deutschen Literarischen Tradition* (Halle, 1979).
Mohanavelu, C. S., 'Karl Graul's Efforts to Promote Evangelical Lutheran Mission in Tamil Nadu, 1844–1864', in Ulrich van der Heyden and Jürgen Becker, eds, *Mission und Gewalt: Der Umgang christlicher Missionen mit Gewalt und die Ausbreitung des Christentums in Afrika und Asien in der Zeit von 1792 bis 1918/19* (Stuttgart, 2000).
Möllers, Benhard, *Robert Koch: Persönlichkeit und Lebenswerk* (Hannover, 1950).
Morton-Jack, George, *The Indian Army on the Western Front: India's Expeditionary Force to France and Belgium in the First World War* (Cambridge, 2014).

Mosse, Werner E., et al., eds, *Second Chance: Two Centuries of German–speaking Jews in the United Kingdom* (Tübingen, 1991).
Mukherjee, R., '"Satan let loose upon Earth": The Kanpur massacres in India in the Revolt of 1857', Past and Present, no. 128 (1990).
Müller-Jabusch, Maximilian, *Fünfzig Jahre Deutsch-Asiatische Bank: 1890–1939* (Berlin, 1940).
Murti, Kamakshi Pappu, *India: The Seductive and Seduced 'Other' of German Orientalism* (Westport, CN, 2001).
Myers, Perry, 'The Ambivalence of a Spiritual Quest in India: Waldemar Bonsels's *Indienfahrt*', in Veronika Fuechtner and Mary Rhiel, eds, *Imagining Germany Imagining Asia: Essays in Asian-German Studies* (Rochester, NY, 2013).
Myers, Perry, *German Visions of India, 1871–1918: Commandeering the Holy Ganges during the Kaiserreich* (Basingstoke, 2013).
Myers, Perry, 'German Travellers to India at the Fin-de-Siècle and their Ambivalent View of the Raj', in Joanne Miyang Cho, Eric Kurlander and Douglas T. McGetchin, eds, *Transcultural Encounters between Germany and India: Kindred Spirits in the Nineteenth and Twentieth Centuries* (London, 2014).
Nadel, Stanley, *Little Germany: Ethnicity, Religion, and Class in New York City, 1845–80* (Chicago, 1990).
Nagel, Silke, *Ausländer in Mexiko: Die 'Kolonien' der deutschen und US-amerikanischen Einwanderer in der mexikanischen Hauptstadt 1890–1942* (Frankfurt, 2005).
Nagler, Jörg, *Nationale Minoritäten im Krieg: 'Feindliche Ausländer' und die amerikanische Heimatfront während des Ersten Weltkriegs* (Hamburg, 2000).
Naranch, Bradley B., 'Between Cosmopolitanism and German Colonialism: Nineteenth-Century Hanseatic Networks in Emerging Tropical Markets', in Andreas Gestrich and Margrit Schulte Beerbühl, eds, *Cosmopolitan Networks in Commerce and Society 1660–1914* (London, 2011).
Negi, S. S., *Sir Dietrich Brandis: Father of Tropical Forestry* (Dehra Dun, 1991).
Nehring, Andreas, *Orientalismus und Mission: Die Repräsentation der tamulischen Gesellschaft und Religion durch Leipziger Missionare 1840–1940* (Wiesbaden, 2003).
Nehring, Andreas, 'Missionsstrategie und Forschungsdrang: Anmerkungen zu Mission und Wissenschaft in Südindien im 19. Jahrhundert', in Heike Liebau, Andreas Nehring and Brigitte Klosterberg, eds, *Mission und Forschung: Translokale Wissensproduktion zwischen Indien und Europa im 18. und 19. Jahrhundert* (Halle, 2010).
Neill, Stephen, *A History of Christianity in India: 1707–1858* (Cambridge, 1985).
Newton, Ronald C., *German Buenos Aires, 1900–1933: Social Change and Cultural Crisis* (London, 1977).
Newton, Ronald C., *The 'Nazi Menace' in Argentina, 1931–1947* (Stanford, CA, 1992).
O'Donnell, Krista, Bridenthal, Renate and Reagin, Nancy, eds, *The Heimat Abroad: The Boundaries of Germanness* (Ann Arbor, MI, 2005).
Oehler, Wilhelm, *Geschichte der deutschen evangelischen Mission*, two volumes (Baden-Baden: Fehrholz, 1949–51).

BIBLIOGRAPHY

Oesterheld, Joachim, 'Zum Spektrum deustcher Eliten im kolonialen Indien: Ein erster Überblick', in Markus A. Denzel, ed., *Deutsche Eliten in Übersee (16. bis frühes 20. Jahrhundert)* (St Katharinen, 2006).
Oesterheld, Joachim and Lothar, Günther, *Inder in Berlin* (Berlin, 1997).
Omissi, David, ed., *Indian Voices of the Great War: Soldiers' Letters, 1914–18* (London, 2014).
Osterhammel, Jürgen, *The Transformation of the World: A Global History of the Nineteenth Century* (Oxford, 2014).
Palmer, Bernard, *Imperial Vineyard: The Anglican Church in India under the Raj from the Mutiny to Partition* (Lewes, 1999).
Panayi, Panikos, 'The British Empire Union in World War I', Immigrants and Minorities, vol. 8 (1989).
Panayi, Panikos, *The Enemy in Our Midst: Germans in Britain During the First World War* (Oxford, 1991).
Panayi, Panikos, ed., *Minorities in Wartime: National and Racial Groupings in Europe, North America and Australia during the Two World Wars* (Oxford, 1993).
Panayi, Panikos, *German Immigrants in Britain during the Nineteenth Century, 1815–1914* (Oxford, 1995).
Panayi, Panikos, *Prisoners of Britain: German Civilian and Combatant Internees during the First World War* (Manchester, 2012).
Panayi, Panikos, ed., *Germans as Minorities during the First World War: A Global Comparative Perspective* (Farnham, 2014).
Panayi, Panikos, '"Barbed Wire Disease" or a "Prison Camp Society": The Everyday Lives of German Internees on the Isle of Man, 1914–1919', in Panikos Panayi, ed., *Germans as Minorities during the First World War: A Global Comparative Perspective* (Farnham, 2014).
Panayi, Panikos, 'Minorities', in Jay Winter, ed., *The Cambridge History of the First World War*, Vol. 3, *Civil Society* (Cambridge, 2014).
Pati, Biswamoy, ed., *The 1857 Rebellion* (Oxford, 2007).
Pennington, Brian K., *Was Hinduism Invented? Britons, Indians, and the Colonial Construction of Religion* (Oxford, 2007).
Penny, H. Glenn and Rinke, Stefan, 'Germans abroad: respatializing historical narrative', Geschichte und Gesellschaft, vol. 41 (2015).
Pax, Elpidius, 'Otto Strauß', Zeitschrift der Deutschen Morgenländischen Gesellschaft, vol. 100 (1950).
Pfleiderer, Hermann, *Gottlob Pfleiderer: Der erste Basler Missionskaufmann in Indien* (Stuttgart, 1929).
Phillips, Howard and Killingray, David, eds, *The Spanish Influenza Pandemic of 1918–19: New Perspectives* (London, 2003).
Pietsch, Tamson, *Empire of Scholars: Universities, Networks and the British Academic World, 1850–1939* (Manchester, 2013).
Poettinger, Monika, 'German Entrepreneurial Networks and the Industrialization of Milan', in Andreas Gestrich and Margrit Schulte Beerbühl, eds, *Cosmopolitan Networks in Commerce and Society 1660–1914* (London, 2011).
Poffenberger, Mark and McGean, Betsy, eds, *Village Voices, Forest Choices: Joint Forest Management in India* (Oxford, 1996).

Porter, Andrew, *Religion Versus Empire? British Protestant Missionaries and Overseas Expansion, 1700–1914* (Manchester, 2004).
Potter, Simon J., *News and the British World: The Emergence of an Imperial Press System 1876–1922* (Oxford, 2003).
Powell, Avril A., *Muslims and Missionaries in Pre-Mutiny India* (Richmond, 1993).
Procida, Mary A., *Married to the Empire: Gender, Politics and Imperialism in India, 1883–1947* (Manchester, 2002).
Proctor, Tammy M., '"Patriotic Enemies": Germans in the Americas, 1914–1920', in Panikos Panayi, ed., *Germans as Minorities during the First World War: A Global Comparative Perspective* (Farnham, 2014).
Purtschert, Patricia and Fischer-Tiné, Harald, eds, *Colonial Switzerland: Rethinking Colonialism from the Margins* (Basingstoke, 2015).
Racine, Karen and Mamigonian, Beatriz G., eds, *The Human Tradition in the Atlantic World, 1500–1850* (Plymouth, 2010).
Raghaviah, Jaiprakash, *Basel Mission Industries in Malabar and South Canara, 1834–1914: A Study of its Social and Economic Impact* (New Delhi, 1990).
Rawat, Ajay S., 'Brandis: The Father of Organized Forestry in India', in Ajay S. Rawat, ed., *Indian Forestry: A Perspective* (New Delhi, 1993).
Rehmer, Hans-Joachim, 'Ein Mecklenburger – Polizeipräsident von Bombay', Carolinium, vol. 64 (2000).
Roeber, Klaus, 'Johannes Evangelista Goßner (14.12.1773–30.3.1858): Skizze eines Lebens', in Ulrich Schöntube, ed., *Zwischen Wort und Tat: Beiträge zum 150. Todestag von Johannes Evangelista Goßner* (Neuendettelsau, 2009).
Roeber, Klaus, 'Missionare der Gossner Mission als Forscher und Wissenschaftler', in Ulrich van der Heyden und Andreas Feldtkeller, eds, *Missionsgeschichte als Geschichte der Globalisierung von Wissen: Transkulturelle Wissensaneignung und -vermittlung durch christliche Missionare in Afrika und Asien im 17., 18. und 19. Jahrhundert* (Stuttgart, 2012).
Rosenberg, Peter and Weydt, Harald, 'Sprachen und Sprachgemeinschaft der Wolgadeutschen', in Dittmar Dahlmann and Ralph Tuchtenhagen, eds, *Zwischen Reform und Revolution: Die Deutschen an der Wolga 1860–1917* (Essen, 1994).
Rothermund, Dietmar, *The German Intellectual Quest for India* (New Delhi, 1986).
Roy, Kaushik, ed., *War and Society in Colonial India* (Oxford, 2006).
Roy, Tirthankar, *India in the World Economy: From Antiquity to the Present* (Cambridge, 2012).
Rüdiger, Klaus H., *Die Namibia-Deutschen: Geschichte einer Nationalität im Werden* (Stuttgart, 1993).
Russ, Charles V. J., 'Swabian', in Charles V. J. Russ, ed., *The Dialects of Modern German: A Linguistic Survey* (Abingdon, 2013).
Said, Edward, *Orientalism* (London, 2003 reprint).
Saldanha, Indra Munshi, 'Colonialism and professionalism: a German forester in India', Environment and History, vol. 2 (1996).
Salesa, Iremina, *Racial Crossings: Race, Intermarriage and the Victorian British Empire* (Oxford, 2011).

BIBLIOGRAPHY

Salmons, Joseph, *A History of German: What the Past Reveals about Today's Language* (Oxford, 2012).
Schirrmacher, Christine, *Mit den Waffen des Gegners: Christlich-muslimische Kontroversen im 19. und 20. Jahrhundert* (Berlin, 1992).
Schlatter, Wilhelm and Witschi, Hermann, *Geschichte der Basler Mission*, five volumes (Basel, 1916–70).
Schöntube, Ulrich, ed., *Zwischen Wort und Tat: Beiträge zum 150. Todestag von Johannes Evangelista Goßner* (Neuendettelsau, 2009).
Schulze, Winfried, 'Ego-Dokumente: Annäherung an den Menschen in der Geschichte', in Winfried Schulze, ed., *Ego-Dokumente: Annäherung an den Menschen in der Geschichte* (Berlin, 1996).
Sebastian, J. Jayakiran, 'The baptism of death: reading the life and death of Lakshmi Kundinya', Mission Studies, vol. 28 (2011).
Sebastian, Mrinalini, 'Localised Cosmopolitanism and Globalised Faith: Echoes of "Native" Voices in Eighteenth and Nineteenth Century Missionary Documents', in Judith Becker, ed., *European Missions in Contact Zones: Transformation through Interaction in a (Post-) Colonial World* (Göttingen, 2015).
Sebastian, Mrinalini, 'The Scholar Missionaries of the Basel Mission in Southwestern India: Language, Identity, and Knowledge in Flux', in Heather Sharkey, ed., *Cultural Conversions: Unexpected Consequences of Christian Missionary Encounters in the Middle East, Africa and South Asia* (Syracuse, NY, 2013).
Sedlar, Jean W., *India in the Mind of Germany: Schelling, Schopenauer and their Times* (Washington, DC, 1982).
Sen, Indrani, *Women and Empire: Representation in the Writing of British India (1858–1900)* (Hyderabad, 2002).
Sengupta, Indra, *From Salon to Discipline: State, University and Indology in Germany, 1821–1914* (Würzburg, 2005).
Sharkey, Heather, ed., *Cultural Conversions: Unexpected Consequences of Christian Missionary Encounters in the Middle East, Africa and South Asia* (Syracuse, NY, 2013).
Shiri, Godwin, ed., *Wholeness in Christ: The Legacy of the Basel Mission in India* (Mangalore, 1985).
Singh, Gurharpal and Tatla, Darshan Singh, *Sikhs in Britain: The Making of a Community* (London, 2006).
Sobhanan, B., ed., *A History of the Christian Missions in South India* (Thiruvananthapuram, 1996).
Soto, Katharina Tietze de, *Deutsche Einwanderung in die chilenische Provinz Concepción 1870–1930* (Frankfurt, 1999).
Speed III, Richard B., *Prisoners, Diplomats and the Great War: A Study in the Diplomacy of Captivity* (London, 1990).
Sprockhoff, Joachim Friedrich, 'Friedrich Schrader zum Gedächtnis', Zeitschrift der Deutschen Morgenländischen Gesellschaft, vol. 113 (1963).
Stache-Rosen, Valentina, *German Indologists: Biographies of Scholars in Indian Studies Writing in German* (New Delhi, 1981).
Stanley, Brian, *The World Missionary Conference, Edinburgh 1910* (Grand Rapids, MI, 2009).

Steinbach, Daniel, 'Power Majorities and Local Minorities: German and British Colonials in East Africa during the First World War', in Panikos Panayi, ed., *Germans as Minorities during the First World War: A Global Comparative Perspective* (Farnham, 2014).

Stenzl, Catherine, 'Racial Stereotypes in the Construction of the Other and the Identification of the Self: The Basel Mission and its Industries in India ca. 1884', in Martin Tamcke and Gladson Jathanna, eds, *Construction of the Other, Identification of the Self: German Mission in India* (Vienna, 2012).

Stibbe, Matthew, *German Anglophobia and the Great War, 1914–1918* (Cambridge, 2001).

Stibbe, Matthew, *British Civilian Internees in Germany: The Ruhleben Camp, 1914–18* (Manchester, 2008).

Stokes, Eric, *The Peasant Armed: The Indian Rebellion of 1857* (Oxford, 1986).

Strachan, Hew, *The First World War*, Vol. 1, *To Arms* (Oxford, 2001).

Stricker, Gerd, ed., *Deutsche Geschichte im Osten Europas: Rußland* (Berlin, 1997).

Tamcke, Martin and Jathanna, Gladson, eds, *Construction of the Other, Identification of the Self: German Mission in India* (Vienna, 2012).

Tampke, Jürgen, *The Germans in Australia* (Cambridge, 2006).

Taylor, Philip, *The Distant Magnet: European Emigration to the USA* (London, 1971).

Thamer, Ulrich, 'Flucht und Exil: "Demagogen" und Revolutionäre', in Klaus J. Bade, ed., *Deutsche im Ausland – Fremde in Deutschland: Migration in Geschichte und Gegenwart* (Munich, 1992).

Torp, Cornelius, *The Challenges of Globalization: Economy and Politics in Germany, 1860–1914* (Oxford, 1914).

Triebel, Christian, ed., *Der Missionar als Forscher: Beiträge christlicher Missionare zur Erforschung fremder Kulturen und Religionen* (Gütersloh, 1988).

Tucher, Paul von, *German Missions in British India: Case and Crisis in Missions* (self publication, 1980).

Tyrrell, Hartmann, '"Organisierte Mission": Protestantische Missionsgesellschaften des "langen 19. Jahrhunderts"', in Klaus Korschorke, eds., *Etappen der Globalisierung in christentumsgeschichtlicher Perspektive* (Wiesbaden, 2012).

Tzoref-Ashkenazi, Chen, 'German Auxilliary Troops in the British and Dutch East India Companies', in Nir Arielli and Bruce Collins, eds, *Transnational Soldiers: Foreign Military Enlistment in the Modern Era* (Basingstoke, 2013).

Upadhyaya, Uliyar P., 'Contribution of the Basel Mission to Tulu Literature', in Godwin Shiri, ed., *Wholeness in Christ: The Legacy of the Basel Mission in India* (Mangalore, 1985).

Urry, John, *Sociology beyond Societies: Mobilities for the Twenty-First Century* (London, 2000).

Urry, John and Elliot, Anthony, *Mobile Lives* (London, 2010).

Urry, John and Grieco, Margaret, *Mobilities: New Perspectives on Transport and Society* (Farnham, 2011).

BIBLIOGRAPHY

Vertovec, Steven, *Transnationalism* (Abingdon, 2009).
Waack, Otto, *Indische Kirche und Indien-Mission*, two volumes (Erlangen, 1994).
Wal, Marijke van der and Rutten, Gijsbert, 'Ego-Documents in a Historical-Sociological Perspective', in Marijke van der Wal and Gijsbert Rutten, eds, *Touching the Past: Studies in Historical Sociolinguisstics and Ego-Documents* (Amsterdam, 2013).
Waldschmidt, Ernst, 'Richard Pischel zum Gedächtnis', Zeitschrift der Deutschen Morgenländischen Gesellschaft, vol. 109 (1959).
Walther, Daniel Joseph, *Creating Germans Abroad. Cultural Policies and National Identity in Namibia* (Athens, OH, 2002).
Wanner, Gustav Adolf, *Die Basler Handels-Gesellschaft A.G., 1859–1959* (Basel, 1959).
Ward, Kevin and Stanley, Brian, eds, *The Church Mission Society and World Christianity, 1799–1999* (Richmond, 2000).
Weidenfeller, Gerhard, *VDA, Verein für das Deutschtum im Ausland: Allgemeiner Deutscher Schulverein (1881–1918): Ein Beitrag zur Geschichte des deutschen Nationalismus und Imperialismus im Kaiserreich* (Bern, 1976).
Wendt, Reinhardt, ' "Reden" und "Schreiben" in den Evangelisationsstrategien von Basler Missionaren und Jesuiten in Südwestindien und im südlichen Mindanao im 19. Jahrhundert', in Reinhard Wendt, ed., *Wege durch Babylon: Missionare, Sprachstudien und interkulturelle Kommunikation* (Tübingen, 1998).
Wendt, Reinhardt, ed., *An Indian to the Indians? On the Initial Failure and the Posthumous Success of the Missionary Ferdinand Kittel (1832–1903)* (Wiesbaden, 2006).
Werbner, Pnina, *The Migration Process: Capital, Gifts and Offerings among British Pakistanis* (Oxford, 1990).
Wilcox, Walter F., ed., *International Migrations* (London, 1961 reprint).
Willson, Arnos Leslie, *A Mythical Image: The Ideal of India in German Romanticism* (Durham, NC, 1964).
Wilson, Henry S., 'Basel Mission's industrial enterprise in South Kanara and its impact between 1834 and 1914', Indian Church History Review, vol. 14 (1980).
Wittke, Carl, *Refugees of Revolution: The German Forty-Eighters in America* (Philadelphia, PA, 1952).
Wulf, Andrea, *The Invention of Nature: The Adventures of Alexander von Humboldt, the Lost Hero of Science* (London, 2015).
Youngs, Tim, *Travellers in Africa: British Travelogues, 1830–1900* (Manchester, 1994).
Youngs, Tim, ed., *The Cambridge Introduction to Travel Writing* (Cambridge, 2013).
Zacharia, Scaria, 'Dr. Hermann Gundert and Malayalam Language: The Context of Understanding', in Albrehct Frenz and Scaria Zacharia, eds, *Dr. Hermann Gundert and Malayalam Language* (Changanassery, 1993).
Zacharia, Scaria, 'Tuebingen Heritage as Reflected in the Dictionaries of Gundert and Kittel', in William Madtha, Heidrun Becker, A. Murigeppa and H. M.

Mahehshwari, eds, *A Dictionary with a Mission: Papers of the International Conference on the Occasion of the Centenary Celebrations of Kittel's Kannada-English Dictionary* (Mangalore, 1998).

Zantop, Susanne, *Colonial Fantasies: Conquest, Family, and Nation in Pre-colonial Germany, 1770–1870* (London, 1997).

Zeuske, Michael, 'Deutsche als Eliten in Lateiamerika (19. Jahrhundert): Regionen, Typen, Netzwerke und paradigmatische Lebensgeschichten', in Markus A. Denzel, ed., *Deutsche Eliten in Übersee (16. bis frühes 20. Jahrhundert)* (St Katharinen, 2006).

Theses

Jones, M. A., 'The Role of the United Kingdom in the Transatlantic Immigrant Trade, 1815–1875' (unpublished Oxford University PhD thesis, 1955).

Mather, B. H., 'The Gossner Mission to Chota Nagpur 1845–1875: A Crisis in Lutheran-Anglican Missionary Policy' (University of Durham MA Thesis, 1967).

Websites

Basel Mission Archive, www.bmarchives.org, accessed 27 January 2016.

Gaebler Info und Genealogie, 'Liste der IndienmissionarInnen der Leipziger Mission', www.gaebler.info/india/leipziger_indienmissionare-1.htm, accessed 23 April 2015.

Leipzig Missionswerk, Missionäre, Indien, www.lmw-mission.de/de/missionare–2-site-1.html, accessed 1 June 2015.

Oxford Dictionary of National Biography, Nicholas Goddard, 'Voelcker (John Christopher) Augustus (1822–1884)', www.oxforddnb.com/view/article/28345?docPos=1, accessed 27 April 2015.

Oxford Dictionary of National Biography, David Prain and M. Rangarajan, 'Brandis, Sir Dietrich (1824–1907)', www.oxforddnb.com/view/article/32045?docPos=1, accessed 27 April 2015.

Oxford Dictionary of National Biography, R. S. Troup and Andrew Grout, 'Schlich, Sir William Philipp Daniel (1840–1925)', www.oxforddnb.com/view/article/35970, accessed 27 April 2015.

INDEX

Abyssinia 43
Achilles, Albert 50
Acts of Parliament
   Aliens Restriction [Britain] (1914) 194
   Basel Mission Trading (1920) 198
   Enemy Missions (1921) 199
   Foreigners (1864) 194, 195
   Foreigners Amendment (1915) 195
   Indian Forest (1865) 100
   Trading with the Enemy (1918) 199
Aden 44, 64
Age of Migration 52
Agra 18, 80, 82, 98, 114, 117, 177, 229
Ahmednagar internment camp ix, xiii, 1, 5, 25, 50, 51, 99, 173, 201, 202, 203, 204, 205, 206–11, 212, 213, 214, 215, 218, 230, 239
   see also internment of Germans in India
Ahmenabad 79
Aldingen 78, 172
Alexander the Great 153
Alexandria 45, 64
Allahabad 21
   Muir College 18
Allgemeiner Deutscher Schulverein zur Erhaltung des Deutschtums im Auslande 113, 237
   Handbuch des Deutschtums im Auslande 113, 114
All India Missionary Conference (1902) 168
Altenmüller, Heinrich 123
American Lutheran Mission 199
Ammann, Johannes 46, 57, 122
Amritsar 169
Amulner 129
Anandapur 92

Ansbach 123
Anton, A. 5, 64, 76, 168, 177
Antwerp 113
Apenrade (Aabenraa) 55, 60
Appelt, David 81, 171
Archaeological Survey of India 83
Archiv der Franckeschen Stiftungen 2, 4
Argentina
   Germans in 28, 111
Arnold, David 76, 84, 117
Asiatic Society of Bengal 21
Augsburg 9
August, Mathilde 171
Australia 16, 18, 29, 51, 81, 189, 194, 229
   Germans in xii, 16, 18, 28, 29, 30, 81, 111, 188, 229, 239
Austria 47
   Germans in 28
Austrians in India 113, 115, 116, 117, 194, 197–8, 204, 207, 212, 213, 214, 216, 229

Bacmeister, Paulina 57
Bade, Klaus J. 42, 52, 235, 237
   Deutsche im Ausland Fremde in Deutschland 235
   Vom Auswanderungsland zum Einwanderungsland 235
Baden 58, 59, 60, 62
Bagchi, Kaushik 160
Bahrain 50
Baierlein, Edmund Raimund 80, 81, 97, 98, 154, 155, 166, 171, 177
Balmatha 57
Bancoorah 75
Bangalore 78, 80, 197
Baptist Missionary Society 12
Bara, Joseph 98
Baroda 77
Basel 3, 12, 13, 45, 55, 57, 96, 134, 167

[273]

INDEX

Basel Mission (German Evangelical Missionary Society) xiii, 1–2, 3, 4, 11, 12, 13–15, 16, 18, 23, 29, 42, 43, 44, 45, 46, 48, 54–5, 56–7, 58–9, 60, 62, 65, 73, 75, 76, 78, 82, 84–5, 92, 93, 95, 96, 97, 98, 102, 112, 118, 119, 120, 121, 122–4, 125, 126, 127–8, 130, 131, 132, 133, 134, 135, 138, 145, 150, 154, 155, 156, 158, 164–5, 166, 167–8, 170, 171–3, 175–6, 178, 191, 197, 198, 199–200, 207, 208, 212, 214, 215, 216, 230, 231, 233, 237, 240
  Album der Basler Mission 2, 3, 148
  Archive x, 1, 4, 14
  Basel Mission Trading Company 96, 198
  Basel Trading Company 198
  Basel Women's Mission Committee 94
  in Coorg 14, 15, 93, 154
  in Canara 14, 15, 57, 78, 96, 176, 200
  in Malabar 14, 15, 43, 57, 65, 75, 96, 200
  in Niligiri 14, 15
  in South Maharrata 14, 15
Basra 50
Batsch, Henry 178
Battles
  Marne 199
  Tanga 50
Bayly, Chris 41
Bauer, Fritz 85–6
Bavaria 17, 59, 60, 61, 123
Becker, Judith 4, 48, 145, 164–5, 170, 176
Beerbühl, Margrit Schulte 19, 53, 234
Beisenherz, Heinrich 80
Belgaum 25
  internment camp 50, 205, 207, 208, 211–12, 218
  see also internment of Germans in India
Belgium 191
  Germans in 28
Belitz 230
Bellary 99
  internment camp 201, 202, 205, 212
  see also internment of Germans in India
Benares 12, 79, 80, 114, 156, 160, 153
  Benares Hindu College 18, 168, 177
Benner, Gotthilf 230
Berckefeldt, Franz von 229–30
Berckfeldt, G. von 197
Berlin 12, 18, 21, 24, 25, 44, 161, 208, 236
  Berlin Missionary Society 18
  Staatsbibliothek ix
Besigheim 234
Bettighery (Betgeri; Bettigeri) 78, 79, 84, 96
Beveridge, Annette 117
Bexell, David 81
Beythan, Hermann 80–1
Birmingham University
  Cadbury Library 2
Bismarck, Otto von 237
Biswas, Mani Mukhta 171
Blackbourn, David 9, 235
Blanton, Casey 6
Blumhardt, Christian Gottlieb 13, 57, 118, 172
Böblingen 123
Boehmer, Elleke 234
Bombay xii, 20, 21, 22, 23, 24, 25, 27, 44, 45, 46, 47, 50, 63, 64, 74, 75–6, 77, 79, 82, 83, 84, 85, 86, 90, 96, 99, 100, 112, 113, 114–15, 116, 117, 122, 128, 129, 137, 151, 159, 160, 161, 163, 169, 195, 197, 201, 206, 207, 209, 211, 213, 215, 216, 218, 230, 231, 232, 234, 239
  Elphinstone College 63, 77, 83, 88, 163, 173
  Jesuit College 83
  St Xavier's College 20
  Watson's Esplanade Hotel 76, 90
Bomwetsch, Christian 171, 172

[274]

INDEX

Bongard, Oscar 23
Bonn 22
Bonsels, Waldemar 23, 150
  Indienfahrt 150
Booth, John 50
Borneo 13, 29, 102
Brandis, Dietrich 22, 63, 100, 101, 151
  Indian Trees 100
Brazil 189, 236
  Germans in 28, 74, 111, 236
Breklum Mission 2, 18–19, 94, 127, 154, 160, 199, 200, 202, 204, 206, 212, 217, 231
Bremen 24, 47, 48, 55, 60
Bristol 43
Britain 23, 53, 64, 74, 111, 189, 194, 218
  emigration from 40, 47
  Germans in xii, 1, 5, 28, 43, 53, 58, 63, 188, 234, 235, 239
  National Archives 4, 187
  South Asians in 61, 236
British Empire Union 213
British in India 27, 29–30, 73, 117, 118, 121, 167–75, 190–1, 200, 231, 238
Brixton 43
Brown, Agnes 172
Brown, Judith 188–9
Brunswick 21, 171
Büchner, Robert 172
Bueltmann, Tanja 40
Buenos Aires 116
Buettner, Elizabeth 117, 118, 122, 238
  Empire Families 117
Bugge, Henrietta 131, 132
Bühler, Georg 63, 83, 99
Bührer, Adam 122
Bulgarians in India 207
Burdwan 12, 56, 75
Burgasalach 58
Burma xiv, 22, 63, 113
Byculla 201

Caemmerer, Friedrich 16
Cairo 45
Calais 43

Calcutta xii, 12, 13, 18, 21, 24, 25, 26, 27, 43, 46, 47, 56, 63, 74, 75, 76, 79, 80, 86, 100, 112, 113, 116, 119, 121, 148, 151, 163–4, 168, 171, 178, 190, 195, 197, 201, 208, 215, 231
Caldwell, Robert 16
Calicut 75, 96, 160, 165, 202
  Calicut College 200
Cameroon 29, 102, 233
Canada
  Germans in 111, 188, 239
Candy 231
Cannanore 9, 165
Cape Comorin 11
Cape Town 215
Caprivi, Leon von 237
Carwitz 171
Cassel, Paulus 161
Castles, Stephen
Catherine the Great 236
Ceylon xiv, 79, 82, 113, 114, 150, 151
Chakrdharpur 88
Chamberlain, Austen 190–1, 214
Chapman, Stanley 102
Chaybassa 127
Chicago 138
Chidabarum 80, 81
Chile
  Germans in 28, 111, 236
China 13, 24, 29, 102, 114, 120, 150, 233
Chinsurah 75
Cho, Miyang 8
Chombala 165
Choné, Aurélie 160
Choudhury, Tarapado 164
Christian Patriot 190
Christian Rede 218
Chunar 12
Church of the Swedish Mission 199
Church Missionary Society (CMS) xiii, 2, 11, 12, 13, 43, 54, 79, 86, 88, 91, 116, 119, 147, 155, 167–8, 170–1, 173, 177, 178, 233
  Register of Missionaries 12

INDEX

Cleall, Esme 169–70
Cochin 9, 47, 48, 151
Coimbatore 58, 81, 230
Colombo 44, 76, 230
Conrad, Sebastian 41, 47, 66, 237
Constantine, Stephen 40, 53
Cordes, Heinrich 16
Cox, Jeffrey 132
Cuddalore 80, 88
Culna 88
Curtin, Philip 83–4
   Death by Migration 83–4

Dagshai internment camp 207
   see also internment of Germans in India
Dahlmann, Dittmar 29, 236
Dahlmann, Joseph 23, 160
Dalhousie, Lord (James Broun-Ramsay) 22, 63
Dalton, Hermann 113, 127, 148
Danish East India Company 10
Danish missionaries in India 4, 132
   see also Tranquebar: Mission
Daressalam 240
David, V. A. 133
Davis, John R. 53
De, Sarmistha 26, 238, 239
   Marginal Europeans in Colonial India 26
Deerr, James 88, 171, 175, 176
De Gama, Vasco 153
de Haas, Hein 52
Delhi ix, 82, 168
   National Archives of India ix, 4, 187
Denmark 44, 60
   Germans in 28
Denzel, Markus 102, 234
deportation of Germans from India xiii, 4, 25, 26, 58, 81, 82, 188, 189, 213–19, 229–30, 239
Der evangelische Heidenbote 77–8, 124, 155, 156, 160, 176
Detzlinger, Johann 57
Deussen, Paul 23, 76–7, 79, 82, 90, 163, 164, 169
Deutshce Erde 114

Dēwasagājam, N. 135
Dharwar 75, 78, 123, 165, 167
Die Deutschen in Indien 230
Dietz, Elisabeth 123
Dietz, Ernst 123
Digel, Friederike 87
Digel, Thomas 123, 176
Dinapur internment camp 204, 206, 212
   see also internment of Germans in India
Dinkelmann, Richard 208
Dodt, Friedrich 46
Dönninghaus, Victor 236
Dr. G. E. Burkhardt's Kleine Missions-Bibliothek 3
Dresden 16, 46, 47, 65
Drewes, Martha 95
Duingen 55, 60
Dürr, Wilhelm 88
Dutton 81
Dwarka 76

East India Company xiii, 10, 11, 13, 21, 43, 44, 50, 76, 153
Echo aus Indien 129
Edwardes, Michael 238
   Bound to Exile 238
Egypt 46
Ehlers, Otto 148
Ellinwood, Dewitt 188
Emmerich 229
Engberts, Christiaan 113
Engel, Gottlob 172
Erfurt 172
Erickson, Charlotte 40
Erlangen 120
Esslingen 57
European Association 190–1, 196, 238
Evangelische Heidenbote 166
Evangelisches Missions-Magazin 124

Fabricius, Johann Philip 11
Falbe, Henriette 171
Fehlberg, Arthur 171
Fellbach 57
Finland 54

INDEX

First World War ix, x, xii, xiii, xiv, 1, 4, 5, 11, 13, 14, 16, 21, 25, 26, 27, 29, 30, 40, 41, 42, 47, 50–2, 57, 58, 61, 64, 81, 82, 94, 95, 99, 102, 112, 113, 116, 117, 120, 122, 129, 138, 147, 160, 161, 165, 169, 173–5, 178, 187–219, 229, 230, 231, 232, 235, 236, 237, 238, 239–40, 241, 242
  confiscation of German property in India during xiii, 189, 196–201, 219, 229, 239
  Germanophobia in India during 189–91
  Indian contribution to 188–9
  measures against Germans in India during 189, 193–6, 239
    Enemy Trading (Winding Up) Order (1916) 196
    Foreigners Ordinance 194–5, 196
    Hostile Foreigners [Trading] Order (1914) 197
Fischer-Tiné, Harald 25–6, 117, 232, 233, 238, 239
  Low and Licentious Europeans 117
Flex, Oscar 5, 153, 162–3, 168, 238
Foertsch, Karl 214, 216–17
Fort William 201
France 7, 191
  Germans in 28
Franckeschen Stiftung 10
Franke, Johannes 123
Frankel, Helene 61, 94
Frankfurt 102
Frauen-Verein für christliche Bildung des weiblichen Geschlechts im Morgenlande 94
French in India 117, 132
Frenz, Albrecht 4, 166
Fritz, Johannes 46, 57
Fröhlich, Richard 171
Fuchs, John 12
Führer, Alois Anton 83, 99
Funk, Johannes 123

Gäbler, Christoph 16, 81
Gäbler, Hermann 46–7, 77, 81
Gaebler, Else 195
Gaebler, Gustav 195
Gaffky, Georg 22
Ganeshan, Vidhagiri 8, 150
Garbe, Richard von 21, 79–80, 82, 113, 160, 161, 164, 169
Garibaldi, Giuseppe 25, 64
Gaya 90
Gazette of India 194
Gehring, Alwin 44, 49, 56, 77, 79, 89–90, 95, 101, 127, 136–7, 150, 153, 158, 159, 176, 179
Gehringen 230
Geiser, Alfred 114
  Deutsches Reich und Volk 114
Geneva 26
Gengnagel, Ludwig 167
Genoa 44
German academics, scholars and scientists in India ix, x, xi, 5, 8, 21–3, 24, 53, 63–4, 65, 73, 79–80, 82–3, 84, 90, 99–101, 102, 146, 151–3, 163, 164, 168, 207, 208, 211, 219, 231, 232, 234, 237, 238, 241
German businessmen and merchants in India ix, x, xi, 5, 9–10, 24–5, 48, 75, 102, 112, 114, 116, 121, 197, 207, 216, 218, 219, 229, 234, 238
German Catholic and Jesuit missionaries in India 2, 19–20, 23, 25, 83, 84, 93, 97, 98, 128–9, 134, 197, 208, 237, 241
German community and identity in India x, xi, xii, 111–38, 175, 187, 211, 217, 219, 230–1, 232, 239
  role of education 121–2
  role of language 10, 111, 123–5, 138, 162–3, 230, 239
  role of nation 111, 112, 113–17, 122, 125, 127, 130, 131, 138, 219, 230–1
    Navy League 111, 113, 115, 116
  role of Nazi party 231
  role of religion 111, 112, 116, 219

INDEX

German doctors in India 10, 17, 84, 96, 130
German families in India xii, 61–2, 65, 112, 117–22, 203
German indology x, 6–9, 21, 63–4, 97, 99, 208, 241
German interaction with Britons in India x, xi, xii, 27, 112, 147, 167–9, 178, 187, 191–3, 232, 238
  intermarriage 116, 169–75, 178, 179, 187, 232
German interaction with Indians xii, 91–2, 131–8, 145–7, 162–7, 178, 179, 232, 238, 240
  hostility from Indians xii, 175–8, 187
  intermarriage 146, 147, 169–75, 179, 240
German Jews in India 112
German Lutheran Mission 92
German mercenaries in India 9–10
German migration to India xi, 9–10, 30, 40–66, 232–4
  causes of 40–66
    forced 42, 50–2, 65
    globalisation 41–2, 52, 66, 232–4
    networks 52–64, 65, 66, 233–4
    Pietism 48–50, 51, 52, 233
    population growth 40, 42
    transport improvements 40, 42–8, 51, 65, 66, 233
  travel within India 74–80
German missionaries in India ix, x, xi, xii, xiii, 1–5, 6, 9, 10–21, 27, 29, 42, 43–7, 48–50, 52, 53, 54–62, 64–5, 66, 73, 74, 75–6, 77–82, 83, 84–99, 101, 102, 113, 116, 117–38, 147, 148, 150, 153–4, 155–9, 161, 162, 164–8, 169–73, 175–9, 187, 189–90, 191, 195–6, 197–204, 207, 208, 212, 214, 216, 219, 230, 231, 232, 233–4, 237, 238–9, 240–2
  educational activity 14, 16, 18, 20, 92–4, 97, 126, 127, 128–9, 130, 132, 133–4, 135–6, 164, 197, 199, 241

Indian converts 79, 92–3, 112, 126, 127, 130, 132–8, 145, 165–7, 178, 240–1
  numbers of 11, 14, 16, 17, 18, 19, 92–3, 130, 200
  industrial activity 14, 73, 96–7
  length of time spent in India 81–2
  marriages 56–7, 61–2, 118–20, 169–73
  medical work 95–6
  research activity 21, 73, 97–9
  see also Basel Mission (German Evangelical Missionary Society); Breklum Mission; Church Missionary Society (CMS); German Lutheran Mission; Gossner Mission; Halle Mission; Hermannsburg Mission; Tranquebar: Mission
German perceptions of India xii, 23, 24, 97, 145–62
  British rule 23, 24, 147, 160–2
  cityscapes xii, 159–60
  disease 147, 160, 178
  landscapes xii, 23, 147–55, 161
  religion 23, 146, 147, 153, 154, 155–8, 160, 162, 178
  women xii, 94–5, 147, 158–9, 162, 178
German prostitutes in India 26, 173
German sailors in India ix, 5, 26, 113, 207, 232
German South West Africa 29
German travellers in India ix, xi, 5, 6, 23–4, 73, 74, 102, 112–13, 116, 147, 148–51, 231
Germany 1, 6, 7, 13, 16, 17, 22, 24, 25, 41, 42, 47, 51, 53, 59, 74, 80, 82, 83, 94, 96, 146, 168, 197, 200, 208, 216, 217, 234–8
  emigration from 27–30, 42–66, 234–7
  Empire 7, 29, 40, 237
  National Archives 4
  Pietism in xi, 10, 48–50, 52
  Poles in 237
Geschichte und Gesellschaft 235
Ghazipur 18, 77
Gießen University 22, 63
Gilmour, David 238
  Ruling Caste 238

[278]

INDEX

Glasgow 5, 28, 53, 235
Gläsle, Hermann 120
Gläsle, Rosmarie 119, 120
Gläsle-Richter, Mathilde Elise 120
Gleeson, David T. 40
Gloyer, Ernst 154
Goch 217
Goethe, Johann Wolfgang von 7
   Westöstlicher Diwan 7
Golconda 214–16, 217, 230
Gold Coast (Ghana) 29, 102, 173, 233, 240
Gonegaon 129
Gooledgood 165
Goruckpur 12
Gossner, Johannes Evangelista 17–18, 237
Gossner Mission xii, 2, 3, 4, 17–18, 23, 46, 88–9, 92, 93–4, 98, 113, 118, 127, 128, 130, 133, 135, 137, 158, 177–8, 195, 197, 199, 200, 202, 203, 206, 207, 212, 214, 231
   50 Bilder aus der Gossnerschen Kols–Mission 2–3
Göttingen 63
Govindpur 88, 137
Grafe, Hugald 4
Grass, Günther 8
Gräter, Benignus 123
Gräter, Mathilde 86–7
Graudens 43
Graul, Karl 3, 16, 21, 23, 44, 64–5, 75–6, 78, 83, 112, 116, 157, 161, 168, 169, 237
Gravesend 43
Greeks in India 26
Greifswald 120
Greiner, Christian Leonhard 13, 14, 122
Greiner-Frohmmeyer, Frieda 62, 122
Greiner-Frohmmeyer, Wilhelmina 62
Grimsby 218
Grote, Margarete 58, 90
Groves, Anton 76
Grundemann, Reinhold 3
Gründler, Johann Ernst 11
Gründler, O. 94, 159
Gudur 19

Gundeldingen 46
Gundert, Hermann 4, 8, 14, 21, 56, 62, 65, 76, 78, 86, 91, 92, 97, 98, 99, 101, 150, 154, 164, 166, 167, 168, 176, 179, 237
   A Malayalam and English Dictionary 98

Haas, Waltraud 118, 119
Haeckel, Ernst 23, 151
Hague Convention 209, 211
Hall (Württemberg) 123
Halle 2, 10
Halle Mission 6
Haller, Johannes 172
Hamburg 24, 47, 48, 55, 99, 112, 218
Hammitzsch, Georg 202
Handmann, Heinrich Paul 120
Handmann, Otto Richard 120, 202
Handmann, Richard 16, 120, 131, 136
   Umschau auf dem Gebiete der evangelisch-lutherischen Mission in Ostindien 131
Hanover 24, 48, 59, 60, 61, 171, 197
Hansewandell, Wilhelm 166
Hara 156
Hardiman, David 95
Harling, G. 50
Harper, Marjorie 40, 53
Hartmann, Athanasius 20
Harvest Field 193
Harwich 44
Hary 58
Haug, Martin 99
Hauri, Rudlof 123
Havelock, Sir Henry 22, 63
Hazirabagh 178
health of the Germans in India xi, 62, 64, 73, 74, 81, 83–7, 101, 129, 210
Hebich, Samuel 3, 13, 14, 54–5, 65, 75, 78, 91, 164, 166
Heckelmann, Wilhelm 172
Heidelberg 21
Heilbronn 123
Heithöfen 55, 60
Hensolt, Auguste 16, 61
Herder, Johann Gottfried 8
Herget, Aurelie 61, 62

INDEX

Herget, Johanna 61, 62
Hermannsburg Mission 2, 19, 55, 58, 60, 85, 86, 87, 94–5, 121, 199, 202, 207
Hernecken, Friedrich 172
Hesse, Hermann 8, 62, 150–1
   Aus Indien 150–1
Hesse, Johannes 62, 165, 166
Hesse, Marie 45–6, 62
Heyer, Gustave 63
Higgs, T. K. 170
Hiller, Johann 57
Hirner, Gottlob 123
Hirschfelde 46, 47
Hirschtal 123
Hobsbawn, Eric 41, 66
   Age of Empire 41
Hoch, Mark 119, 123
Höchst am Main 24
Hoerder, Dirk 42
Hoffmann, Johannes 169
Hoffmann, Wilhelm 94, 95
Honore 165
Hoobly 78
Höppner, Heinrich 46
housing of the Germans in India xi, 74, 76, 77, 87–90, 126
Hübener, Berta 61, 230, 231
Humboldt, Alexander von 22
Huschke, A. H. 24

Imhoff, Jorg 9, 22
Indian Mutiny xii, 168, 176–8
internment of Germans in India xiii, 1, 4–5, 25, 42, 50–1, 188, 189, 197, 199, 201–13, 231, 239
   numbers interned 204, 207, 212, 213, 217–18, 229
   see also Ahmednagar internment camp; Belgaum: internment camp; Bellary: internment camp; Dagshai internment camp; Dinapur internment camp; Kataphar internment camp; Ramandroog internment camp; Sholapur internment camp; Waltair internment camp; Yercaud internment camp

Irion, Christian 97, 158
   Malabar und die Missionsstation Talatscheri 97
Irish migration 52
Isenberg, Charles 62
Ispringen 120
Italians in India 26, 117
Italy 25, 64
   Germans in 28, 116

Jamshedpur 24
Japan 29, 150
Japanese in India 173
Jaus, Jakob 166, 202, 212
Java 22
Jelke, Gustav 25
Jenkins, Jennifer M. 45
Jenkins, Paul 167, 170
Jerusalem 234
Jessen, Otty 217
Jeypur 18, 79, 163, 200
   Sanskrit College 163
Josenhans, Joseph 131
Juneja, Monica 165
Jürgemeier, Ernst 55, 60

Kabis, Johannes 77
Kade-Luthra, Veena 8
Kalashti 19
Kannanur 75, 167
Kant, Immanuel 8
Kanundinya, E. 172
Kanundinya, Hilde 240
Kanundinya, Lakshmi 172
Kanundinya, R. 172, 240
Kanundinya, Rani 240
Karachi 20, 234
Kastens, Elise 95
Kataphar internment camp 205, 213
   see also internment of Germans in India
Die katholischen Missionen 129
Kaufmann, Oscar 82–3, 84, 151, 160
   Aus Indiens Dschungeln 151
Kaundinya, Anandrao 134, 165, 172–3, 176, 179, 240
Kellenbenz, Hermann 9

INDEX

Kempten 75
Kendel 129
Kenny, Judith T. 131
Kerberg, Emma 61
Kerr, Ian 76
Keti (Kaity; Kety) 87, 118, 126, 127, 148, 165
Khelde 129
Kiautschou (Tsingtau) 201, 208
Kielhorn, Franz 99
  Sanskrit Grammar 99
Kiel University 23, 163, 208
Kilkenny 216
Kilossa 240
Kirchberger, Ulrike 9, 12, 22, 53, 62–3, 64, 234
Kittel, Ferdinand 97, 98
Kittel-Eyth, Julie 62
Kittel-Eyth, Wilhelmine 62
Knabe, Wolfgang 9
Koch, Robert 21–2, 84
Kodaikanal 121
Kodur 19
Koenigsmarck, Count Hans von 23, 112–13, 162, 169
Köhler, Andreas 87, 118
Kohlmeier, Christian 55, 56, 60
König, Heinrich 24
Königsberg 79
Konrad, Dagmar 4, 46, 85, 233
Korntal 45, 57
Kotageri 121
Krapf, Johannes 123
Krueder, Richard 210
Kudelur 177
Kulladghee 100
Kumar, Apurla 164
Kumbakonam 150
Kurlander, Eric 8

Lahore 234
Lamu 50
Layer, Johannes 123
Lechler, Johannes 76, 172
Lehmann, Arno 4
Lehner, Johann Christian 13, 14, 88
Leifer, Walter 9, 231
Leipzig 231

Leipzig Mission x, 2, 3, 4, 6, 16–17, 18, 55–6, 58, 59, 61–2, 65, 77, 78, 80–2, 85–6, 88, 89–90, 91, 94, 95, 97, 98, 101, 118, 119, 120, 121, 122, 127, 130, 132, 133, 134, 135, 136, 138, 155, 157, 165, 170, 171, 178, 199, 200, 202, 207, 217, 230, 231, 237, 240, 241
Leonberg 134
Leonberger, Johannes 78–9
Leupolt, Charles Benjamin 91, 155, 177
Leupolt, Martha 177
Leutkirch 95
Liberia 102
Liebau, Heike 3–4, 97, 112, 131, 132, 133, 165
Liebendoerfer, Eugen 95–6
Limbach, Samuel 156
Lisbon 9
Liverpool 218
Lohardaga 121, 134
Lohn 122
London 1, 9, 29, 43, 44, 46, 47, 50, 55, 64, 83, 99, 102, 112, 116, 198, 200, 216, 239
  Alexandra Palace internment camp 1, 216
London Missionary Society 11, 12, 56, 191
Lorbeer, Helene 158
Lübeck 54
Lübeck Missionary Society 54
Lucas, Anna 159
Lucas, Bernard 193
Lucerne 45
Lüchow, Peter 56, 87
Lucknow 12, 83
Ludwigshafen 218
Luebke, Frederick C. 125, 236
Lusitania 189, 193, 198, 203
Luxemburg
  Germans in 28
Luxemburgers in India 129

Mack, Julia 155
MacRaild, Don 40

[281]

INDEX

Madras xii, 16, 21, 22, 24, 25, 43, 44, 45, 46, 47, 56, 58, 63, 64, 74, 76, 77, 78, 79, 80, 81, 82, 90, 99, 100, 113, 114, 116, 161, 172, 195, 202, 208, 215
   Adyar Library 64, 99, 208
   Fort St George 202
   Presidency College 63
Madras Mail 189, 190
Madras Representative Council of Missions 192, 199
Mafia 50
Magazin Neueste Geschichte 88
Magee, Gary B. 40, 53
Mahabelashwar 100
Main 218
Malan 129
Malaysia 10
Manaveram 76
Manen, Johan van 208
Mangalore (Mangalur) 44, 75, 76, 87, 88, 93, 96, 119, 120, 121, 122–3, 124, 127–8, 130, 134, 172
   Karnataka Theological College 93
Manila 114
Manjapra, Kris 8–9, 146, 231
   Age of Entanglement 231
Manktelow, Emily J. 118, 119, 121
Mann, Michael 9–10, 29
Männer, August 123
Mannheim 43
Manning, Patrick 52
Manz, Stefan 5, 28, 53, 111, 113, 117, 125, 235, 237
Marchand, Suzanne 7
Margorin 171
Marschalck, Peter 42
Marseilles 46
Marshall, P. J. 73
Marshman, Joshua 63
Marshman, Rachel 63
Matheran 191
Mathusamy, Mauelmedu 136
Mattweil 123
Maue, Jakob 1, 191, 208, 216
May, Andrew J. 125
Mayavaram 231
McGetchin, Douglas T. 6, 8

Mecklenburg 216
Meerut 76
Menge, Carl 62
Menge, John 62
Merkara 93
Metz, Johann 122
Meugert, Johannes 46
Meurin, John 20
Mexico
   Germans in 236
Meyberg, Anne Marie 95
Meyner, Theodor 230, 231
Milford Haven 43
Miller, Jon 48, 54, 62, 66, 233
Miller, Mark J. 52
Mizutani, Satoshi 146, 169
Mögling, Hermann 44, 55, 57, 65, 75, 92, 93, 97, 99, 123, 154, 164, 165, 166, 172, 179, 240
Möllenkotten 123
Montagu, Edwin 204
Mombassa 50
Montenegrins in India 213
Morgenländische Frauenverein 18
Moriaro 92
Moscow 236
Mosse, Werner 235
Mueller, Max 21, 63
Mukli 57
Müller, Herbert 208, 216
Munich 99, 208
Münklingen 172
Murree 114
Murti, Kamakshi 8
Muzaffarpur 92
Myavaram 134
Myers, Perry 7, 150, 160–1
   German Visions of India 7
Mylius, August 86

Nadel, Stanley 28, 58, 122
Nagel, Silke 236
Nairobi 50
Naples 44
National Christian Council 168, 191, 199
National Missionary Council 168, 200
Nayudupetta 19

INDEX

Neesbach 172
Neuffen 123
Nehring, Andreas 4, 98, 132, 146, 154, 155, 231
  Orientalismus und Mission 98
Nepal 26
Netherlands
  Dutch East Indies 18, 29, 219
  Germans in 28
Nettur 95
New Guinea 22, 29
New York 28, 58, 102, 116, 122
New Zealand 18, 30, 146, 188, 194
  Germans in 12, 18
Nilagiri 168
Nimburi 129
North German Missionary Society 18
Nostitz, Grafin Pauline 23
Noti, Severin 84
number of Germans in India 1, 27, 113, 197–8, 214, 229, 238, 240
Nuremberg 9

Oberurbach 123
Ochs, Carl 46
Oehler, Wilhelm 29, 64–5, 102
Oepke, Albrecht 202, 203
orientalism xii, 4, 7–8, 98, 132, 145–7, 148, 149, 155–9, 164
Osnabrück 55, 99
Osterhammel, Jürgen 41, 52, 66, 233
Ottoman Empire 7, 188
Oxford 63

Pākiam, C. 135
Pakistan xiv
Pamperrien, Karl 77, 120
Pamperrien, Maria 120
Pamperrien, Martha 120
Pandur 133
Panrutti 130
Paris 7, 63
Pathre 129
Patna 18
Patricia 218, 229
Paul, Carl 214
Paul, V. A. 133
Penny, H. Glen 235

Pereira, Anna Mercia 172
Peshawar 79, 234
Petersen, Otto 55
Pfander, Karl Gottlieb 98, 155, 176
Pfleiderer, Deborah Johanna Hoch 119
Pfleiderer, Gottlob 96, 120
Pfleiderer, Karl 123
Pfleiderer-Werner, Johanna 120
Pietermaritzburg 216
Pietsch, Tamson 234
Pilley, Tandvaran 134
Pischel, Richard 21
Plath, Karl Heinrich 23, 44, 49, 77
Plieningen 12
Plütschau, Heinrich 9, 10, 241
Poland 41
Poles in Germany 41
Poona (Puna) 25, 99, 100, 128, 129, 206
Poona College 99
Pope Gregory XVI 20
Porayar 120, 231
Port Said 44, 218
Portsmouth 43, 44
Portuguese Empire 9, 40, 145, 169
Pöthig, Otto 25
Prahan, S. D. 188
Prisoners of Britain ix
Probst, Hans Georg ix, 208
Prussia 24, 42, 43, 59, 60
Pudukotei 127, 136
Purselbākum 135
Purtschert, Patricia 233
Purulia 120, 127, 128
Puttur 120

Queen Mary 46
Queen Victoria 63

race and racism in India xii, xiii, 132–3, 145–7, 162, 164, 170, 175, 209, 232, 239, 240
Ramandroog internment camp 205, 207, 213, 218
  see also internment of Germans in India
Ramawarma, Jakob 167
Ramona 43

[283]

INDEX

Ramsgate 43
Ranchi 18, 88, 94, 127, 178, 197, 203
Rangoon 195, 197
Ratnagiri 209
Rawalpindi 114
Red Cross 207, 209
Reinhardt, Marie 172, 240
Remo, Paulus 135
Reulaux, Franz 23, 163
Rhenius, Charles 12, 43-4, 49, 88, 168
Rhineland Mission 48
Ribbentrop, Berthold 22, 63, 100-1, 151
  Forestry in British India 101
Richter, Julius 93, 154
Richter-Hoch, Hanni 119-20
Richter-Hoch, Hans 120
Rinke, Stefan 235
Ritter, Gustav 57
Roeber, Klaus 98
Roer, Hans 21
Rome 237
Rosenberg, Peter 125
Rosenberger, Edwin 26, 159, 170, 173
Rosenthal, Berthold 197
Ross, Henry 191
Rotterdam 43, 44, 113, 218
Ruckdäschel, Johannes 202
Rupur 19
Russia 189, 191, 195, 207
  Germans in 27, 28, 29, 57, 74, 111, 125, 235-6, 237
Russians in India 26, 207

Sadras 80
Said, Edward 7, 146
Sakchi 201
Salurpetta 19
Samoa 29
Samocin 171
Sandegren, Carl 81
Sandys, Thomas 79
Santipore 171
Saxony 24, 46, 60, 61, 122, 233
Schaeuffeln, Eugenie 23
Schäffer, Eduard 62
Schäffer, Martin 62
Schaffhausen 122
Scheide, Carmen 29
Schelling, Friedrich Wilhelm Joseph 8
Schlagintweit, Adolphe 22, 23, 79, 82, 99-110, 117, 151
Schlagintweit, Emil 148, 151, 158
  Indien in wort und Bild 148, 151
Schlagintweit, Hermann 22, 23, 79, 82, 99-100, 117, 151
Schlagintweit, Robert 22, 23, 79, 82, 99-100, 117, 151
Schlatter, Wilhelm 3, 66, 102, 233
  Geschichte der Basler Mission 3
Schlegel, Friedrich 7
  Über die Sprache und Weisheit der Inder 7
Schleswig Holsteinischer Evangelical Lutheran Mission
  see Breklum Mission
Schlich, William 22, 63, 100
Schmid, Ludwig Bernhard Ehregott 86
Schmidt, Käthe 61
Schneider, Frederic Edward 177
Schomerus, Hiko 62
Schomerus, Rudolf 62
Schopenhauer, Arthur 8
Schorndorf 171
Schrader, Friedrich 63-4, 99
Schrader, Otto 25, 208
Schraut, Isabella 26
Schroder, Ernst 25
Schüler, Elisabeth 61
Schultze, Benjamin 11, 97
Schulze, Winfried 5
  Unter indischer Sonne ix
Schunermann, August 25
Schwartz, Christian Friedrich 11
Sebastian, Mrinalini 165
Second World War 236
Secrole 177
Seeadler 115
Sengupta, Indra 6-7, 8, 63, 64
Sharkey, Heather 145, 170
Sholapur internment camp 51, 205, 207, 208, 212-13, 218
  see also internment of Germans in India

INDEX

Siam 42, 50, 65, 212, 218–19
   Germans in 42, 51, 212, 218–19
Sicandra 18
Sierra Leone 44
Sigra 18
Simla 114
Singapore 150
Soto, Katharina Tietze de 236
South Africa 18, 201
   Germans in 188, 201
Southampton 22
South India United Church 200
South Indian Missionary Association 168
Spanish Empire 9
SS *Dinsamud* 51
SS *Pinsamud* 51
Stache-Rosen, Valentina 21, 234
   Scholars in Indian Studies Writing in German
Stahl, Luise 87
Staib, Ferdinand 123
Standing Committee of the Conference of British Missionary Societies 192
Stenzl, Catherine 172
Stern, Henry 12
Stierlin, Freidrich 123
Stierlin, Luise 62
Stierlin, Lydia 62
Stock, Eugene 12, 233
Stokes, Mary 172
Stork, Marie 172
Stosch, Georg 44, 49, 56, 92, 157, 158
Stosch, Johannes 197
St Petersburg 18, 54, 236
Straits Settlements 51
Strasburg 43
Strauß, Otto 208
Streng, Lisa 58, 61
Stricker, Gerd 236
St Thomas 9
Stuttgart 43, 57, 123, 131
Suez Canal xi, 8, 44, 45, 47, 48, 51, 64, 65, 150, 215
Sutter, Georg 57, 93, 123
Sutter, Julia 123
Sweden 16, 54, 61

Switzerland 13, 14, 16, 94, 112, 122, 123, 124, 125, 171, 233
   Germans in 28
Swiss in India 112, 113, 115, 116, 117, 122, 123, 129, 171, 200
Sydney 239

Talatscheri 45, 158, 161
Taliparambu 91, 156
Tampke, Jürgen 29
Tanjore 58, 120
Tehran 114
Tesch, L. 201
Teterow 25
Thibaut, Georg 21
Thompson, Andrew S. 40, 53
Tilbury 215, 216
Tingamonar 162
Tinnevelly 12, 76
Tirhoot 92
Tirunelveli 168
Tirupati 19, 95
Tiruvallar (Triwallur) 81, 214
Togo 29, 102
Torp, Cornelius 234
Tranquebar 9, 10–11, 56, 77, 80, 81, 91, 94, 97, 165, 177, 241
   Mission 4, 10–11, 16, 76, 112, 131, 168
Travancore 136
Trichinopoly 120, 176, 201
Trieste 45, 64, 86
Tripumtura 167
Trumpp, Ernst 234
Tübingen 55
   Deutsches Institut für ärtzliche Mission 85
   University 55, 97
Tuchtenhagen, Ralph 236
Turkey 114
Turks in India 212
Tuticors 77
Tyrell, Hartmut 54
Tzoref-Ashkenazi, Chen 10
   Transcultural Encounters 8

Udapi 14, 57, 176
Uffmann, Heinrich 120–1
Uffmann, Johannes 120

INDEX

Ujjain 90
Umballa 177
Unterweisach 57
USA 7, 40, 42, 43, 74, 189
   Americans in India 129, 132, 168, 173, 229
   Germans in ix, xii, 5, 28, 29, 40, 42, 43, 74, 102, 111, 229, 235, 236, 237
Utakamand 121

Vaiyolagam 136
Vakadu 19
Venkatagiri 19
Vijayanagara 9
Vilupuram 77, 81
Vincent, Robert 25, 64
Vlissingen 216
Voelcker, Augustus 22–3
   Report on the Improvement of Indian Agriculture 23

Waiblingen 123
Wain 123
Waltair internment camp 202, 203, 204, 212
   see also internment of Germans in India
Waurick, Bernard 208
Wazīrābād 64, 76
Wegener, Georg 161
Weigle, Christian 123
Weigle, Gottfried 46, 54, 57, 93, 97
Weigle, Pauline 123
Weitbrecht, John 12, 43, 49, 54, 56, 75, 76, 79, 86, 91, 119, 153–4, 155–6, 157, 168, 170–1
   Protestant Missions in Bengal 153
Weitbrecht, V. D. M. 97, 154, 158
Welsh Calvinistic Methodists' Foreign Missionary Society 125
Wendt, Reinhardt 165

Werner, Johanna 57
Werner, Karl Friedrich 57
Wernicke, E. A. 190
Wesleyan Mission 200
Westmann, Theodor 197
Weydt, Harald 125
White, Mary 171
Wilhelm II 237
Wilson, John 75
Wilstedt 55
Windsheim 60
Wirruttsalom 81
Wirth, Alfred 114
Witschi, Hermann 102, 233
World Missionary Conference (1910) 29, 168
   Continuation Committee 192
Wörrlein, Johann 55, 56, 60, 94
Würth-Leitner, Fanny 45, 46
Württemberg 1, 12, 13, 14, 41, 42, 43, 45, 48, 57, 59, 60, 62, 65, 78, 96, 122–3, 171, 172, 230, 233, 234
Wüstenroth 123
Wutow, Jacaues 197

Yercaud internment camp 205, 207, 212–13, 218
   see also internment of Germans in India
Youngs, Tim 6

Zanzibar 50
Zeuske, Michael 102
Zibel, Emilie 171
Ziegenbalg, Bartholomäus 9, 10–11, 97, 154, 155, 189, 192, 229, 241
Zielenzig, Barbara 171
Zimmer, Max 23
Zimmermann, Johannes 173
Zirke 80
Zitelmann, Katherine 114, 116, 137
Zöllnitz 230

EU authorised representative for GPSR:
Easy Access System Europe, Mustamäe tee 50,
10621 Tallinn, Estonia
gpsr.requests@easproject.com

www.ingramcontent.com/pod-product-compliance
Lightning Source LLC
Chambersburg PA
CBHW051602230426
43668CB00013B/1952